'If you are an academic teaching in/through/despite psychology, this book refracts like a fractured mirror and feels like a colonoscopy. If you are an academic who has been betrayed/fired/attacked/exposed by your university because of a radical scholarly project, you will feel heard, seen, archived and in very good company. If you are a student of psychology, the volume blinks like a beautifully curated, auto-ethnographic yellow light. Beware. The Psychology Stories narrated by Ian Parker – an exquisite and painful auto-ethnography; a careful disciplinary dissection, and a skillful institutional autopsy – unfold crucial counter-narratives about what it means to live a life of willful passions, witness the disciplinary erasures and decadence of psychology and be consumed by surveillance and the carnivorous appetite of the neo-liberal academy. Read the book. You may not love all parts; you may not agree; you may have a different story of psychology to tell. You will, however, not easily forget the brilliant path Ian has carved through the psy complex and you will most definitely applaud his stunning "walk off" song.'

– **Michelle Fine,** *Professor of Critical Psychology, Urban Education, Gender/Women's Studies, The Graduate Center, CUNY, USA*

'Subjectivity is arguably the "theme" of psychology. Yet, as Ian Parker's autoethnography shows, mental life is not just intra-subjectivity when sharing personal experiences but also intellectual influences and networks in psychology and related fields. Particular interactions in the context of the academic and cultural-historical developments of Britain since the 1970s and around the world, and academic and activist responses, point to the significance of inter- and socio-subjectivity. We learn about the hyperreality of an academic discipline, to which all critical psychologists can relate, and come to appreciate the sometimes unintended agency that shaped Ian's project. A daring instructor might use this historically systematic book for educational purposes; one can enjoy reading about persons, times, and locations that have remained either intriguing or influential; or the book can be understood in terms of the author's attempt to understand the psyche and its nexus to social and institutional struggles since, unsurprisingly, the psychological remains political. Clearly and beautifully written, drawing on an impressive memory, and generous to people who co-constructed shared activities, Ian Parker lays out a stream of reflexivity and interferences that confirms that critical psychology stems as much from necessity as it does from personal experiences that make subjectivity not only societal, but also unique and irreplaceable.'

– **Thomas Teo,** *York University, Canada*

'Parker tells an intriguing, insightful and very personal story about his journey through becoming and being a psychologist – in harsh and cruel times. Its telling is woven through with an erudite and fascinating account of the creation of "critical psychology", its triumphs, troubles and troubling. This book is intended to set several cats among an awful lot of pigeons, to awesome effect! Its critique of the harms being done by the neoliberal destruction of all that was best in the academy (including the governmental power of pretty well everything that is "psi") – is a compelling call for action. May its impact live long and thoroughly prosper.'

– **Wendy Stainton Rogers,** *Professor Emerita,*
The Open University, UK

'This is the story of one of our most prominent critical psychologists whose journey into and eventually out of psychology serves as both lesson and cautionary tale. Ian Parker's long trajectory through contemporary psychology is a fascinating reminder of the pitfalls and seductions of a discipline that serves still to befuddle and bewitch rather than liberate and deliver us from a narrow individualism. His story is an ultimately hopeful tale of one psychologist's struggle to make a difference.'

– **Hank Stam,** *Psychology, University of Calgary, Canada*

PSYCHOLOGY THROUGH CRITICAL AUTO-ETHNOGRAPHY

This unique book is an insider account about the discipline of psychology and its limits, introducing key debates in the field of psychology around the world today by closely examining the problematic role the discipline plays as a global phenomenon.

Ian Parker traces the development of 'critical psychology' through an auto-ethnographic narrative in which the author is implicated in what he describes, laying bare the nature of contemporary psychology. In five parts, each comprising four chapters, the book explores the student experience, the world of psychological research, how psychology is taught, how alternative critical movements have emerged inside the discipline, and the role of psychology in coercive management practices. Providing a detailed account of how psychology actually operates as an academic discipline, it shows what teaching in higher education and immersion in research communities around the world looks like, and it culminates in an analytic description of institutional crises which psychology provokes.

A reflexive history of psychology's recent past as a discipline and as a cultural force, this book is an invaluable resource for anyone thinking of taking up a career in psychology, and for those reflecting critically on the role the discipline plays in people's lives.

Ian Parker is Fellow of the British Psychological Society, Emeritus Professor of Management at the University of Leicester, and Co-Director of the Discourse Unit, where he is Managing Editor of *Annual Review of Critical Psychology*.

PSYCHOLOGY THROUGH CRITICAL AUTO-ETHNOGRAPHY

Academic Discipline, Professional Practice and Reflexive History

Ian Parker

Routledge
Taylor & Francis Group

LONDON AND NEW YORK

First published 2020
by Routledge
2 Park Square, Milton Park, Abingdon, Oxon OX14 4RN

and by Routledge
52 Vanderbilt Avenue, New York, NY 10017

Routledge is an imprint of the Taylor & Francis Group, an informa business

British Library Cataloguing-in-Publication Data
A catalogue record for this book is available from the British Library

Library of Congress Cataloging-in-Publication Data
A catalog record for this book has been requested

ISBN: 978-0-367-34418-4 (hbk)
ISBN: 978-0-367-34417-7 (pbk)
ISBN: 978-0-429-32568-7 (ebk)

Typeset in Bembo
by Apex CoVantage, LLC

CONTENTS

INTRODUCTION

Control and confession

Quick souls have their intensest life in the first anticipatory sketch of what may or will be, and the pursuit of their wish is the pursuit of that paradisiacal vision which only impelled them, and is left farther and farther behind, vanishing forever even out of hope in the moment which is called success.

(George Eliot, *Felix Holt, the Radical*, 1866)

How do people get into psychology? What is psychology really, and how do psychologists try to make sense of other people, the ones who, they think, are quite unlike them? And then, how might they get out of it again? This book is about how I got into psychology, and out the other side. Along the way I will show you how I discovered that psychology operates as a research apparatus that turns people into objects, but also that it is not so much better when it tries to accord these objects some sense again in line with its own reduced image of what it is to be a human being. You will see how psychology works and what it does, and why you should beware the many different contradictory forms of social control the discipline imposes on psychologists as well as on those they study.

The overriding aim of psychology as a discipline is to construct a scientific account of what we are as individuals, in line with a declared 'predict and control' ethos. Usually the focus is on how we behave, with observations of behaviour seen as the most scientific route to a workable theory of mind. I will describe how psychologists themselves behave, and you will see that what they say about what they are doing is always contradictory and sometimes unpleasant. In the process I have had to talk about myself, to put myself in the picture, so you are in a better position to evaluate what I say.

Accounts of this kind are clearer if you know where the author is coming from, and that is something that psychological studies usually shut out. I retrace my steps through psychology here as a kind of ethnography, reflecting on what I was doing as well as describing what others around me did. In this sense I am like an anthropologist on a strange planet, but I am inside a discipline that has reached around the globe and insinuated its ways of thinking about people almost everywhere. The 'auto-ethnographic' aspect appears at those moments when I include myself in the story, and it is here that I also risk being drawn into the shadow side of the more quantitative control aspects of the discipline, into the more qualitative aspects intent on making subjects confess. I will describe later in the book how qualitative research is grudgingly allowed in some psychology departments, even to the point of allowing a little auto-ethnography, which psychologists often mistakenly portray as being no more than the researcher talking about themselves, as amounting to no more than a restricted version of 'reflexivity', an account of personal experience. Here in this book it means attending to the conditions in which knowledge is produced, to the entwinement of subjectivity with social institutions and cultural practices. Being critical as I confess to you my role in events I describe will not always save me from reducing things to the activities of individuals, but it should better help you know what is going on.

This reflexive history of the recent past and present of psychology is about the academic discipline, but you will also see how the academic research intersects with professional practice. The book is in five parts, and the narrative goes like this.

I begin by tracing what led me into psychology, and describe how undergraduate students are taught to focus on behaviour, disregarding what people say, disregarding the psychologist's powerful role in setting up studies; they thereby construct and enforce models of how people think reduced to 'cognition', and try to sort out what is nature and what is nurture. This part of the book in the first four chapters is about the induction of the student into the strange version of science that psychologists imagine they are adhering to.

The second part of the book, Chapters 5 to 8, is where I am really hooked, but where I think I am doing something better than mainstream psychology as I study for my PhD. You will learn something about different competing models of science, and about attempts by some psychologists to grasp how important language is to what we are as human beings, to what we think we are. This part of the book opens up some of the contradictions inside psychology.

The third part, Chapters 9 to 12, is about the shift from studying to teaching psychology. Here you can see how the disciplinary boundaries that separate psychologists from those they study are complemented by boundaries that shut out other approaches to experience, from sociology, for example, and from the domain of practice. It becomes clearer as we go through this part of the book that it is more useful to think of the different psychological stories that comprise the textbooks as 'discourses', ways of speaking and writing that have a peculiar power to shape people's lives.

Part IV, Chapters 13 to 16, is where we really go critical, and we also begin to come up against the limits of a critical approach inside psychology. Various alternative frameworks, including the study of discourse, are themselves embedded in institutions which place severe constraints on what can be done to change things. I map out some of the different conceptual and practical moves that are made by different kinds of critical psychologists to notice what is happening, and the countermeasures that are put in place to hamper the critics, and, crucially, to turn critical accounts back into real psychology again, into something that can be absorbed and neutralised, made manageable.

The fifth part of the book describes in the final four chapters the intimate and necessary interrelationship between psychological knowledge and contemporary management strategies, and the demand that people talk about themselves in ways that will adapt them more efficiently and thoroughly to abusive power structures. This final part of the book builds to a crisis in which the individuals involved are expected to behave in line with psychological theories, but in which some of them choose to take that path and some of them do not.

The psychology that I describe in this book is of a specific time and place, but that is part of the argument. Psychology as a discipline desperately tries to transcend specific local conditions in which it develops its theories and gathers together the 'facts' supposed to support them, but it is always rooted in the particular conditions and biographies of those involved. This is an intellectual autobiography focusing on one part of my life and on the illusion that this supposedly scientific discipline could account for the behaviour and internal mental life not only of one individual but of all human beings. I tell you something about myself, of the kind of personal choices that are usually missing from psychological textbooks, and I describe theories and attempts to gather evidence that give its practitioners the idea that they are scientists. I chart my anthropological auto-ethnographic journey through psychology, through strange academic terrain. I hope thereby that it will seem strange to you, reader, either because you know little about psychology or because I make something you think you know very well seem other than it seems, other than what you think it is. This is a story about the discipline of psychology and a warning.

I'll start at the beginning, so here we go.

PART I
Studying psychology

1

EXPERIMENTS

Cold method

In which we encounter psychology for the first time, and discover how attached this strange discipline is to an experimental method which reduces personal experience to the link between cause and effect. We also make connections between the separation of the individual from context, and the isolation of people from each other outside in the real world.

I know this is a strange way to begin a psychology book, and in a textbook for students it is unthinkable to directly reference the author at the outset in the first person. Even though it is the case that as we go up the hierarchal structure of the discipline it becomes permissible for venerable professors to say 'I think' this or that, the message conveyed to students is that they must blot out what they think or feel in order to be more objective, more scientific. I learnt this from my first false start as a student of psychology, something I describe in this chapter.

Delusions

It is freezing here, and the rain drives us all into our homes, those who have them. We shiver inside, alone if we are unlucky or if we are new to the city, away from home. Psychology begins for me in Newcastle in September 1975. Here I am inside my lodgings. I am not sure why I chose psychology, but it had a lot to do with being with friends. This is paradoxical because psychology usually separates people from each other in order to study their behaviour. I arrived here to take a combined honours degree in botany and zoology. It was bitterly cold from the start. My oversize dark blue greatcoat and long thin hair were little protection against the chilly wind cutting through from Jesmond Dene in the east across to the university campus. Newcastle-upon-Tyne is a city in the north east of England, almost as far away from south London as you can get. I knew no one. I was in a strange city and I was lost.

I did not know what I was getting myself into. I was a year older than most of the other first-year students on my course. Maybe that helped, though I don't think I would have been better prepared for life here in the far north if I'd come here the year before, if that had been possible. I hadn't done well enough in school, and even now I had some catching up to do. It was a lucky break for me that biology was introduced as a new subject in my secondary school when I was thirteen, my third year there. I did well at the subject, and the new teacher liked me, I thought. I liked him, and even if he didn't like me, he was willing to give extra lessons to two of us in the fifth year who sat the O-level exam. If I hadn't passed that particular exam I would not have progressed into sixth form. Those two years of biology class meant at least that I had some attention away from the bewildering chaos that was my form, 4F and then 5F. The form letters ran from B to F. The A was missing, I guess, to disguise the ability grading system the school used to sort out who would make it through to A-levels and who would not.

I loathed school. I wanted to die. I still sometimes dream that I am trying to find my class in the empty sprawling modern buildings of Ravens Wood at Keston in Kent, not being able find my way around, anxious that I am late, lost. Biology was better. We sat side by side in the unnaturally quiet classroom when school was over, me and Johnson – second names were how we knew each other at school and outside it – while Mr Hocking, the biology teacher, guided us through the syllabus every Thursday afternoon. We both made it through, but when I went back in September after the summer's O-level exams I was the only student carrying on. I took botany and zoology O-levels in the first year of sixth form and then A-levels the year after, in summer 1974. I wore a white lab coat. I dissected animals, even eventually Bertie rat who had become a little too plump after being pampered by the biology technical assistant, and whose lucky escapes from the knife did come to an end. I worked on assignments in the school library, on my own because there was no class to attend.

My other classes were disastrous, first mathematics and then English. I muddled through mathematics for a couple of weeks before transferring into English literature, scraped through a re-take of the O-level to be able to do that, and then failed the A-level. I could blame it on *Mansfield Park*, which I was supposed to read but didn't, or *Lord of the Rings* which I did, but which was not on the syllabus. You will have got the impression so far, perhaps, that I wasn't the most sociable or socially competent of boys. Psychologically difficult, perhaps, or stupid, or maybe there was just no psychological mindedness as such in me at all.

Ravens Wood was the new name for Bromley Technical High School and was in transition to becoming a Comprehensive, and so open to all abilities. Some pupils, those who had failed to get into a grammar school, made it through this one, and then to university. The biology, botany and zoology funnelled me in that direction, though it mystified other school friends that I might do this, that I could go on to take a degree.

I discovered when I began to think about this next step, that I needed chemistry O-level to get into university. Newcastle's offer of a place for the following year gave me time to pass that exam while still living at home in Bromley and working in a furniture shop. I would walk in to work and spend the day arguing with the manager who was in the Communist Party. I would work on my chemistry lesson book in the lunch break and walk home at the end of the day to work on coursework assignments for the correspondence course. No classes and no experiments, but plenty of brown paper envelopes. That year, 1975, I turned from being pretty clueless politically, conservative even, to being shocked by the brutality of US imperialism in Vietnam and inspired by victory there. I wasn't impressed by the Soviet Union or its satellite states, but I was reading about Marxism and up for finding out more about politics. Newcastle would be the place to do that.

The rain is busy outside, and here I am in the sitting room of my terraced-house lodgings off Heaton Road beyond Jesmond Dene. It is just after breakfast. We were in the house in September, were served a cooked breakfast every morning, which always began with porridge, porridge which made me retch but which I struggled to eat because I had not told the landlady the first mornings that this was something I really disliked. I didn't want to upset her. She is a Geordie, a local of Newcastle. She is perhaps in her seventies, with tightly-curled grey hair, wire-rimmed spectacles and a flowered pinafore. She has looked after generations of medical students, she says, and I think she is disappointed with us. She likes medics. She doesn't hear about what they get up to in the university. She brings trays with toast and tea and in the afternoons she sometimes sets the table for home-made scones. She hooks her foot around the door to pull it closed behind her when she leaves the room. The yellowing flower-pattern china is assembled on doilies and they compete for attention with the lace tablecloth. By the side of my sitting room chair I have a few books on the sideboard; some Thomas Hardy and then, a little later, there will be a couple by Lenin.

At least I now have a bedroom to myself. At the beginning of term I was sharing a bedroom with Dave from somewhere near London. He had two lime-green check shirts that he hung to air at night in the wardrobe. Dave studied civil engineering, had soldier-style Brylcreemed-hair, short-cut and shaved at the back of his neck, buck teeth and acne. He looked like a giant spotty rabbit. We shared the bathroom, which has a big cold bath and coughs out water as brown as the tea along with little bits of pipe. The other guy is from Leeds, has his own room, and he has a girlfriend from Manchester here at the university who is living nearby. They are Nigel and Sandra, they study psychology and they both wear duffle coats. Here are my first friends in Newcastle.

It seems like psychology could be interesting, they say, though they don't know much about it yet. The main selling point is that you can do experiments on people. You apparently measure people doing different things and study what they are thinking. It does sound fun, white-coat stuff, and, most important, it is something to do as a third subject. That's what it is for Nigel and Sandra, something they have chosen alongside their other main degree interests. It's not exactly psychiatry, they say, which is about dealing with mad people. I knew that already, about psychiatry. My mother and then school classmates used to joke about who might end up at

Colney Hatch, the old mental asylum in north London. That's where they locked people up who acted too weird and bothered other people. And that was it, though even that didn't connect with or threaten my own weird sense of myself because I had learnt not to be too weird around others and not to bother them too much. Neither psychiatry, which was one of the names for prison, nor psychology, which was a complete mystery, had anything to do with me. Psychology itself doesn't at all seem to be about helping people. If anything, it seems close to astrology, perhaps with a harder edge, for it is about spotting personality types, working out how different people behave, guessing how they think. Now I've arrived here I realise I need to find a third subject to study for my first year of the degree course along-side botany and zoology. It is not going to be chemistry.

There is another possible option. That is anatomy, which will be taken alongside the medics and will specifically focus on the hand. It will involve dissection of a hand. Within a few days of arriving in Newcastle we hear stories about two of the most obnoxious upper-class gangs at the university, students of agriculture and medicine, these are the 'agrics' and the 'medics'. They fight, usually with each other, which is fortunate. But it reminds us who is in charge of the place. Newcastle is a city divided along class-lines, between the town and the gown, and between the university and the Polytechnic, which does not, we assume, have gowns. And the university is also internally divided, between students from privileged backgrounds who are more likely to end up in agriculture or medicine, to follow in the footsteps of their fathers, and some of us who are here on sufferance to study the lesser and less serious subjects. So, would it be a year of the hand, anatomy in a part of the university that I don't know and guess I won't like, or could I go in to campus the following morning with two new friends who have told me that they think there are still places on the psychology course? It's a no-brainer, it seems. I have the idea psychology is about people, perhaps like the Marxism I was into, and that it is a science, so I could study plants, animals and human beings.

This is what I said the next day to Professor Max Hammerton in the psychology department during his brisk assessment of new applicants. I didn't mention the Marxism. He let me in. Hammerton had close-cropped hair, an amazingly big chin, a buttoned up tight check shirt and looked at me in a funny way, which, I realised in the first lecture of the course, was because he had one eye. He had delivered his inaugural lecture at Newcastle the year before on psychology as, the title had it, 'A science under siege', and he was quick in the first-year lectures to tell us who the enemies were. Many people believe that there are fairies at the bottom of the garden, he said, but they have no proof that these little beings exist, which sounded fair enough, true even.

Psychology isn't fooled by such ridiculous beliefs, he continued, and as he warmed to his theme in the first lecture he mentioned other enemies of reason that sounded a good deal more interesting. A "French punk" called Jean-Paul Sartre was especially dangerous. Hammerton spat out the word 'punk'; this was clearly his party piece, one that he probably always opened the course with, and he was evidently enjoying himself. The existentialist Sartre, he told us, was not only a lousy philosopher but a lazy novelist. In one of his "so-called novels" he wrote of a character with one eye unable to detect the murderer who was standing very still and blending into the wallpaper. Hammerton finished off his tirade with a killer blow which combined scientific expertise with what he himself knew. Science plus professionalised personal experience gave him the edge in dispensing with Sartre. Anyone with the most basic understanding of perception would know that this storyline was quite impossible, he said, for a one-eyed man would be well able to distinguish figure from the background. This was where we began our search for knowledge about the mind: in the land of the blind where the one at the front of the class was king.

Here was a double hook. It was thrown out for all of us in the class, and it sure was for me. One message was that psychology can tell you the difference between what is true and what is false. Here is the science, and the Marxist classics I was reading also promised to dispel superstition. Lenin often cites Tolstoy who writes of a confusing scene in which it seems as if a madman is crouching and gesticulating in the street, but when he comes closer he sees that the man is sharpening a knife on a stone. The message is that the closer you get, the more you know. Many people believe things that are false, and even this famous French philosopher I'd barely heard of was fooled. It seemed now that Sartre not only had a lazy eye, but was also a lazy novelist, though I couldn't track down the story of the killer hiding in the wallpaper. What I did know of Sartre was that he was an atheist who questioned what we can know of reality. I'd been taught at home to scoff at religious ideas, even to be wary of religious people when they came together in groups. That much had been brought home to us by my mother who embarked on a teacher-training degree when I was in my teens. Existentialism had been a seminar topic on her course, and we picked away at it around the kitchen table. Hammerton's attack on Sartre at least acknowledged his existence, and that made psychology as a subject immediately more attractive to me. The idea that there was a nauseating nothingness to our little lives was one I had obsessively circled around in various dramatic suicidal fantasies. I declared myself to be a 'solipsist' at school, by which I meant that this world around me and all the other beings in it were figments of my imagination, that only I existed. Buried in this claim was the glimmering paradox that this should also mean something to the few friends I had, even when I was boring them to death.

My mother used to comment scornfully whenever there was a disaster reported on television, that she bet the families would all be praying again, clearly out of their minds. When my sister had a brain tumour, my mother would return home from the convent school where she taught and mutter contemptuously 'they're praying for her again'. I was given licence by my parents to be late at school and so to miss the Anglican mass assembly before classes, and that again separated me from the rest of the dangerous deluded religious fools, a separation I liked. Sometimes, if I timed it right, I could make it to Ravens Wood in time to pick up the class register that had just been delivered to the main reception office, tick my name as present, and then sit and chat outside the assembly hall with the one Catholic and one Jewish pupil excused from attending assembly.

At the same time, there was a second message in Max Hammerton's tirade, which was that psychology could key into your own sense about what might be true about yourself. Here is an appeal to personal experience, another hook that is closely attached to the scientific one. Psychology is not just brute science, but latches into something deeper, and that's what makes it seem so magical to so many of those who encounter it for the first time. Even in a university department like Newcastle's which prided itself on scientific method as the basis of psychology, there was an appeal to what someone might feel about the matter to ground knowledge in reality, to give an objective account the stamp of approval. Who that someone was, whether they were a professor who was able to make that connection and give it some authority, or whether they were everyday folk who turn out to be mistaken about fairies at the bottom of the garden, was unclear. This double appeal of psychology – that it combines objective truths built from scientific experiments that all psychologists should know about combined with what each individual might feel to be true – was a winning combination, but sometimes an unpleasant one. And that's where I was up to, attracted and repelled.

Here we three are then. The rain is picking up speed, and back in the sitting room in Heaton this morning, we are chatting after breakfast. Here's how psychology works, an example. This is now me and Nigel, and Sandra just arrived from her place before we get the bus together into class. Dave has left these lodgings now, and this is just before we will disappoint our landlady again, abandoning her house to move in together into a tiny downstairs flat on the other side of the city in Benwell near the old shipyards on the River Tyne. The evening before, we had picked up a Scientology leaflet and had a long argument about it with one of their flock. Scientology is one of the other worlds running in parallel to the discipline of psychology, and some psychologists are attracted to it because it looks like it does the same kind of thing, linking science with personal experience. It is a rival approach but excluded from academic study, and it's rather more obviously made up than psychology, written as an elaboration of 1950s science fiction before claiming to be a religion. Anyway, this morning when I refer to our argument the previous evening I'm blanked by my two friends. "What are you talking about Ian", they said, "that never happened". When I turn to the mantelpiece to take down the leaflet which I had put next to the clock, the leaflet isn't there.

For a moment I'm overwhelmed with uncertainty, with the possibility that my memory of the evening is wrong, or, worse, that I hallucinated it all, and I protest all the more to get some acknowledgement that it really was so. They are good actors, these two, and they are playing it straight as I shift to and fro; from anxious appeal to their memory of what happened to insisting that I am right, that I have not lost leave of my senses. In that oscillation between my two desperate attempts to put things right we have both sides of the equation that makes psychology as a discipline so powerful. On the one hand, there is shared knowledge about what is real, a reality enforced by agreement between at least two others which here throws what I know into question. On the other hand, there is my own sense that what I have experienced is true, that this is some kind of game and I need to find a way of making what I know count. There is an unstable shifting balance of power between agreement about what had happened and what I remember and feel to be the case.

In scientific psychology the route to agreement about what has happened is given a structure which the psychologists call their method, and that's what we are learning to follow in our experiments. Fortunately, there is a more human dimension which psychology often needs in order to obtain support for what it says about people. Nigel and Sandra eventually cracked when we got into university and reassured me that their story about my story was untrue, a game. I was relieved. I felt my own reality and that of other people begin to align again. The problem is that this science of the mind picks and chooses the stories that will fit its own story, those that confirm what it says it has discovered.

Here already in our first lecture by Max Hammerton was a rather surprising combination of scientific knowledge and personal experience. But it is sometimes the case that scientific knowledge as a shared enterprise among those with power overrides the personal experience of an isolated individual. My anxiety that morning impressed this on me. In the case of psychology, this is especially dangerous. Psychology claims to link the two, what you didn't yet know with what you already sensed to be the case. In the course of the year we were invited as students to make that link as we learnt about psychology, and this is a link that again and again binds psychologists to their own discipline and then to a particular way of looking at the world.

Dreams

It wasn't always so bad. We had some lectures on Sigmund Freud by Vincent Deary, a nice guy with a tangled beard and baggy jumper who giggled a lot as he talked about free association, the linking of one word to another. The idea was apparently that this linking became more risqué the more some kind of internal censorship was relaxed, and then, for Freudian psychoanalysis, we were told, this train of associations invariably eventually involves sexual symbolism. Vincent gave examples of innuendo in film, his favourite case being the scene in *The Thomas Crown Affair* from 1968 where Faye Dunaway is flirting with Steve McQueen over a game of chess and suggestively strokes the bishop piece. The connection with psychology as we should approach it in class, however, was made by way of dreams, and these would be dreams that we should record and correlate with things that had occurred during the day, more specifically with what we had eaten. The psychology textbooks reminded us that as far back as Aristotle there was the idea that a bodily sensation might be converted into an aspect of the dream; phlegm sliding down the throat might appear in the dream as the swallowing of honey, for example.

Freud himself discussed such historical speculation about the meaning of dreams and then tried to distance himself from any universal map of dream symbolism, from dream analysis based on the decoding of symbols. *This* might mean *that* in a dream, but the connection is idiosyncratic and depends on the personal history of the dreamer and, crucially, on what they specifically do not want brought to conscious awareness, what they may have repressed. It is one thing for Faye in the film to communicate sexual attraction to Steve through the turning of the bishop chess piece into a symbol of male genitalia, but quite another to know whether a bishop is sexually charged and repressed for either Faye or Steve. So, for our own study we decided we should ask people what the sexual symbols in dreams meant to them. That would surely be a 'psychological' way of connecting what was meant with what people thought.

We didn't know how we would do that for the practical assignment which was linked to this part of the course. It was embarrassing enough talking about it among ourselves, even though there seemed to be something in what Freud was saying. Perhaps there was something in it precisely because it was embarrassing. We were guided onto safer ground by the method that we would use in our own experimental study to be carried out in small groups, away from what the sexual images might mean and from what might cause sexual thoughts. This iteration of the method resolved itself into asking people whether or not they had eaten cheese before they went to sleep, and whether they had dreamt. No sex.

This is where we learnt one crucial lesson about scientific psychology, which is that what is most important is not what the content of the theories might be but how to test them; not what it is about but rather how to examine it. This is where we learnt what experimental method is, and why psychologists are so attached to method. When we got together in small groups to carry out our investigation into the effects of eating cheese on whether you dream we were, of course, focusing only on what we could see. You can't see what has been repressed, what psycho-analysts believe to lie in the unconscious, but you can see what people write about what they remember about their dreams after eating cheese the night before. It's not much, but it will have to do if your method is to be based on accurate observation of reality, if it is what psychologists call 'empirical'. Scientific psychology is fully empirical when it observes and measures behaviour. In our case we were looking at writing, at little diaries of dreams, which is clearly second-best. It means that there is still what psychologists call a 'black box' between the eating of cheese and the report of the dream. This black box is what other people think of as their minds, all of the thinking that goes on in the midst of behaviour that cannot ever be observed and recorded.

Then you need to know what it is you are going to observe and record, and empirical scientific method tells you what steps to follow so that you know where you are in the process of setting up and carrying out your investigation. There is plenty of activity going on inside the black box, but we needed to leave that aside, try to forget it and instead just home in on what was recorded in the diaries. Our task was to treat what went on the evening before, one aspect of it, eating cheese as the 'cause', and the report of the dream as the 'effect'. Even if there wasn't a black box in between the cause and effect we still wouldn't have been able to directly link the two. Even when you see a billiard ball hit another one that then shoots off into the pocket you can't be absolutely sure that the first ball caused the second to move. The eighteenth-century Scottish philosopher David Hume, someone who psychologists much prefer to Jean-Paul Sartre, insisted on this point as part of his argument that what counts is the *correlation* between what we take to be cause and what we assume to be the effect. Your own common sense, and that of everyone else around you, will tell you that you saw that connection between the two billiard balls happen, that one ball really did push the other one into action. However, while psychology needs shared common sense to make sense of things in the world, it is sceptical about what you can see. It is the method that is in command, and that method gives the psychologist the means to sort out what is there and what is not. Somewhere along the line, experimental method in psychology will invite you to believe that the things it describes as being inside you really are there and that the things that you used to think were there inside you are not. We had to trust the method to link cause and effect in our investigation. Once we set things up like that, we could call it an experiment.

Another way around and eventually, we thought, into the black box, was to put together our record of observations of cause and effect from lots of different people. In Newcastle we were told to refer to the people we studied in our experiment as our 'subjects'. This keeps things neat and tidy because then you know exactly what you're talking about when you describe what the subjects did, even if you don't know why they did it. You dispense with the huge variety of reasons why they might have done what they did, why they might have dreamt after eating cheese for example, by grouping them into what we were told to call our 'sample'. It was rather a small sample size, and we couldn't pretend that the subjects in our sample were representative of any kind of population, of psychology students or university students, let alone people from Newcastle, Britain or the world. That's what we had to remember, even if we claimed to have something like a 'representative sample'. Even if, through some amazing and improbable selection procedure we had the same proportion of people in our experimental group from every imaginable cat-egory of person as there were in the world outside, once they were in our study they would no longer be distinct people, they would, aggregated together, become our subjects.

We also needed a group of subjects so we could divide them into those who were going to eat cheese, which was our experimental group, and those who were not, our 'control group'. The experimental rationale was that we needed to home in on the precise variables we wanted to measure, and once we followed that logic, which I did, then we are led into a certain way of viewing the world and the kinds of people who live in it. The advantage of being in a control group is that you don't have to do anything in particular, apart from carry on as usual, and fill out a diary or questionnaire, which, of course, calls for reflection and report to the researcher, something quite unusual. The disadvantage in this case was that if you normally eat cheese before you go to sleep you must have an evening off. As well as being an experimenter I was one of the subjects, which is bad practice in real psychology because that meant that the subject bit of me knew what the experimenter bit of me was up to. Psychology specialises in separating out these two functions, conceal-ing what the experimenter is up to and deceiving the subject; this is one reason, perhaps, why the discipline dislikes philosophers who insist that there must still be some hidden connection between the two functions, the two roles. That night I ate cheese and didn't dream anything worth reporting, and, worse, there were no significant differences between the two groups. That's Freud for you, we thought, and that was psychoanalysis done for us too as far as the psychology course at Newcastle was concerned. Freud was too hot, perhaps, too fascinating, but whatever was of interest melted away when we subjected him to our cold method.

Getting people to be subjects who would do strange things while we were watching them is one part of psychological research. Another is learning how to link the causes and effects we were observing and recording with existing knowledge, with records of behaviour made by other psychologists before us. Those records are ordered according to the questions they thought worth asking and the methods they were using, which puts all sorts of obstacles in place of working out what was really going on. One part of our course was on correlations between left-handedness and different psychological characteristics. The question here was whether being left-handed was linked with different levels of intelligence or kinds of personality or forms of behaviour.

One lesson drummed into us from our cheese dream study and from every other experiment reported in the lectures was that 'correlation is not cause'; psychologists will often repeat this mantra while implying all the while that they can find the causes for human behaviour. They evoke and repress what they are told in their undergraduate classes about what Hume wrote. For example, if you find that left-handed people are more resentful of others, you cannot then conclude that it is being left-handed that leads to that resentment. It might have been something to do with the way that left-handed people were treated or any number of other things, other 'variables' as they are called in psychological method terminology. Newcastle University library had shelves upon shelves of psychology journals going back to the time where the pages were almost as thick as the covers, and the dust had settled into the rough-cut edges.

Past studies of left-handedness were interesting, but not for what they revealed about the correlations between that sinister condition and bad behaviour, bad personality or stupidity. Those grimy dark red, blue or green-backed journals on the sagging wood and sharp metal shelves in the lower levels of the library were a goldmine, revealing not what left-handed people thought but what psychologists thought about them. Because it was once assumed that children should learn to write with their right hands, left-handedness was often suppressed with force, by tying the left hand up behind the back, for example, or punishing pupils who broke the rule. Then the correlation between being left-handed and such abnormalities as homosexuality was indeed treated by many psychologists as a cause, and sometimes as a cause running in the other direction; why not that you could be left-handed because you were gay?

The insistence on correlation in psychology opened up more questions than it solved, which led to further research. The faded fine print sinking into the grain of the old pages in the library stacks told many such stories of correlations and what they might mean. Article after article took a description and found ways to enforce it as if it were a universal norm. Each turn in the argument sought to identify behaviour that strayed from the norm, to name those that could be captured in psychological categories that named forms of abnormality. It was depressing and enthralling reading. One little project on left-handedness for the psychology course at Newcastle involved hours of research. Gloomy narrow corridors of journals and books barely lit by low-voltage fluorescent light were at that moment my object of study, and it was as if the psychologists who produced them were my subjects. There were no windows to be forced open in the basement rooms of the library, but here were windows onto psychology itself. For those moments, psychology was worth studying.

Meanwhile, I had to deal with botany and zoology classes, places where social classification seemed almost as powerful as sorting objects into genera and species. The botany course exposed me to people who already knew all the names of the plants from their country estates. One Saturday we had a field trip outside the city to pick mushrooms, and while the other students seemed at home I was out of my depth, outclassed. For the zoology course my tutor was Lord Richard Percy who was jolly enough but seemed mystified that everyone in our little group was not as fascinated by fish fossils as he was. His room was up some winding stairs in a turret. His eyes swam around his spectacles. I never saw the Northumberland coast while I was based in Newcastle, but our botanical and zoological specimens all seemed to be squidgy wet things that looked like nothing I'd studied at school; well, to me they looked like nothing. These were other worlds, and I didn't put time into finding out how they worked. I felt anxious in class and in the laboratories where the dark wood benches and microscopes projected their gloom into me. I could not make what I peered at on the slide adjust to what I saw in the textbook. I left the classes early, mystified as to how these people around me seemed to be having so much fun. I escaped into the city. I wandered aimlessly around Newcastle city centre avoiding classes, sometimes I whiled away the time catching an afternoon film show, found the best places to buy stotties, the local speciality heavy round white bread-cakes. I shouldn't have passed the exams for botany or zoology, or the re-sits at the end of the summer of 1976, and so I didn't.

Psychology was the one course I passed at the end of my first disastrous year at university. I found some anchor points for alternative perspectives which helped, little books in a Methuen 'Essential Psychology' series – we were told to buy the lot – by Nick Heather on *Radical Perspectives in Psychology* and a terrific one by John Shotter, *Images of Man in Psychological Research*. I'm not sure who I could blame for messing things up, but high up the list would be drinking too much Newcastle Brown Ale, cause and consequence of a chaotic household and bad sex, good sex with the wrong people, out in the west of the city. I was almost teetotal for years after that. When I joke that I am careful not to get drunk and abusive, it is not so much that I fear I'll turn my anxiety outwards, direct my hostility at other people at all, it is rather that I'll turn in on myself and ruin my life. I knew by then that the fact that 'solipsism' is a disastrous mistake did not mean that I could not be tempted again to enact it, to make it so, and to cut out the others I need around me to stay human. I didn't know that my turn to psychology would lead me into a dense meshwork of names for what I felt, that would name the despair I encountered when I made the mistake of turning in on myself, still less that this naming of it could make it worse.

Reality

I did learn something while I was there. I found a bookshop near campus that sold left journals. Reading and political meetings gave some structure to my time. I learnt a lot about Marxism in Newcastle, and about other kinds of politics, but not in university courses. I spent some time in a reading group run by Maoists based at the Polytechnic. We read Lenin and then Stalin, and then I left. There were jokes that the group I eventually joined had entrance exams, which wasn't true. My new comrades were Trotskyist, that is, Marxists who were Leninists who still wanted to stay true to the promise of more democracy after the revolution, not less. There was an internal educational bulletin and classes, and internal and international internal discussion bulletins. Wading through reams of smudgy cyclostyled stapled pages took much time. Nearly every contribution was profoundly pedagogical, rehearsal of a line which was pitted against the others, reminders of debates from around the world through which I learnt more about geography and history than I had ever done at school.

In this political group there was another aspect to the debate over how to build a revolutionary party that I didn't anticipate before I joined, and this aspect also made some surprising connections with psychology. This was feminism, which was present not only in the women's liberation movement but was also emerging as a rebellious force inside some left organisations. There was an argument as part of the critique of traditional Leninist 'democratic centralist' groups that personal and everyday life was part of the political process itself. This was the argument summed up in the slogan that 'the personal is political'; the way we related to each other in our meetings and our bedrooms, the argument went, reflected power relations between men and women in society, a society that turned people into objects to be bought and sold, one in which women were objectified, reduced to their household labour and their sex. Those power relations reflected and reproduced the systematic distortion of human relationships under capitalism as an economic system based on exploitation and under patriarchy which privileged male power.

These arguments made internal discussions inside the Newcastle branch of our group very uncomfortable. I didn't understand the difference between the minority tendency that I signed up for at that year's upcoming conference and the leadership, let alone where feminism came into it. There were recriminations that these kinds of feminist debates had nearly destroyed our French sister organisation, and then counter-charges of sexism. In the midst of all this there were several internal conference discussion bulletins about the personal and the political. These included analyses of the way that this sick society not only treats those who rebel as if they were the ones who were sick, but also how pathological relationships between men and women were showing us something about the way we treated each other and treated ourselves. That is, our delusions and dreams were grounded in social relationships shaped in a particular way by political-economic structures. These delusions and dreams were important to what we ordinarily think of as our 'psychology', but psychological research methods never seem to actually touch on that.

The distortion of experience when we treat others and ourselves as if they and we are objects is described in Marxist theory as 'alienation'. We are alienated under capitalism, alienated from who we are or who we could be, prevented from working together to recognise each other's value as human beings. The internal discussion documents on the link between the personal and the political pointed to the way that alienation as a weird kind of separation from each other and from our feelings took its toll on women, but also pointed to how people who were so physically close to each other in modern cities could, even at the very same time, feel so isolated.

There are consequences of this alienation and separation for how individuals then relate to each other in groups they join, including in political organisations that aim to change society. As I read these documents, I thought of my relatives who lived alone and then talked at us when we visited them instead of with us. We would give friends who were lonely little time not only because we had little time ourselves but because they drained us of energy as they demanded to be heard. They wanted to make the most of their rare opportunities to speak to someone else, to anyone. The left groups were also part of the problem; they either blocked people who wanted to talk more about themselves, or they degenerated into places where people endlessly and hopelessly and fruitlessly complained about how they felt, turned over their frustration at not being able to change the world.

I sensed the isolation of people from each other and from their collective shared experience of the world. People wrenched from the social relationships that made them human became individuals who then ended up very much like the objects we called 'subjects' in our psychology experiments. The subject that psychology seemed to be studying was not in fact an individual in the sense of being something singular to be valued in relation to others, but an individual who was separated out and then aggregated into a sample so that their very individuality was lost somewhere along the way. When people who are alone and feel lonely join groups on this basis and try to make sense of their lives when they are using psychology as a guide, they don't solve the problem but intensify it.

Good grades in some of my psychology essays for assignments set and marked by postgraduate students encouraged me to meet my tutor after the sit and re-sit exam fiasco. He was a young lecturer in developmental psychology with a boyish pudding-bowl haircut and a cuddly jumper. I went to ask him what he thought I should do. Now it was at the end of the summer break. The new academic year was about to begin in late September. His office was next to a laboratory observation area where children were brought in to be watched and their behaviour recorded.

I had moved on from my shared house after failing the re-sit examinations in botany and zoology. I was signing on for unemployment benefit and sleeping on the sofa in a comrade's house. I walked up Westgate market street into the city centre, bought a loaf of Mother's Pride white sliced bread for 13 pence on the way, popped into the student's union building to check upcoming political meetings, and arrived at the psychology block in the late afternoon. I wondered if there might be a way of transferring into the psychology degree. My tutor looked at me for a while and then said slowly and clearly that he thought that I should consider applying to a polytechnic if I wanted to do a course like that, a polytechnic because I had clearly failed to make the grade at university. I didn't like this reality check, but it was good advice, not psychologically oriented at all, but focused on the practicalities of a rather lonely isolated student coping with academic life.

My first introduction to psychology had been a bruising and puzzling one, and it made me wonder all the more about the nature of this strange discipline, and what those who spent their time inside it were up to. There were clearly connections between my own restricted sense of who I was as an individual and the discipline's image of individuals as isolated objects, as subjects of experimental research. Those were the kinds of connections that left politics was trying to grapple with, alienation that various political groups aimed to theorise and put an end to but which they unfortunately also tended to reinforce in their own practice. This encounter made me appreciate how important psychology was, not as a place to solve the riddle of how to connect personal experience with social processes, but as a network of theories and practices that perpetuated alienation. I was hooked, wanting to get inside this thing and work out how it operated. That was where my anthropological journey into the discipline really began. I will describe, in the next chapter, my second more successful attempt to learn about psychology and reflect on how it subjects students to its own peculiar forms of knowledge.

2

COGNITION

Sex and race

In which we notice how approaches to politics are marginalised in psychology, a discipline that tries to forget its own past, and how this politics returns unbidden. Psychologists use the reductive notion of 'cognition' to describe memory and perception in order to frame human action, and these limited accounts of the way we think and feel operate in relation to deeper more threatening ideas, with connections between fascism, race and sexuality.

I enter the test department in this chapter and show how quickly and easily psychologists slide from description to prescription. They know well that an experiment is not a test, but something in the logic of the method they use leads them to assess how well their subjects have performed, and part of the problem is that their subjects also know this. You can see here how this works for undergraduate students, how subjectivity is avoided in the name of a concern with objective investigation. At the same time, psychologists try to avoid another domain, one in which passions seem to them to run riot over calm clear reason – politics. I discovered that however much psychologists try to steer clear of political controversy, the right has often found psychology to be a useful and dangerous tool for dividing people from each other and ruling over them.

Test

We travel to Plymouth Polytechnic next, for a place on a course there, in early summer 1977. I wanted to get away from London again, and this was the furthest-most possible place with a psychology degree course, down in the south west of England. The other end of the country to Newcastle seemed ideal for a fresh start, a warm and sunny city in Devon, by the sea. It seemed perfect, but first I needed to get through the interview. I reckon at least two things worked against me that day; what

I looked like and what I knew. Or, rather, the mess that I was when I turned up, and what I could not remember about the psychology I had studied so far. I had messed up enough job interviews by that time to know that appearance and preparation were important, but I seemed to have learnt nothing. My attempt to join the civil service the year before hit the rocks when I turned up with long hair and couldn't think of anything diplomatic to say when asked what I thought about what was then the third 'Cod War' between England and Iceland.

By now I had work and was saving hard to get out of it again, to get back into full-time study. Because I was saving money, I took the nine-pound nine-hour bus journey from Victoria Coach Station in London down to Plymouth, arriving near midnight before the day of the interview. I was fortunate that it was warmer than London because I had nowhere to stay. I climbed over the wall into Beaumont Park, locked for the night, found a bench and settled down, and tried to sleep. In the early morning I walked around Plymouth Hoe, the terraced area facing the sea which was alive with the sound of gulls but not much else, and read some of Liam de Paor's republican history of Ireland, *Divided Ulster*.

By the time I got to the psychology department mid-morning I was a rather scruffy unshaven sight compared with the other candidates, some of whom had travelled down that morning on the train from London, a special return deal that was apparently the same cost as my bus journey. I felt stupid, and knew I should have checked those rail prices. One of the applicants was wearing a suit and carry-ing a briefcase. The highpoint of the day was participating in what I still thought of as a psychology test. Experiments are not supposed to be 'tests' of ability and that is why psychologists tell participants that there are no right or wrong answers. That is also why most times the participants conclude that the psychologist is lying to them and assume that it must be a test. They assume that this or that answer is what the psychologist is really looking for, and that's the game they play. If you are an experimental 'subject', you behave like it's a game, and usually, if you are not very stubborn, you do your best to win. Either way, the psychologist thinks they have won, when they have actually lost, failing each time to obtain meaningful results from these rigged games.

This experiment was a perfect example of psychological research as a test and a game, and the frame was perfect too. When the 'experimenter' cajoles or threatens their 'subjects' there is always a risk that something will go wrong, perhaps that some of the 'data' will have to be discarded as a result. In this case, however, we were good subjects. We all had good reason to do the best we could and behave well. A cognitive psychologist, Ian Dennis, was waiting for all the applicants after our tour of the department. The tour amounted to being shown a lecture theatre, a laboratory and a corridor with staff office doors on either side. There wasn't much to see, so a cognitive psychology experiment was also something to do to fill the time. Ian spoke very slowly, as if he was thinking about each word and phrase, a deliberate and slightly dopy manner, and made his pitch to enrol us as subjects in his experiment. Since we were all keen to get a place on the degree we all, of course, agreed to take part.

This experiment was such fun because Ian instructed us one-by-one to carry out a task I was already very well practised at. It was a version of a game my sisters and I had played at home to deal with the boredom of repeated advertising on the one commercial channel. We would shout out as quickly as we could the name of the product, and meantime speak out loud the commentary. What went in the ears came out the mouth in one seamless babble while we tracked what we heard and competed to guess what was being advertised. If advertising agencies knew we played this game they could have adapted and pitched their message to us as an ideal-typical audience. Our family comprised obedient-enough consumers of the message as it was, but, at last, here it was payout time.

If cognitive psychologists knew we did this they might have built into their research plans a filter of some kind so we less than ideal-typical subjects wouldn't mess up their experiments. The problem this poses for psychology is a general one, that discussion of different strategies that we each used to perceive, remember and repeat things – that is, what is termed 'cognition' in psychology's textbooks and journals – would help screen out some people, people like me for instance, but then the results could not claim to be about everyone. The psychologist can never know exactly which of their experimental group is a 'sample' of what. This is one of the binds that the experimental psychologists tussle with but cannot escape. So, Ian told me to put on the headphones, to listen carefully to what I heard and repeat it out loud. He seemed nervous enough at the beginning of this little game, and by the end was very concerned. A psychology experiment is usually designed to distract attention away from what the research question really is, which is why subjects usually feel deceived somewhere along the way. They *are* deceived, and they usually only find out what the real aim of the study is at the end, during what is called a 'debriefing'. Even then, the poor subject doesn't know quite what to believe, and what they are told is often not plausible enough to make sense of what they have been through. Most student subjects disregard or disbelieve what they are told by psychologists, and are all the more likely to be sceptical because most student sub-jects are on a psychology degree course themselves.

The common exception to the rule, perhaps, is the particular kind of subject who really wants to become a psychologist, who laps up the explanation during the debriefing and is then more liable to believe every word they are told. That's what I did. When I was debriefed I discovered that this experiment was about what is called 'echoic memory'. One of the building blocks of cognitive psychology, and one of the little boxes in the diagrams that litter journal articles about how people remember things, is the 'auditory store', that imaginary little mechanism that holds what we hear for one or two seconds as what is called 'sensory memory'. You get a picture here, perhaps, of these bits and bobs also as slotting together like files in folders and then in the drawers of a filing cabinet, and the point has oft-times been made that the world of the cognitive psychologist is rather like that of a bureaucrat's office. The researcher sorts and files their data from their experiments on people, and so they are very comfortable with a model of the mind that depicts it as also being like a little office. This is one reason why the ideal psychological subject is a white-collar worker. The point of this experiment was to measure the duration of sensory memory – that is, what I heard – under different conditions in which there were different kinds of 'task interference', things to make it more difficult.

Cognitive psychology, with Ulric Neisser as one key figure here, is composed of a series of models of thinking, of how we perceive and remember. Then the models are broken up into little bits so that each element, each box in the diagram, can be disassembled and tested in the laboratory on people like me. Well, not exactly on people like me because, by chance, I'd already rehearsed this task at home while I was growing up. And, it wasn't that I was an exception that proves the rule, but an exception in the way that every particular human being is an exception to the model of thinking that the experimental psychologist patches together from all of the unusual people they gather together in their laboratory. Psychology is never exactly about anyone in particular. It is about no one, but it pretends to be about everyone. Ian told me that my results were very unusual, and I received this information with mixed feelings; I was pleased to have done so well – I must have passed this test that should not have been a test with flying colours – but I was also now anxious that this result might be fed through to the interviewers.

I didn't know what Ian might do with the data from this experiment. It is still not easy to predict what the psychologist will do if things don't go as planned, what happens if they get an unusual result in an experiment. If they get some very anomalous results, they usually discard that record of the encounter they call their 'data' and try and forget it happened. They can smooth things over. This is not recommended in the textbooks, because the researcher is told that they should not try to confirm their prediction or 'hypothesis' but rather look to try and disprove it. This is why they are taught to test what is called the 'null hypothesis', which is that there is no difference between the groups of subjects in their experiment.

This is a real bind for the diligent experimenter. No difference means that there is no significant result, but if they do come up with a difference between the 'experimental' and 'control' group they have to be sure both that it happened all by itself, that the results are really statistically 'significant'; that is, that it could not merely have happened by chance, or, worse, could not have merely reflected what they themselves had engineered. The experimental researcher in psychology is in the impossible position of both setting up the precise conditions in which their subjects behave and having to disclaim any responsibility for what happens, for what their subjects do. The experiment works because it is carefully planned, but it should not be planned to work out exactly as it does for it to produce a convincing publishable result. If all worked out as claimed, it would mean that the articles in psychology journals, articles that have supported a hypothesis, have been astoundingly lucky results that have gone against what the researchers have been aiming at. The journals very rarely publish studies which show that there is *no* significant difference between experimental group and control group, and maybe this is because, however much the psychologist likes to be neutral and objective they also deep down imagine that they are the 'cause' of changes in behaviour and that the 'effects' they describe are down to what they have done to their subjects. A psychologist wants to make a difference in the world, but the apparatus that they use, the experiment, often prevents them from doing that or it distorts what they do, and it distorts how we all understand our own behaviour. Sometimes this is with a political agenda which is also driving that distortion, something psychological supposedly 'scientific method' conveniently obscures.

The year before, in 1976, the story broke in the press that one of the leading British psychologists, Sir Cyril Burt, had fiddled his experimental results and even made up data from fictional research assistants to support his claims about the inheritance of intelligence. As the first and then most prominent educational psychologist working for London County Council from just before the outbreak of the First World War, Burt was in a powerful position, not only to continue his early work in rooting out 'feeble-minded' children in line with the Mental Deficiency Act of 1913, but also to argue for a segregated school system that linked intelligence with class. My own 'technical' high school, for example, was a notch below a 'grammar' school, but a step up from the 'secondary moderns'; this tripartite secondary school system was a legacy of Burt's work which the new inclusive 'comprehensives' should have replaced. Burt was later appointed Professor of Psychology at University College London and served as President of the British Psychological Society, so this story was extremely embarrassing for the public image of psychology as a whole. His fateful slip between an 'experiment' and a 'test' in line with a politically motivated attempt to use experimental data to support eugenic arguments about the inheritance of ability, drew attention to how tempting it is for psychologists with career ambitions to find evidence to support their own pet theories.

Even before this kind of scandalous deliberate distortion of the data, however, the experimenter makes a multitude of little choices, often in good faith or without even thinking through the consequences. These are choices that also cover over inevitable discrepancies in their research data. There is another option to deal with anomalies in the results that is always open to even the most well-meaning experimental psychologist – in fact, to some extent or another, this is standard practice, following implicit unspoken rules that the student is inducted into, and the experimental method would fall apart if they did not do it. This is so that, instead of discarding any results, the researcher can quite legitimately smooth out the measurements so that all the results are put together and then divided out again. Each subject is treated as one in a 'sample' that should be as large as possible to enable statistical analysis, and then it is the abstracted average individual, someone who does not really exist, who is described in the psychology textbooks. Then we, as readers, puzzle about what we read as an account of how we think and feel; we find just a little bit of it that makes sense to us, just enough to draw us in but not quite enough to complete the picture. Then it seems as if everyone perceives the world, thinks about it and remembers it in the same kind of way. In this standard approach different kinds of people with different kinds of experiences then disappear into the mix. Until, of course, that overall account defines what is 'normal' so that those who don't correspond to it are viewed as odd. I consoled myself with the thought that they might want unusual people on the course.

It was time for the double-interview. The fun was over. Paul Kenyon commented that I was "a difficult case" and he would have to consult with his colleague. We had been told that Paul worked in the animal laboratory, and this led me to think that he might be the bad cop. I didn't know where the other interviewer, Michael Hyland, was coming from, but he also looked pained at my answers. It wasn't good. I wasn't at my brightest when I was asked what it was I remembered and liked about psychology at Newcastle. In fact, after a sleepless night in the park and the excitement of the echoic memory task experiment, I could hardly remember anything at all.

The Zeigarnik effect sprung to mind. I remembered the name, and that it was a description of the way we remember things that are unfinished or interrupted, how they stay with us, even that we carry on working at them without being consciously aware of what we are doing. The Russian psychologist Bluma Zeigarnik had been cued into this phenomenon by her supervisor, the Gestalt psychologist Kurt Lewin, in Berlin in the 1920s. Lewin pointed out that good waiters remember unpaid orders, but when bills were settled up the waiter then let them slip from their memory; it is as if the completion of the transaction finally resulted in a 'Gestalt' or a completed 'shape' or 'form' of it that had been awaiting resolution. This description had made sense to me. It fitted with my experience of arriving at solutions to problems, as when I woke in the morning after failing to solve a crossword the night before to find the answer magically bubble into consciousness.

The Zeigarnik effect could be a way of describing how I began a psychology degree in one city and then remembered elements of it sometime later. It was nice to remember the effect in Plymouth during that interview, but it is actually also an example of our experience of memory that cannot be captured by experimental research in psychology. This is one reason why Zeigarnik is of more interest to historians than to cognitive psychologists today, and maybe her 'effect' was already more interesting to me because I focused on how ideas in psychology appeared at different points in history and how they might tell us something more about that historical moment than they did about timeless and universal aspects of the way we think. She tried to find experimental support for the effect, but failed, failed because it is what is meaningful and important to people that is interrupted and then remembered, and the meanings we attach to things always muddle up what the researchers are trying to quantify and measure.

Not everyone thinks in the same way, a piece of information or a task does not mean exactly the same thing to each person, and an experiment that relies on the accumulation of results from a large 'sample' of subjects to prove a theory – or disprove the 'null hypothesis' that the theory is wrong, if we are to believe the textbook description of the experimental process – cannot capture that. This, even if, perhaps, it does also capture something of the always unfinished effect of reading about our own psychology in the textbooks and sensing that something is missing, wanting more. Bluma Zeigarnik moved back to Russia and continued her work in a tradition of psychological research following the revolutionary scientist and writer Lev Vygotsky through the Second World War and way beyond that. It was a tradition of research very different from that in the English-speaking world, a tradition that even now reinterprets her work in order to frame the effect as a memory problem that psychological training can put right. She died in Moscow in 1988, which completes her story for now, but is not a reason to forget her.

Result

I was offered a place on the course, but suspended beginning that same year in Plymouth until the following September of 1978 to give me time to save enough money to live while studying for the first year, that is, until my local educational authority would resume my student grant, forfeited for a year after I dropped out of Newcastle. I lived at home and worked, able to save enough to get to Plymouth and survive for the first year thanks to my mother and stepfather tolerating their regressed unhappy son hanging around the house again. Time out of higher education, working a year before Newcastle and then for two years after that, meant that by the time I arrived in Plymouth I was what was called a 'mature student'. This also meant that when the student grant was resumed in my second year I got a little extra money. I didn't do paid work while at Plymouth, and I vowed to myself that I would never work again. It helped that I was a little bit older and more politically experienced than my classmates. This time I was better prepared for what it was to be a student away from home.

My two years away from academic life were spent in political activity, and in gathering together some few texts I could find on links between psychology and Marxism. I was warned by my political comrades that I shouldn't get involved in psychology because it was, they said, a 'bourgeois discipline'. I agreed with them but argued that this was precisely why it was important to get inside it and find out how it worked. Adjacent disciplines like sociology or history provided competing accounts about the shifting relationships between the individual and culture but tended to avoid examination of the domain of personal experience. When psychology did look into the individual, it did so with the aim of discovering what was 'normal', and marking out abnormalities that needed to be fixed. More important, the discipline had the power to do that, but how was it that psychologists assumed they had that right to determine what was good and bad behaviour, good and bad ways of thinking about the world?

I thought I would find some resources to reflect on limitations of psychology at the Tenth Communist University of London in summer 1978 because they had a session on psychology, but was disappointed. This summer university was run by the Communist Party of Great Britain, then already in the throes of debates over 'Eurocommunism', a shift away from Marxism to reformism which my comrades also warned me against, but the party at that point was therefore also more open to questions of culture and to debates happening in different academic disciplines. One session with Andrew Sutton was on tests used by educational psychologists, and although there was some agonising about categorising children, there was little reflection on how educational psychology had developed and what role it played in society. The contribution by Susan Michie on the mental health system in Cuba, which relied on the Soviet bloc for material support, was really grim, keen to defend the gains made by the revolution but uncritical about the use of medical psychiatry in the hospitals. Given the awful record of psychiatrists in the Soviet Union in diagnosing and incarcerating dissidents, I expected a sharper critique of standard medical approaches and how they meshed with power.

The presenters and participants seemed torn between being loyal to uses of psychology in the so-called socialist countries on the one hand, and finding ways of working with ideas and techniques developed in psychological services in Britain on the other. What was being played out in miniature was the line of the Communist Party's latest revision of what they called the 'British Road to Socialism' which had been published the previous year. On the one hand there was an attempt to distance the party from the Soviet Union and the legacy of Stalinism, but, on the other hand, the alternative was to seek alliances with what were seen as 'progressive' politicians in the mainstream of British society. Instead of a critique of psychology we had the worst of both worlds at the Communist University; that is, some tentative disagreements with the use of psychology in the 'socialist' world and some tentative engagement with psychology at home. As a result, the discipline of psychology itself was treated as a form of knowledge to be appreciated, with underlying assumptions about what it was up to left unquestioned.

The other resource I found was in Collet's, the bookshop linked to the Communist Party on Charing Cross Road in central London. There were stacks of left-wing newspapers and magazines, and among them I found a journal called *Radical Philosophy*, and another called *Ideology & Consciousness* which had started in 1977 and styled itself on the back cover as "a marxist journal in the theory and practice of psychology, psychoanalysis, linguistics and semiotics in the family, the school, the media and other areas". Linguistics and semiotics were completely unfamiliar to me, but I assumed that I could skip those subjects, skip the articles about Ferdinand de Saussure or Valentin Vološinov, for example, and perhaps also the articles on psychoanalysis, focusing on the ones to do with Marxism and psychology. I subscribed and had three issues of the journal by the time I arrived in Plymouth. From *Radical Philosophy* I learnt about different debates in Marxist thought, and in philosophy itself, which I knew nothing about. I used that journal to try and make sense of what I was reading in *Ideology & Consciousness*, which I would skim but not really understand at all.

The journal was an incomprehensible mélange of different ideas, referring to writers who were mainly French such as Louis Althusser, Michel Foucault and Jacques Lacan, characters I had never before heard of. I couldn't even say their names correctly. The journal included polemics with other writers in sociology and cultural studies such as Antonio Gramsci, who I recognised from some the debates about Eurocommunism. I had read how his approach to politics involved a turn from old Marxist attempts to reduce political explanation to economic processes, 'economism', and toward a study of culture. At least, that is how he was framed by the Communist Party at that time, by those inside it who were trying to distance themselves from their historic links with the Soviet Union and with Stalinist forms of Marxism that, paradoxically, insisted on a scientific understanding of economics as the 'base' of society while turning Marxism itself into a kind of religion. The opening essay in issue number one of *Ideology & Consciousness*, on 'Psychology, ideology and the human subject' included all of these names, and more, but I couldn't work out what it had to do with psychology at all.

The fourth issue of the journal arrived that autumn, after I started my degree in Plymouth, and I carried on reading it as a parallel track to my main studies, worrying about what the connection was. I wondered if the problem was the theoretical level of the debate; not so much that it was at a higher theoretical level than I could follow, though that was a problem in itself, but that it was pitched at issues that called themselves 'Marxist' but were not so much concerned with Marxist politics. The references to 'practice' made my doubts about the connection with actual political activity all the more confusing.

In the first induction sessions for the degree in Plymouth we were told by a cognitive psychologist Jonathan St B.T. Evans that it was an empirical fact that if we got involved in student union politics we would obtain one degree grade less than we would otherwise. This pronouncement didn't seem to be meant as a threat. Evans, a tall imposing man with a strong jaw leading out from his angular face, seemed friendly enough and he occupied the position of academic leader of psychology at Plymouth. He was rather aloof, and students made fun of his name, 'St Bartholomew', for surely this surname was rather too aristocratic for a polytechnic, and his presence then served to confirm rather than take the edge off our lesser status, as not quite a real university. Evans was a more influential figure, perhaps, than the titular head of department, Phil Wookey, who was a very smiley behaviourist, someone who told us to disregard what people said they did and focus on the consequences of certain kinds of reinforcement. I was wary about what consequences Evans' warning might have.

There was, however, already a political link between what I was reading and practice. There was a new link that *Ideology & Consciousness* discussed, between politics and pathology, and it connected, in turn, with a real threat that some psychologists were starting to discuss and do something about. The new link was in what *Ideology & Consciousness* referred to in its opening position piece in the first issue as 'biological essentialism'. This ran alongside complaints about Marxist 'economism' – reduction of explanation to the economic level – as a form of essentialism.

On the one hand, the line they took from their reading of Gramsci, which led them to take cultural debates seriously, did also make them more open to feminist arguments. It allowed them to see that there was more to power than capitalism as such understood only as an economic system, and that feminist analyses of patriarchy – the power that men had over women, and that older men enjoyed over younger men – should also be part of political struggle. This opened the way to an analysis of other forms of power, such as the racism that flowed from the continuing legacy of colonialism. On the other hand, my own comrades reacted strongly to the attempt to junk the old Marxism altogether, to abandon class struggle and to treat economic analysis with suspicion as if it must always be 'economist'. There was the economy, however much you disliked what effect it had on our lives, and there was biology, there in the bodies we inhabited. The problem wasn't really at this simple level of 'biology' at all, but was to do with how some writers understood biology and turned it into some kind of quasi-spiritual force. For some writers, sexual energy was a creative force that was repressed in capitalist society, repressed by individuals who 'armoured' themselves against it, and repressed by authoritarian institutions that preferred the status quo to rebellious freedom. That approach boiled down to a version of psychoanalysis that was antithetical to psychology, to the ideal of self-governing well-behaved individuals, and it also seemed antithetical to the psychoanalysis we read about in our psychology textbooks. I was not even sure it was even psychoanalysis as such at all.

Freud himself was less fun at Plymouth than he had been in Newcastle, and the emphasis seemed to be less on putting aside psychoanalysis as a playful indulgence than making sure he was really dead. That was not so much by insisting that he was unscientific and out of date but by presenting the ideas as the most deadening of psychological models. The lectures were by Reg Morris, a bearded ginger-haired behaviourist who was clearly already bored senseless by the psychoanalytic story of the id, ego and superego. He gazed out the window of the General Teaching Block as he drained the topic of any interest. In other contexts Reg was helpful, while serious, but we did have the impression that this was the graveyard slot of the course, an ordeal for the teacher as well as the students.

For the behaviourists like Reg and Phil, it just didn't make sense to ask what was going on inside peoples' minds because that wasn't what interested them. The problem for them was that thinking as it is actually experienced wasn't reducible to observable behaviour to be reinforced or tabulated in an experimental study. Best to ignore it. For the cognitive psychologists like Ian and Jonathan, on the other hand, the egg-shaped box called 'ego' in Freudian diagrams of the mind was itself rather empty and useless, and didn't show us exactly how one stage of reasoning led to another, nothing to be tested there. Psychological models should be clearly described, they said, and it should be possible to spell out what you expect to happen if people behave in line with them. For all my suspicion of psychology, I could give it that, and this clarity and appeal to evidence made it more straightforward to learn and discuss in essays and prepare for in examinations. One experiment claims this outcome, and then the next contradicts it or refines the claim. The sequence of claims and counter-claims can then be organised in a narrative, and then it is possible to play the rules of the game, tracking these different narratives in psychology, better if you can also get a grip of the statistical rules used to analyse the results of the studies.

I learnt to string together little descriptions of experiments in cognitive psychology into a sequence that would serve well enough as an essay, and liked some of the lecturers who could also treat it as if it were a game. Ken Manktelow, a PhD student, lectured us, helping us remember that the classic *History of Experimental Psychology* was written in 1929 by the aptly-named 'E. G. Boring' and that the 'Aha-experience' in apes discovering how elements of a unfamiliar situation fit together was described, Ken said, by Herr Köhler. The problem was that this abstracted mechanical image of the human being left out all of the messy complicated and paradoxical experience of being human that had led most of us into psychology in the first place.

The General Teaching Block, the GTB, was a brand-new building which was wittily designed so that the arrangement of the windows took the shape of a computer punch card, cardboard rectangles riddled with a slot pattern that would give the computer information. In the basement, that is, underneath all the cognitive paraphernalia displayed on the outside walls of the building and taught in the classrooms, we would find the statistics teaching staff. They were dragged up into the classrooms to get the first-year psychology students through their end of year examinations, examination results that fortunately didn't count toward the final degree grade. It was as if, in the dungeons of psychology, we won't find the unconscious but systems of mathematical rules.

I went down to the GTB basement to find out what was likely to come up as a stats question in the exam, and it was there that a young man with spectacles sighed as he told me it might be worth learning what a 't-test' was. I recognised him from one or two of the statistics classes I had been to, but nothing he had said there had stuck. "It could be a 't-test'", he said. I looked it up. Are the results of two sets of data, from two groups we have studied for example, significantly different from each other? The test was developed by a researcher at the Guinness factory in Dublin and is sometimes known as the 'student t-test' because the researcher took the pen-name 'student', not because it was made up for students to use. It seems reasonable, when looking at beer, to assume that results should follow what is called a 'normal distribution'. This distribution is what is represented in the 'bell curve' in which the spread of probable results clumps around a central average hump on the graph while the low and high extremes tail off on either side. Whether what goes on inside a human being's head is distributed in this kind of way, when drunk or not, is another matter.

It was clear that these are the rules of distribution that underpin what goes on under the surface as far as most psychologists are concerned. Maybe that explained why psychoanalysis that was turned into psychology was so much of a problem. It was a problem for the psychologists and then a problem for me. I found Freud dry and boring, and it was a focus on social processes of repression and liberation that brought some of the ideas alive again. We set up a 'Sex-Pol' student society which was inspired by the 'Sex-Pol' movement that had been built in 1930s Germany to embed the fight for sexual freedom with political struggle, and this became the base for lesbian and gay politics in the union. That tradition of research and activism close to the 'critical theory' of the Frankfurt School rather than any version of psychology would also, I thought, help me remain true to my aim of understanding how psychology as a bourgeois discipline worked from the inside. This political tradition drew attention to the fact that psychology as a disciplinary and ideological apparatus was not merely bourgeois but was caught up in something worse, fascism.

Consequences

The real threat indeed came in the form of a revival of fascism in Britain in the shape of the National Front. The Labour Party in government had bowed to the diktats of the International Monetary Fund in 1976, and such political defeat of the left at the hands of finance capital institutions made the rise of fascism almost inevitable. At least, economic restrictions and the image of a foreign power ordering poor little England around did fuel conspiracy theories and the search for scape-goats at home who could be blamed for rising unemployment. The National Front were classically fascist, hostile to open expression of sexuality, actively involved in physical attacks on gay people even at the same time as some of their leaders had covert same-sex relationships. The organisation itself as well as the wider political climate was a seedbed of repression and hatred of those who seemed to be free. At the same time, the main thrust of the National Front's propaganda was racism, against Asians and Black people and, as a deeper sub-text, against Jews. The bat-tleground of the anti-racist movements in organisations like the Anti-Nazi League and Rock Against Racism was also, then, around the question of 'race', something which connected directly with critiques emerging inside psychology which con-cerned some of its dominant traditions of work.

Scientific racism is one of the most obviously nastiest legacies of psychology in the first half of the twentieth century. Psychology students through the 1970s could not avoid this issue, and especially so when fascist movements were now quoting the old research on the inheritance of intelligence. We could see other psycholo-gists, our teachers, desperately trying to disentangle their own research from the history of IQ, the so-called Intelligence Quotient that was supposedly distributed in the general population as if in a 'bell curve'; they characterised that history as a terrible mistake rather than as an integral part of what psychology was up to in its attempt to categorise people; we were encouraged to abstract the technical debates over how the thing should be measured from the political debates over whether the thing, intelligence, existed as such at all. The debate over the measurement of 'intelligence' was one of the set pieces for essays in the first year of the degree at Plymouth, and this meant that books like Leon Kamin's *The Science and Politics of IQ* were required reading, reading which drove home how psychologists in the United States in the 1920s had been actively involved in identifying 'feeble-mindedness' among immigrants and former slaves and in promoting eugenics programmes well before the rise of fascism in Europe.

A new generation of scientific racists in the United States – Arthur Jensen and William Shockley, who was not a psychologist – were arguing that nature had 'colour-coded' individuals so that the 'man in the street' could make predictions about who was statistically likely to be more or less intelligent. In Britain, the Cyril Burt scandal was breaking in the press, a scandal about the rigging of research purporting to show a genetic link between intelligence and class. This was not just about the past, not just about the history of psychology. It was also about the present, and the way the worst of psychology kept repeating itself. One of Burt's students and most vociferous defenders was a well-known populariser of psychology, Hans Eysenck, who was keen to draw out the implications for personality, criminality, and for 'race'.

Inside British psychology there were voices against this resurgence of fascism. There were, crucially, some attempts to carry out research that would investigate and undermine it, radical work I will describe in Chapter 4. We desperately needed something to counter the big glossy psychology textbooks from the United States – the favourite assigned text at Plymouth was Hilgard and Atkinson's *Introduction to Psychology* – in which 'social psychology' was included as just another version of psychology but one in which behaviour was carried out on groups of people co-present to each other. That it was behaviour that could be observed as carried out when others were present was what qualified it as 'social', as if most of the other things we did, and thought about, and fantasised about did not involve others too. Most history of what had happened in the discipline hadn't found its way into what we were taught and so an important aspect of present-day context was missing. The history of racism inside psychology and the threat of fascism in the real world made it all the more clear that 'models of mind' were not enough, that there must be more than this.

In the late 1970s the political climate changed rapidly in Britain; psychology as a discipline benefitted from that change and grew in strength. We were beginning to sense this, and it became even more urgent to find something more than this, some progressive alternative that would mean moving beyond and then against traditional experimental methods in psychology. I knew there was something wrong, but could not see a way to put it right. I had been well behaved enough to get onto a psychology undergraduate degree, and along the way had experienced some of the ways that psychologists treat people they carry out their research on. They treat us as objects rather than as human beings. I was to find out more about their underlying assumptions about our brute nature, and will describe those assumptions about our underlying beastliness in the next chapter.

3

BIOLOGY

Performing animals

In which we encounter biological arguments in psychology, attempts to reduce human beings to animal behaviour and attempts to reduce animals to biological matter. After meeting Pavlov, Skinner and Chomsky, we find some surprising alternatives to popular stories about aggression among woolly monkeys in Cornwall, and we explore some questions concerning the nature of experience, our experience of nature.

I wanted to like psychology, and I must admit I was enjoying learning about the surprising variety of explanations for human action that were jostling for attention in the lectures and the textbooks. It was not an enemy as such, but felt like a very strange enigmatic friend. Some of my friends, fellow students, settled on a particular conceptual framework and then used that as a resource base to assess the value of the other rival accounts. We were expected to compare and contrast theories in our essays and exams, and that comparative work was a skill we were explicitly schooled in. I too grasped for an approach to psychology that I would be happy with, whether it was one of the stories about behaviour or cognition, but each option was problematic, and especially so when it was presented as universally applicable. It was worse when we were told that because it was 'natural' it could never be changed; our 'animal nature' is often viewed by psychologists as the bedrock and limit of human potential.

Nature

In April 1979 the Conservative Party triumphed in the British general election, and Margaret Thatcher inaugurated a new period in British politics. She did help marginalise the National Front, the main fascist party, but she did this by taking on board their main argument about immigration. She argued that it was understandable that white Britons felt 'swamped', as she put it, by people of a different culture coming to Britain. It did feel like we were being thrown back into the worst of the history of xenophobia that marked the old Empire, a history that psychology had played such an active role in as the Empire disintegrated.

Psychologists who were seeking out those of lower intelligence, seeking them out in order to sterilise them and stop them breeding, and those who endorsed divide and rule strategies which pitted different categories of people against each other because they were supposed to be from different 'races', often got themselves off the hook, avoided the accusation of racism by saying that they were merely describing what was actually there and that it was 'natural'. We learnt from the history of intelligence testing that moral and political choices were being made all the time by psychologists. We could see this, for example, from the selective decisions that they made in the United States to alter the specific items in the early intelligence tests that appeared to show that women were brighter than men. It was surely just not possible that this was so, the psychologists reasoned, and so the conclusion was that there was something wrong with the test. Not so, of course, when people from 'inferior races' scored worse, and so, in that case, the test items which obviously corresponded to white common sense were retained. Psychologists routinely evaded responsibility for what they did by insisting that they were just going along with what was thought at the time to be normal and natural.

We had already learnt something about common sense, about what is taken to be normal and natural, in our lectures. Common sense is eaten, regurgitated and fed by psychologists – they need the contradictory networks of necessary false consciousness that we all use to find our way around the world – but the 'commons' as our shared natural resources that sustain us as human beings is systematically corroded by them. Psychologists peddle the myth that the so-called tragedy of the commons – conflict between individuals over these shared resources – is inevitable, overlooking the scientific research in other disciplines that shows that cooperation is more common than competition. Psychologists lapped up the argument of Garrett Hardin, a white supremacist and eugenicist who coined the phrase 'tragedy of the commons' but overlooked the counterarguments by Nobel prize-winning ecological activist Elinor Ostrom in her 1990 book *Governing the Commons*.

It is 'common sense' for many people that there are such things as race differences, and psychology mines that field, searching under the surface, inside the head for evidence of such things. Similar embarrassing false starts to intelligence testing were made in South Africa when 'poor white' descendants of settlers, particularly those from impoverished farming backgrounds or the unemployed working class, scored badly compared to African indigenous people or migrants from Asia. Again, the offending items from the tests were removed or amended so that the results would come out in line with what psychologists already knew to be true.

In South Africa things took an even more unpleasant turn than in the United States and Europe, and in a way that fuelled ideas about what was 'natural' and biologically wired into human beings of different kinds, the human kinds made to look like the natural kinds of things that were described by psychologists. Instead of covering over the past or regretting past mistakes as being 'unscientific', which was the narrative in most of the histories of testing that we were assigned as reading in Plymouth, scientific psychology in South Africa confirmed and then underpinned the founding of the apartheid state. The architect of apartheid as a theory and practice of 'separate development', Hendrik Verwoerd, was once Professor of Applied Psychology at Stellenbosch University in the Western Cape. He provided the rationale for segregation which was then implemented mercilessly by the South African state after the Second World War.

1950 was the watershed year for South African legislation to put in place a fake-scientific project for a racist world, one in which different categories of human being described in psychological research was turned into grim reality, made true. The enforced division of the population into four different 'racial groups' – White, Black, Indian and Coloured – by the Population Registration Act gave the stamp of government approval to what psychologists were happy to describe as natural differences, and the Group Areas Act restricted movement around the country, with the Black population being divided into a further ten separate groups. An Immorality Act criminalised sexual relationships between the four main racial groups, and resistance to these laws was dealt with by the South African government passing, the same year as the other three legal instruments, a Suppression of Communism Act. Communism threatened to change this world.

We knew about this in Plymouth, not from what we read in the psychology textbooks – they were silent about this history – but from our discussions with activists from the Anti-Apartheid Movement. This was a boycott movement that came to visit the city to mobilise against sporting contacts with South Africa. In October 1979, just after term started for my second academic year, the South African rugby team, the 'Barbarians', played Devon up the road in Exeter, which was about fifty miles away, but not without a fight, not without invasions of the pitch by anti-apartheid protestors. Three days later we travelled down to Camborne in Cornwall, the south-western-most county which Plymouth borders, and made plenty of noise demonstrating outside the ground.

We met with South Africans in exile who explained how academic freedom was violently suppressed in order to silence any voices opposing apartheid, and how academic contact between British and South African institutions served to make this state of affairs look normal and natural. The sending of a 'multiracial' rugby team to Britain by the Barbarians that year was a cynical cosmetic device very similar to the parading of members of separate 'races' in South African propaganda, and it needed to be exposed as such. The boycott movement isolated the mainstream apartheid institutions, those that deliberately maintained apartheid or those that kept quiet about what was happening, and it gave confidence to those who spoke out, whether they were forced abroad or were still at home working with the African National Congress or with other opposition organisations.

Academic disciplines, including anthropology, which you would think would be generous in its portrayal of different cultures, do not come out of this history looking good. Psychologists were not the worst of the bunch, but they did fall in line with the apartheid state, and it was a discipline that was a valuable ally to those in power, not only because of what psychology says about human nature but because of what it can do practically to divide people from each other on the basis of spurious test results. When psychologists claim to discover what they like to call the 'biological basis of behaviour' they are most times simply rediscovering what real biologists have long been working on – physiological mechanisms and evolutionary processes – but then pretending that there is something distinctively 'psychological' at play. When they stitch together a biological account of who we are with our experience of living in our bodies, of our embodied nature as human beings, they slide from one version of a 'basis' for our behaviour, that which is necessary for us to be able to think and behave, to another, to a story about how biology produces our thoughts and comes to define who we are.

It is that story about biological effects, as if our biological heritage is responsible for our behaviour, which then leads to the fantasy world of 'evolutionary psychology', a malign twist on cultural differences noticed by anthropologists, and on biological characteristics noticed in the natural sciences. Here in evolutionary psychology – a bizarre melding of biological and cultural data so that the nature of each kind of human being is summed up as if in a Rudyard Kipling Just So Story – there is a movement backwards and forwards, from the way we behave and experience ourselves to what biologists have found in other species. Part of the illusion that evolutionary psychologists create is facilitated by the way in which they frame what biologists find in other species, and sometimes even by the way biologists themselves frame what they find as they anthropomorphise their findings to make them more understandable to the general public. The claim that animals are just like us, the kind of anthropomorphic representation that frames many nature documentaries, confirms not only that what we do is universal and unquestionable but also that we are just like them, trapped by nature. The danger is not only that we get caught in a loop between psychology and biology, tautology masquerading as explanation, but that the biological account limits what we dare to imagine about how we could be different and dare to relate to each other differently from the way we do now. Searching for biological foundations for psychology, and the even more restrictive version in evolutionary psychology, thus functions as a profoundly conservative enterprise.

The most prestigious university psychology departments had animal laboratories, and it is often assumed that the closer the animals are to human beings the more valid the results of the studies. Best if they are monkeys, though that caused some unease among psychologists who were concerned about the conditions in which the animals are kept. There were already rumours in the 1970s that several British psychological research animal laboratories had to be closed down after the psychologists 'went native', it was said. That is, they became unnaturally close to the chimpanzees in their care. The more lurid gossip had it that some of these psychologists were becoming very close to their inmates. There were stories of one psychologist who gave up his licence to do animal research after becoming vegetarian, and another who converted to Buddhism. These little crises of conscience over animal research rippled through to Plymouth, but the objections to this research mainly came from the students.

One of my classmates in the first year of the course was Danny, who didn't make it through the exams at the end of the year, and who did object very strongly. I went with Danny to see *The Deer Hunter*, a post-Vietnam veteran trauma movie released in 1978 which includes a scene in which Robert De Niro kills a deer with 'one shot'. That's a motif that recurs in the film through to the Russian roulette scenes in the Vietnamese prison and consequences of this treatment for the three main characters. It was a powerful disturbing narrative, but Danny was most enraged, gasping with horror at the killing of the deer, and refusing to let this go in our long after-show discussion as what he saw as the main problem with the film. There was a question for him here about the link between the representation of the death of the deer and what actually happened in reality. The shooting of the deer was, as far as Danny was concerned, unforgivable, and I was quite exasperated eventually at the end of the evening way after we had left the cinema by him repeating angrily "the poor deer". In fact it was a trained deer, an animal actor we might say, who was helped along in the scene by a strong sedative, and it was the staging of the incident that enabled the deer to play its part so convincingly, or, at least, for us as audience to experience it as real. Dealing with Danny after the film forced me to think about what some minimal version of 'animal rights' might mean for psychology, and where research on animals led to in terms of the system of knowledge psychologists were piecing together.

Danny was also vociferous in class when we discussed the famous cases of monkeys learning language. We learnt about Washoe, the chimpanzee caught in Africa for use in the space programme of the US Air Force and taught American Sign Language by Allen and Beatrix Gardner. The Gardners reasoned that earlier attempts to teach chimps to speak had failed because of the animals' inability to physically produce the sounds for spoken language, and so sign language seemed the next best option. Washoe did combine signs, though there is much debate as to whether she did this by chance or design, and it is such a rich study for undergraduate teaching precisely because it is so ambiguous and inconclusive. The research project lasted a few years in the 1960s before the Gardners moved on to other work, and Washoe ended up in an institute for primate studies in Oklahoma after having been raised as a child in the household, sharing meals, wearing clothes, and going on outings in the family car. She had been inducted into human culture from nature, and then thrown back into a version of 'nature' again, now confined in a cage. It was a similar sad story for many of the other 'subjects' of monkey language studies. Nim Chimpsky, named after the famous linguist Noam Chomsky, was another.

Chomsky himself was something of an inspiration and an enigma for us in Plymouth. On the one hand, his 1959 'review' of B. F. Skinner's book *Verbal Behaviour* that had been published the year before seemed to demolish behaviourism altogether; Chomsky tried to demonstrate that you could not give a convincing explanation as to how human beings produced complex grammatical statements about the world by simply tracing through what the history of behavioural 'reinforcement' had been for each individual. Skinner's perspective did seem a bit dehumanising, leaving little room for reflexive engagement of people with others or with their own thoughts, and his approach could lead to a manipulative approach to human behaviour. Social reform would thus amount to little more than arranging 'contingencies of reinforcement' that would hold a community together, and it would also put psychologists like Skinner in the powerful position of deciding the shape of those contingencies of reinforcement. That would be bad reactionary psychology and politics.

On the other hand, Chomsky didn't offer a more convincing account, claiming that the innate Language Acquisition Device he posited appeared somewhere in the brain at some point in human history, just like that, even perhaps as a result of a strange meteor shower or sudden genetic mutation that was then passed on to the rest of our species. Chomsky was completely disinterested in evolutionary explanations of the emergence of language. In fact, despite the Chomsky-Skinner debate being a set-piece in class discussion, Chomsky himself was also against experimental or any other empirical test of his constantly mutating theories of language. For Chomsky, the capacity to elaborate syntactical structures in language was there in the head, each individual head, and that was that. Even concepts like 'carburettor', quite a complex piece of machinery in an internal combustion engine, were wired in, Chomsky claimed; they were quasi-linguistic concepts waiting for the words to articulate them. This quite weird account of the origins of human creative language also seemed to leave us trapped in exactly the kind of individual psychology that could never be changed. This was an updated and quasi-scientific version of the mind-body dualism proposed by René Descartes, a quite explicitly Cartesian account of language as operating in the mind with no immediate connection to practice or social relationships. Chomsky was active politically, speaking out against exploitation and oppression, and had been a particularly vocal opponent of US intervention in Vietnam, but there seemed to be a deep separation between his linguistics and his politics, a separation that he explicitly maintained and refused to reflect upon.

Chomsky was involved in politics but never addressed the politics of research. His name may have been inspiration for the attempt to show that Nim Chimpsky had the same underlying linguistic abilities as human beings, but he would never offer critical reflection on the supposedly 'scientific' basis of that research. Nim was in a bad state about ten years after having been raised in the family of research assistants to the improbably named Herb Terrace. When the funding ran out, and the researcher's interests moved on, Nim was also carted off to the Oklahoma institute for primate studies. He died in 2000, age 26. Washoe made it to 42, she died in 2007.

The point my friend Danny made again and again in class, and he rather pushed it beyond the bounds of credibility when he extended the argument to all other animals, was that there is a creative imaginative capacity that the psychological studies always overlook, and that these studies lead to suffering instead of knowledge. This suffering dehumanises those who carry out the studies, and it is demeaning of the animal participants themselves. Animal actors often seem to be better treated than animal experimental subjects, including Jiggs IV who played Cheeta in many Tarzan films and TV series, and who ended up in a retirement home in Palm Springs, watching television, painting and producing a ghost-written autobiography. Perhaps we would do better to treat these animals as performers, and for sure the poor chimps had to live up to their roles in the families they learnt to 'speak' in. Better to treat them as performers, even following scripts that are not of their own making, than experimental subjects.

There was a strong strand of animal research at Plymouth, but the evolutionary psychologists there had to make do with rats, which is the favourite fallback non-human subject of many studies. Some of the earliest studies of conditioning, the linking of stimuli and responses, had actually been carried out on dogs. Ivan Pavlov's experiments in St Petersburg before the Russian revolution conditioned his canine subjects to salivate at a chosen sound, which psychology textbooks tell us was the sound of a bell, after linking the sound with the presence of food. Pavlov was not a psychologist, but a physiologist, concerned with interplay of biological processes and observed behaviour, and carried out surgical externalisation of the salivary glands of the dogs and then vivisection. Pavlov's 'classical conditioning' experiments laid the basis for later work in the Soviet Union that then came closer to something we could recognise as psychology, and to some parallel strands of work later on in Britain by the biological psychologist Hans Eysenck and his followers. Rats became the favoured psychological subjects in the United States, most notably in the studies of 'operant conditioning' carried out by Skinner. The 'operant' part of the equation refers to the prior activity of the animal which is then rewarded, reinforced and moulded by the consequences it brings about. Some of the earliest studies of 'operant conditioning' carried out by E. L. Thorndike were on cats, and many of Skinner's experiments were on pigeons, but it is the rat that emerges as the hero in the history of psychology in the US in the twentieth century.

The white rat thus became the emblem of psychology in the popular imagination. J. B. Watson, a psychologist who also carried out studies of conditioning, the most popular being the case of 'Little Albert', had obtained his doctorate in 1903 for an account of the 'psychical development' of the white rat. The white rat in general, note, not a particular white rat. The assumption underlying all this animal research was that the experiments carried out on one sub-set of the rat population could be generalised to all rats and then read back into the behaviour of each individual rat. This is, as we have seen, a model of research popular in psychology, one in which we bring together a number of subjects in our 'sample' in the study, combine our observations and then expect that each member of the group will act along the same lines. The logic and lesson of the study is then easily transferred, psychologists think, from their rodent subjects to the human population, and it should then apply to their colleagues and human friends. Once you buy into the idea that segments of behaviour can be separated off and experimentally manipulated and measured, you will be more willing to accept that these apparently abstract segments of behaviour are functionally the same in different animal species.

The formal arrangement of behaviour patterns, which are patterns that are carefully arranged by the researcher in their experiments, are what count, and so it shouldn't really matter, if this approach is right, whether it is a rat or a cat or a pigeon or dog, or a human being, who is operating in accordance with those patterns. This attempt to set aside nature and to focus instead on 'conditioned' or 'nurtured' behaviour set the pattern for much US-American psychology in the last century. The attempt was disrupted from time to time by those who noticed that the different results obtained in different research laboratories could be explained by the slightly different breeds of rats, and by those who pointed to some of the ideological undercurrents in this research, covert racism in which, it was said, as the title of one book by Robert Guthrie, one of the few Black psychologists during the rise of psychology had it, *Even the Rat was White.*

Nurture

My friend Danny had a get-out from our first-year 'practicals' in the rat lab, which was his allergy to the animals, and this may have been one of the many contributing factors to him failing to continue on the course after the first year. One of our tutors, Paul Kenyon, also had an allergy to rat urine, but he ploughed on with his research nonetheless, and it was this research linking evolutionary psychology with developmental psychology in the department that also framed what we were supposed to do in our own training. The topic of most of the experiments carried out there, including ours, was on the relationship between lactation, the production of milk by the mother rats, and 'attachment'. The production of the milk and the attachment of the baby rat 'pup' to the mother could be disrupted in different ways by us, and so we could thereby learn something about attachment, it was claimed, and then something more about the mother's and pup's behaviour. Attachment in this case had to be restricted and 'operationalised', that is, given a clear limited behavioural description. In this case it was operationalised as 'nipple attachment'. If a noxious chemical is put on the mother rat's nipples, for example, then the pup won't suckle, and there will, as you might expect, be consequences of that. Those aren't consequences you can explore by giving the pup or mother a questionnaire, but by noticing changes, sometimes pathological changes in 'maternal behaviour'.

Research being carried out at that time by Paul, our rat-man, and Stephanie Keeble, who taught us developmental psychology, was even more drastic than this. They were busy injecting a local anaesthetic into the mother's face, pulling out her whiskers – 'vibrassal removal' – and cutting, 'transecting' they would say, the trigeminal nerve of the mother rat, that is the bit of the nerve running around the face that leads to the snout and lips. The good news is that 'normal retrieving' of the pups did resume after being 'initially disrupted'. We students weren't actually cutting up the rats, but we were cutting out aspects of the behaviour so that we could study it, and that's what giving an operational definition of 'attachment' as 'nipple attachment' entails. I plead guilty to having done these practical assignments which removed pup from mother to observe what she did, with the only mitigating factor being that I did it in a group, so I didn't interfere with the rats but gathered the background research for writing up the project.

This did all seem rather gruesome, but we managed by compartmentalising what we did in the animal lab and what we learnt in our lectures about animal behaviour, which was mainly in line with the Skinnerian operant conditioning approach. This compartmentalisation was what enabled the different theoretical approaches to peacefully coexist with each other in the psychology degree, as well as to enable the tutors to be able to teach what they were comfortable with. The idea was that if Paul and Stephanie were doing research that would be published in respectable journals this would strengthen the department, as would cognitive experimental research carried out by Jonathan or Ian. We had space to discuss some of the political dimensions of theories of the attachment of baby animals to their mothers on condition that we bracketed out what was being done to animals in our labs.

The political dimension was itself also troubling, and we focused on the topic of 'nature versus nurture' to try and unravel it in class and in our assignments set by the social psychologists. This question – over whether the underlying drivers of human behaviour and our cognitive abilities are biologically wired in over the course of evolution or whether it is the specific changing environments that human beings are raised in that are most important – is a favourite one in psychology undergraduate textbooks. The question pops up in studies of personality, intelligence, and the causes of aggression. Brian Champness, my first-year tutor, was a social psychologist who encouraged us to think about these issues, as well as introducing us to alternative approaches in psychology to those based on laboratory experiments, including anthropological research. The question of aggression doesn't seem to have been solved there either.

Some of the anthropological research seemed to link up with biological perspectives in psychology when it came to the descriptions of 'attachment', though these descriptions didn't always entail interfering with rats. Instead of direct biological experimentation, an influential strand of work called 'ethology' built up detailed observations of animal behaviour, and noticed patterns across species that then, it was thought, could be generalised across to human beings. The Dutch ethologist Nikolaas Tinbergen, for example, drew on his ethological research to develop a complex model of the instincts, though in the process he added to the commonsensical everyday use of the term 'instinct' a series of internal 'stimuli' and 'releasing mechanisms' that look very much like some of the flow-diagrams representing internal mental processes produced by cognitive psychologists. Tinbergen also carried out experimental studies to intervene in behaviour, and these studies complemented the ethological research. The most well known of his studies, of the red spot on the mother herring gull's beak which 'releases' certain kinds of responses by her young, drove home the idea that there are certain images that produce certain kinds of behaviour, or that 'release' that behaviour. It looks like Tinbergen was as fond of a good story as any other researcher, and the 'red spot' seems not to be more important than other colour markings on the mother's beak. This isn't to say that Tinbergen massaged the evidence, but he did know how to make a point.

When Tinbergen made links with human behaviour he was quite cautious, and he used his Nobel Prize acceptance speech to discuss the work of F. M. Alexander, founder of the eponymous postural technique that had more to do with performance to an audience than behaviour in line with natural imperatives. Tinbergen shared the 1973 Prize for Physiology or Medicine with Karl von Frisch, well known for studies of the 'waggle dances' that bees use back at the hive to indicate the direction and distance of food sources, and with an altogether dodgier character, Konrad Lorenz. Frisch was an Austrian ethologist who was forced into early retirement under the Nazis after accusations that he would not dismiss Jewish co-workers and was therefore practising some kind of 'Jewish science'. Lorenz, in contrast, was an Austrian who joined the Nazi Party and then the Wermacht, and who worked as a military psychologist studying what he referred to as German-Polish 'half-breeds'. It is his ethological studies of birds that are cited, but it should also be remembered that quite early on Lorenz argued that his work on greylag geese was evidence that the breeding of 'bird hybrids' led to a consequent deterioration of 'social instincts', an argument that chimed with Nazi warnings against 'race mixing'.

The standard image of Lorenz in psychology textbooks is of a smiley grey-bearded old rogue followed by some of the goslings that had an 'imprinted' image of him in place of that of their mother. This imprinting was engineered by hatching eggs away from the mother, and so, in a very brief period of time, Lorenz was effectively the goslings' first figure of attachment. These ethological studies of behaviour that, in this case, Lorenz insisted, was 'species-specific', quickly caught on in psychology, and some psychoanalysts also picked up the notion. The imprinting of the image of the object, the image of the mother goose as first love object that Lorenz described, could then be linked to accounts of 'attachment' of the human infant to their mother or primary caregiver. The psychoanalyst John Bowlby, for example, was much taken with these ethological studies, and made 'attachment' central to his story of child development, attending meetings with Lorenz organised by the World Health Organization in the early 1950s.

This notion of 'attachment' both anthropomorphises animal behaviour, making it seem as if it is equivalent to human child rearing, and naturalises the way children relate to their caregivers, as if they are no more than little animals. Such anthropomorphising and naturalising become increasingly more powerful when they operate together in an observational and then conceptual loop. Bowlby had already published a classic paper in the *International Journal of Psycho-Analysis* called 'Forty-Four Juvenile Thieves: Their Characters and Home Lives' ten years before, and his emphasis on the 'attachment' of children to their mothers is sometimes blamed for British government policies after the Second World War which pushed women back into the home to be good mothers after they had, out of economic and military necessity, been drafted into the workforce.

This was the kind of psychoanalysis psychologists liked. The small influence of psychoanalysis in psychology departments by the 1980s was, however, waning even further, and one of the few times we heard about it in lectures outside the 'personality' course at Plymouth was in accounts of the influence of ethological research on Bowlby's ideas. This story was told with the moral that the real underpinning of the best research, even in Bowlby's psychoanalytic work, should be traced to careful observation and experimentation in the ethological tradition. Which is a curious moral, given that Lorenz's theories, which were picked up and extended by his good friend Tinbergen – of biological imprinting, accumulation of 'action specific' drive energy and its 'release' in the presence of the right triggers – is a hydraulic model that owes a lot to the popular psychoanalytic ideas around him when he was developing the theories in the first place. That hydraulic model, of the drives pushing for release, was exactly what was mocked as characterising Freud's own work by psychologists.

This was perplexing to us as students trying to work our way through the tangle of ethological research and its influences and, for me, trying to work out what the political consequences might be. This detection of political traces in psychological models seemed as useful a way as any other to at least find my bearings in the debates, though it was just as easy to be disoriented by some of the surprising sideways moves and odd personal choices made by researchers when it came to social issues. It did seem that research into the political judgements and misjudgements of psychologists and their friends in other disciplines turned up some worrying trends. Lorenz did, after the war, 'regret' his membership of the Nazi Party, for example, but the links between particular views of human nature, of what the human being is, and varieties of fascism still run deep.

One of the themes that Lorenz continued to write to for a more popular audience was on the biological basis of 'aggression', and such biological explanations also posed a challenge to social psychological approaches. It did seem as if the peaceful coexistence of psychologists in the Plymouth department rested on mutual tolerance between, not so much different theoretical approaches, but different aspects of psychology itself, as if the different sub-disciplines jostled alongside each other, and caused each other trouble only when researchers strayed across the sub-disciplinary boundaries into another camp. Perhaps this was one reason why the link with anthropology was so disturbing, for it was another discipline entirely that should have shared its natural borders with social psychology. In fact, a lot of the anthropological research we learnt about supported a more biologically-reductionist explanation of aggression.

One strand of laboratory-experimental psychology, for instance, saw the occurrence of aggression as arising from the inhibition of natural impulses and their eruption in certain kinds of situation. In this 'frustration-aggression' strand of work we could see reappear the old hydraulic model of biological drives and triggers to action. This, again, was the very hydraulic model we had been taught to deride in Freud's theory of the mind, in which, we were told, instincts for sex or food or aggression bubbled around in the 'id' and were repeatedly pushed back there by the 'superego'. Only the 'ego' saved us from useless id-sourced antisocial behaviour or from superegoic crippling guilt, an ego that was suspiciously like the moderating agent that the judicious psychologist aimed to be, weighing up what was from nature and what was from nurture, what was inside us and what we should respect in other people.

There is plenty of anthropological work that contradicts the biological story about human behaviour, including the idea that aggression is something hard-wired into our biology, ready to fire into action if the appropriate triggers come in sight. The humanist anthropologist Dennis Child pointed out that if aggression was really an instinct, it should be found in every member of the species, and that since it was patently the case that there were human beings who were not aggressive, that biological inheritance argument fell to the ground. Our favourite authors in this strand of anthropological research, for their names rather than their arguments, were Robin Fox and Lionel Tiger who, in separate research and in a joint book called *The Imperial Animal*, traced through the evolutionary roots of human behaviour. Fox and Tiger laid the basis for 'sociobiology', mainly by spawning a generation of student researchers who became key figures in that sub-discipline. Robin Fox had carried out ethnographic research, including on fighting, in the 1960s on 'Tory Island' just off the north coast of Ireland, which also amused us. This, after all, was the year the British Tory Party took power in Britain under Thatcher.

The quasi-Freudian, or at least the pop-Freudian hydraulic model of the mind, which was relayed out into anthropological research on aggression and then back into psychology again, carried with it another moral message about human beings, one which ran alongside the caution that we should beware of our biological heritage because it might explode in our own faces and between us and in others at any moment. This was the general message that our nature was suspect and needed to be tamed, and it reinforced a suspicion that the closer we came to being like animals the worse it would be for us. Perhaps we should indeed tame our animal nature, tame the wild animals and, why not, experiment on those animals to save life from itself, from life in the raw. If this was right, then Danny must have been mistaken to look for creative reflexive activity in an animal kingdom that we human beings had almost managed to transcend.

Culture

We needed a break from all this, and one day a group of us housemates hired a car to travel over the county border into Cornwall. This took us back into a land of pixies, disused silver and tin mines, over which there had been rebellions against the British Crown in the fifteenth century when Henry VII increased taxes to pay for war against Scotland, and a still-active Cornish independence movement Mebyon Kernow that leans to the left but in the 1980s also had members with some worrying links with English fascist groups. We arrived in the parish of St Martin near the small coastal town of Looe and spent some time in the Monkey Sanctuary founded by Leonard Williams.

Williams was an extraordinary man with a project that connected with and then subverted what we had been learning about animal and human behaviour. He was a respected jazz musician in the 1950s in London, founder and head of the Spanish Guitar School, but then Williams became enamoured with woolly monkeys from the rainforests of South America. His neighbours in Chislehurst in south London protested against his attempts to raise and look after a community of woolly monkeys in his house, and so he decamped to Cornwall. One of his books, *Challenge to Survival*, published in 1971, was on display at the monkey sanctuary and there was a copy in the library at Plymouth Polytechnic which I seized on as a source for a counter-story to the miserable evolutionary psychological and sociobiological accounts of aggression in the animal world, aggression that was supposed to be simmering away inside each of us, pushing to be released, ready to erupt in acts of vindictive rage at any moment.

Leonard Williams' book rambles through prehistory, philosophy and politics, with some quite wild sideswipes at behaviourist and psychoanalytic psychology, but he succeeds in reframing what is too often seen as intrinsically antisocial animal behaviour pitted against human civilisation. For Williams, it is not only the separation of the human animal from other species that is the cause of conceptual errors and disastrous dehumanising practices in research on the 'lower' animals; that separation also prevents us from learning about the positive channelling of what we call 'aggression' into the formation of social bonds and communities, both among animals and among human beings. There is an impassioned plea for us to take seriously, for example, what Williams refers to as the 'defensive aggression' of the Viet Cong against the brutal machinery of US-American occupation in Vietnam or of the Black Panthers resisting racism in the US itself.

One message of the book is that we human beings draw on our biological heritage as part of the animal kingdom to configure 'aggression' in many different innovative and sometimes horrific ways. That innovation and horror is a function of what it is to be a human being, one of the peculiar twists that we add to our biology as we experience it, try to make sense of it, and then make use of it. What is 'instinctual' about aggression is a resource for us, but it cannot itself serve as an explanation for how it manifests itself amongst us or even inside us now. This also means that we should not see other animals as lesser beings than us, as if they are driven by those selfsame forces. This is the paradox of the book, one that Williams does not really grapple with. Animal research provides us with intriguing examples of what it is to live collectively, but human beings do not directly live out their animal nature, precisely because they reflect upon it, creatively draw on it and sometimes turn it in the most dreadful directions. This means that the woolly monkey examples cannot really be taken as offering guidelines for how we should live more authentically, true to our 'nature'.

The book works as an argument against biological psychology all the more powerfully if it is read alongside Williams' practice as a researcher and guardian of the woolly monkeys at the sanctuary. Groups of volunteers lived with the monkeys, who were not prevented from leaving the sanctuary's premises and the monkeys could be seen swinging around in the trees as we arrived and when we left their home after our visit. Williams assembles a strong case for radicals who would speak with nature rather than against it, but that also makes for some bizarre attacks on student revolutionaries of the time who he sees as 'cluttered up' with drugs, Zen Buddhism and pop-art, to name just three malign influences singled out by him in the book. It makes for some equally bizarre claims about his book as providing what he saw as a Marxist 'historical–materialist' account. Yes, that claim to Marxism was one of the hooks for me, and it led me to an argument about biology that was almost diametrically opposite to the one spun by psychology, including to an enduring suspicion of approaches that claimed to provide a 'Marxist psychology'.

It was clearly not good enough to try and wish away our evolutionary heritage and all of the messy contradictory biological processes that enabled us to act or that limited what we could do. That was the mistaken path taken by the behaviourist psychologists, and it eventually led to an attempt to abolish experience and reflection about what we are altogether, an attempt that became explicit in the decision by some behaviourists to abandon psychology and try to found an entirely different field of research they called 'behaviorology'. As a counterpart to behaviourism, the attempt to explain away what we did with reference to what was found in animal behaviour was another dead end; that reductive tradition of so-called animal psychology merely replaced our experience of what it is to be psychological beings with a description of what animals do. As it works its way around an increasingly tight feedback loop between what it describes and what it claims we can do, it does human beings a disservice, demeaning us and animals alike.

Memories and dreams of the monkey sanctuary stayed with me, and the book was my bedfellow for quite a while after our visit. Leonard Williams' insistence that we need to live with what is given to us by our biology rather than reacting against it was impressive, and the way he developed his project as an alternative to the mainstream accounts in biology and anthropology raised questions that could not, I suspected, be answered by the discipline I was supposed to be studying.

I cannot pretend that I was disenchanted, for I have already told you that from the start I was suspicious about what the psychologists were claiming. Each possible progressive way of reconfiguring psychological theory so that it would operate in a progressive rather than a reactionary way was being closed off. As an undergraduate student I was being led around the prison house of psychology. Psychology is a multifarious, contradictory discipline, but even though, or perhaps because, it is so divided, it defends itself fiercely against those approaches it views as non-scientific. As we have seen, it shuts out psychoanalysis, treating it as a form of science fiction rather than as guided by empirical observable fact, and when psychoanalysis tries to play the game it comes up with some bizarre ideas that are just as unpleasant as the kind of psychology it apes. As we will see in the next chapter, science itself becomes something very strange in the hands of psychologists, and something to be jealously guarded against outsiders.

4

SCIENCE

Breaking up madness

In which we encounter alternative methods that break completely from old paradigm laboratory-experimental research in order to surf through the crisis to a supposedly more scientific 'new paradigm' focused on language as a defining characteristic of human psychology. By way of distress, we encounter other, more traumatic ways of making and breaking the rules, by Scientologists and by Michel Foucault.

What a reasoned well-balanced account I have given so far of my time as an undergraduate student, telling you how I was subjected to psychology but saying little about the anguish I felt surrounded by people who turned everyone else into objects or animals. Every pathological label cut, for it spoke of distress while marking it off as something 'other', as if anxiety and unhappiness were signs that one was not fully human, still less that I was not really, could never really be a psychologist. I was behaving like an insider, that is what this ethnography speaks of, but I was profoundly alienated from the discipline. Sometimes I felt quite mad, and every attempt to bring science to bear on madness compounded the problem. The language psychologists use to speak about people in distress is quite appalling. I felt that, knew that, as I tried to take my distance from it.

Faith

There were alternatives to the psychology we studied in class in Plymouth, and plenty of distraction from the quasi-scientific fairy stories we were told there. Over the road from the Polytechnic student union building was the local Scientology headquarters. Comrades from the 'Sex-Pol' society spent a while in there taking the personality tests and baiting the staff. We managed to distract the Scientologists' attention by messing around with their 'E-meters'. These devices, made out of cardboard and wire, then enable a trained 'auditor' to see your thoughts. We made off with a pile of questionnaires. We planned to pick our way through the items and work out which pattern of responses would make you come out 'clear' rather than set you off on an expensive course of treatment. This was a fruitless task, for all the patterns of response indicate things that need to be put right, but there was something endlessly appealing about Scientology, especially the way it mimicked and unwittingly parodied mainstream psychological techniques. I read avidly about Scientology, a theory that was more fantastic and so more alluring than most cognitive psychology, talked to adepts, including fellow psychology students looking for something more coherent as a guide to life, and gathered together insider accounts from those who had left in horror at what they had been subjected to inside the faith and willing to spill the beans. I was distracted for a while, becoming an anthropologist in the field of the enemy, even behaving like an investigative journalist.

The standard version of the history of the scientific discipline of psychology in textbooks is that it has roots going back to the Greeks thousands of years ago but that things really got going in 1879 with Wilhelm Wundt's 'experiments' in the attic of Leipzig University. In fact, Wundt's experiments were very different from those hailed as exemplifying scientific method in present-day psychology. Wundt used an 'introspective' approach, asking for a detailed description of the subject's experience of perception and cognition. This kind of introspection is a no-no in psychology today, now intent on getting behind the back of what people think they are thinking. Wundt also swapped places with his subjects so they could each experience and report what they observed, though these were subjects who had been trained how to speak about what they saw and what they thought. The game was rigged from the start. Psychologists today like their subjects to talk in psychological terms, but not too much, rather in the same way that doctors expect you to tell them about your pain but without utilising their own complicated medical terminology. Uneducated use of specialist vocabulary breaches the professional-client relationship, and they, the doctors and the psychologists, often get uncomfortable about that.

Wundt's quasi-experimental work on introspection was only one part of his research programme into psychology. He also explored what he saw as the higher mental functions through studies of 'folk psychology' which was shared collective symbolic matter, the explanations and ideas that circulate through a culture. When psychology was transplanted from Germany to the United States, the new discipline in the English-speaking world forgot about folk psychology and focused only on individuals who were manipulated in the laboratory, treated like objects. When we complain about US-American psychology as a global force that is then translated into local contexts, we should also remember that it was itself once an immigrant constellation of approaches to understanding the person in social context, translated and adapted to its host culture, masquerading as a science of the individual.

Let us turn for a moment to a clone discipline that accompanies and battles against psychology, an approach which hovers on the boundary between science and faith, reason and madness, Scientology. We may then better understand some of the contours of the science of mental life I am focusing on in this book. The underlying theory in Scientology is intriguing too, as intriguing as the strange ideas that found their way into our discipline. Scientology begins with a mixture of personality assessments in the Oxford Capacity Analysis, a weightier name perhaps than the original American Personality Analysis, and with lie detectors, the different versions and upgrades of the E-meter or Electropsychometer. Those are the bits of technology that draw people into the local store, gadgets we disassembled. This apparatus of testing and mind-reading is part of an altogether wackier blend of psychology and science fiction that outdoes any of the theories we were mugging up on for our exams, and it leads acolytes through a series of 'levels' in which high-ranking 'Thetan' Scientologists themselves conceal what they know from those lower down the food chain. In this respect, Scientology perhaps has some valid claim to the status of religion as well as science and protects its own esoteric knowledge as carefully as do Freemasons. The reasons for this are eminently 'psychological' and that's another reason why the tidy shop over the road was so interesting. At the very same moment it operated as the site both of psychology in reverse and in extremis – the opposite of real psychology, whatever that was, and the logical end point of what psychology did to people – it made visible some of the rules of the game in the discipline we were supposed to be studying and adhering to.

One reason the Scientologists keep secrets from the public, and from most of their own members, is, for them, a profoundly psychological reason that is bound up with an implicit theory of trauma. This psychological reason, the rationale for hiding the truth from those who are not yet fully functioning conscious Thetans, is that this truth is so amazing that normal folk who come into the shop, or even those who are starting to work their way up the levels, would find it too shocking to believe. That's no great shakes in itself, but the nature of that truth is also bound up, Scientologists believe, with our deep memories, and this is where the theory turns into a psychological story about trauma. L. Ron Hubbard, the founder of Scientology, who was still alive and head of the church in the 1980s, had been a science fiction writer who first came up with 'Dianetics'. The 1950 book *Dianetics* – subtitled *The Modern Science of Mental Health* – was Hubbard's first stab at a complex cosmological theory of who we human beings are. The secret story goes something like this; we humans, the core of who we are, were brought to earth 75 million years ago by the dictator of a galactic confederation called 'Xenu'. This, after his mass murder of his own subjects, us, but Xenu failed to destroy us; our immortal souls, called 'Thetans', live on inside human bodies, attached to these human shells. What 'auditing' does is to detect and clarify that traumatic history, and so unveil a story so incredible that only those who have reached Operating Thetan level OT-III should have that revealed to them. This is also why Scientologists spend much time and energy denying that this is the story, denying even that they believe Xenu existed, pointing out that, indeed, it doesn't make sense, threatening legal action against non-Thetans who reveal it.

The Plymouth student union newspaper *PAKT* was a bit nervous about publishing my account of Scientology in 1979, but editor Keith was also amused enough by the story, and that overweighed his doubts. For me, this was psychology, but even better. As someone who only passed Religious Knowledge first stage O-level exams at fifteen by learning about the New Testament as a series of stories, and who grew up in a house littered with yellowing spine-cracked classic science fiction paperbacks by authors like Philip K. Dick, I loved this. It was not only because Hubbard and his followers told a cracking story. The layers of deception, initiation and revelation were, for me, a living case account of how a belief system can be constructed and lived as real, even with reformation and counter-reformation movements inside and against Scientology that compressed the history of the other major Western religions into a period of little over half a century. I wondered why we should believe what psychologists thought was going on inside our minds any more than their enemies, those who had a belief system just about as watertight, if not more so.

The Scientologists are the enemies of the kind of 'scientific' psychology that aims to treat people and enforce its own particular rules about rational thinking and behaviour, and sworn enemies of the discipline, not so much because they opt for irrationality or 'unreason', but precisely because their idea about how to divide reason and unreason is so different while just as certain. That is, the psychologists and the Scientologists can't even agree on the ground rules for how we might try to have a debate about how to be reasonable, how to think clearly or how to 'go clear'.

This is where we come to the deepest psychological reason for concealing the truth about Xenu and who we really are, the event that configures our innermost psychic being. That truth is so mind blowing that to be exposed to it unprepared would, they claim in their internal high-level restricted documents, most likely be as traumatic as the historical events they describe. You must be led slowly to the truth, they believe, and so the process of 'auditing' and induction into their church is a journey through which the painful undigested mental images, or 'engrams', which lie inside our 'reactive' minds should be detected and neutralised. This is where Hubbard's Dianetics, and then Scientology, operates as a psychological theory itself which revolves around some notion of a dynamic unconscious – the reactive mind in which debilitating engrams do deadly irrational work – and trauma. In this case, the trauma also includes the terrifying incomprehensible events in which we relive in our own personal history our annihilation by Xenu. This is their 'chosen trauma', we could say, one that Scientologists use to constitute their identity as a distinct community and faith.

This psychological theory of trauma, of the defences we put in place against our reactive minds and against the truth, is uncannily close to the versions of psychoanalysis we were learning to parrot and dismiss in our essays and exams. These are themselves versions of psychoanalysis that had already worked their way into popular culture, and against which the discipline of psychology protected itself by way of caricature and the setting up of its own criteria for evaluating whether the theory was correct, criteria that were built into the methods it used to assess it. And, as with the 1956 film *Forbidden Planet* in which 'monsters from the id' that destroyed the ancient indigenous Krell civilisation now besiege the new visitors to planet Altair IV, this theory of the unconscious is also a theory of a very deep past, a theory Freud himself dabbled with in his off days when he speculated about the present-day impact of a prehistorical 'primal horde' on our relationships today.

One of the key procedures of cultural filtering and distortion of psychoanalytic ideas as they seep into everyday life and then circulate in psychology, as well as in the neighbouring disciplines of psychiatry and psychotherapy, is not only that Freud's ideas are simplified to make them fit with common sense but also that some of the key terms are replaced. It was convenient, for example, to convey to us students the psychoanalytic theory of the unconscious by saying that the mind is like an iceberg of which only ten percent is above the surface, but that quantitative representation of amounts of different kinds of thinking here and there in parts of the mind is misleading. Even more misleading was the use of the term 'subconscious' favoured by Carl Jung, and we used this word as a litmus test to detect whether it was psychoanalysis as such that was being described or some second-hand account, not that this distinction really mattered to the Scientologists. Freudian and Jungian theories are invariably muddled up together in the outside world, as is psychology and psychiatry, and the Scientologists' hatred of psychiatrists also made them very wary of us student psychologists when we visited them.

Psychiatrists are medically trained mind doctors who spend much of their time diagnosing 'mental illness' and prescribing drugs or physical interventions like electroconvulsive 'therapy' – ECT or electroshock – or even leucotomies and lobotomies, the cutting into or cutting out of bits of the brain. The Scientologists were suspicious of us psychology students, partly because psychology was a rival approach to the mind and behaviour, and partly because we teased and harassed them, but psychiatrists were something else. For the Scientologists, psychiatrists are evil, subjecting people to inhuman treatments, many of which have disastrous life-long consequences, and their hatred of psychiatrists is also rooted in the distant past, in their darkest days millions of years back when the psychiatrists were allies of Xenu, aiding him in his deadly genocide. Psychiatrists persecuted Thetans 75 million years ago, and so now it is payback time. But be careful, the enemy of your enemy is not necessarily your friend. I do not like psychiatry, as you already know by now.

Reason

As well as the Scientologists, there were other alternatives in Plymouth that also seemed to tip over from science fiction into something much crazier. Down on the harbour-side Barbican area of Plymouth was the studio of artist Robert Lenkiewicz, a wild grizzled shaggy-haired character who had recently been invited to give a seminar in the psychology department and, it was said, frightened the students before taking two of them home to bed with him. His fantastic gigantic mural, *The Last Judgement*, on Southside Street was one of many around the city, and on the corner of Southside Street and Blackfriars Lane was a studio shopfront with the artist's name on it and, above that in huge letters, the legend 'The Portrait Painter'. In the centre-front of the dusty window full of bits of canvas and assorted curiosities was displayed a book called *Madness and Civilization*. The book, subtitled

A History of Insanity in the Age of Reason, was by someone with a mysterious name, Michel Foucault, but it looked useful for an essay on 'models of madness'. I knew that name, it was one of the unpronounceables from the journal *Ideology & Consciousness*, and so it was time to check the book out. I found a copy for £3.50 in Chapter & Verse bookshop on Eastlake Walk in the shopping mall on the underside of the Poly campus. *Madness and Civilization* was a deep history of the exclusion of 'unreason' and the developing power of psychiatry to define what rational thought and behaviour should look like.

Foucault's wasn't as deep-time a history of psychiatry as the Scientologists would have liked, and the message was that practices like psychiatry had not always existed. It also seemed to be that something like madness had always been with us and once roamed free, but that it was not like the madness we thought we knew today. I couldn't understand the book, and fished out quotes from it for my essay, turning its poetic evocative account into a standard historical narrative. Even at those moments when there was something recognisably 'historical' in it, Foucault's writing was disturbing; the book conjured up images of the fear of contamination by the madness-inducing fumes wafting out from the old houses of confinement, of the ships of fools in which the mad travelled the oceans, and of the rise of the doctors who aimed to free the mad only to enmesh them in the new chains of reason. It was partly because the book was on display in the Lenkiewicz studio window, but also as reflection of my own confusion about what I was trying to make sense of, that I assumed that this writer Foucault must himself be mad, and that he was speaking from inside the insanity he described, railing against rational discourse. This was madness of a different order than either Scientology or the unconscious that psychologists thought Freud was describing.

Something in Foucault's book usefully jarred with descriptions and diagnoses of disordered thinking we were being taught in the abnormal psychology classes. I sat in seminars listening to Phil Ley, a bluff no-nonsense rotund bearded cognitive psychologist telling us what depression is, what might cause it and how we might help people cheer up. Phil's favourite anecdote was about a woman who was given a diagnosis of depression after she had a leg amputated, and we were told that it was quite understandable, it wasn't rocket science, he chuckled, for we too would be depressed if we lost our legs. Then Tony Carr, a calmer, leaner more serious quietly spoken behaviourist, took over Phil's lecture slot and the focus shifted from what people felt to what schedules of reinforcement might give rise to different patterns of behaviour, including patterns that we might then describe as being 'depressed'. We were tossed from common-sense-coated cognitive psychology into radical behaviourism, but neither captured what I felt.

Student life in Plymouth was good for me. I lived in a shared house with good friends on different courses at the Poly, and I quickly developed circles of comrades in Sex-Pol, Soc-Soc, the Socialist Society, among radical social work students, and with the anarchists who ran the local Anti-Nazi League who were great, hilarious pot-heads who would smoke or ingest anything they could get hold of, especially magic mushrooms. Some of my best friends in these circles would eat up any plant seeds going and then sick them up after hallucinating for a bit; morning glory seeds were apparently particularly cheap and potent. Other friends on my course spiralled down into more severe drug use, and eventually disappeared altogether. I wasn't drinking alcohol or doing drugs at that time, and I guess I worried they would lead me down if I did. My double life as busy activist encouraging protest and critique and as isolated and conscientious student was, at moments, what psychologists might call 'manic' and at others what they might call depressed. I could deal with this most of the time as just being the way I was, as normal for me. But I began to notice that it was under the gaze of psychology that this normal was turned into something else, something that could even be seen as a problem.

In the midst of all the jollity there was an enduring and suffocating pressure to enjoy, and a question why, when everyone else seemed to be happy, I often still felt isolated, and sometimes sunk into nothing, or wanted to sink down there. I coped with lectures by dividing my time between taking notes and gazing at the breeze-block walls, imagining an invisible space opening up through which I could dive and disappear. I wondered why I was not having fun like everyone else, and I feared being discovered, dragged off and drugged, destroyed. One of my housemates, Chris, whose room was next to mine, started shouting prayers to exorcise evil spirits when he came home, and we did not know what to do. Chris was a devout Christian, we argued about religion, and he did not feel safe being in the same house as unbelievers. He was taken off to the local mental hospital and reappeared at Poly a few months later, slow, overweight and medicated, and then living in a church residence. I disliked jokey dismissals in class of the experience of depression and the calm rational procedures used to treat it. I quite liked those two lecturers on psychopathology, different avatars of reason, but I was not sure which of them made me feel worse.

Psychology experiments in which we volunteered as 'subjects' to help our fellow students or postgraduates doing their PhD research or lecturers writing a journal paper were occasions when I could feel myself tip into despair. I had had a good experience with the cognitive memory encoding experiment, but not so good with some of the other later pieces of research. In one study I had to fill out a questionnaire about changes in mood, and marked high on the scale for indicating depression, yes to questions that asked if I often felt unhappy, things like that. The student researcher who was carrying out the study, and who was a friend on my course, took the questionnaire away for scoring, and I could see him reading through my responses as he walked away. He shouldn't have done that, of course, but it is a rare researcher who has not wanted to have an early peek at the data to see how the study is going, sometimes even to peer into their subjects' secrets. I felt worse, a sense that I was now to be viewed as depressed, and wanted to grab back the questionnaire. Too late, but it served as another lesson in labelling, labelling others, and the consequences of the labels one gives to oneself within an expert system of knowledge about distress in psychology.

This double life was one that I recognised as being divided; between, on the one hand, reasonable argument which I could follow and reproduce myself well enough in class discussion and essays, rational discourse, and, on the other, something closer to the hallucinatory malaise that Foucault wrote about. The social work students, including those who were taking the course because they were socialists or feminists, were the ones who pushed us psychologists most to reflect on the terms we used to speak about 'madness'. We discussed anti-psychiatry, protests against the way that women, gay people and black people were incarcerated and pumped with drugs in the mental hospitals, and I found an issue of the journal *Race & Class* in the Poly library in which Hussein Bulhan described the work of the radical psychiatrist Frantz Fanon who worked with the national liberation movement in Algeria. A few of us more radical psychology students had good discussions at least about the politics of naming people who didn't fit in to society in line with medical or other pathologising labels, categorising those who were different so as to bring them to good order again.

I reminded myself again, that life here was good, that I was happier now than I had been at school, much happier than I had been during my first disastrous attempt to take a degree course, and during the years out from education, immersed in alienation and anxiety. Before I found Foucault, it was Sartre who kept me company. He described the tension between underlying impulses that felt as if they came directly from nature and the yearning for some kind of transcendence. His work counters the biological reductionism of those who claim that there is innate animal aggression waiting to be spit out at others, and argues instead that the drive to hurt others is bound up with the continual self-punishment we exact on ourselves to keep ourselves in our place as good obedient well-behaved individuals.

The argument is similar in a number of writers in the tradition of German Critical Theory, that the traces of inhuman disciplinary control work themselves into the way we configure ourselves as self-limiting and self-destructive, hating others who seem to be free, for they remind us of what we have set ourselves against, of what we have lost. The defences we erect against others also lock ourselves in, and it is only by reaching out and connecting with others that we will find a way out of our own little prisons. Like Sartre, the Critical Theorists also provided a more optimistic picture of the possibilities for change.

Michel Foucault was something else. Foucault's history of insanity in what he called our 'age of reason' in the Western world collided with what I was being told about abnormal behaviour or 'psychopathology' in class – our lecturers seemed to think that if we were well-behaved and cheered up then all would be well – but in a peculiar way Foucault's account also illuminated the shadow side of the well-meaning and eminently reasonable messages about the self peddled by psychology. He was arguing in his own delirious way against rules for behaviour and rules of discourse that were themselves, I thought, quite mad. There were times I felt quite frightened that I could end up confined in mental hospital if I didn't play by those rules, and moments when I felt pushed to the edge, but held back from protest for fear of the consequences. The psychologists who chuckled about other people feeling depressed because bad things had happened to them but couldn't make sense of the obvious link between those bad things and their sense of hopelessness; the psychologists who thought they could arrange systems of reinforcement that would make us play the game and insist that it had all worked out fine and that now we were happy – these psychologists systematically reduced others to being objects rather than human beings.

Ideology

There were spaces in the course that gave voice to alternative dimensions of psychology, but even the social psychology lectures were mainly taken up with descriptions of experiments carried out on people in different situations, and usually with the message that human beings do what they are told, obediently hurt other people, and might even behave worse in groups than when they are left on their own. The social psychologists in Plymouth were sympathetic to criticism of those experiments. Fraser Reid, an energetic check-shirted bloke with an impressive short-cut densely-tufted ginger beard, was very encouraging when I tried to bring in some of the names I'd been reading about in the journal *Ideology & Consciousness*, and, with Brian Champness, he supported the reading I was doing which connected work on 'intergroup conflict' with contemporary politics. The debates inside social psychology seemed sealed off from the other material I was reading, but there were at least debates, and two lines of conflict among social psychologists that were interesting.

The first was the conflict between US-American and European social psychology. This was a fairly easy dispute to get a handle on, and the way the debate was set up played too easily into our English prejudices about how bad the United States was generally, and it still didn't seem as if the 'European' researchers were getting much further than their 'American' counterparts. The conflict boiled down to an opposition between those who had an explicitly individualistic understanding of 'social behaviour' and those who searched for something more positive in collective activity. As an alternative to reductionist US-American social psychology, there were European researchers who attempted to bring in a more radical social dimension. They described what Serge Moscovici in France called 'minority influence' in which opposition groups who challenged dominant ideas were more powerful if they acted in concert or they studied 'social representations' which were shared ideas about what was significant among people and their identities. Inside the 'European' tradition there was something even more interesting happening in a series of books by the British social psychologist Michael Billig.

Billig carried out his PhD research with Henri Tajfel in Bristol as his supervisor, and we had one of Tajfel's ex-students, Mike Hyland, with us at Plymouth. The Tajfel tradition of research on 'minimal groups' showed how the categories that we are provided with to demarcate ourselves against others can then play out in the way we will choose to prefer people in 'our' group category. These are 'minimal' groups because in the experiments Tajfel carried out in the early 1970s, the 'subjects' – Bristol comprehensive schoolboys in the first classic studies – were assigned groups on the basis that they preferred paintings by Paul Klee or Wassily Kandinsky. Mike took us through the complicated 'matrices', grids that represented how the subjects assigned rewards which favoured members of their own group, even if it was clear that they themselves would not benefit. Mike told us that Tajfel didn't like the Welsh.

What Billig did was to bring in the dimension of ideology, and he traced through how the one who set up the experiment in the first place is then invariably invisible to those who take part and to those who read about it in the social psychology journals. Billig attended to the third invisible power that sets up the categories and gives the rewards not only in the 'European' experimental tradition of his mentor Tajfel, for whom he also worked as a research assistant, but also in the many studies of 'group conflict' in the United States.

For a while Billig's 1976 book *Social Psychology and Intergroup Relations* – a hefty red hardback from Academic Press at £35.00 – was my bible, and I bought his 1978 *Fascists: A Social Psychological Study of the National Front* as soon as it came out. There Billig sets out a history of studies of fascism within the 'critical theory' tradition and shows how the key researchers, Theodor Adorno and Max Horkheimer, adapted to the US context they fled to from Germany, and became known inside social psychology after the Second World War for carrying out questionnaire studies on what was then called 'prejudice'. Billig combines this critical history with an account of an interview study with members of the National Front which shows how a deep underlying core of Nazi ideology was at work inside this group. Billig's research was carried out at a moment when the main efforts of the Anti-Nazi League and Rock Against Racism were directed at exposing the National Front as a dangerous fascist organisation, not just an over-the-top eccentric group of little-Englanders.

Better still for those of us inside psychology, Billig produced a pamphlet in 1979 for the anti-Fascist magazine *Searchlight* called *Psychology, Racism and Fascism* which made clear the links between racist theories of intelligence in the discipline and fascist organisations outside. It was possible to see from this how important psychological research was to those who wanted to divide people from each other, how it was a tool for oppression and hatred. We tried to get Billig, who was by then working in the University of Birmingham as a lecturer, to come down to Plymouth to speak at a meeting of the local Anti-Nazi League; I phoned him from the student union but he said he found these kind of talks stressful and declined the invitation. That's all I had from the encounter then, his voice, but it was something, and he was still there on the radar, his presence a sign that something radical, even explicitly political in social psychology was possible.

The other conflict in social psychology didn't seem so immediately political, but it cut into the way the discipline treated people as if they were objects, and it offered an alternative way of carrying out research. This second line of debate took up the question of psychological 'science', and it aimed to outwit the psychologists who thought that people had to be treated as push-pull mechanisms. The lines of division here were inside British social psychology itself. The main representative of the experimental tradition of social psychology was Michael Argyle in Oxford University whose books on nonverbal behaviour and social skills helped define those fields of study for British researchers. His books on the social psychology of religion and happiness found that Catholics were likelier to be happy, as were those who liked Scottish country dancing; Argyle participated in both practices, so there was perhaps a covert personal experiential factor at work in the research. However, the patterns of nonverbal behaviour he reported from hundreds of little experimental studies, and then the prescription for good social skills that would lead to good mental health, had little to do with experience as such, except insofar as his 'subjects' would report how they were feeling by filling in questionnaires.

This laboratory-experimental tradition in social psychology was dubbed the 'old paradigm' by a philosopher of the natural sciences and language also at Oxford, Rom Harré. We learnt about the 'paradigm revolutions' in science from Mike Hyland who ran a course on the history and philosophy of psychology, learnt how the shift in astronomical science from a worldview or 'paradigm' that saw the earth as the centre of the universe to a paradigm in which the earth revolved around the sun enabled the scientists to account for the anomalies in their observations up to that point and to take forward their research. The passage from periods of 'normal science' governed by paradigmatic assumptions about the nature of the world through to 'paradigm crises' where revolutionary science broke from those assumptions and opened up new ways of seeing, and new research questions, was outlined in Thomas Kuhn's 1962 classic study *The Structure of Scientific Revolutions*.

Rom Harré's bold argument was that we needed a shift in psychology from the old paradigm in which people were treated like objects, put in laboratories and have things done to them so their behaviour could be measured. This old paradigm is 'empiricist', which means that only behaviour that can directly be observed counts in the results, and 'positivist', which means that worthwhile knowledge is supposed to be the accumulated total of those quantifiable results. The shift needed to be to a 'new paradigm' in which people should be, for scientific purposes, Harré said, treated as if they were human beings. This revolutionary shift in the times of 'crisis' in social psychology that we were living through then would enable us to make sense of anomalies in our observations of people confined in our laboratories and confined within the assumptions we made when we carried out laboratory-experimental style studies of them even when they were outside the labs. Irritating aspects of the way that people behaved in experiments, such as the tendency of people who seek approval to participate, 'volunteer characteristics', or their tendency to do what they are told, which are known as 'demand characteristics', now made sense.

We need to treat people as if they are human beings for 'scientific purposes', Harré argued, because good science has a theoretical model of what its object of study is. Our object of study is a subject, he insisted, a subject very much like ourselves, puzzling about what the experimenter wants, and striving to confirm the hypothesis, if this subject is in a good mood, or messing it up if they are not. Human beings are reflexive beings, engaging in what Harré, writing with a social psychologist Paul Secord in 1972 in *The Explanation of Social Behaviour* still rather mechanistically called 'second-order monitoring', perhaps framed like this because he felt he had to use a language that social psychologists would take seriously. The argument elaborated in later books was that human beings follow social rules in order to be taken seriously, to be accorded recognition for being good people, rules which vary from situation to situation, and they adopt social roles rather like those performed by an actor on a stage.

The accounts that people give when you ask them what they are doing will render explicit what those rules and roles are, for the actions and accounts draw on the same symbolic material, the rules and roles defined through those explanations offered to others. This is an unthinkable suggestion for psychologists, those who usually don't let their subjects know what is being done to them and often deceive or mislead them. Harré's new paradigm was 'ethogenic', that is, it is a bit like animal ethology, but with the added dimension of meaning, of exploring what sense is being made of what is going on by those working in line with this 'role-rule' model of human action. Traditional research neglected important aspects of our activity as human beings and it reframed linguistic and reflexive capacity as 'nonverbal behaviour' and 'social skills'. The ethogenic new paradigm, in contrast, aimed to bring our activity as speaking beings to the forefront of research, to show how accounting for action was crucial to the action itself.

In the final year of the course at Plymouth I had to carry out an empirical study to be written up in a dissertation which was heavily weighted alongside the second- and third-year exam results toward the degree grade. Tim Auburn arrived at Plymouth to take over from Brian Champness for a year, and I was lucky that Tim, who was very familiar with the role-rule alternative, was willing to supervise my work. Without Tim, or Brian, who had also given lectures on Harré's arguments for a new paradigm, or Fraser, who was happy to discuss links between these theories and some of the weirder ideas in *Ideology & Consciousness*, I wouldn't have been allowed to carry out research for my degree that was not experimental. My dissertation was an 'ethogenic' study of the rules and roles that structured the activities of the student's union executive, a body that I had been part of briefly as Vice President for External Affairs. The dissertation broke the rules about what counted as research, and did that by asking people about the rules they followed, and the roles they adopted. I can't honestly say that the description I gave of that added to the sum total of human knowledge. And to get through the degree I still had to conform to some fairly inflexible rules about assessment, criteria which define what it is to even begin to be a psychologist.

Everyone in my shared house was taking finals exams in summer 1981, and whether it was psychology, geography, physics or environmental studies, we had to bend to a routine – rigid systems of rules – and at least pretend that we knew what it was we were cramming into our heads in order to expel it within a timed interval of only a few hours on a given day. The exam routine replicates exactly the worst of the empiricist, positivist old paradigm way of treating people as if they are objects. We had to treat ourselves like objects, our bodies at that crucial time of revision and exam had to function, could not break down, for this time when we were being observed and assessed counted for everything, and we knew that. Instead of alcohol we – me and geographer Jon, my housemate – drank orange juice because, we were told, the vitamin C burnt off the adrenalin, and we ran around the block every day to keep us alert and help us sleep at night.

Each day in the crucial two weeks, the exam hall was organised as a grid, the little square desks on tubular frames set a precise distance from each other, and we sat separated one from the other as if we were a group in an experiment and as if we were in competition with each other. It is not only the organisation of space that is rule-bound, but the meshwork of interactions, sometimes voiced through the instructions by the invigilators but mainly, as Michael Argyle might have said, 'nonverbal'. Through those rules we obediently took up our roles as good students, the knowledge locked inside our heads, ready to let it out into the answer booklets.

The final paper in psychology had a rather unusual format, with general questions that were designed to show that we could think across the sub-disciplinary boundaries that divide psychology against itself. I chose to answer a question which began with a 1972 quote from the chemist and artificial intelligence researcher Christopher Longuet-Higgins, a quote which seemed to suggest that words operated as windows into the mind. This was my chance to make use of material I had been struggling with in the journal *Ideology & Consciousness*, and I turned around the question to rehearse arguments put forward by Ferdinand de Saussure on the relation between words as sound images and concepts that are attached to these words to form 'signs'. This was the opposite of what Longuet-Higgins was arguing; for him words expressed thoughts, and so we students, for example, were supposed to be expressing what we thought and remembered. In this environment we had no choice but to appear to do so, as if that is how thinking actually happens in the flow of life, in relationships and by circulating elements of language that we have not ourselves defined and that we do not fully control. It occurred to me then that this examination room was also, like most psychological laboratory experiments, configured as a silent world, operating as if human beings did not speak to each other to form relationships and work out who they are and what is important to them. I pushed aside that reflexive thought, kept to the task, and looked forward to life outside and after the exam when I would be able to speak again.

This is where the journey ends for most of those who take a first degree in psychology. They have had enough of it, but they still carry what they have learnt into other places, becoming relays for psychological knowledge, for psychological ways of describing the world, categorising those who do or do not fit into it. I had not had enough of it, as you can tell. This is the end of only the first part of my journey. I was, for all my depressive doubts, a good student, obedient enough and conscientious enough, and a little elated at the appearance of a 'new paradigm' which was, for me, a door into the next level in the game. What could there be next for those who go deeper into the discipline? For one partial take on that question, turn now to Part II, the next four chapters in which we explore the world of a postgraduate researcher who has a PhD as a life goal.

PART II
Psychological research

5

PARADIGMS

Performing student

In which we search for a place to continue to study the limitations of psychology, and encounter the strictly-policed borders between academic disciplines, demarcating those that cleave to science from those that are more suspicious of it. We explore the role of performance in navigating applications for postgraduate research. After a journey around the country, we begin research in a new home.

The production of a doctoral thesis is an oft-times lonely and occasionally frantic occupation, and marks the transition from being a student learning about a discipline to being a researcher, from being entirely dependent on the knowledge of others to taking some responsibility for the production of knowledge. The ambiguous nature of this transitional period is marked by the confusing juxtaposition of terms for someone struggling to really get into the discipline of psychology; in the United States they are termed a 'graduate student', which is confusing to the Brits who refer to this status as being a 'postgraduate'. You will see in this part of the book what it takes to absorb and display the cultural conventions of academic knowledge and scientific selfhood, what you need to do to become an academic psychologist. It is difficult to enter this terrain, and more difficult still to obtain funding. I describe how I did it in this chapter. I was lucky.

Rules

Psychology students do not, as a rule, become psychologists. This is an unpleasant cold reality that slowly dawns on those who have embarked on a first degree course with a view to beginning a career. I saw around me many hopeful friends on my course who thought that they were taking the first steps to becoming qualified psychologists, in most cases aiming to be clinical psychologists. Their realisation that this was most probably not going to happen was difficult, even painful. Perhaps it was because I was, from the beginning of my studies, a little more distanced from the claims to knowledge about people made by psychologists that I noticed how quick the transition was during the first months of the first year; a transition from my fellow students speaking about themselves in seminars to then getting more used to only speaking about others. That, they seemed to think, would put them on the clinical track; they would perform an identity of 'psychologist' that would differentiate them from those who didn't really understand what behaviour, cognition and emotion really were.

I was interested not so much in how psychology could be used to describe what I personally thought and felt as in what that psychology was saying about all of us, the claims it made about what we were thinking and feeling. I found the musing about personal experience that went on in the very early weeks of the course as peculiar and unsettling as what came next. First my classmates talked in seminars about the meanings of their dreams, for example, and even though they didn't yet have the words to fully convincingly show it, they were clearly looking to psychology to help them understand themselves. I didn't want to play that game, but much preferred it to the way they then began to censor themselves. They learnt that reflective self-understanding was viewed by most of our lecturers as self-indulgent talk that was not at all scientific. What was worse was that the switch of focus, from speaking about the self to speaking about other people who were not psychologists, often didn't even include understanding other people but, instead, modifying their behaviour or the way they thought. That's what it would mean to help people, they said, what it would mean to become a psychologist.

The nastiest twist to this lesson about the difference between a psychologist and the rest was that most of us going through the course would end up on the side of the rest. One reason is that there are just not enough psychologist posts for the students spilling out from the degree courses. Another reason, particularly in Britain, is that most degree courses are not professionally validated trainings, and so after the degree it was necessary to find a training course to become a clinical psychologist, say, or an educational psychologist. It is in the specialist training after the first general degree that you really become qualified, and it is quite difficult to get onto one of those postgraduate training courses. So, one by one, most of my friends at Plymouth resigned themselves to going into personnel management or advertising, or perhaps into nursing or other care work. This is a process of discovery that is common to most academic disciplines, but something that seems to hit psychology students hardest. I suppose one thing they learnt was that they were not psychologists. They had been subjected to what Michel Foucault called a 'dividing practice'.

I did want to learn about psychology, but had no ambition to become a psychologist. This made things easier for me at the beginning of the course, and more than anything else my time on the degree was, it seemed to me, another escape from work. But then I did start to wonder what I could do next. The beginning of my final year, a time when I was working on my dissertation study of the roles and rules that structured the life of the student union executive committee, was when

I asked my tutors what I might do to carry on studying psychology. Their cautious suggestion was that one possibility was postgraduate research, perhaps studying for a PhD, and this opened a door that I didn't even realise was there. They were sceptical about the possibility but supportive; it was worth a try. It was difficult to get a PhD place, they said, and they were even more doubtful about getting funding for it. I knew for sure that I wouldn't be able to pay for it myself. Life after psychology at Plymouth forced a choice between paid work and another student grant, an unlikely pot of money to keep me going for another three years. There were grants, I was told, but they were few, and usually given direct to university departments. What I should do, they said, is write a 'proposal' which described what I wanted to do for my research and send it to lots of likely departments and see if I got lucky, which is what I did.

It was not clear to me what such a proposal should look like, but my tutors told me that two pages should be enough to get the attention of anyone willing to supervise the work, so I sketched out a little essay which point by point described what I might look at – 'investigate' was the word I should use if I wanted to fit in with the old paradigm experimental approach. Saying what I wanted to focus on was the easy bit. The idea that there was a 'crisis' in social psychology seemed a good place to start, and the 'new' paradigm might perhaps be connected with other kinds of revolutionary challenge to dominant taken-for-granted knowledge in other disciplines, and, why not, in society. This could also, I thought, be connected with phenomena of power and ideology, with the question as to who could make the rules and what playing along in line with certain kinds of accepted role would mean for peoples' experience of their place in the social order. When Rom Harré talked about 'structure' he talked about it in terms of interlocking sets of 'respect-contempt' hierarchies, but never in terms of power. Following the rules and playing your role in a little social world, on a football terrace or in a student union executive meeting for example, would place you in a pattern of relationships with others where you sought someone's approval or disdained those who were seeking your approval. But surely that was not all there was to it.

Rom Harré visited Plymouth to give a seminar talk about the new paradigm during my third year. Because I was carrying out an 'ethogenic' study for my dissertation research, I was invited along for dinner after the talk. I was awestruck, and perhaps this was partly because I didn't know how – felt unable – to ask critical questions about these issues of power and ideology. I carried around with me in my head a complete set of analyses of power and ideology from the other part of my double life as a student activist, but could find no way to make all of that fit with what I was doing in my own little bit of social-psychological research for my degree. I couldn't articulate it. And it was all the worse that Harré was such an important reference point for an alternative perspective to the rest of the psychology I was so suspicious of. Harré was a small bright sprightly figure with a mop of grey hair swept over in a side parting, quick and sharp with the social rules he described so well in his books, sure of himself, for sure surer of himself than I was of myself.

Brian Champness, who hosted the dinner, described how his chickens were locked into patterns of dominance and submission, a pecking order. This 'chimed with', as Harré liked to say – it was one of his favourite phrases – other kinds of socially maintained respect-contempt hierarchies. I respected him but didn't want to get pecked, so I stayed quiet, not knowing how to challenge the way this picture of biologically wired-in social relationships might function ideologically. I'm sure they already knew this was an important question, but I was uncertain how to tackle the way they were talking about the chickens as if they were human beings, and as if we were like them. It was an agonising evening and I was glad when it was over.

Shortly after that, Harré's rival in the paradigm wars in social psychology came to give a seminar. Michael Argyle was a tall, slow and rather ponderous character with an oblong carved face; he bore an uncanny resemblance to former Rhodesian Prime Minister Ian Smith, mistaken for him on occasion. The story of the 'crisis' in social psychology during the 'paradigm revolution' was personalised during our lectures on the topic. It was told to us as a story about Harré as a canny philosopher of the natural sciences at Oxford stumbling by chance on what Argyle was doing in social psychology and, appalled by the conceptual errors, trying to find an alternative to the rather ridiculous experimental studies. One of the jokes often made about the sparring match between the two was that Argyle struggled to follow what was going on in the new paradigm and seemed only able to understand the issues in terms of the old paradigm. An apocryphal tale circulated that when Harré accused old paradigm positivist psychologists of being 'Cartesian' – splitting mind from body as René Descartes had done in the seventeenth century – Argyle had searched and, of course, failed to find this 'Cartes' fellow in his dictionaries of philosophy. This wasn't so much a stupid misunderstanding, of course, as what you would expect if the issue really was a paradigm clash as described by Thomas Kuhn; a dispute between radically different ways of understanding the world.

Argyle's talk at Plymouth was about the 'rules' of family life which he described, true to form, by way of responses he had gathered from questionnaires about how members of families made sense of how they should behave to be good mothers and fathers and so on. This was very different to the way that Harré would go about collecting accounts from people by asking them directly what they were up to, treating those accounts that people gave as exemplifications of the rules they followed. For the new paradigm researchers, the real nature of the family was in these rules rather than inside the heads of the individual members. Even if the rules were also inside the heads of the individual members, you wouldn't be able to get inside their heads by asking them to fill out a questionnaire. All you would get would be agreement or disagreement with your own questions, with your own presuppositions about what was going on. Harré described, for example, how 'memorial rights' in a British family were often distributed through the rules that people followed such that the mother eventually determined what was to be counted as an accurate account. A memory in a family is not something that immediately and easily pops out of someone's head, but is assembled, negotiated, and at some point given a stamp of approval as the real thing. This way of looking at 'memorial rights' in a little social world like a family shifts focus from the old paradigm individualistic way of doing cognitive research on memory. In addition, and this is something that Harré didn't take further, it draws attention to the power structure inside a family.

These issues chimed with, we might say, not so much the big issues about class power and ideology in society that Marxists grappled with but the smaller stage of interpersonal interaction that feminists have been more attuned to. This is where the pecking order is felt day-to-day, moment-to-moment, and where men and women learn their place, not only in the family, but also as what it is to be entitled or not to partake of and enjoy wielding power in the wider world. In the question time after Argyle's lecture I asked about the question of ideology and power in the historical role and function of the family under capitalism and patriarchy, and how the rules that governed the family maintained oppressive social roles. Argyle very slowly, in a deep quiet voice, mused over the question and said that he would certainly give it some thought and see whether it would be possible to put in some additional items in the questionnaire about rules concerning power and ideology. I'm not sure what I expected him to say, and he was friendly enough in the free drinks after the seminar, amused that I was carrying out Harré-style ethogenic research. I wasn't invited to dinner.

One of the outcomes of these encounters was that I realised that it would be the feminist questions rather than explicitly Marxist ones that would give me an angle for my proposal concerning the political context for the kind of research that the so-called new social psychology might carry out into power and ideology. Since I knew that I needed to include something in the proposal about what I would investigate, what actual empirical research I would do to make it a PhD, I settled quite quickly on the topic of how men became men, learning to follow certain kinds of rules to behave as men should and adopting certain kinds of roles. A little reflection on my first brush with my academic heroes – a battle of ideas in a seminar followed by dinner parties in which status was both a topic of discussion and the resource base of the encounter – made me acutely aware that the world of psychological research was itself quite a macho place. I needed to take care as I trod a career path that was among men and might be about men. I reckoned that one way into that topic would be to look at the attempts by men to change those rules and roles in alliance with feminists, particularly in the 'men's groups' that were around at the time as a complement to 'women's groups' that emerged from the 1970s women's liberation movement.

These men's groups were not always operating in a complementary way to the women's movement, and there was sometimes a tendency for these groups to develop their own ethos which then brought them into conflict with feminism. Delving into the hurt experienced by having to be a man, by having to be the breadwinner, and by having to exert power over women, did sometimes lead these men to claim that they too were oppressed. This problem, one in which the personal psychological experiences of what was felt to be immediately oppressive about having to adopt a certain kind of limited social role then took precedence over the political problem which had led them into the groups in the first place, seemed to me to be interesting. This problem, of a switch of perspective from oppression to the suffering of the oppressor, also seemed to raise broader questions about the relationship between the psychological level, the kind of question my degree course was mainly about, and the social level which feminist and Marxist politics was concerned with. So, the proposal for PhD research on power, ideology and new social psychology was initially for an empirical study about men. It was kind of about me and not about me at the same time, so it still fitted the bill for a piece of psychological research that was also sceptical about the role psychology itself was playing.

Roles

I sent the proposal to departments of psychology, sociology and philosophy – to philosophy because there seemed to be connections between what Harré was talking about and philosophical debates concerning 'structure' and 'agency'. He occasionally referred quite explicitly to some of the theories I had tried to make sense of in the journals *Radical Philosophy* and *Ideology & Consciousness*, theories from social anthropology and literary theory concerning 'structuralism' and the bad old rival approach it tried to displace, a 'phenomenology' that valued personal experience and agency. Most of my proposals and covering letters asking for a grant-funded place weren't answered. Some quick replies from Marxist philosophers politely pointed out that this was not for them. Then came some replies, four, calling me for interview.

First stop was a sociology department, and a lesson about academic disciplinary boundaries. The university in York was in a modern campus on the outskirts of the city, so it was a long day's train and bus ride for an interview that lasted less than half an hour. I was invited in by Andy Tudor, a young guy a couple of years older than me with long hair and a beard who told me he did media research and that he would be the chair of the interview. We sat on low seats in a small square office, and he introduced me to Peter Martin, a balding middle-aged man with black-rimmed glasses who was sitting quietly and quite enigmatically in the corner. This potential supervisor was a 'symbolic interactionist', and although I knew roughly what that meant, I didn't know how it functioned in the fraught relationship between sociology and psychology. Symbolic interactionism was one of the theoretical resources that Harré borrowed from different places to build his 'new paradigm' in psychology, but symbolic interactionists were very suspicious of attempts to import their work from sociology into a rival discipline that was historically focused on individuals separated from social context.

Symbolic interactionism was developed inside sociology in the 1960s as an attempt to think through how meaningful action between people is mediated. And it is about how that mediation by way of language in the broadest sense of the term – language as a symbolically structured medium which includes spoken and written communication and also nonverbal and visual cues – gives shape to how individuals come to understand themselves through their relations to others. The roots of this understanding of social life as a network of interactions that are symbolically structured lie as much in phenomenology – the study of how we give meaning to our lives and ourselves – as in the study of what we do with the world through our behaviour as social beings, something that is sometimes referred to as a 'pragmatist' approach. So, masculinity in a symbolic interactionist perspective is seen as a set of shared meanings through which those social beings called men come to understand who they are and how they relate to others.

This much I knew from reading my potential supervisor's work, but what I didn't know was how the acquisition of these sociological ideas by theoretical magpie Rom Harré across the disciplinary boundaries in psychology would be viewed. And the answer was, badly. There was nothing new about what I was saying, I was told, it had been discussed very thoroughly years ago in sociology, and insofar as Harré and his colleagues were doing symbolic interactionist research it was distorted and muddled up with other things. A brief explanation of what I couldn't offer to sociologists and my inability to give account of myself beyond being another dubious psychology student brought the interview to a close. I did at least have the presence of mind to ask what else there was to see in the campus, and I was told that the duck pond could be quite nice at this time of year. It wasn't so nice.

Second, I visited a social psychology department, which should have been more promising, but could not deliver. The department at the London School of Economics was distributed around a warren of little wood-panelled rooms connected by narrow corridors and dangerous stairways. I had been to political education meetings in the basement of the building on Houghton Street in my year before going to Plymouth, so it wasn't such a strange trek to get there, not such an intimidating place to go for interview. Roger Holmes and Bram Oppenheim found a room, apparently by chance after I arrived, and we sat together in the dull light filtering through the lead-etched windows, Holmes with a large book that looked like an accounts ledger open, ready to take notes. The first question, a good one if they hadn't read my covering letter, was how I was going to fund myself to do the PhD. No, I could not pay, I said, and this news that I needed a grant meant the big book was dramatically slapped shut. Even so, we had a discussion about what I wanted to do for the research which was good rehearsal time for the remaining two interviews. "Well, you know", Oppenheim said, "Harré is pushing at an open door here at the LSE, we have no problem with these ideas, but what key concept do you think Marxism has to offer that would add to his account". My silence, and then more silence. I gazed at the closed book and I wondered what that concept could be. They saved me eventually, and came up with an answer; "class?" They fed me the right answer, but they still didn't have the money, so that was that.

The third and fourth interviews were both in departments of psychology, one at Durham and the other at Southampton. These two places were both in the running for Social Science Research Council PhD studentships, grants which were awarded first to departments and then assigned to students there. Durham is up in the north east of England, a stretch further than York, almost Newcastle; it was a long journey, including a walk from the station to the sound of the cathedral bells in the fog. The visit included a night's accommodation in a university residence, and then a trip to the experimental laboratory site of the psychology department in the middle of a field for an interview in the morning with a possible supervisor, Jim Good, and, for the first part of it, also with the head of department Michael Morgan.

This was the closest I got to an argument in an interview, at least with Morgan who was playing the bad cop and quality gatekeeper. It was also one of the times I've been directly challenged about what this new paradigm research has to offer psychology as a scientific discipline, but was an occasion very different from my York interview fiasco, one in which I felt I was arguing on home turf. I knew the ground rules, and I could make use of Harré's status as a philosopher of science, of the natural sciences, something that cut no ice in sociology. The problem in the old paradigm is not that it is scientific, according to Harré, but rather that it is not scientific enough. The paradigm revolution is a way of reckoning up the costs of treating people as if they are objects, and of coming to the conclusion that this way of carrying out research doesn't really tell us much beyond how people behave in artificial situations that psychologists themselves have set up. Morgan was guarded, suspicious, and, after grilling me about what I was up to, said that he had heard enough and left the room, leaving me with Jim. I hoped this was not a bad sign.

Jim Good, a bespectacled very image of a scientist with a trim moustache who would have suited a laboratory white coat in a sepia photograph, was working on the sociology of scientific knowledge, on the way that scientists give account of their work as if they really are discovering things, which they sometimes are. Jim was rather apologetic about Morgan's role in the interview, but explained that that's just the way he is, and that we were, after all in a department of experimental psychology. The interview now turned much more into something that felt like a conversation. We chatted about symbolic interactionism and other ideas borrowed by the new social psychology, and how these ideas took different forms outside psychology. A decision about whether I would be given a funded place would very much depend, Jim said, on a number of different factors to do with the internal politics of the department. I left Durham that day feeling that I was in with a slight chance, and very much hoping they would say yes.

Audiences

It was Southampton next, my last chance, again a department I knew nothing about. Southampton is on the south coast, capital city for Hampshire, and is a seaport, one with a naval engineering and military history, still with dockyards and a navy base. The city is quite close to London, just over an hour on the train from Waterloo, with the campus a bus ride from the station. The interview was with the possible supervisor Roger Ingham and was very different from each of the other interviews. By now I knew that the best prediction I could make about these events was that it was impossible to predict what they would be like. And what I also learnt from the process was that the 'proposal' I sent was no more than a working document, a bit even like a Rorschach inkblot for a potential supervisor to see something in it that interested them and that would then need to be talked through. I suppose this meant that, in the worst of cases, the 'interview' negotiation about the uncertain ambiguous shape of the research at the beginning was as much about what a supervisor wanted the work to be about as what the student did. I was learning that being a PhD student also involved adapting perspectives so that what I was keen on would fit with what a supervisor liked enough.

The story at Southampton was similar to that told me at Durham, that internal politics, including over whose turn it was that year to take a funded postgraduate student, would determine whether I got offered a place or not. Of course, I hoped I would, and Roger Ingham also liked bits of the proposal. The bits he liked were exactly those to do with the new paradigm research, not so much because of its political impact but because of what it enabled us to see when we did fieldwork interviews. This meant that the empirical work on men's groups would be most interesting, he thought, because of what it would show about accounts of masculinity in different methods of research. Roger said that he had been a PhD student at Oxford supervised by Michael Argyle, but that although that had been within the frame of laboratory-experimental social psychology – in the frame of what we now saw as the old paradigm – toward the end of his PhD the paradigm wars had broken out, and Roger himself shifted paradigm under the influence of Harré's work. The favourite narrative around these events was that Roger was Argyle's thirteenth PhD student, unlucky for Argyle when his student had gone over to the camp of his rival. Roger had light sandy hair and complexion, clean-shaven. He was casual in manner and dress, a relaxed quiet presence with a sarcastic edge and anecdotes aplenty to illustrate slow, thoughtful and carefully unrolled questions about where different ways of carrying out research might lead.

There was a question here for me about the status of the empirical work in the PhD, something that was important to Roger, who had by then, after his own time with Argyle, gone on to carry out research inspired by the classic 'new social psychology' studies on football fans. One of the weaknesses of the argument for a new scientific paradigm was that, over a decade after the revolution had been proclaimed, there were very few research studies that would show in practice what the alternative to laboratory experiments and questionnaires would actually look like.

One of the few examples, one that was trotted out again and again but was already looking a bit worn at the edges, was one about football fans at the Oxford United ground, published in 1974 by Harré and co-workers Elizabeth Rosser and Peter Marsh as *The Rules of Disorder*. The second chapter of the book is about the rules and roles that operate in the classroom, and this often overlooked ethogenic research in schools was followed up a few years later in another book focusing on the way that children give each other nicknames. Or, if they are very isolated, something that this group of researchers using 'sociograms' of the social links that individuals have with each other uncovered, make up nicknames that no one else knows. This book *Nicknames*, by Rosser, O'Neill and Harré, was effectively the only other full-scale practical example of what the new paradigm might look like. The second chapter of *Rules of Disorder* figures in the book as one example of how apparent disorder is really underpinned by a complex network of rules, an underlying order that gives structure to the classroom as a little social world. The football terrace is a more dramatic example, and is used to drive home the point that outbreaks of violence do not so much spring from biological instinctual aggression triggered by rival fans wearing different patterned scarves, but emerge through the fans' understanding what they are expected to do in that particular context, as performers on that particular stage.

The young fans, or 'novices', thus spend their first season at the front of the stand, but not watching the match itself; instead, they turn back to watch fully fledged fans, all the better to know what they should wear next season, where they should stand and what they should chant. Among those senior fans are those who perform the different roles taken up by those who lead the chants, and those who chase the opposing team's fans. This is a little social world structured in such a way that, as a fan works their way through it, they trace through what these researchers call a 'moral career'. This was empirical work that drew on aspects of symbolic interactionism and, much more so, on work by a sociologist, Erving Goffman. Goffman was often seen as a symbolic interactionist by outsiders not clued up on the finer points of distinction between different traditions in micro-sociology and the competition between these traditions.

Goffman's studies in *The Presentation of Self in Everyday Life* back in 1956 filled out the metaphor of the human being as an actor on a stage with others as their audience, showing through careful detailed observation and description how it is that we arrange the objects in our personal space to give an impression to others of the kind of person we would like them to think we are. He described how we move through the world accounting for our actions to our audiences, accounting through detailed explanations or, more subtly, through hints and nonverbal cues. This is life as drama organised around what Harré refers to time and again as the 'dramaturgical' metaphor. One only has to watch someone walk down the street and turn back, apparently changing their mind because they have forgotten something, to see how people even then publicly 'account' for their actions, perhaps through clicking a tongue, patting a pocket or glancing at a watch. Even if the audience is one's self, it is always there as an 'other' for whom we perform who we are. Goffman's study of asylums, in which he posed as a cleaner to get closer to what he called, to follow his dramaturgical metaphor, 'backstage', showed how the patients know how they must perform, what role they must adopt to be considered to be a 'good' patient in order that they can fit in or, perhaps, get out of the place.

At some moments Harré claimed to be drawing on Goffman to build the new paradigm, developing from Goffman a distinctive account of the self as an alternative to the image of the human being as a kind of push-pull mechanism in mainstream psychology. At other moments Harré claimed to be providing a theory for Goffman himself, a 'role-rule' model of social research that would more scientifically ground the many different empirical studies that Goffman provided. The subject in a psychological experiment who is keen to obtain the approval of the experimenter will then behave in a certain way, for instance, and this is all part of the performance. This is not to say that they are being dishonest, or that the right research techniques would get 'backstage' and find out what the subject is really thinking. Instead, the shift of perspective that is opened up as we shift from one paradigm to the next makes sense of all of the attempts by those who have been inside experiments to fit in with what the experimenter wanted, and it makes all the more clear that most of the 'findings' from such experimental studies are therefore quite worthless.

The notorious experiment carried out by Stanley Milgram in 1961, for example, was designed to show how the phenomenon of 'obedience' could be replicated in the laboratory, but it can be read as showing us something more about the power of the scientific psychologist. That surely is the figure in the white coat who tells the subject to 'please continue' administering electric shocks at 15-volt intervals even though the confederate of the experimenter was apparently in pain. About two thirds of the subjects followed the instructions by the experimenter to administer electric shocks to another participant, another participant who, unbeknownst to them, was pretending to be shocked. Humanist critics try to find comfort in the fact that a third of the subjects refused to obey the experimenter, and, more than that, there were clear indications that many of those who did obey found it a distressing experience. In this sense the term 'subject' is appropriate, for these people were indeed subject to a frightful situation in which the rules seemed arbitrary and their roles quite undefined. Afterwards, some of the participants claimed that they had suspected all along that it was a set up, that it was very unlikely that they would actually be asked to electrocute people in a university laboratory, and that they were being well-behaved 'subjects' to humour the experimenter.

It does indeed take a good deal of ingenious stage-setting and convincing role play on the part of an experimental team to set up a scenario like that to be found in the Milgram experiment. The companion study in the social psychology textbooks, the Stanford 'prison experiment' carried out by Philip Zimbardo ten years later was even more elaborate. Those who had 'volunteered' to take part were not told before the study that they would be assigned roles of prisoner or warder, and they were expected to play out their roles in a university basement area kitted out like something from a kidnap horror film. The study had to be abandoned, and it is surprising that those involved lasted as long as they did. You don't need psychology to tell you that being subjected to this kind of situation will result in some bizarre behaviour as well as extreme anxiety about what is going on. Other less dramatic experiments have had to be equally careful about the staging of the tasks, restricting what the participants can do in order that extraneous influences can be screened out, itself an almost impossible task. These extraneous influences are called 'confounding variables' in the jargon of the laboratory-experimental old paradigm. Sometimes these confounding variables will be aspects of the situation that the psychologist can 'control', such as the level of lighting or noise or the presence of other people, but often a confounding variable only becomes apparent well after the rigging up of the study and often cannot be controlled. Both Milgram and Zimbardo screened their subjects for signs of what they called 'mental illness' so that only 'normal' people took part, but there is little one can do about the variety of other agendas that people bring to the setting, and how they understand what it is going on.

One curious and slightly embarrassing aspect of the Milgram study, and this is the case for many of the most memorable studies in psychology, is that it was not really structured around a series of 'hypotheses' which could then be investigated and tested against the standard base-line assumption that there will be no difference between experimental and control group. When it comes down it, Milgram seems to have simply been curious about what would happen in this strange situation, and he justified that with some extrapolation to other more horrible historical events. The studies that have been most influential in the history of psychology haven't been carried out in line with the methodological procedures demanded in the psychology textbooks. The old paradigm only seems to have delivered something of interest when the rules that govern it were broken. A telling 'finding' by another researcher, Don Mixon, was that it was not necessary to deceive people at all, and it was possible to arrive at the same proportions of 'obedient' and 'disobedient subjects' discovered by Milgram. Mixon asked all his participants to act out this bizarre scenario, and they acted it out so well, playing the roles and following the stupid rules of a psychology experiment, so well that they came out with the same results, the same statistical proportions.

I had to make a choice when I was offered a funded place at Durham and at Southampton. It was at a time when being closer to London was important to me, and that became the deciding factor. I accepted the place at Southampton, and the prospect of a PhD place that now depended on getting at least an upper second class degree added some pressure as well as some incentive in the final stages of the dissertation and then the exams. These last stages of my time at Plymouth required not only 'performance' in the sense in which it is usually understood by mainstream psychology, attainment of a grade in a test, demonstration of aptitude at study and proof that I would be a good postgraduate student. What was more important was the performance of self, a performance that was to a slightly different audience at each point in the process, a performance that was coordinated with the way that interviewers and potential supervisors were each performing their roles, on the stage for the other as audience, and also on the stage of the university as an institution which framed what rules and roles were acceptable and which were not.

My proposal, the one that eventually went to the internal institutional committees in the university at Southampton still included the word 'Marxism', though the head of postgraduate research in the psychology department there, an experimental developmental psychologist George Butterworth, told me that he changed it at the last minute, replacing 'Marxism' with 'political'. He did me a favour, unsympathetic though he was to the kind of work I wanted to do in his department. He played his part as a good academic and was one of the characters on the next stage of this auto-ethnographic journey. We were all set to play our roles in this academic social world, patching together our jointly assembled moral careers for different kinds of audience as I performed being a good student.

6

PERCEPTION

Boxed beetles

In which we settle into a new academic home, watch colleagues carry out empirical investigations, and also find out, now from the inside, how a psychology department works. Here structural family therapy provides a description of relationships and a lesson in what qualitative research might entail, and we also notice better the ways in which psychology really functions as a discipline.

Now it is possible to look around this strange social world of a psychology department as an insider. A psychology textbook and an undergraduate course stitches together a variety of different contradictory approaches and is barely held together by its experimental method. A psychology department is more diverse still. This department comprised some psychologists who were very sceptical about that method and others committed to it. The conceptual tensions were matched by the interpersonal tensions between colleagues often working at cross-purposes. Nevertheless, you can also begin to see in this chapter how the institution of a psychology department is structured in such a way as to enable each approach to be slotted into place, and for an illusion of coherence to then operate for everyone as if, and only as if, they were all working together on some kind of common project.

System

I learnt to touch type. It was clear that I wouldn't get away with writing out the PhD long-hand, so I spent the summer on my mum's massive Adler typewriter that she used for paid secretarial work from home when we were young. I repetitively typed A with the little finger, SDF with the others on the left hand, and so on until it I got it half-right, but with not enough time before the autumn to get to working on the numbers without looking down. Perhaps if I were to do statistical analysis, quick access to the numbers would be necessary, but that was not on the cards, and, with luck, never would be. Then birthday money was enough to buy a very heavy so-called portable, an Olivetti Lettera 35, which I used until I graduated to a computer, a Commodore 64 I bought in Southampton, from which I could print out pale drafts in slow dot matrix on lengths of folding paper. Work on these machines occupied much of my time for the next few years, and I may have spent more time gazing at the brand names on the machines while thinking what to write than reading academic texts.

Shackleton Building at Southampton University was a modern low-rise office block on the edge of the campus. I had an office, a space in the corner at the end of the psychology department fourth-floor corridor which I shared with a couple of other postgraduates who started the same time as me. This office had a desk with three empty drawers down the right-hand side. I put some paper on the desktop and some pens and pencils in the top drawer, and looked out of the window. More blocks. I accumulated photocopies of journal articles, but kept most of these in my rented room a twenty-minute cycle-ride down in the city. These photocopies were marvellously unwieldy sheets the size of a broadsheet newspaper that the university library would provide on request. I spent much of my time in the first year finding my way around the much older redbrick ivy-fronted library in the centre of the campus, locating the books and journals. The card index boxes were on the ground floor, and the service department would produce photocopies of articles from journals in the library or send for copies from other libraries on interlibrary loan. Or, worst option, I could look at blurred images of an article on a microfiche, a little strip of photographic film badly backlit, and then have it printed out on shiny paper that was almost as difficult to read. This was my research.

My fellow students seemed much busier than me. Their desks were covered with files, and they commandeered filing cabinets in the room which filled up at an alarming rate, and they were often either there at their desks when I went in, or were rushing in and out, looking for 'subjects' or writing up their field notes. Those looking for subjects to take part in experiments began by asking the undergraduate psychology students, appealing at the beginning of the lectures for volunteers, and then wandered around the campus trying to persuade other students to take part. In US-American psychology departments the undergraduates are usually compelled to take part in a certain number of experiments to obtain course credits, but even then the researcher either has to attach themselves to a senior member of staff to get priority or pitch their study to the 'volunteers' to choose them over their rivals. There was much agonising in the office about whether using psychology student volunteers would really come up with the same results as with 'normal' people, agonising that then sometimes appeared in the write-up of the research. They knew that this particular sample, of people who knew something about the theories that were being tested would 'skew' the results, shift the hump so it would not look so much like a bell curve. They knew that trawling the university for other students wouldn't be much better. But, what could you do? Most psychological research is carried out on this skewed sample, and most psychology is actually about what the researcher thinks a psychology student thinks, and so they carried on.

The PhD research closest to what I was supposed to be doing was an observational study of families. Shirley Reynolds was funded by a huge research project based in the department concerned with family therapy in which the approach of the 'structural' Argentinian family therapist Salvador Minuchin was a key influence. The Southampton project was overseen by one of the professors, Tony Gale, and a senior researcher funded to run it, Arlene Vetere, who had already got her PhD in that department. So, Tony and Arlene were Shirley's supervisors. Minuchin's 'structural family therapy' shifted attention from the individual patient who first manifested a problem and might turn up in front of a psychiatrist, often to be given therapy, if they were lucky, or given medication if they were not. It shifted attention to the family itself. The word 'structural' in this approach caught my attention because it chimed with the descriptions of family structure and role-rule structures that Harré and his colleagues had been giving of the distribution of 'memorial rights' in their own studies. Minuchin's understanding of the importance of the 'structure' of the family was much tighter than Harré's account of little social worlds, but then the family therapists were dealing with systems or structures of relationships in which the different actors were more closely tied together. It was precisely because they were locked into the structure that the problems or 'dysfunctions' in the system manifested themselves as what a psychiatrist who still focused on individual pathology would view as mental illness.

The shift of focus, from individuals remembering things inside each separate head – the subject of most classical 'memory' research in psychology – to the social world of the family in which there were shared and distributed 'memorial rights' in the new paradigm, threw mainstream old paradigm psychology into question. In much the same way, structural family therapy was a way of thinking about distress not as a psychological 'illness' but as a feature of the social world of the family and how it was organised at the expense of some of the members who made it up. What Minuchin did not do is step back and analyse the problematic structure of the close-knit nuclear family itself. Instead, his concern was with what went wrong; with the dysfunctions in the system when its supposedly balanced 'homeostatic' nature was disturbed.

This term 'homeostasis' was a clue that Minuchin saw the family structure as operating well when it was in an organised stable state. The problem, as he saw it, was that the family members often tried to patch things together themselves and restore order by setting up pathological alliances within and across different 'subsystems', between the parents or between siblings. The task of the structural family therapist was to draw attention to these pathological aspects, facilitating communication between members of the family and making new alliances that would restore its balanced homeostatic functions. For some families Minuchin was indeed a saviour, and there were stories of him being greeted by Spanish-speaking patients as 'Salvador', which was his name, and which indeed translates into English as 'saviour'. The question remained as to what it was exactly that he was saving when he sought to restore the family to its balanced natural state.

These family therapy alternatives to the way that psychologists thought about problems with relationships were impressive, as were some of the problems with simply turning from the individual to a bigger 'structure'. When I had carried out my own little study of the student union executive committee I had built up a picture of the role-rule 'structure' that gave it a reality for its members, but I had the nagging feeling that the approach I'd taken could make it seem as if that structure did or should run smoothly, as if it were some kind of efficient mechanical apparatus. Now I was faced with an approach to family therapy that underpinned Shirley Reynold's research, one that did even more so treat the structure as if it were, or could run as a well-oiled machine. Even more impressive was the research that Shirley was carrying out, for it was a project in which she had to go and live with families and notice the operation of the family structure and different sub-systems. Living with the families, of course, made her into part of the system she was investigating, and different family members did their best to recruit her into their own understandings of the problems they experienced, to make alliances or even to draw her into closer relationships with them. It was a time-consuming and sometimes nightmarish process, with some difficult situations she had to extract herself from. And that difficulty, along with the difficulties faced by the other students who were running around collecting 'subjects' made me think twice about whether I really wanted to do 'empirical' research for my own PhD.

I thought about joining a 'men's group' to carry out research with, but couldn't find a group in Southampton. I'd read about other such groups in magazines like *Achilles Heel*, mainly based in London. These were supposed to be leaderless groups that would operate free of patriarchal structures, free of the kind of male-centred power structures that underlay the Western nuclear family. The claim that they were leaderless, non-patriarchal and so, they sometimes claimed, 'un-structured', was exactly what was interesting about them. What I read was not appealing, however, with the key participants and spokesmen certainly appearing to act like leaders, and the ones I met were insufferably smug. Not only were they self-satisfied at supposedly having broken from the stupid familial ideology that the rest of us were still trapped in, but they viewed any questioning of what they were up to as at best indicating betrayal and at worst amounting to a manoeuvre by their enemies to discredit them. I had the sense that trying to do research in these groups would be as time-consuming and difficult as it was for Shirley living inside her target families. The closer I came to the practicalities of getting into the men's groups the less keen I was. I wondered whether I really needed to subject myself to the experience of being among these men, whether the studies I wanted to refer to had already been done, and whether I would have more scope referring to those studies and lots of other different kinds of studies if my time wasn't drained away in empirical research.

Would reading about existing research and writing about it be 'empirical' enough? This was something I talked through with my supervisor Roger Ingham in our first meetings, meetings which were sometimes weekly, depending on whether I had things to report about my thoughts or plans. Psychology prides itself on being a 'science' because it is 'empirical', but just as it has a flawed understanding of what 'science' is – that's something Harré had shown – so it also had a restricted view of what was and what was not 'empirical'. By 'empirical', psychologists usually mean regularities of behaviour that they can actually observe. That's why they are most comfortable with the kinds of experiments in which the subject is made to carry out a particular task, and measurement can be made of the extent to which their subject did or did not do it. Behaviourism of some kind is thus the baseline of psychological research, and second-best research into what people are thinking – into cognitive and perceptual psychology – has to make do with evidence that they are mentally processing events in this or that way, evidence that comes from their behaviour, behaviour as responses to images or accomplishment of tasks, which is then observed 'empirically'.

The ethogenic studies in the new paradigm were also, of course, in some sense 'empirical', but the data they produced consisted of accounts rather than meas-ures of behaviour. They were not 'empiricists', not conforming to the caricature of empirical research that most traditional psychologists collude in. Traditional psy-chologists dislike this kind of research even more because there is evidently a layer of interpretation that cannot be cleaned away to show you what is really there, regardless of what the research says about it. One of the big differences between the empirical ethogenic studies – whether they were of classrooms, football grounds or families – and old paradigm laboratory-experimental studies was that we weren't pretending that we could get rid of systems of meaning, of interpretation as we gathered our material. In fact, in the ethogenic research studies where we became part of the little social world we were studying, we could get closer to what was going on than the experimental psychologist who saw their subject only briefly to measure their behaviour, and who sometimes got a research assistant to do even that bit of the work. At least we could say that we had really been there, and had some-thing to say about it from our own experience of what was going on. However, we would never pretend, if working in the new paradigm, that there was not an interpretive gap between what we thought we saw and what was really, underneath it all, happening.

These were exactly the issues I struggled with in my supervision sessions with Roger at the beginning of the first year. He liked research, finding out things, but as the weeks went by it became clearer to me that what I liked more was the reading I was doing. My first major piece of writing was about the history of social psychol-ogy and the role of experiments in it. Eventually we agreed that my thesis was to be primarily 'theoretical' and that if it was 'empirical' it would be through analysis of other existing studies. Making this decision was a great relief.

Supervision sessions with Roger were very unlike the guidance sessions I'd had back in Plymouth. Back then, only a year before, I would come in and describe what had happened in one of the student union executive meetings or what had been said in one of my interviews, and Tim Auburn would patiently explain an aspect of Saussure's so-called structuralist theory of language and semiotics as a theory of sign systems. A tradition of theoretical and historical research unfolded from this theory of signs that comprised language. This was a tradition that was sometimes described as 'structuralist' or then 'post-structuralist', even though Saussure himself used the term 'system' instead of 'structure' and the different researchers influenced by him never signed up to be part of a group agreeing to a common conceptual framework. Tim would sometimes draw again on the blackboard in his office the 'paradigmatic' and 'syntagmatic' axes of signification; that is, the dimension from which items are chosen as alternative options to put together a representation of things outside language and the dimension along which the items are arranged in a sequence. For example, I can choose the word 'Tim' or 'Roger' as alternatives from the paradigmatic axis, and then structure a sentence to say that I listened to 'Tim' or that 'Roger' listened to me along the syntagmatic axis. These were lessons in semiotics, the only ones I had during my course, lessons designed to help me make sense of what I was encountering in my research.

Supervision sessions with Roger operated according to another kind of intersection of meanings, a different kind of logic in which I had to try and explain what I was reading and what it meant. Perhaps it would be possible to say that there was a meeting and crossing of the different paradigmatic and syntagmatic axes of meaning. We had different sets of terms to choose from, and spun quite different narratives about what the research was about. I would try and explain what I was reading, and Roger would associate to what I was describing and offer alternatives for me to go away and think about and account for in the next meeting. Comparing notes with other PhD students I knew that my supervisions were very different from theirs, but also that their own meetings with supervisors were also very different from each other. There was no common format. For some, the supervisor had a plan, a schedule of tasks, and there was a clear track that led from writing a background 'literature review' of the existing research on their topic to finding subjects to take part in the study, to analysing results and then 'writing up', producing the dissertation. For others, the supervisors were at times disinterested, and at other times seemed in a panic about the production of upgrade reports and the validity of the data that had been collected so far. Some students had supervision teams where it was sometimes difficult to deal with competing views about the best way forward. That kind of team supervision might work if the plan of work was set out for me at the outset in line with a research project, but then I would have felt that the research was not my own. Those students working on already-formulated research projects had to struggle to find a new aspect they could work on within the parameters of what was given to them. Sometimes it meant that they had to effectively carry out two pieces of research, the one for the project and their own for a PhD. I was grateful I didn't have to deal with that.

Structure

I was reading research literature that Roger clearly had no knowledge of, theories of structure and 'structuralism' in cultural studies and literary theory, of research in the human sciences well beyond psychology, about 'modernity' and 'postmodernity' as descriptions of our place in history. I was reading while trying to find other people who were reading the same kinds of thing. What I learnt from the supervision meetings was that Roger was not going to teach me, but that he could see that I was working, that I was already learning, and what he knew I needed was supportive discussion and constructive challenge to the ideas I was coming across. I was reading more about the historical studies by Michel Foucault on prison systems, translated into English a few years before, and on sexuality, just translated. I wanted to use some of the descriptions of power in his book *Discipline and Punish*, for example, to understand the laboratory experiment in psychology.

Discipline and Punish traces a dramatic historical shift at the end of the eighteenth century from a time of 'sovereign' power that targets the body to 'disciplinary' power that targets the mind. The book opens with the horrific botched execution of Damiens in France in 1757, punishment for attempting to kill the king. It then contrasts this exercise of sovereign power, which is power wielded as if it were something to be exercised over others, with the new disciplinary regime instituted barely fifty years later in which the prisoners walk obediently around the prison yard. This prison regime is organised around Jeremy Bentham's design for the 'Panopticon', a central guard tower from which it is possible to see the movements of the prisoners in their backlit cells ranged around it in a circle. This 'regime of truth' infused by a disciplinary kind of power that relied on minute observation of behaviour is there in the prisons, but the message of Foucault's book is that this regime of truth is now the model for the kind of society we live in today. Foucault himself had worked as a prison psychologist before he went on to write his history of madness for his own doctorate dissertation and then a series of other studies, including this one about prison systems. Could we not see in the psychologists' attempt to set up studies in which they controlled all the 'variables', down to the lighting and layout of the laboratory cubicle, a version of this Panopticon, as replicating in the experiments they conducted this new historically-specific form of disciplinary power?

I wrote about this, printed it out as smudgy dot matrix, and discussed it with Roger. His comments were detailed, necessary and unexpected, the first being to ask me whether this is really how you spell 'Foucault' and how you pronounce this name. I knew I was right about the spelling. These were good questions, and it took a lot of asking around in the university, turning from history and philosophy and then eventually to the English department to find out how to say the names of the authors I was following. I would try and persuade Roger why the debates in structuralism and post-structuralism were relevant to debates in the new paradigm, and he would raise more questions, demanding clarification. His musing and anecdotal associations to issues in social psychology worked across my narratives about the history of the human sciences, always making me ask myself whether this, happening inside the discipline of psychology, was the same or different from that process that was happening in the broader culture outside it.

My 'advisor' or second supervisor was Alan Costall, not a social psychologist and so with a very different perspective on these debates. Roger and Alan were friends, but they did not work together as a team. Alan was there to provide a reality check for the work I was doing with Roger, and he certainly elaborated an alternative reality, one that was in some strange way in tune with the critiques I was reading about and, in other ways, in complete contrast to them. I couldn't work out what to make of what he said, but trying to do so was worth the effort. Alan had a deserved reputation as an eccentric in the department. We could access the Shackleton building at any time of day. I was told that Alan had lived in an experimental cubicle when he started teaching at Southampton, packed up his bed and clothes each morning, using this little box as his home until he found an apartment in the city. Meetings with him would oscillate between him cackling away at some remark he was reporting from Ludwig Wittgenstein and staring at me severely waiting for me to saying something sensible about what I was doing. Alan needled me about two main issues, one was conceptual – that's where Wittgenstein comes in – and the other was political.

One of Alan's favourite Wittgenstein comments was that a thought is not inside the head like a beetle inside a matchbox. This cryptic comment expressed a key concern underlying his own research, a concern about dualism which neither the new paradigm psychologists nor post-structuralist social theorists were giving him a satisfactory answer to. Or, at any rate, my understanding of what they were saying was not giving him anything like a good enough answer. One problem was dualism between what was individual and what was social, and it looked as if simply swapping talk about little social worlds or structures in groups or families for individual cognitive processes would not solve the problem. There were clearly still people inside these social structures making sense of the social order and either repeating it or speaking against it. We researchers were also trapped in psychology and social psychology, and sociology for that matter, with a language that made it seem as if we were each individually rattling around inside those structures. Rattling around them like beetles inside a matchbox.

The deeper problem was about psychology itself, and I think that's what the beetle in the matchbox metaphor was really designed to cut against. Here the problem of dualism concerned what was going on inside our heads as we made sense of the world and what was happening in the world itself. At the heart of psychology, Wittgenstein seemed to be saying, there is an irresolvable split, a split that is repeated every time the psychologist tries to discover what someone is thinking, as if the task is to discover what is going on inside their head, and as if that 'inside' is something different from what is going on 'outside' it, something different that only the language of psychology can describe. Alan gave me some new conceptual resources from inside US-American psychology. I didn't really know what to do with them. But I knew they were attempts to give a non-dualist account, and they ended up giving alternative accounts that were not really 'psychological' at all.

One alternative account was in the work on 'perception' by J. J. Gibson, who pointed out in the 1950s that the mainstream perception experiments were misleading us about how we viewed the world because they relied on laboratory-experimental studies in which the subject had to sit still and look at the visual display offered to them, a display on a machine called a tachistoscope. Technical storerooms in psychology departments housed rows of these bulky machines which operated like giant stereoscopic display units but without the 3D effect and without holiday views. The tachistoscope allowed the experimenter to flash images on the screen at specific intervals and periods of time, a stimulus in response to which the subject had to respond by clicking on a button. However, Gibson argued, there is a problem here in this arrangement, a problem built into the machine, and then into the relationship between the subject and the image. Gibson pointed out that this isn't the way we see things in the real world. In the real world we move around, and so the 'visual field' changes as we engage with it. We are not the passive observers of an external reality presumed by experimental psychology, not the kind of observer whose passivity is enforced by the experiment. If Gibson's argument was correct, which I think it is, the results of most perception studies tell us very little about how people really see things in everyday life. Instead, the descriptions in the specialist journal articles are entirely artificial, artefacts of the experiment.

Gibson's non-psychological account of perception made sense, and chimed with Wittgenstein's argument that our minds are not like beetles inside the box of our heads. We move around actively engaging with the things around us, we are not inside our heads, but in the world itself. I assisted with undergraduate practical classes on perception which were overseen by Alan. These were classes in which we tried to persuade the students that something quite different emerged if you allowed your participants to move around the world. This was hard work, partly because I kind of got what the argument was, but still found it difficult to spell out what the consequences were to the students.

Part of the problem here was that the 'practical class' still had to design a study and produce results, and the students believed that we should all know our place and stick to it. They wanted to know how to fit into our view of the world, the view of psychological experts they were learning from, not to actively engage with it and change it. You couldn't blame them for that fixed limited perception of who they were and what they had to learn. Even when we took them away from the tachistoscope they still assumed that they should be passive observers ready to absorb information. They would stubbornly insist on their role as obedient students and follow what they thought the right rules were. One student had been in another perception experiment a few days earlier, and still had the plaster on his finger that had been used to hold a bit of the measurement apparatus in place. He told me that he thought that perhaps the air was being sucked out of the experimental cubicle, and that part of the experiment was to see how long he would keep the plaster on. In this way, for example, a version of 'psychology' was built into the teaching and learning environment inside Shackleton Building. Architecture was at the core of Foucault's analytics of power, the architecture of the built environment and of modern social relationships.

Perhaps the political question Alan kept raising was connected with this critique of mainstream psychology many years before the new paradigm was dreamt of. "Why are you doing this research?" he asked, surely this is "not just because of some kind of idle curiosity". That was his phrase, 'idle curiosity'. He said it again, and it stung. And he was right. His was a question about political consequences of the critiques we make of psychology, one that was as important as the question about how we treat psychology as part of an apparatus of power and ideology. In different ways, other members of the department I respected raised this question, though in gentler form, whether from a behaviourist perspective in the case of Bob Remington or from a social-developmental one in the case of Paul Light.

Family

I got to know who liked who in the department and, more importantly, who disliked who. Even though most of the lecturers were careful not to air the shared history of grudges and slights – complaints about being blocked for promotion and annoyance that their own work wasn't taken seriously – these petty conflicts did sometimes surface and were sometimes quite intriguing and revealing. There was often a whispered hint that this or that colleague with an office further down the corridor didn't understand psychology properly, that they were not even on top of their own area of work. As an undergraduate student I had been shielded from this kind of thing. On more than one occasion I heard verbatim reports of conversations in which senior researchers carrying out mainstream quantitative research who disparaged those of us doing qualitative research would themselves muddle up what statistical tests they should be using and pitifully have to ask another colleague for advice. It did seem as if the problem of psychologists misunderstanding the scientific method they claimed to be using – a problem Harré drew attention to – ran much deeper than the new paradigm critics suspected. The old paradigm psychologists were all the more touchy about the role of statistics in their kind of research because they didn't really understand it at all, and had to take a lot of the claims for it on trust. Where could we discuss this? We talked about it among ourselves behind closed doors but we never discussed it in departmental forums.

There were occasional research seminars at Plymouth, but at Southampton such events were a bigger deal. There were more of them; visiting speaker seminars were often weekly, and there were lunchtime seminars where people in the department were expected to talk about what they were doing. Organising meetings was something I had been trained to do during my involvement in left politics, something which carried on while I was in Southampton. A psychologist might describe my involvement in organising meetings in terms of learnt patterns of behaviour, and that would be a reasonable way of describing it if they were a behaviourist. Psychodynamic explanations that delved deeper would attend to something more compulsive, perhaps. I can't pretend that such theories don't make sense; of course, they each tap into one aspect of our lives, but each and every apparently 'psychological' account needs to be embedded in a particular social context. At this point in my career I guess it would also make sense to say that I felt I knew what was going on when I could make this little social world of the university department into something meaningful, structured, where I knew what my role was and what rules to follow. Helping organise seminars was something I could do and wanted to do. It helped me feel at home. Perhaps one didn't need to go and stay with a family to observe behaviour and spot affiliations and rivalries inside the structure. A psychology department, and perhaps any institutionalised group, will serve just well, serve itself up as an object of research, which is what it is now in this auto–ethnographic account.

This kind of activity works very efficiently when it is in a department structured according to different alliances and sub-systems, one in which competition is justified in line with a researcher's allegiance to a chosen field of psychology. The research seminars were one place where this kind of structure could be exemplified and reproduced. The visiting speaker seminar was viewed as a thankless task because whoever was invited to speak would, of necessity, be from a particular area of psychology that was of no interest to other members of the department, or at the same time, and worse, be from a specific theoretical position that everyone else viewed with suspicion if not hostility. All varieties of excuses would be made by the staff for not being able to attend the seminar, and while we were waiting for the speaker to arrange their notes so they could begin, the eyes sweeping round the room were not so much to see who was there but to mentally note who had not turned up. At Southampton they had settled on 4.15 every Thursday afternoon during term-time as a regular slot. It was a finely calculated arrangement, regular so there could no doubt when it took place, a quarter past the hour so there was no way to blame non-attendance on a lecture over-running. It was late enough for the students, who we wanted to attend, to disappear for the day and miss it, and early enough for the speaker to stay for an early dinner before they set off back home.

If the speaker was one that we'd suggested, then we were expected to take care of them afterwards. While it was good that rivals who did attend quickly disappeared afterwards, and would never come to ruin the dinner, it did mean that sometimes we had to entertain people at a restaurant who we had already been thoroughly disappointed and irritated by during their talk. We had often already exercised our social skills, sometimes to exhaustion, before the event, explaining that there were only ten or twenty people in the room because it was a busy time of year or because there was this or that competing event, expressing surprise that the turnout wasn't higher, reporting the great interest that people had expressed in the talk beforehand, even though these people hadn't actually turned up to it. And so on. What constituted sufficiently low numbers to give rise to such anxious justification and mollification of a visitor would vary depending on how famous or self-important the speaker was, but somehow the level was always just low enough to trigger that anxiety and embarrassment.

Being involved in these seminars was also a way of dispelling the myth that there was somewhere a 'backstage' behind the roles and rules that the characters in the department followed in corridor-conversations and departmental events, that is, a backstage where people would drop the mask and be spontaneous and authentic with each other. What went on in and around these public performances were just as much displays of power and vanity as in the classroom, what Erving Goffman called 'impression management'. There is no backstage. For waiters returning to the kitchen to talk about 'the pigs on table four', for example, the kitchen is just as much a performance area as the dining room. The dinner was sometimes a trial, and it did sometimes also reveal better what these characters thought they should be up to as famous academics. If it was three or four people including the visitor there could be a chance to exchange gossip, which itself is a performance of ownership of knowledge and display of being in on what was happening, of course. Or, as the most excruciating worst performance, it could be an opportunity for the guest to mark territory and remind you how important they were. One eminent social psychologist, Jos Jaspers, came down from Oxford. He ponderously described the different funded projects he was involved in, and we were asking for the bill when he turned slowly toward me and said slowly "you may talk about your research if you wish". Fortunately, we both knew that it was too late to take up the offer. Another visitor, Bill Noble from Australia, who was working in the tracks of Gibson's theories of perception, responded more abruptly when I described work I was carrying out on the history of the experiment as an instance of disciplinary surveillance drawing on Foucault; he simply snapped back "fuck-all", so that perhaps could have been one way to say the name of my hero of the moment.

I never saw an open argument in the discussion time at a seminar, but a question might sometimes have a sharp edge, at which point the audience would glance at each other, and ruminate about it after the thing was over. There was certainly nothing like a cut and thrust of debate, the contrasting of opinions or the thrashing out of differences in a psychology seminar. Being in a seminar was more often like being trapped in one of the paragraphs of a textbook, wanting to turn the page and being led instead around a repetitive and tedious account of what had been done and what had been found. That was the case most often in the old paradigm 'empirical' research that was reported by visitors. I loyally attended these seminars in the first year at least, even if they looked bad, and got used to a narrative about questions arising from previous research and 'findings' from a study, and to the rather desperate last-resort question to break a silence after the talk was over as to whether there were any 'sex differences' in the results, by which they meant whether the researcher had noticed a difference between the way men and women participated or performed.

One peculiar thing about this 'sex differences' question is that it pops up in psychology when it is not necessary and is overlooked when it plays a serious role in theories of gender. One would have thought that cognitive psychologists, for example, would have noticed that the 'Turing Test', which is supposed to determine whether a machine could pass as a human being, does not in fact ask the participants to guess whether they are asking questions of a man or a machine but whether it is a man or a woman that they are communicating with. It is on that basis of the determination of gender that the machine passes the test and becomes accorded humanity. This guess, however, is a guess about 'gender' not biological 'sex', and psychologists routinely confuse the two, so when they are doing research on people they do assume that they must sort them into two real body categories rather than in line with what social convention has taught us to make of bodies as we live them out as our gender.

The lunchtime seminars were a shorter and gloomier version of the main event, and here the difficult task was not only to get an audience, but to get a speaker, someone willing to spend an hour talking to usually no more than four or five people who came along to confirm for themselves that their colleague was doing nothing of interest. It came round to my turn to do a lunchtime seminar toward the end of the first year, so I read out my paper on the history of experimental social psychology which tried out some of Foucault's ideas about the Panopticon and disciplinary power. George Butterworth, the portly developmental psychologist who had seen through my research proposal at the university committee, sat eating a sandwich while I spoke, the rest of his lunch laid out on the table around which we sat. When I finished speaking, he wiped some of the filling off his moustache and asked, "What's the point?"

I liked George. Not a lot, but enough to recognise in his question at least an attempt to make sense of why I was doing this work – and it's a question that had already been raised by Roger and, more intensely and repeatedly, by Alan. It was a question that made evident the difference not only in 'paradigm' but in frames of understanding that we used in the department to explain to each other what we were up to. It was at moments like these that I really felt as if I was inside psychology, and that, just as the memorial rights to say what had actually happened or not are distributed in a family, so the rights to think this or that are distributed around the discipline, and then, in miniature, around a psychology department.

I had, of course, been outside the departmental family, if that's what it was, at Plymouth, for an undergraduate student is, at best, like a neighbour asking for help or causing trouble. They are not inside the structure itself. Southampton was my first psychology departmental family, held together by overlapping and cross-cutting histories of annoyance and tolerance. This meant that, in a peculiar kind of way, even those that annoyed me became points of reference, those for whom I was writing. Now, to be fostered into this family for a few years became one metaphor to understand who I was in it, and what I was doing.

I wasn't contributing to the knowledge that psychology thought it was accumulating about peoples' behaviour or to the way that psychologists usually described how other people thought. In that sense, there could be no way to answer the question posed by George to his satisfaction, within his frame of reference for what psychology was about. I had never wanted to be inside psychology at all, but now I had to account for what I was doing in terms that they would understand, and having a real hard time trying to do that. Perhaps this would be an impossible task, and, to make sense of how impossible it was, perhaps I would have to step outside psychology altogether.

Why did I stick with the PhD programme? It is a difficult question to ask of someone who has a funded place to carry out research for three years, and there are clearly vested interests, material economic interests at play for everyone in the discipline of psychology, whether they are funded on an undergraduate degree by their parents or by grant or whether they are employed to carry out research or to teach. I stuck with it because I had no choice – that's one bad-faith answer – and because I had access to conceptual resources that enabled me to step back from what I was doing from time to time, conceptual resources I will describe in more detail in the next chapter.

7

ANALYSIS

The continental selection

In which we find theories outside psychology that replace the way we talk about individual selves with new descriptions of who we are in different language games. To do this we turn to European traditions of work, including that of Jean Piaget who was adopted by the discipline as its favourite developmental psychologist, and discover something about the way that our fake science works to blot out signs of the human subject.

I rail against what psychology as a discipline does to human beings in this book, the way it turns us into objects to be experimented upon, subject to methodologies and social policies concerned with prediction and control. That aspect of the discipline, its power, was what drew me into it. But there is another conceptual theme that started to emerge as I learnt more about psychology, one that I explore in more detail in this chapter, something that became an important focus of my time as a postgraduate. This concerns the nature of the 'subject' that psychology works upon, and how we respond as human beings to those images of ourselves that psychological researchers circulate and demand we conform to. European continental philosophy opened up some new ways of thinking about that.

Predictions

A copy of *Ideology & Consciousness* arrived in the post just after I arrived in Southampton. This issue number 9 included articles on transformations of the way that 'work' had been conceptualised and discussed in the previous ten years in France, and on 'orientalism', with a review of the recently published book on that topic by the Palestinian activist and literary theorist Edward Said. I had assumed that it was a weird kind of radical psychology publication when I first started reading it before I started my undergraduate degree, but now there were only occasional references to psychology in the journal. There were but glimpses of critical perspectives on the ideas around me in the department in Southampton, so I had to piece together what I was reading in the journal with how it applied to my own research. It was harder work to explain how these ideas fitted with what I was supposed to be working on to my supervisors. The articles seemed, as did the debates in the journal *Radical Philosophy*, as if they were taking place in another world. Academic disciplinary divisions run deep, even in critical work, and the borders they build are often modelled on and reinforce linguistic and national boundaries.

This journal *Ideology & Consciousness* was, however, still a key reference point for me, for it was one of the few places where there was an opening to different ideas about the human being, very different to those inside psychology. It was reflecting back on the assumptions that we psychologists made about the 'self', preferring instead to talk about the 'subject'. I picked up some bad habits from the journal, apart from referring to an array of esoteric French authors. The way that 'work' was described in France in issue number 9, in an article by Jacques Donzelot, referred to 'discourses' about the topic. I adopted this way of writing and speaking about how things are represented, and maybe it isn't such a bad habit, but to refer to 'discourses' of this and that can still sound pretty strange to people outside that particular way of speaking about things, outside that 'discourse' discourse. I also learnt to speak about the opposition between 'the individual', which people around me in psychology thought they knew plenty about, and 'the social', which nominalised, or treated as a thing the domain of experience and society in a rather strange way, strange to many of those around me. This opposition between the individual and the social was, of course, one of the dualist discourses employed in psychology and also in neighbouring disciplines.

Since it began in 1977, *Ideology & Consciousness* had included articles on discourse analysis and psychoanalysis and feminism, introducing me to the work of Michel Pêcheux, Jacques Lacan and Luce Irigaray, among others. There had been articles about G. H. Mead and his 'social behaviourist' approach, and that approach had also been an influence on the development of symbolic interactionism in sociology and on research inspired by Jean Piaget in developmental psychology. Piaget's description of what he referred to as 'genetic epistemology' – a study of the origins of our knowledge about the world – was turned into a version of developmental theory inside psychology. It became a form of 'developmental psychology' as it appears in the textbooks, with a series of ages and stages that were then treated as chronological wired-in steps we could learn about and repeat in exam answers, very different from the logical sequences that Piaget himself was describing. In developmental psychology, textbooks and degree courses represent Piaget as the good experimental researcher who tells us how the child 'develops' by going through distinct cognitive stages which allow it eventually to use language and put its thought into words, and this theory is often contrasted with the romantic Marxist Lev Vygotsky. Even though Vygotsky's work was also tamed as it was translated from Russian into English in the early 1960s, it still smacked too much of Marxism for many psychologists; they felt there was too much emphasis on the way that the child learns to think by speaking – thought, for Vygotsky is viewed as being 'internalised speech' – and Piaget seemed more systematic.

Vygotsky's work got a warm reception in some of the new paradigm writing. Rom Harré waxed lyrical about the compatibility between Russian work in the 1920s and his own approach, sometimes claiming that his own work was close to what Vygotsky himself must have had in mind. What is sometimes overlooked in the too-neat contrast between Vygotsky and Piaget, however, is that Piaget was also from a continental European tradition of work which baulked at mechanistic positivist psychological research methods. Piaget's 'clinical method' wasn't experimental or quantitative in the way that developmental psychology lecturers and students at Plymouth and Southampton understood method, but ethnographic and qualitative. There was more going on in this mistranslation of Piaget's work into Anglo-American mainstream psychology than first appeared. Not only was he concerned with forms of knowledge, something that made him interested in theories of language like structural linguistics and then structuralism, topics that he devoted book-length studies to, he also working in a continental European tradition that was diametrically opposed to some of the assumptions about the nature of the individual separated from social context that were routinely made in the English-speaking world.

I knew the journal as *Ideology & Consciousness*, but in 1979, issue number 6 carried the abbreviated title *I&C*. This issue still used the full title in the back-cover blurb, and carried an article by Foucault on 'governmentality' as well as a Foucauldian study of the development of the school classroom as a manifestation of 'disciplinary power'. Replacing the 't' at the end of Foucault's name with a 'd' made it sound a little more French when you pronounced it, I discovered, and I think this is the main reason why some writers, me included, preferred to write about our approach as being 'Foucauldian'. It is by way of a concern with 'governmentality' that I learnt to refer to my history of the experiment in social psychology as being Foucauldian, though I had the uncomfortable sense that, if Foucault was right about the prevalence of the Panopticon prison regimes in modern society, then anything and everything could be treated as disciplinary power. I had noticed that after issue number 3 the journal no longer proclaimed, in large lower-case italic letters arched across the back cover, that it was 'a marxist journal'. The 'm' was, from the first issue, in lower case, a cute reminder that the editors were already close to some recent revisions of Marxist theory that had developed on the continent. The Marxism they were most engaged with was theory cut off from the practice of class struggle. Some other writers in the same academic circles spoke of 'theoretical practice'. Issue 7 and then the next two issues simply used the title *I&C*, the terms 'ideology' and 'consciousness' disappeared altogether from the journal, and then it stopped. It stopped arriving.

There were mailing addresses in the journal, I managed to track down one of the founding editors, Valerie Walkerdine, and she agreed to meet me to talk about my research and how some of the ideas in *I&C* might be of use. I went to her flat in north London one Saturday morning, and talked with her and Couze Venn. Valerie with shoulder-length flame-orange curly hair and bright red lipstick leant against a radiator with a rather pained expression on her face as she tried to make sense of what I was trying to do. It was clear that the 'new social psychology' debates had little connection with the theories that inspired the journal. I knew that, but hadn't appreciated until then how big the gulf was between the attempts to reform or bring about a 'paradigm revolution' inside the discipline and the debates about subjectivity and power that were raging outside it.

Valerie Walkerdine made some links in her own research on power and gender in the classroom, between the questions in the journal and what I was reading in social psychology. She warned me how difficult it would be to get this kind of work published in a psychology journal, and gave me a copy of her recent article, 'Sex, power and pedagogy'. It had been rejected by different mainstream journals on the grounds that it was not 'psychological'. She had eventually been able to place this article in a journal called *Screen Education*, which, along with the journal *Screen*, was where some of the first discussions of subjectivity in France were translated into English. Film theory, cultural studies and literary theory was where these debates were being elaborated, and so it was clear I would need to go well outside the dualist couplet 'psychology-sociology' to get at what I needed for my own work. Her article on sex, power and pedagogy stepped back from the way developmental psychology was understood in psychology to look at how the ideas functioned in 'discourse' in the classroom. I suppose what annoyed the psychologists who rejected the paper from their own journals was that it wasn't fitting into or adding to what they thought researchers like Piaget said about children's development. In a curious and roundabout way, it was, even so, also about 'development' because the article showed that the descriptions taken up by psychologists had an impact on how teachers understood children and also on how they understood their own position in relation to the children they taught.

The centrepiece of the article was a piece of transcript of classroom interaction in which a young woman teacher tells a little boy not to knock down an assemblage of toy building blocks; the boy responds with a stream of sexist abuse, and then the teacher shrinks back from admonishing the boy. Was her feeble reaction because she assumed that the boy's gender and particular stage of child development called for a more supportive response? Walkerdine then explored the way that discourses about development that are influential in teacher training entailed a version of developmental theory that rendered this teacher powerless in the interaction. The 'pedagogy' in the title of the article therefore referred to the educational practices to which the teacher had been subjected, and so we could see how she became positioned as a certain kind of subject who experienced herself in relation to the little boy who, within the discourse of developmental psychology, was being treated as another particular gendered kind of subject. Subjects were called into position, hailed by dominant discourses to respond in a certain kind of way; they were, as *I&C* liked to say, 'interpellated' – addressed, arrested by discourse – so that the positions they were then slotted into made sense to each of them and to each other. Both of them, teacher and boy, were evidently treating each other, and also learning to treat themselves, as 'psychological' subjects. The interpellation of a subject into discourse sometimes includes a barely conscious reflexive puzzling about who we are to respond to this call into position. It is in this sense that it includes in it something almost psychological. It was then possible to link this with the account given by other Foucauldian historical accounts of subjectivity in *I&C*, including the article in the final issue number 9 in which Donzelot describes how 'psychological' notions of subjectivity are mobilised in discourses of work in French society in the late twentieth century. This new kind of contract that seems necessary to hold 'the social' together Donzelot named as being 'neo-liberal'.

I could see now why the psychology journals had rejected the Walkerdine article. It wasn't only because it was not explicitly 'psychological'; it was not attempting to explain what was going on for the teacher by way of what was supposedly going on inside her head. We really have no idea what that teacher is thinking but can only describe how she is 'positioned' and how she positions herself within the discourses that are available to her. It may well be that if the teacher had read Valerie Walkerdine's work, or had other discursive resources to hand, she could have responded in a different way, and perhaps she would even respond differently the next time round after having been thus subjected, and after having subjected herself to sexist abuse from the little brat. The paper was also rejected, I guess, because of the underlying assumptions about what constitutes 'method' in psychology. If the teacher did respond differently the next time this kind of thing happened to her then that would, for psychologists, disprove the interpretation offered in the paper. The interpretations the psychologists value are those concerned with 'predicting' what will happen, with predicting behaviour, and to do that they have to control for all the other possible 'confounding variables' that might be influencing the situation. Those underlying assumptions about prediction and control in the method of psychology were being challenged in Walkerdine's paper, for she was concerned not with what will happen next but how we might understand the conditions which made those things happen then.

Our understanding of what Foucault called the 'conditions of possibility' for certain kinds of events is what makes it possible for us to change how we act. For this continental European tradition of work, the question of change is prioritised over the rather static and fixed picture of the world in psychology that will allow us to predict and control behaviour. Psychology is a ragbag of different rival theories that is held together by the kind of predictive method that fits us up for a world that does not change. Couze Venn, a slim quiet guy in a white polo-neck jumper and rimless spectacles, sat on the couch. Valerie struggled to translate what I was saying into a more Foucauldian discourse and back again, and from time to time he tried to further complicate the story. I found it difficult enough to read the articles in their journal, and was completely at sea making sense of what Couze was saying to me about the historical constitution of subjectivity in contemporary discourse. Valerie made it a bit clearer, but I was completely out of my depth, and they both knew it.

This field of work was obviously important to me, and so my supervisor Roger Ingham agreed to have Valerie invited down to give a seminar about her research in Southampton. It was a typically agonising occasion in which the developmental psychologists that did make an appearance kept quiet, waited for the session to end, and then disappeared quickly before we went for dinner, at which the discussion between Roger and Valerie was a good opportunity to see two worlds meet, to see differences between those two worlds and their contrasting concerns with knowledge and how they functioned.

We discussed trade union activity, and Valerie told us she had abandoned participation in Camden Trades Council in north London because the discourse there was so stereotypically macho. She talked about the way her students referred to her as 'aunty', and how this 'positioned' her as a sympathetic gendered subject with particular responsibilities, as if it was more important that she care for them than teach them. In the process, her expertise was overshadowed by a form of familial discourse. I am aware that I have shifted quite quickly in the course of this account from referring to Walkerdine, the researcher author, to Valerie, the person I knew who tried to explain to me more clearly what she meant by what she wrote. I wonder if it is familial discourse that also frames that shift to a more personal reference, and I mark the names of those still distant to me and those more familiar in different ways in this book. I position them in this text, and so I am complicit in some of the work of positioning that goes on in language whether we think we are in control of it or not. There were evidently consequences of this turn to positioning in discourse beyond academic re-description of what was happening in a piece of classroom transcript. Valerie's reflections were methodological, and had a bearing on how we psychologists were positioned, and how we positioned ourselves in teaching and research.

Descriptions

The bad news was that *I&C* was finished. The good news was that there was a book on the way. The disappearance of the term 'Marxism' from the discourse of the journal was, it turned out, connected with the disappearance of 'ideology' and 'consciousness'. The various French theories that underpinned the journal were each, in very different ways, indebted to Marxism, but the theorists themselves were slowly disentangling themselves from that political legacy and forging alternative descriptions of society and the individual. Foucault, for example, had been a member of the French Communist Party in the 1950s, and one of his first books, on *Mental Illness and Psychology*, refers, in the first published edition, to 'social classes', this substituted a few years later with 'social groups'. There were good reasons for him to leave, some commentators putting it down to the Party's attitude to homosexuality, assumed to be a symptom of the degeneration of bourgeois society, and others to the prevalence of antisemitism following the so-called doctor's plot in which Stalin lashed out at 'cosmopolitan' enemies who, he said, were trying to kill him. At any rate, the question of power, and of the Communist Party itself as a power apparatus which was little better than the capitalist society it pitted itself against and worked alongside in government whenever it had the opportunity, loomed large in Foucault's work ever since.

Different forms of power and discourse at different points in the history of Western Europe were, according to Foucault, tied up with knowledge and subjectivity, both with how we understand the world and how we understand ourselves as human beings in it. That's what gave Valerie Walkerdine's study of the woman teacher and boy child such bite. It wasn't about what young women and children were always like, their unchanging psychological attributes, but rather about how they had come to be formed, or 'constituted' as Foucauldians would put it. If we could understand the way that little world was constituted, then perhaps we would be a step further towards changing it. What that link between power, discourse, knowledge and subjectivity also did was throw into question the claims to 'truth' made by disciplines like psychology. Foucault's argument was that different 'regimes of truth' made certain kinds of objects and subjects visible to us. Once we were constituted as a particular kind of subject inside a regime of truth, it was very difficult to break out of it. It was difficult but possible, possible when our reflection on the conditions of possibility for a new analytic discourse was tied to action, to resistance.

A consequence of the argument was that, over time, we might shift from one kind of system of knowledge to another, but we do not thereby arrive at a definitively true account as such. The cultural-historical frame of epistemology Foucault referred to as 'epistemes', and he described in his book *The Order of Things* how the last three major epistemes had lasted around a century and a half each, landing us in the latest 'modern' system of knowledge. The upshot of this cultural-historical account is that there is no entirely accurate or correct representation of reality outside discourse. We cannot expect one representation of reality to resolve all the problems we face as human beings but can only expect to encounter different regimes of truth. This also throws into question the opposition dear to much Marxist theory between 'ideology' on the one hand and 'truth' on the other. Foucault and other theorists breaking from orthodox Marxism became increasingly reluctant to use the term 'ideology' because it had so often, in that political tradition, been used as a term of abuse by those who thought they did really have access to the truth. Marxists can't directly see the world or real things hidden in it any more than psychologists can, and so this term 'ideology' itself became seen as suspect, as a term that was part of a particular kind of discourse, of a particular 'regime of truth' that became so powerful in the historical disaster that was the Stalinised Soviet Union.

The other term linked to ideology, one that seems closer to the concerns of psychologists, was 'consciousness', but while that term was initially useful in the title of a journal that tried to intervene in psychology, it was also fatally compromised, caught up in the network of assumptions about knowledge and experience that the French theorists wanted to challenge. The phrase 'false consciousness' was employed by many Marxists, for instance, to describe how people were bewitched by ideology, even though Marx himself never used the phrase. Then there was a temptation to imagine that it would be possible to break from this false consciousness and arrive at an authentic consciousness that grasped the complete truth about society and about the human condition. French theories led their master thinkers and followers to conclude that there was no such thing as 'true consciousness' or even a kind of correct 'class consciousness' that saw through the illusions that held capitalist society together. Instead, the notion of consciousness itself was seen as a conceptual trap and was best avoided.

These different theories were grouped together by many of their followers outside France, and even more so by their enemies, as being 'structuralist', and then brought under the more popular catch-all category of 'post-structuralism'. While the older more reputable philosophical approach to how people made meaning that was called 'phenomenology' was of interest to some psychologists, this new 'post-structuralist' approach was dead set against investigating our conscious meaningful engagement with the world. *I&C* never used this portmanteau term, and none of the various French theorists they included ever signed up to it as a school label for what they did. But the journal did flee from old Marxist categories of 'ideology' or old psychological notions of 'consciousness', and it looked for different ways of talking about experience, and alternatives to what we in psychology usually referred to as the 'self' or as a person's 'identity'.

There were people who called themselves 'post-structuralists' around Southampton, even if they were quick to unravel what the term meant if they were asked to explain it. They were in the English department, and so this was one port of call to find out more. One of them, Robert Young, edited a book in 1981 called *Untying the Text* which styled itself, in its subtitle, as *A Post-Structuralist Reader*, and there was a group of postgraduates that included Joe Bristow and Judith Squires. Along with a postgraduate student from philosophy, Geoff Gray, we set up a reading group which looked at some of Foucault's work and that of Jacques Lacan. So-called 'post-structuralist' ideas about who we are as human subjects focus not on experience that can be gathered together in one place, gathered together in the mind of the individual or inside the self, but on 'subjectivity' which is assembled from different discourses. These ideas were important to those of us who participated in the reading group, underlying assumptions about language and subjectivity.

That different way of reading and untying text also poses a problem for empirical psychological research that would like to come up with 'results', and preferably results that could be quantified. The concern with 'results' in psychology is in line with the, at best, prospective and, at worst, predictive nature of its method. The alternative ideas we were looking at in the reading group were rooted in a study of language that was retrospective; for example, looking back and understanding what has happened so that we might ourselves do it differently the next time. This way of approaching meaning and action is very frustrating for the mainstream psychologists, and that's why it sometimes seems like we, the critics, and them, the psychologists, are speaking different languages. Even qualitative research could then only claim to be a tentative account of the process of making, repressing and remaking meaning, not an account of what things really meant as such, as things that could be made fully present to consciousness. This put the spanner in the works, not only for traditional psychologists who aimed to discover what people were thinking, but also for some of the new paradigm psychologists who were concerned with structure but who still wanted to know how people made meaning, how they followed the rules in little social worlds and performed their roles on the different stages of their life. The 'subjectivity' that the different post-structuralist theorists were trying to describe was something that was always already broken into fragments, and patched together moment-by-moment. It was the process we needed to track rather than the end product that was important; the end product that psychology expects at the end of a study is, as English literature readers and researchers in Southampton delighted in saying, fictional; and the pleasure of reading lies in the construction and 'deconstruction' of literary fictions, of texts.

Prescriptions

I spent a lot of time in London, staying over in Southampton only as often as I needed to fulfil the requirements of my studentship grant and to be able to participate in reading groups, departmental seminars and some teaching, assisting in practical classes. There were crucial theoretical resources in London, including events at the Institute for Contemporary Arts on The Mall, Madan Sarup's introductory evening course on structuralism and post-structuralism at Goldsmiths College and, most importantly, a series of the University of London's Extra-Mural Studies sessional classes on structuralism and post-structuralist theories run by Peter Dews. Peter gathered around him a little group of students who would faithfully attend each version of the classes, on 'Language, History, Politics: Developments in Post-War Continental Philosophy', 'Problems in Post-War Continental Philosophy' and 'Philosophy and Modernity' in successive years from 1982 to 1985. These were classes that traced the work of different theorists from debates in phenomenology and existentialism, in the work of philosophers such as Jean-Paul Sartre and in the lectures on Hegel by Alexandre Kojève in Paris that many influential figures, including Sartre and Jacques Lacan, attended. Peter set out this history as background context for an account of the impact of the structural anthropologist Claude Lévi-Strauss, and then the emergence of structuralist and post-structuralist theorists like Foucault, Lacan and Jacques Derrida, doyen of deconstruction, among others.

These classes gave me my main grounding in the debates, and over the years of these London classes during my PhD work I encountered researchers from different academic disciplines. There were no psychologists there, but students from other human sciences. Georgina Born from cultural anthropology and Michael Newman from art history attended, as did others from film theory and philosophy. We gathered in little basement rooms in Birkbeck College in groups that hovered around the ten or fifteen number mark. Peter Dews was a young lecturer with fair hair who had studied for his PhD in Southampton and who had a quizzical air about him, especially when he gazed up into the corner of the room and, as if making it up as he went along, lucidly explained how this theory developed from and in response to that one. The philosopher Anthony Grayling attended some of the sessions, and this enabled some intriguing though inconclusive connections with the 'analytical philosophy' tradition that he specialised in. Grayling was a friendly and patient presence in the classes, peering at us through rimless specs and often also through a mass of hair that he had to repeatedly and nervously sweep back. At one end-of-term drinks together just off the Old Kent Road he anxiously inquired whether we thought the publisher Duckworth was respectable and would be good for his career. His slightly fussy and pedantic demeanour made for an ethos of constant clarification, which was very useful. The debates in class between Peter and Anthony also lured some of us into his own classes, including a Saturday course in November 1984 on 'Truth and Meaning' where we were subjected to some of the more complex algebraic and logical positivist arguments about the nature of language.

The classes with Peter Dews, and, even more so, the contrast with the approach taken by Anthony Grayling, impressed on me that the disputes between paradigms inside psychology were mirrored in some way across academic disciplinary boundaries. These disputes were even more evident than in my encounters with the English department people in Southampton where it seemed as if post-structuralism ruled the roost, and its influence spread across to neighbouring departments. At a seminar in February 1984 even Tony Manser, a professor of philosophy who specialised in existentialism tried, when under siege by his sceptical colleagues, to persuade them that Derrida was really saying the same thing as Sartre had already said. These disputes inside philosophy were additionally interesting because the 'analytical philosophy' and then 'ordinary language' traditions were influential background frameworks for Harré's new paradigm critiques inside psychology. Furthermore, those debates gave me some better grasp of what Alan Costall, my thesis advisor, was going on about when he kept citing Wittgenstein.

What eventually became apparent was that Wittgenstein was not so much a bridge between the two traditions in philosophy, traditions which were rather misleadingly known as 'analytical' as opposed to 'continental' philosophy, but marked something of a break between one and the other. Wittgenstein's only book, the *Tractatus Logico-Philosophicus*, had been mentioned to me in one of my few encounters with Tony Gale, professor of psychology at Southampton, one of my fellow student Shirley Reynolds' supervisors. Tony said he preferred Bertrand Russell and Alfred North Whitehead's positivist bible *Principia Mathematica* as he slowly closed his office door, shutting me out. I came to see why he thought *The Tractatus* might be relevant to his own discipline when I realised that this book was the work of the 'early' Wittgenstein of the 'analytical philosophy' tradition he contributed to along with Russell. In that early Wittgensteinian argument, the structure of language was thought to map directly onto the structure of things in the world. If this were true, then not only would the rather mechanistic procedures of laboratory-experimental psychological research make perfect sense but the sense they made would conform to how things really were, whether those things were outside in reality or inside the head.

The analytical philosophy tradition thus corresponded quite well with the tradition of mainstream research in psychology, and the conversation between the two shared some common assumptions about the status that should be given to clear speaking and clear thinking. This connection also reinforced the connection psychologists liked to make between research in the natural sciences and research into the way an individual spoke and thought in everyday life, in 'ordinary language'. The method that was built from this way of approaching language was 'logical positivism'; that was the methodological approach that was explicitly claimed by many psychologists to back up their experimental research, and attacked as the background assumption underlying laboratory-experimentation by Harré and his followers at the time of the 'paradigm crisis'.

Wittgenstein himself was never really happy with the assumption that there should be a correspondence between the methods of the natural sciences and the social sciences, but his later work completely broke with Russell and with logical positivism. The 'later' Wittgenstein to be found in *Philosophical Investigations* assembled and published after his death in 1951 presents a very different picture. Words and sentences do not now provide an accurate picture of the world, but, instead, language becomes seen as something more slippery and fluid, a characteristic expressed in the phrase 'language games' that Wittgenstein employed to speak about the construction of reality. Language also becomes viewed as something rulebound, where it is the following of rules and the elaboration of what a rule is in social life that holds our relationships together. Games, as we know, are not always as mutable and playful as we would like; a game is a structured set of rules, with consequences for those who break them.

Among the many consequences of this rupture in analytical philosophy that Wittgenstein engineered when he moved on from the *Tractatus* to his later, quite different work in *Philosophical Investigations*, are two that are relevant to debates about language and social life inside psychology. The first consequence was to be felt inside the new paradigm in psychology, for alongside and against Harré's emphasis on 'structure' in his role-rule model of social life – something he hoped would also provide a theory for the work of the sociologist Erving Goffman – there was another strand of work which was more phenomenological, an approach to meaning and action to be found in the writings of John Shotter. Shotter, who was based in Nottingham, emphasised the experiential and mutable nature of social interaction, and he often utilised Wittgenstein's arguments to show how the meaning of something could only be found in its use. That is, instead of looking to the way that meanings are given by the structure of language in a society or in any particular social situation, we need to look at how meanings are elaborated momentby-moment as part of the life project of a person. Shotter's concern was with the way that we accounted for our actions and with how the process of accounting for action had implications for our conceptions of who we were, for our 'selves' as located in the to and fro of a conversation.

A second consequence of this dramatic shift from a logical positivist way of looking at the world, one in which you could treat the world as a set of objects to be experimented on to discover what they were really like, to the later Wittgensteinian way of accounting for action in a complex interlocking series of language games, was that philosophy itself connected once again with the 'continental' tradition. That term 'continental' had always been a bit of a misnomer when it was applied to what was viewed as the bad new wave of structuralist and post-structuralist theories sweeping over the Channel into literary and film studies. After all, when the logical positivist philosophers escaping from fascism on mainland Europe arrived in Britain and the United States in the 1930s, they were at that time themselves referred to as the 'continental' philosophers. Furthermore, the new French theory that was named as 'continental' was actually very soon much more popular in English Literature and in some philosophy departments in Britain and the US than it was back in France, where analytical philosophy is still the dominant tradition. The point is that the later Wittgenstein functions as a critique not only of psychology, but also of old analytical philosophy, and there have been many books and journal articles which read Wittgenstein as if he himself anticipated arguments in what we knew as 'post-structuralism'.

Muddy and muddled is a fair way to describe how all this appeared in the human sciences, in which we should now include cultural and literary studies and philosophy itself, as well as in psychology, a discipline that would have much preferred to steer clear of the human sciences but now found itself dragged closer and closer to them. That mess of cross-cutting debates about language and action, and about what scientific inquiry should look like, also raised questions for what Rom Harré was up to as a philosopher of science. He made a keystone of his argument in psychology the claim that we should move into a new paradigm and treat people as if they were human beings, for scientific purposes. He used Wittgensteinian arguments, but instead of taking psychology into the realms of literary and cultural post-structuralist theory, he still wanted to make the discipline more genuinely scientific.

I had one post-structuralist literary-theoretical reference group at Southampton, another philosophy reference group in Peter Dews' classes in London, and a third reference group composed of those of us inside psychology who had been reading *I&C* and work by some of the editors while we were waiting for their book to appear. This third loose network was not really so interested in social psychology, and one of the things I learnt from that group was how limited and parochial the new paradigm was. I read about a 'revolution', but it became more and more untenable to write and speak about that when other people doing radical work in psychology often didn't seem to have heard about it. That didn't stop me from referring to it though, and one thing a three-year funded PhD does is to commit you to the frame of reference you've been given the grant for. So, I stuck with it, branching out at one moment, and returning to my specific research topic at the next. This third reference group included developmental psychologists like Erica Burman who was in Manchester, and social psychologists like Sonia Livingstone and Peter Lunt who were based in London.

Another reading group I was part of which overlapped with this third network focused on 'semiological' arguments and included Corinne Squire, who was doing her PhD at Exeter on Lacanian psychoanalysis and gender. The term 'semiology' was itself what we came to refer to as a 'signifier', that is a term in language whose meaning is a conceptual keyword defined by its place in a linguistic structure. The so-called father of structuralism was Ferdinand de Saussure, and his work became a reference point for the structural linguists and for the first generation of structural anthropologists, particularly Lévi-Strauss. In his lectures, which were put together for publication in 1916 by his students after he died as the *Course in General Linguistics*, Saussure argued that language was made up of 'signs' and that these signs were composed of the 'signifier' or the sound-image – the word we hear when we say the word 'post-structuralist' for example – and the 'signified' which is the concept attached to it, which might be a shaved-head French guy wearing a polo-neck jumper.

The signifiers we use to refer to things are not always linked to the same concepts – for other readers the signifier 'post-structuralist' might bring to mind a debonair figure with black eye-lashes and curly white hair – and they certainly do not reliably refer to things walking around in the world. Those things in the world were what Saussure called the 'referents'. Saussure called for a new 'science of signs' which, he said would be called 'semiology', and this semiological study was taken further by the literary and cultural theorist Roland Barthes who proposed that there was a 'second-order' system of signs that he called 'myth'. I carried around the little Barthes book *Mythologies* for many months, reading about aspects of French culture that he analysed semiologically. This term 'semiology' was one of the key 'signifiers' which made it clear that we were much taken by the French post-structuralist debates, and we chose to use the term quite deliberately, preferring it over the US-American linguistic term which ran in parallel with semiology which was 'semiotics'.

'Semiology' was one of the signifiers that gave us some kind of badge of shared identity. We never settled on a name for our group inside psychology working with these ideas, but referred to it as our 'circle of sympathy'. This informal name is so curious because it is so misleading. To call it a circle makes it seem as if it was a wholesome complete thing, a holistic little universe of meaning where everything fitted together and we could agree on what it was that united us. To say that we were in 'sympathy' with each other makes it seem, even though we deliberately avoided the term 'empathy', as if we were some kind of new-age humanist group, sharing our feelings, sensing what each other felt, and creating shared meaning between us that would also serve to sum up what each of us individually felt.

The post-structuralist and semiological theories we were reading about were explicitly in opposition to that way of thinking about groups or, for that matter, about individual selves. In place of the 'self' we learnt to talk about 'subjects'. We were reclaiming the signifier 'subject' from experimental psychology where it so often meant 'object' – treating people as if they were objects. When we said 'subject' we didn't mean something complete and self-conscious of itself, but we were referring to how people were torn between different discourses, divided by language, and perhaps also divided between what was conscious and what was unconscious about was happening to them and inside them. There was a political aspect to all this. Perhaps that was an aspect of this work that we did share, even if we didn't agree on what it would amount to; we didn't simply want to describe the subject, we wanted to change it.

I wanted to change the subject, but I am not sure I really thought I could change psychology as such. That seemed a futile exercise, impossible. I was in it up to my neck, and time was running out. Whether I would succeed in getting the PhD or not, my time as a postgraduate was soon going to come to an end. I was writing, but not fast enough. There is something of the rhythm of academic life in this that goes beyond psychology, though I could step aside at odd moments to look at what I was doing. I could step aside and look at academic work as if I was an anthropologist rather than a psychologist. But those moments were shrinking. I needed to produce a thesis. I will show you how I did that and what the thesis looked like in the next chapter.

8

SOCIAL

What is a dissertation?

In which we learn how to piece together many different ideas from outside psychology into something that will look like a doctoral dissertation, and then defend it in an examination, this time in the unusual closed small space of the viva. And, along the way, as we complete postgraduate research, we must attend conferences and give papers, and negotiate different political conflicts that also enter into the academic world.

If the writing of a PhD is a mysterious and stressful process, then the viva voce examination is even more cloaked in secrecy and anxiety. I step back in this chapter to look at how the pressure of thesis work is, towards the end of postgraduate research, intensified by the requirement that the student attend conferences where they engage in ghastly self-promotion, networking in order to be able to continue working in the discipline. This kind of career progression is a little more complicated when scholarly debates become tangled up in the broader social questions that psychology usually tries to avoid. Psychology claims to tell you why people behave and think as they do but, as you will see, the discipline is framed by forces that take on a brute reality well beyond what a simple focus on the individual can disclose.

Thesis

I was fortunate to be given time in the first year at Southampton to read around and decide what shape the thesis would take. Many of my fellow students, particularly those on PhD programmes funded by large-scale research projects, were slotted into a rigid grid of work and pushed quickly along the tracks toward a final product which began with a review of the existing literature, described exactly what they did to work at a gap in the research, analysed the data they had gathered, and then arrived at conclusions of the work. Even when they didn't put their subjects in experiments and do things to them, the overall ethos of the study was 'experimental' in the sense that hypotheses were made at the outset about what might happen and then results gathered from measurements of behaviour, questionnaire results or quasi–ethnographic observations. That kind of ethnographic work – close study of the way that a group, community or organisation functions and how the participants make sense of what they are doing – most of the time in psychology takes the form of a rather dry 'objective' description. This is very different from ethnography in anthropology or social geography where there is, in the best work, a rich account and compelling narrative which holds the description together. The shape of the thesis was, in this standard psychological research, a frame which reinforced the 'experimental' character of the product, whether the work had been carried out inside a laboratory or, as some of my colleagues liked to say, 'in the field'. That is, they were working within a framework or 'paradigm', whether they liked particular bits of it or not.

I wanted to work outside the experimental paradigm, and also wanted to discuss limitations of the new paradigm from inside that, so I needed a different shape to my thesis to do that. I had so far managed to negotiate a change of focus for the PhD with my supervisors, from being an empirical study to a theoretical one, and we had managed to convince the department, and the Faculty of Social and Human Sciences, that historical and theoretical research would in some sense meet their requirements. A theoretical PhD in psychology was unusual, but being located in this particular faculty helped, even if social sciences at Southampton also tended to be quite quantitative. Assembling an argument from existing theoretical resources was, we argued, 'empirical' in a very broad sense, stretching the meaning of the word beyond observations of actual behaviour. We had to be clear in end-of-year reports that I was, nevertheless, going to make 'an original contribution to knowledge', a phrase often used to specify what a PhD should amount to, across this university and in most others in the UK.

My funding was for three years full-time study. By the time I got down to 'writing up' I was out of money, and went onto unemployment benefit, the dole, as I had done after I left Newcastle. The 'dole' in Britain, which refers to the doling out of charity to the deserving poor, was a safety net, as necessary for me to be able to finish the PhD as undergraduate and then postgraduate grant funding had been for me to begin it. I now lived most of the time in London, and was registered at different addresses in Southampton and then Camden in north London to be able claim benefit. That gave some routine to my time, cycling to London Waterloo station, travelling by train to Southampton, and then pedalling to the dole office and then up to the university campus for supervision, and meantime, of course, writing the thing, the thesis. This 'writing up', however, was not merely reporting results and drawing conclusions. I had to patch together different theoretical arguments that I had been picking up through the three years.

This is what it eventually looked like. I had to outline the arguments for the 'new social psychology' as a paradigm that was very different from the kind of old paradigm research that had supposedly been displaced during the 'crisis' or 'revolution' in the discipline, research that was alive and well all around me in the department at Southampton. This included an account of the 'realist' arguments made by Rom Harré, arguments that were crucial to his claim that, while the old paradigm psychologists kept referring to the natural sciences and used them as benchmarks for the experiments they carried out, they misunderstood how the natural sciences worked. Realism is usually counterposed to 'relativism', to the idea that there are multiple accounts of reality, none of which can be accepted as definitive truth. Most adherents of the new paradigm pinned their hopes on realism as an epistemological approach that valued discoveries in the natural sciences, and then looked for ways to carry out social scientific research that would be credible as an alternative to the logical positivist tradition in psychology.

Instead of accumulating factual observations about behaviour in the laboratory or in 'the field', which was the way of the old paradigm logical positivists, some realists led by Harré aimed to produce models of underlying 'generative mechanisms' or 'patterns of action'. A role-rule account of action in a little social world like a classroom or football ground, for example, would describe a structure that held that world together. I also had to review some of the ways such a 'realist' approach had been taken up in Marxist theory, since that was the political-theoretical stance I was taking towards all these debates. That was just a little bit easier, more plausible, because one of Harré's PhD students, Roy Bhaskar, had explicitly elaborated a realist Marxist account of scientific inquiry. All of that background work was crammed into chapter one.

Then I had to deal with an approach to language that had developed inside social psychology that ran parallel to the new paradigm 'linguistic turn' but didn't buy into either the realist approach or the emphasis on qualitative research. That alternative approach, the study of 'social representations' proposed by Serge Moscovici, was becoming increasingly popular in social psychology in Britain. A massive edited book on social representations had appeared in 1984 edited by Moscovici and Rob Farr who was based at the London School of Economics. Farr had managed to draw in some experimental social psychologists to work in this new framework, and, in the process, win some of them to forms of qualitative research. So, in the second chapter I contrasted the social representations approach to shared social meanings in society – one that borrowed its notion of 'representation' from the sociologists Émile Durkheim and Max Weber – with the notion of 'signification' to be found in Saussure's proposals for a new science of 'semiology'. This semiology, Saussure argued, would be 'a science of signs in society' that, I argued, was more compatible with the new social psychology and that called for qualitative methodological inquiry rather than the quantitative approach favoured by the laboratory-experimentalists. This chapter also led me into some of the highways and byways of structuralism and post-structuralism, and this account gave some warning to the reader about what was going to come later when I went into more detail about those theories.

Because the title of the thesis was 'Power, Ideology and New Social Psychology', I had to deal with the way that 'power' was understood in mainstream social psychology, and this was even more important given that Harré's new social psychology didn't really seem to take power very seriously. There was plenty of discussion of power in sociology, but that discussion rested on quite reductionist and psychological assumptions. That is, power was still assumed to be something that was possessed by individuals and always deliberately wielded by them over others. When an account of 'ideology' was brought into the equation things got even worse, even more psychological, for not only was there the assumption that some individuals really had power, packets of pure force in their pockets, there was a correlative assumption that the others they wielded their power over were dupes, mystified by it. This view of society as consisting of canny power holders and a population afflicted by some kind of 'false consciousness', under the sway of ideology and so unable to see the truth, was surely exactly what Foucault had described as being a regime of 'sovereign power'. I went through some of the experiments carried out on power by social psychologists in chapter three, showing how they fitted with these quite mistaken assumptions about how power operated today, how this image of power operated as a disciplinary mechanism or structure in which those who thought they were wielding it actually had little more room for manoeuvre than those who were subject to it.

These contrasting conceptions of power also raised the question of human agency, and this itself was a question that psychologists should have had something to say about. Inside the discipline of psychology there was a long-standing dualistic opposition between the bad old 'scientific' experimentalists and 'humanistic' psychologists who valued the meaning that people gave to their lives and the choices they made. A psychologist is often torn between a mechanistic dehumanising view of human beings and a rather idealistic romantic one, one which unthinkingly reproduces existing power relations or one which tries to wish them away and pretend that ideology is unimportant.

I tried to find a way through this simple opposition between scientific description of behaviour and subjectivity in chapter four by showing that even inside the hard-line 'radical behaviourist' theoretical system of B. F. Skinner there was an implicit account of human agency, and that this could be highlighted by comparing Skinner's theory with that of the psychoanalyst Jacques Lacan. Lacan was someone who focused on the repetition of signifiers in a person's life and who was consequently sometimes presented by enemies and even followers as himself being rather behaviourist. If Lacan was in any way 'behaviourist', however, it was because he refused to delve under the surface of language into the thoughts or wishes that were usually assumed, especially by psychologists, to be driving the behaviour. For Lacan, human action in language was crucial, and so, insofar as it was focused on the surface of language it unravelled some of the assumptions made by those behaviourists who reduced language to 'verbal behaviour' instead of taking it seriously as such. Perhaps it would be possible to say that Lacan's was an already deconstructed form of behaviourism.

As Saussure's structuralism gave way to 'post-structuralist' theories of language there was a greater emphasis on the indeterminacy of meaning in texts and society, and, in the work of Derrida, an emphasis on a kind of reading and intervention in texts that became known as 'deconstruction'. So, chapter five was about deconstruction. The interplay between the way people were 'constructed' and made to play out their lives in line with structures of shared social meaning, on the one hand, and the way people challenged those structures and 'deconstructed' them, on the other, was, I thought, to be found in 'micro-sociological' theories like symbolic interactionism and, even more so, 'ethnomethodology'. That is, these sociological frameworks that homed in on the construction and deconstruction of our individuality described who we are without prescribing who we should be; this is very different from the way psychology endorses taken-for-granted shared culturally and historically-specific representations of the individual and tells us how best to conform to those representations. The neologism ethnomethodology, which describes an approach developed inside US-American sociology from the 1950s, is designed to explore the framework of methods, the 'methodology', that people, the 'ethnos' as ordinary folk, use to create and maintain meaning and social order.

Ethnomethodology had its origins in some of the 'structural' traditions in sociology, but its founder Harold Garfinkel reacted against those traditions by taking a more phenomenological standpoint. Garfinkel, born in 1917 and carrying out his most fruitful work during the Cold War in 1950s US America, had successfully disrupted mainstream sociological assumptions about method, sociology as a discipline that most of the time was as devoted to stable structures and good behaviour as psychology. He did this by refusing to buy into reified descriptions of what people did, that is, descriptions which turned what we do in the flow of activity into static entities independent of someone's own action. There was a political element in this argument, but for Garfinkel it played out as a defence of ordinary activity that was suspicious of any sociological or political theory, and he was hostile to those who might turn his work into 'theory' that would then be 'reified' and turned against people. Towards the end of his life at academic conferences, for example, he would refuse to be recorded in case, he said, 'the communists' got hold of it. There was, then, in ethnomethodology, opposition to the kind of individualistic reductionism and reification of cognitive structures to be found in psychology, but Garfinkel was still devoted to a reduction of phenomena to a micro-sociological level, the ethnos' own methodology which he fiercely defended.

Jacques Derrida, on the other hand, steeped in the Marxist debates that surrounded the emergence of structuralism and post-structuralism in France in the 1960s, was concerned with the nature of 'text'. Although he was accused of reducing political context to the level of the text – mocked for the slogan that there is 'no outside of the text' – Derrida saw deconstruction as a political project that was compatible with an open form of Marxism. Marxist analysis for him was itself an analysis of the systems of meaning that held us in our place – what is usually referred to by Marxists as 'ideology' – and so he was concerned with what was woven into the texture of our everyday lives under capitalism. Capitalism itself was inside the text, not outside it at all, and the illusion that there was an 'outside of the text' was part of the problem, a philosophical problem.

Derrida himself always refused to fall in line with Cold War anti-Marxist propaganda, and he did put himself on the line in speaking out for dissidents in the West and in the East. He was arrested in Prague in 1982, before the fall of the Soviet Bloc, for example, on the trumped-up charge of drug smuggling after going there to speak about bureaucracy and the work of the Czech writer Franz Kafka. Derrida elaborated deconstruction out of debates about language in structuralist theory, but the role of phenomenology was just as important as a background to his work. I wanted to show how his approach complemented some of the micro-sociological ideas that the new social psychology inside psychology was drawing on, and how deconstruction could take those ideas further.

Chapter six of my thesis tried to put those ideas to work in a study of one of the most popular standard experimental social psychological theories at the time which was 'attribution theory'. Social psychology specialises in taking up one little element of our lives that people have noticed and spoken about in everyday life, giving it a name and then doing it to death in countless pieces of research which make people carry out tasks while the researcher tabulates their responses. In the process, that little named element is drained of meaning and the social psychologists themselves eventually get fed up with it and move onto something else. 'Attribution theory', as a case in point in the 1960s and 1970s, was the study of how people make sense of the contribution made by a person or a situation to a series of events; they will, so the theory goes, make an external or 'situational' attribution if they believe that the circumstances led to the behaviour of someone else, or an internal or 'personal' attribution if they believe that specific individuals were themselves responsible.

The early phenomenological roots of the approach in the work of the Austrian Gestalt psychologist Fritz Heider were quickly forgotten by social psychologists who turned this description into a theory about cognitive errors, the most important being what they called the 'fundamental attribution error', which is the tendency of people to make personal instead of situational attributions. We can easily see, or, at least, this is what I wanted to show, that from this history of reduction of everyday shared accounts to psychological mechanisms there are some paradoxes at work that can, perhaps, be 'deconstructed'. The most evident paradox is that these social psychologists kept making exactly the same kind of 'fundamental attribution error' – focusing on persons rather than situations – as the poor subjects they were studying in their experiments. In fact, this 'error' is built into the research paradigm that guided them to look at 'attribution' in the first place. The error was a function of the way they conceptualised and investigated the phenomenon and not an individual mistake made inside the heads of each one of them; it was an institutional problem to do with the framing of research rather than a psychological one.

Chapter seven was devoted to a history of the experiment in social psychology as a form of disciplinary power in line with Foucault's analysis of the importance of the model of power based on the Panopticon inside prisons and in Western society. Then the final chapter returned to some of the differences between the more phenomenological versions of new social psychology in the work of John

Shotter and the more structuralist versions in Harré's writing. More explicitly than in the other chapters, I also discussed political dimensions of the critiques made of the old paradigm, and some possible political consequences of the new one. Here Marxism came back into the story, with some discussion of recent debates around a 1979 book by an ex-Marxist Jean-François Lyotard called *The Postmodern Condition* which had just been translated into English. Foucault's historical account which formed the basis of *The Order of Things*, an account of forms of knowledge or 'epistemes', was often seen as pertaining to 'modernity'. That Foucauldian historical account opened the way to a question which it never really answered as to what came next. In the sequence of 'epistemes' that ran for about 150 years apiece – the Renaissance from about 1500 to 1650, the Classical Age from 1650 to 1800, and then the Modern Era – something new could have been expected to erupt to replace the 'Modern' age in 1950.

Lyotard's book, which was originally written as 'a report on knowledge' commissioned by the Canadian government concerned with the impact of new technology on society, seemed to some people to provide a way out of the grim modern world. Perhaps it was a way out of language treated as an iron cage that Foucault described, taking us into a more playful 'postmodernity' where post-structuralist deconstruction might be the order of the day. Some Marxists, such as the cultural theorist Fredric Jameson, loved this idea and Jameson wrote a glowing preface to Lyotard's book when it was published in English linking the account of cultural and technological transformations with the analysis of 'late capitalism' that had been provided by the Trotskyist Ernest Mandel, but most hated it. I had both responses to all this, mixed responses, just as I had mixed feelings about a 'new' social psychology that pretended to solve all the problems of the old one.

Did this look like a thesis? It certainly didn't in early chapter drafts, and even less so when printed out in dot matrix and photocopied as two sheets to a page so that different friends and colleagues could read it and give feedback. It looked like a mess, and the argument was even clumsier and patchier than the narrative I have given here. Final drafts were printed on an electronic typewriter which I hitched up to the Commodore 64 computer, and which maddeningly tapped out the characters at the rate of about three a second, and which needed each sheet of paper fed separately into the carriage roller. While I was engaged in this writing and complicated time-consuming mechanical production process, I was meeting people who might throw more light on the arguments; I was attending seminars and conferences, and I needed to find paid work.

Antithesis

I was encouraged to go to academic events not only inside the psychology department, but also outside Southampton. It had already been made clear to me at Plymouth that it was important to meet other people doing similar work and to share ideas. My first and only visit to Oxford, for example, had been in 1980, to a small day conference on attribution theory, an event that did at least make me think that this experimental tradition was already on the rocks. It was a dismal experience in a large wood-panelled hall where everyone else seemed to know each other, and there was no sign of the new paradigm revolutionists. I carried a copy of Roland Barthes little book *Mythologies* in my pocket, and read that in the coffee breaks. Henri Tajfel was in the audience and intervened at one point in the afternoon to make a point about group processes. There were drinks afterwards, and I asked Peter Collett, a behavioural psychologist who specialised in nonverbal behaviour, the way to the station; he staggered away from the wine bottles and gestured through the doorway telling me that I would have to 'go walkies' to get to it.

The Southampton department participated in a series of 'Wessex' undergraduate psychology conferences which included the universities of Reading and Surrey; these undergraduate cross-university link events included postgraduate students, so as they moved from one host campus to the next over the years I gave papers about aspects of my research. It was at one of these conferences in 1983 that I first saw Celia Kitzinger speak about her postgraduate work at Reading on the social construction of lesbianism, work using an approach called 'Q Methodology' that enabled her to gather together quotes from participants in interviews, an approach that seemed very close to new paradigm qualitative research, but which was using some quantitative techniques tactically to tell a story. There were also national postgraduate psychology conferences each year. I spoke about Barthes and semiology at the one in Canterbury in 1982, and about Foucault and power at the one in St Andrews in 1983, which is where I first met Jonathan Potter and Margaret Wetherell. I was keen to meet them, for I knew they were doing some work on language which also used ideas from structuralist and post-structuralist theory.

I liked them a lot and felt we would be great friends; Jonathan, with spiky hair so black it might have been dyed, was a very quick funny character who told me Foucault had just been arrested for picking up a boy on the streets of Paris, which I wasn't sure was true; Margaret Wetherell was a quiet thoughtful calmer person still with a noticeable New Zealand accent, even though she had spent some time in Bristol working in the Tajfel 'minimal group' tradition of research. Tim Auburn at Plymouth had given me a copy of a paper that Jonathan presented with Peter Stringer at the British Psychological Society social psychology conference in 1980. The paper was on the way that landladies in the UK used different notions of roles and rules than those used by students visiting from New Zealand. It was one of the few accessible accounts of how a role-rule approach might be used in practice, a useful guide in my undergraduate dissertation research.

The postgraduate psychology conferences were also places where our little 'circle of sympathy' network met, at the April 1984 meeting in Nottingham, for instance. These meetings mimicked the structure of a real research conference, but were run by postgraduate students with visiting speakers, and there were opportunities to present our research in a friendly supportive atmosphere. At this Nottingham conference I sat next to Erica Burman and babbled on about Derrida. I had been reading about the 'deconstruction' of the binary opposition between speech and writing, an opposition which privileged speech as being closer to consciousness.

This link between speech and consciousness in many traditions in Western philosophy also, of course, bore fruit in the study of psychology, as if what we thought was directly expressed in words. The binary opposition between speech and writing haunted psychology. It troubled psychologists that much of their research was conducted using written tests and observational grids, and they wondered if they would ever get access to the most important mechanisms, thoughts. Derrida took this critique of 'logocentrism' – the focus on the word as access to thought – further, noticing that this was also a kind of 'phallic logic' which also privileged men's voices. The organisation of meaning around fixed points, words for which meaning must be fixed and guaranteed, went hand in glove with a view of power as a property to be accumulated and wielded over others. I can go on. I told Erica that deconstruction could be a critique of masculine power, and this included a critique of traditional Freudian theory which, Derrida said, was often 'phallogocentric'. She said the critique didn't sound very original, and that feminists had been making much the same argument for many years. You will meet Erica again later in this book.

Nottingham was where an elderly Alan Gauld, who had written a book with John Shotter called *Human Action and Its Psychological Investigation* back in 1977, spoke about parapsychology. It was a weird event, all the more so because there was a clattering of furniture coming from behind and above the venue throughout his talk that accompanied very well his references to poltergeist. At the following year's postgraduate conference in London I gave a paper about attribution theory, and that conference brought together quite a few of us who were just finishing our PhDs, including Nick Pidgeon and Jane Ussher. It was the last one in that series of events for many of us who were ready to move on to teaching or research posts. There was much talk among this cohort about where jobs were coming up and how we might fare if we applied for them.

The student conferences were stepping stones to submitting a paper to a proper grown-up conference, one where you might really have your ideas torn apart. At least, that's how it seemed. I had seen Halla Beloff, who was visiting speaker at the 1982 postgraduate psychology conference in the University of Kent at Canterbury in action, exasperatedly shouting out during one paper about an experiment measuring behaviour in group processes "Why didn't you ask them?" Halla had played a very important role during the recent British Psychological Society investigation into the 'Burt scandal', editing a special issue of the *BPS Bulletin* which reviewed the evidence and which included analysis of the way that Cyril Burt had invented research assistants as well as data to promote his own political agenda concerning the inheritance of intelligence and segregated schooling. I was very glad that Halla seemed to be on the same side as me in the paradigm wars, though after my paper on semiology she commented to me that she didn't like the kind of "frightful post-structuralists" her daughter, a film student, was hanging about with, they all seemed to have shaved heads and wore black polo-neck sweaters. She wrinkled her nose in distaste as she said this, but was clearly, even so, fond of her daughter, and of those arguing for alternative perspectives in psychology, even for semiology. In reality, the worst that could happen most of the time at these conferences is that what you said would be politely ignored.

I had a proposal for a paper on discourse and power accepted for an international conference organised by Terry Honess and Krysia Yardley, the British Psychological Society conference on 'self and identity' at Cardiff University in July 1984, so this would be my first chance to try out the ideas in front of a more mainstream audience. It was more of an alternative than a mainstream psychology audience as it turned out, which was fortunate. As usually happens in these larger conferences, however, there were parallel sessions, different streams of the conference which ran at the same time. This means not only that you will most likely be separated from the famous people who you wanted to see speak and see you speak, but that your own session will most likely be quite small. And so it was, though I did meet in my session John Shotter, avatar of the phenomenological version of the new paradigm, and Ken Gergen, the leading social constructionist US-American psychologist who was kicking off something like the new paradigm on the other side of the pond. They asked me if I would like my paper to be included in a book they were editing on *Texts of Identity*. Well, yes of course I would. If it happened, it might be my first publication, and I knew that I needed to have some publications if I was to get a job in an academic department.

The Cardiff conference on self and identity was also a place where the academic world and politics came crashing up against each other. I noticed that there were two papers in the conference programme by psychologists from South Africa, Don Foster and Peter Du Preez, both from the University of Cape Town. These must be two dodgy characters, I thought, most likely hardened racists. By 1984, we were in the midst of the academic boycott of South Africa, an academic boycott of the apartheid regime that went alongside the sports boycott I had been involved with while at Plymouth and the cultural boycott. The cultural boycott was building up steam, with many protests against artists who travelled to play in Sun City in the Bantustan of Bophuthatswana, for example. Surely, we should make some kind of statement about the presence of these academics who were effectively giving credibility to apartheid South Africa. I talked to other participants and organisers, including silver-haired and smoothly therapeutic Ray Holland, who was more sympathetic than the other organisers, and who agreed to facilitate a meeting of conference participants who wanted to discuss the situation and what might be done about it.

We set a time and quickly publicised the meeting in the conference. Ray was unsure what to do; having brokered the meeting, he explained that he was in a difficult position, and that the main organisers were now apparently very upset that this protest was brewing. It was a tense situation, and I too felt pulled between wanting this to be an academic conference where I would just give a paper, meet some colleagues and maybe even advance my academic career on the one hand, and being drawn into a political battle which was all too familiar to me from events outside the world of psychology on the other. Only a handful of people turned up to the meeting, less than ten, and among them was one of our enemies, Don Foster.

Don was short, slightly built with thinning light hair, and an intense expression of concentration on his face as he listened to our concerns and then responded. I was surprised at what he said, and it was a political lesson for me.

Don began by thanking us for arranging the meeting and telling us that it was really important that we had done this. I was gobsmacked. What manipulative rhetorical moves would this guy make next after turning up to sabotage our protest? But he then said very clearly that he supported the academic boycott, and that we were right to try to exclude him as a representative of an apartheid regime university. He would continue to make applications for funding from his university to attend such events, he said, and he would speak out against apartheid when he did attend. It wasn't his task to boycott himself, he reminded us, and that would be rather ridiculous, but it was indeed our task to implement the boycott, and we should do that. I was impressed. Don told me afterwards that his colleague Peter didn't feel the same about the boycott but was not in favour of the regime either, but this is why he had avoided our meeting. It then became clear that Don was doing work with the African National Congress, he was with the resistance. He gave me his contact details and asked me to send papers I was writing. When I wrote to him, though, I explained that I couldn't send him academic articles, because that would break the boycott. It was rather a comical end to an unpleasant situation. Our little group had sent a message to the conference organisers asking them to make a statement about the boycott, which they did not do.

Synthesis

Changing the Subject, the book we friends of post-structuralism in psychology had been waiting for, arrived in 1984. It was a heady mix of Foucauldian ideas about discourse and power and psychoanalytic discussion of subjectivity drawing most on the work of Lacan, and this was combined with recent Marxist debates about the construction of the subject by forms of ideology and feminist critiques of the image of the alienated abstracted individual researcher disconnected from the things they examined. The chapters were marked as being by the different co-authors – Julian Henriques, Wendy Hollway, Cathy Urwin, Couze Venn and Valerie Walkerdine – and the ideas were woven together in a quite brief introductory chapter. The style of the chapters varied, as did the theoretical resources used by them, some of them sticking to a discussion of the interplay between subjectivity in research and material gathered in interviews, others revolving around intricate discussion of Freudian theory, and others going on more exotic journeys into the history of psychology and postcolonialism. I wanted this book to work as one coherent text, as an argument that we could take up and use to critique mainstream ideas inside the discipline, and others of us in our little network who carried it around with them also hoped that it would work like that. It did not.

For me, the book provided two things. One was an argument against dualism in social psychology, in particular against the split between the individual which was assumed to lie in the domain of psychology, and the social which was studied by sociologists. Social psychology promised to hitch the two together, and there were repeated attempts to overcome dualism inside psychology, of which Moscovici's theory of 'social representations' was just one valiant attempt, but time and again the split between what was going on inside the head and what was happening in 'social context' reappeared. At least this named the problem, and gave a reference that we could cite for that, and the fact that the book had the subtitle *Psychology, Social Regulation and Subjectivity* helped immensely. Too often we were told that critical resources we cited were just sociology or philosophy, and told that that's just what you would expect those who were not psychologists to say about a discipline they didn't really understand from the inside.

Another thing the book offered was a series of contradictory theoretical resources for addressing and trying to transcend this dualism, and in particular it targeted the problem of the 'individual' abstracted from context in psychology. So, when the authors said they wanted to 'change the subject' they meant the discipline of psychology – that was an argument that chimed with the one made by the paradigm revolution researchers, of course – and they also meant that, rather than focusing on the individual, we should conceptualise our object of study as the subject. The individual was, of course, already a subject, and, in that sense, to refer to it as such in descriptions of a laboratory experiment was correct, but that was only one particular kind of subject, someone who was trapped in an artificial environment and made to appear in the journal articles as if it was either itself some kind of machine or was a mere bony shell housing different kinds of mental mechanisms. Those two options, the machine model of the body portrayed in behaviourist psychology or the fleshy container of thoughts that was described by cognitive psychology, posed a false choice.

So-called third force humanistic psychology didn't offer anything much better. It might have made people feel better to insist that human beings were active agents, but what we knew about the operations of power, ideology and the countless self-destructive things that people did to each other and to themselves in capitalist society and under patriarchy didn't really make this romantic idea about people having full self-conscious holistic understanding of their actions very credible. All three mainstream images of the person – behaviourist, cognitive, humanist – were, in different ways, versions of what *Changing the Subject* called the 'rational unitary subject'. The question was whether it would be Marxism, feminism, post-structuralism or psychoanalysis that would solve the problem, separately or welded together.

The question of the 'rational unitary subject' loomed over the argument in my PhD and was not at all resolved by it. I sat with Peter Dews one evening with cans of beer in his east London flat as he mused over the draft manuscript trying to make sense of an argument that was not really philosophical, but borrowed from the ideas he had been teaching us in the extra-mural classes. I had some brief feedback, via my comrade Martin Roiser, from Roger Andersen who had written a marvellous book in 1988 called *The Power and the Word*; his message was that he thought I would just about get it through, but that I would have a hard time in the viva.

And the viva was looming, with someone who was a quintessential rational unitary subject, Rom Harré, appointed to be the external examiner.

The PhD was in equal measures admiring of Harré's contribution and critical of it, and so I approached the morning of the viva in Southampton with some trepidation, travelling down from London the night before and spending a sleepless night at Roger Ingham's house. I waited in Roger's office while Harré and Alan Costall prepared their questions. I wasn't exactly sure what the format of the viva would be, and not reassured by Roger's account of what might happen. I couldn't help imagining it would be like an examination, and that I would be asked questions about the theories that I would be expected to give factual answers to. This is why I quite unnecessarily re-read the thesis over and again until I was sick of it. We sat in low chairs, and I listened in some disbelief as Harré said he found it a very interesting piece of work, had no doubt that it was of PhD standard, and that he wanted to use the time of the viva to have a discussion about the arguments. I was asked to say something about why I had chosen the topic and how the shape of the thing had changed as I had read different things, and later in the viva I was asked to say a bit about how I might approach it differently if I was to start the work again now. That question I experienced as the most dangerous one, surely a trap in which I would say what I would do differently and then they would make me go away and do it, and that would mean 'major' corrections instead of 'minor' corrections that could be done in a month or so. My anxiety was that the examiners might ask for it be worked at again and 'resubmitted' or even resubmitted for a re-examination. I tried not to think about the possibility that it might be failed.

Roger sat in silence – that was the deal for him to be able to attend, that as supervisor he wouldn't be allowed to contribute to the discussion – and then, after a few hours, we were both asked to leave the room. We waited in Roger's office and ran over what Rom had said and what Alan had said, and what I had said, and hadn't wanted to say, and wished I'd said. Rom had been nice, and I guess one aspect of this rite of passage is that I now felt entitled to call him by his first name. Admiration manifested as respect, but shadowed by the concern that it might be complemented by contempt. I was called back into the room, told it was passed, and that there some corrections, which I should do with Tipp-ex on the copies of the thesis immediately so they could be handed in later in the afternoon. There were some spelling errors, and I had to change the word 'critique' to 'criticism' throughout.

I was in a daze over lunch, and don't know what we talked about. Rom made some comments about the importance of what he called 'parish pump politics' over big government. I kept quiet at this explicit manifestation of liberalism, of just the kind of approach to power and ideology that I thought I had critiqued, or criticised at least, in the thesis he had examined. Just before he drove off, Rom had what he called a 'precautionary pee', and I needed to go to the loo as well. As we stood washing and drying our hands, I commented that he had asked questions about all of the chapters except chapter four on behaviourism and subjectivity in Skinner and Lacan. I didn't really want to continue the viva there and then, and so said nothing when he replied that he hadn't thought it was important and asked me whether it had been a joke. We went outside, he got into his car, and we waved him off. This was done, and so now this really was goodbye to the thesis and to Southampton.

This is also the end of postgraduate research, the end of any research for the time being, and we must move on now into the world of work, teaching; move on to the next part of the book. There we will examine how, when we teach psychology, we transmit all we do not know about human beings to the next generation, inducting them into all the stuff we have already had to wade through ourselves.

PART III
Teaching psychology

9

EMPIRICAL

Mapping the quadrangle

In which we begin teaching psychology, and learn to find our way around the inside of another academic department. We discover how psychology relates in practice to other subjects taught in the university; with professional courses that often call upon psychology as a resource, and with sociology, in which it is tangled in a fraught relationship of jealousy and rivalry.

The four chapters in this part of the book are concerned with how those who teach psychology must navigate a complicated network of contradictions, and how that complicated network comprises conceptual debates, practical academic tasks and interpersonal disputes which slowly but surely draw us deeper into the discipline. Psychologists who teach psychology need at some level to believe what they say about it to their students, and so we are faced, time and again, with ethical questions about how we challenge what is wrong about psychology and how we collude with it. In this chapter I describe how I began teaching and, in the process, how I had to persuade my new colleagues that I was at one with them, enough at least to maintain the illusion that we were talking and listening to each other.

Trapped

I find myself locked into a psychology teaching department at Manchester Polytechnic. I am in room E23, a room which is in the corner of what we called the 'quadrangle' on the first floor of a new purpose-built block for the psychologists. This quadrangle is a bare roof space on the inside of the block which the corridor windows open onto on each of its four sides. We look into the building onto nothing. Our offices are ranged around the edge so we have a view looking out of the building through the fixed-frame double-glazed windows, either of the original

Brook House and Shepherd's House listed buildings of the Elizabeth Gaskell campus, or the tower block which houses nursing studies, or the old building containing the library which was once a School of Domestic Economy for young ladies learning how to cook and manage the home. The domestic science department still shares the tower block with the nursing staff whilst awaiting relocation to the refurbished Hollings campus a mile down the road. Hollings boasts a witty piece of pop architecture comprising a tower block with a concrete frame on top which is known locally as the toast rack and a flat round building next to it supposed to look like a fried egg. The one campus photocopier is downstairs in the main building just off the 'link corridor', and the glass platen is often covered with flour because the domestic science lecturers use the machine to make images of pasta shapes and pastries to show in class.

This is my office, room 23 of the E block; the letter E stands for 'experimental'. Below me, on the ground floor, is the psychology department technician's office which is cluttered with racks of bits and pieces of experimental equipment, tachistoscopes and suchlike, rows of cubicles for carrying out experiments, and E16, a social-developmental laboratory with a one way mirror into which we could gaze, if we opened the curtains, from a little lecture theatre next door, E17. Nearby, off the side corridor leading to E16 and E17, are sound-proof booths for detailed physiological measurements, silent spaces that tempted students anxious to carry out their interviews without the intrusion of what they called 'confounding variables', little realising that this would make the situation less like the real life they were trying to capture than more like it. The first-floor offices arranged around the square empty space have solid wooden doors, which give us some privacy and it makes this bit of the building rather like the Panopticon in reverse. We know that no one is in the centre watching us; we are the only ones who can look in at this small bare world. This time I am the prisoner looking in. This evening I cannot get out of the building because the door at the opposite corner of the quadrangle which leads to the stairway is locked and no one answers the phone. No answer from reception where Patsy the caretaker sometimes sat of an evening, nor from the post-room where craggy-face Geoff sometimes worked on his sideline job sorting stock photos he leased out for commercial use when he was not away from campus acting as an extra in Coronation Street; everyone in the campus has gone home.

I have been tidying up after a day's teaching, doing some essay marking and writing tomorrow morning's lectures. I arrived in Manchester in August 1985, well before the beginning of the academic year at the end of September. My plan was to find out exactly what I had to teach and be prepared for the new term, but no one was around then either. I'd come north again for a job after countless applications for lectureships in different places and three interviews. The first two had been disastrous, and in both cases there had been other candidates who were obviously much more suitable than me. One, for a social psychology teaching post in Hull, barely happened at all. I got lost and waited in the wrong place while the interviewers marched backwards and forwards and sometimes past me before we realised who was who. The rival candidate, Julie Dickinson, I had met earlier and

I already knew there was no way this place, Humberside College of Higher Education, would take me on. We went through the motions of the interview, and then the interviewers told me that I would be more suited to a sociology department. The other interview was worse, in the sociology department at Exeter University where I claimed to know about Durkheim, Weber and the rest, and was directly challenged about this. This was for less than a year-long post to replace the teaching of the Norbert Elias scholar Stephen Mennell who would be on sabbatical leave. Mennell, the secretary said, writes about food, something I tried to factor in to what I already didn't know about sociology. When they asked if it was the case that I knew virtually nothing about sociology I had to agree. They didn't ask me about the sociology of food. At least they still paid my travel expenses.

I borrowed a car and drove up to Manchester Polytechnic for my interview here shortly before my PhD viva. This post was altogether more promising. There were two posts going, both one-year fixed-term contracts, and we were told before the interviews that this meant that the panel could be flexible about how the teaching was to be allocated. The interviews were in the John Dalton Building on Oxford Road up at the All Saints Campus just south of Manchester city centre, and the psychology staff rooms were already being emptied out ready for the summer move further out of the city, to Gaskell Campus. The interview process and the interviewers too, it seemed, were being managed by the secretary Hilary Garrett, a brisk jolly woman who made us cups of tea while we were waiting. Opposite me sat John Cavill, a quiet bristle-hairy man with a slow and rather indistinct West Country burred accent who worked on perception and cognitive psychology. Next to me sat another man who anxiously tapped his rolled-up newspaper on his knee, and who leapt up after the interviews were over to push open the door into the room where the panel was deliberating to tell them that he wasn't sure when he would be able to start if he was appointed and that he had some other interviews lined up.

This was an auspicious moment; me and John Cavill exchanged a glance and shared the thought that this guy was out of the reckoning; if we didn't mess this up, these two jobs would be ours. This was a time for good obedient behaviour, for accepting another cup of tea from Hilary and agreeing with almost everything the panel said. I wore a white shirt and a jacket and tie. But I had already slipped up once during the interview, I thought, when I said I didn't really want to teach behaviourist approaches on the third-year counselling option on the psychology degree for 'moral' reasons. That sounded bad as I said it, and it went down badly with the panel. Dean Johnson who was chairing the process in the centre of the table directly opposite me looked to his colleagues either side, first at Peter Banister and then at Jeremy Foster. They frowned and scribbled. They had given me a sheet of paper which had a draft teaching timetable on it, and I could see lectures and practical classes and acronyms like BASS and BAPA written in to most of the slots. They had asked me if I would be happy with this timetable and I imagined that I should say something more engaged with the process than that I would be delighted to do whatever they asked. By now I was pretty anxious, and really needed the work.

I guessed I should be keen but not desperate, which I was. Manchester was a long way from home, and although it was the north west of England rather than the north east, on the other side of the country from Newcastle, Durham and Hull, it was still way up over the historical cultural divide between north and south. When I was called back into the room I was asked by the man in the middle if I would take the post were I to be offered it. I thought his first name was Dean, and couldn't shake this thought until he was replaced shortly afterwards, but it named his position, the Dean. I asked if I could phone a friend in London to discuss it, and Dean leaned away from me on the two back legs of his chair shaking his head slowly in disbelief and telling me that there were plenty of other people who would very much like this job. I quickly, but not too quickly I hoped, said yes I would take it. Outside in the main office was the lecturer I would be replacing for a year, and it was then I was told for the first time, and certainly not the last, that I was now Sue Lewis. With Sue was another social psychologist, Carolyn Kagan. We went to a café nearby and they explained some of the acronyms to me while assuring me that the actual teaching timetable for the year would look nothing like that. I didn't know how to decode it, and they were right, it was nothing like that, it was worse.

I had got my thesis viva examination in Southampton out the way in July, and I moved some books and other possessions up to Manchester in August, staying with another lecturer, a developmental psychologist Carol Lomax, while I looked for somewhere more permanent. I had helped out in Alan Costall's perception practical classes but had never done any teaching. Yes, I'd given some papers at conferences and that may have counted for something in my applications, but it was hardly surprising I hadn't been able to get a lecturing post. I didn't have a clue where to start, and having attended plenty of lectures and seminars myself was of little use. My conference papers were about twenty minutes long, painfully and slowly put together as complete scripts, and painfully and slowly read out before the audience asked one or two questions and we shuffled around so the next speaker could come up to the front and do their bit. Carol Lomax showed me some handouts that she used in her teaching, beautifully hand-written pages illustrated with diagrams and cartoons. I went to the Poly library and got out textbooks on psychology, the ones used for undergraduate teaching on the BA in the Social Sciences, that was BASS; and on applied psychology which was to be for the BA in Public Administration, BAPA.

In a few cases there were lecturers at other campuses of the Poly who wanted to be sure that the Sue Lewis replacement knew what they were doing before they would agree to let me into their classes in September. But in most cases the contracted 'service teaching' I was doing outside the psychology department, teaching for which resources were transferred back and forth across the Poly, would have to make do with who was available on the day, in this case with me. There was a counselling diploma programme four miles south of the central campus in Didsbury, where I was supposed to be teaching personality theory, and I was told I should go down and talk to the course leader to reassure them that I was suitable. A guy with a beard and a piercing gaze called Frank Ashton asked me what I knew about counselling – nothing – and what theories of personality I liked; well, I said, I didn't like behaviourism much, and that was the right answer. He was a humanistic counsellor in the tradition of Carl Rogers, and he told me that you don't have to tell people what to do because they already know. I must have looked sceptical because he repeated it more slowly and insistently until I agreed with him. One of Carol's hand-drawn cartoons came to mind, one which illustrated Rogerian 'unconditional positive regard' and depicted a counsellor leaning forward and beaming at a client who was shrinking back alarmed. I wondered if this is how Frank conveyed to his clients that they already knew what to do. Anyway, my new head of department, Peter Banister, told me the next day that Frank had said I would do, and that he would let me loose on his students.

The new department here at Elizabeth Gaskell combined the psychologists moving down from the All Saints campus John Dalton Building with speech therapists, so it was given the new title 'Department of Psychology and Speech Pathology'. I rather liked this way of accentuating the sinister side of the discipline – the search for pathology – and because I was supposed to be teaching on personality, counselling and psychopathology courses I styled myself as a 'lecturer in social and abnormal psychology'. The title of the post and of the department neatly expressed what I was in and what I was against. The first meeting in Gaskell on 23 September was just before the beginning of term, and it was the first time many in the different sides of the new department had encountered each other. The speech therapists were women, some of them very middle-class with cut glass accents who reminded their students to dress appropriately on placement, that is to wear a nice dress or a skirt.

The psychologists were divided on many issues between the women and the men, not least over what the priorities of the department should be, and they were divided over who should or should not have been appointed new head of department. Jeremy Foster, the cognitive psychologist on my interview panel who was in the running for the post of head, had recently made the tactical mistake of leaving the country on an exchange visit when Steve Stevens, a colourful character known as 'Fred' who flew a little airplane at weekends and often offered to take me up for a spin, had been removed by management for incompetence after complaints from students and other staff. Peter Banister had moved up to fill the position. It was neither an elected nor a rotating post. Peter was there for good, and so there were scores to settle and no obvious or immediate way to settle them. This did not stop them working together, and there were times when the rivalries dissolved under the pressure of other self-imposed tasks. We were told in early 1989, for example, that as part of the 'Europeanisation' of the institution, Manchester Polytechnic had decided to offer language courses to staff. All we had to do was choose which European language we wanted to speak, and someone would be dispatched from languages to our department to run a course. Peter and Jeremy and I chose German, and so in May that year we three assembled in Peter's office ready for our first class, and pressed ahead, even when we were told at the first meeting that the Polytechnic was actually restricting their generous offer to six classes in total. We were, at least, able to greet each other and say goodbye in German, and this linguistic bond stuck us together for a few months after the course was over.

I was told early on by Carolyn Kagan that Peter was not really a manager or a leader, and that there needed to be some direction given to the department. Peter managed the situation by letting everyone pretty well get on with what they were attracted by, throwing in the occasional comment about different mooted plans and projects that it wouldn't do any harm trying, but adding that they would never work. Carolyn's corridor-conversation complaint about Peter's lack of leadership became a sometimes amusing and sometimes wearing refrain, accompanying whatever was being discussed in the department. I was always impressed by the way she used her position to support other people, but I worried what would happen if she ever got her hands on the levers of power. It sometimes seemed as if, for her, strong management of any kind would be preferable to a diverse and pluralistic department, and this gave a strange inflection to her 'community psychology'; it was a contradiction that resolved itself in a peculiar but still contradictory style of command politics and admiration for strong leaders around the world. She exemplified the best of community psychology, but also expressed its contradictions, the way it operated not only as an opening to community but also still as a form of psychology. I was confused by its mixture of progressive potential and reactionary practice for many years.

The first new departmental meeting was downstairs in the main building of the campus, where I was introduced as Sue Lewis. I proposed that we set up a series of undergraduate psychology conferences, one at the end of each year for students to present work from their final year dissertations. The conference could be coordinated with the other universities in the north west of England, rather as we had done in the south of England, in the Wessex region, and I said I would be prepared to coordinate it. There was a rather startled reaction, and I was told afterwards by Carolyn that not only had I broken a rule by speaking in a first meeting when I was a new member of staff, and a good thing too she said, but I had implied some coordination with the university up the road, something that was very unlikely to succeed given how superior they were toward the Poly, how they looked down on us. Peter had muttered in the meeting that it was an excellent idea and that I should go ahead and organise it but that it would never work.

Mapped

I made contact with radicals in psychology in Manchester. John Churcher was in the psychology department at the university. Alan Costall told me that John was active in European Nuclear Disarmament as well as in the union. When I met him, John said he had been invited to be a discussant, along with John Shotter, at the International Society for Ecological Psychology conference hosted by Jim Good and Arthur Still at Durham University on 28 September. Alan Costall was co-editing a Gibsonian-oriented book called *Against Cognitivism* together with Arthur Still, one of the psychologists at Durham who had given up his animal experimentation licence for ethical reasons, and Alan would be there giving a paper too, so me and John Churcher decided to drive up together. We borrowed Erica Burman's car – Erica was one of John's PhD students – and I drove, leaving very early on a cold foggy Saturday morning. John complained that working in Manchester was viewed as being stuck in a "provincial university," which I heard as an attempt to comfort his driver who had just started work in the Polytechnic. We arrived at the conference just about on time, but after getting lost, during which time John observed that this surely showed the limitations of ecological psychology, for we did at least need 'cognitive maps' to get around the world. I'm not sure he really meant it, for his interest was more in unconscious processes than rational thinking, but it was a good provocation to think. I was too tired to concentrate during the day, and we had a long drive home, but thought about his comment for some time.

John's comment kind of seemed to make sense, but I wasn't sure that a 'cognitive map' inside our heads would have made any difference. Clear signage on the roads might have helped, but then they would have been part of the terrain we were navigating, precisely part of the 'ecological' layout that cued us into the right direction. We puzzled about which way we should go during the many detours, and that included puzzling over a map together. An absolutely accurate cognitive map of the journey would only have helped if we could be sure that it was the right one, and if there was a direct one-to-one correspondence between it and the real world outside the car. Ecological psychology could encompass the disputes between people and shifts of perspective as we encounter the world and make sense of reality, while the 'cognitive' approach seemed to lead to the dead-end of certainty and fixed truth from one perspective. The worst end point of that game would be in the clinic where the cognitive-behavioural psychologist would be the one who thought they knew which was the correct map and would make their poor client conform to it. Here, now, in room E23, it was not the cognitive mapping of the space I was locked into that was the problem, but the real obstacles that lay in my way.

I was extremely busy in the first weeks of term, with the plans for the annual undergraduate research conference, and with reading and preparing for lectures day by day, I usually wrote them the evening before. I was often here in the building in the late afternoon and early evening on my own. Everyone else seemed to have their lectures ready and prepared from years ago. Steve, the ex-head who was still in the department, told me that he loved teaching the history of psychology because nothing changed and there was nothing that needed to be updated in his lectures; Freud was born in 1856, he said, and that was that, for example. We knew, for he told us, that the centrepiece of his lectures about psychoanalysis was the information that Melanie Klein had once visited Manchester, though he hadn't seen her, and that she wore big hats. Another older member of the department, Taysir Kawwa, taught about behavioural techniques for stopping enuresis, bed-wetting, and encopresis, uncontrolled defecation, year after year. Often the normative agenda for psychology was not set by the psychology lecturers themselves, but enforced by those in professional training bodies who had absorbed the key lessons of psychology – that certain childhood experiences lead to particular kinds of character, say – and then enforced a model of teaching about the self that the psychologists were expected to conform to. When Taysir Kawwa was teaching developmental psychology in the health care studies department, for example, he had to track through stages of 'development' in his lectures that followed the national nursing curriculum. These two – Steve and Taysir – were the old guard, and everyone knew they were on their way out. The filing cabinet in Peter's room had dents in the side. This was from when Taysir used to come in to complain about his teaching load, shout and kick it. These people went home early. Carolyn Kagan told me that in the good old days when Steve was head of psychology nearly everyone went home early, and on some days when they were supposed to be teaching they would all go off together and play golf.

The third-year students on the psychology degree needed, in line with British Psychological Society requirements for Graduate Basis for Registration with the BPS, to carry out an empirical study for a dissertation which was heavily weighted toward their final degree grade. I had barely scraped through my statistics examination at Plymouth, and my dissertation was qualitative, but now I had to supervise some students who had already been signed up by Sue Lewis – the norm then was six dissertation students per member of staff – whose own research was mainly quantitative. I was able to steer one or two of the students to carry out interviews rather than subject their participants to a pointless questionnaire which would merely get tick-box replies to what the researcher thought was most important. Even this kind of qualitative interview research was unusual in a psychology department, and most of the students were anxious to come up with real results that they could then discuss in the final section of the dissertation, real numerical results. One of them, the first I met at the beginning of term, was measuring 'stress', and was determined to do this by comparing different groups in a school, keen to use a sphygmomanometer. I was able to order one of these medical pieces of equipment from the technicians downstairs, and when I got it back to my office, me and the student spent a while wrapping the bladder cuff round our arms to measure our blood pressure. He got some correlations between this and that and blood pressure readings for his dissertation, and it served as a 'psychology' study that had not a glimmer of psychology in the thing.

Here still. Down the corridor on the left, just after John Stirling's office is a fire-door. There is a handle for this door inside a glass-fronted box which can be smashed in case of emergency. But I'm not sure whether this is really an emergency. I want to get out and get home, of course, and I go back to my office and search for something that will serve as a screwdriver, find a knife and return to slowly work at the screws at each corner of the glass over the door handle. It is getting late, and I have an early start next morning. My bike is padlocked round at the front of the main building, so, while I unscrew the glass, I'm trying to work out how I'll get my bike out of the campus if the main gates are locked. I teach at three of the campuses of Manchester Poly, and on my busiest days that means cycling up to All Saints to teach either BASS or BAPA students and then down to Gaskell to teach a class on the psychology undergraduate degree and then four miles south to

Didsbury campus to teach on the counselling diploma. There is evening teaching at Didsbury one day a week on the MA in Art and Design, and also up at All Saints on the Diploma in Higher Education, classes that run until 9 pm. This first winter in Manchester there was heavy snow, but the bike was still a much better bet for making it between campuses in time to class than public transport.

It was the service teaching around the Poly that made me realise how much psychology there was around in other academic and professional courses, what an influence psychology had well beyond its own discipline. *Changing the Subject* had raised this issue, that psychology was a much more widespread practice in society than it seemed, and that's why a key concern of the book was with 'social regulation' and 'subjectivity'. The year I started teaching at Manchester Poly this practice was named in a couple of articles and books as the psy complex. The term 'psy complex' made much more sense now, for it described not only where I was, here in one of the places where psychological research and teaching took place, but also how it operated as a powerful discourse and practice in so many other places ranging from counselling to education to social work. We psychologists, even very junior lecturers like me who were reading the textbook one day to regurgitate its contents in front of students the next, were viewed as having some expertise about what people were thinking and why they behaved as they did.

On the Diploma in Higher Education classes, for example, I was supposed to be teaching a class about psychology and social context, but it was only the bits about social context that were treated with suspicion by the students. The empirical evidence about gross inequalities in society around axes of gender or culture was disputed by the students, but the psychological theories about prejudice went down very easily. It was difficult, in this class, to teach one aspect without the other, I thought, but it seemed that reference to the persistence of institutional racism or sexism and different life opportunities of different groups was to be treated as something up for debate by them. The stories about the psychological side of the equation, on the other hand, were treated as facts, discoveries that had been made by experts who know how we all think.

The BA Public Administration degree, BAPA, was even more difficult. My teaching was on the part-time course attended by police officers. Some of the senior officers spent most of time gazing out the window waiting for the class to end, and had no interest in engaging with discussion, even less so with junior colleagues in the room. This was time out from the office or off the beat for these lower orders, but they would all react badly if psychologists were moving out of their own domain of expertise into the world the police knew how to handle. I was much younger than them, and that made it even easier for them to dismiss what I was saying when they didn't like it; mostly I probably did know less about what I was teaching than them, only having read about it the night before. I grew a beard to try and gain some authority in class.

There had been disturbances referred to in the tabloid press as 'riots' a few years before, including in Manchester in 1981 when black youth protested against the police in Moss Side district just south of the city centre. White youth had come up from the estates further south in Wythenshawe on the second day, but instead of clashing with the black youth, which is what the journalists predicted, they joined with them and together they attacked the police. There was a similar story in the so-called St Pauls Riot in Bristol which had been documented by the social psychologist Steve Reicher. Steve was studying for his PhD with the Tajfel minimal group tradition researchers at Bristol University. Contrary to what the commentators in the newspapers and television reported, these clashes were not at all between black and white residents.

Equally striking, it didn't seem that people participating in the riots were acting as psychologists had often assumed, out of control and as if they had lost their minds in the midst of a mob that unleashed irrational emotional forces. Instead, there was coordination between white and black youth, and while the police, banks and supermarkets were attacked, local shops and private houses were left untouched. Steve Reicher was once challenged by Michael Argyle at a social psychology conference where he spoke about this research, and Argyle wanted to know what hard evidence there was that the targets of the mob were chosen rather than random targets, as we would expect if it was just an explosion of irrational mob violence. The research touched a raw nerve for Argyle, because it seemed to repeat some of the arguments that had been made about football crowds by Rom Harré and his colleagues when they argued that there were 'rules of disorder' rather than the expression of disordered thoughts and emotions in and around the grounds. Fortunately, knowing that mainstream experimental social psychologists were likely to be in the audience and anticipating this objection, Steve Reicher had carried out a chi-squared test on the number of windows broken in different categories, and he was able to reassure Argyle that this confirmed that there was indeed a statistically significant difference between residential and commercial broken windows and between outside and local businesses.

There was a background context for the events, and those involved knew what they were doing. Whether you agreed or disagreed with what they did was a political question, but you should leave that aside while you are looking at the evidence that would help you decide whether or not there were 'psychological' causes. It didn't look as if searching for psychological causes would get you very far in making sense of what was going on. My policemen didn't like this message at all. One of them offered to take me out in the police vans one night so I could see for myself, not only how reasonable the police were as they went about their work, but also how unreasonable many of those they referred to as 'civvies', civilians, were – particularly the black kids with an inexplicable grievance against the police who were then more likely to act out of order, out of control. The offer was a nice one, and meant well, but I thought it would not be a good idea to be seen being driven in a police van around Moss Side district of central Manchester where I then lived.

Other objections my policemen had to psychology weren't on the basis that it was wrong but that it could be dangerous if this knowledge fell into the wrong hands. I was also supposed to teach them at least the basic ideas about quite standard Argyle-style 'social skills training', or SST. SST is not only about how certain kinds of behaviour enable individuals to fit in, but also how training in 'assertiveness skills' enable people to stand up for their rights. The class narrowed their eyes and asked me if I was also teaching this to the civvies, because if I was teaching this to 'chummy', one of the civvies they had brought in for questioning, then that would make police work more difficult, I was making their job more difficult.

This isn't to say that there weren't limits to the power of psychology to define what was true and what was not, and I had mixed feelings in the evening classes on the MA Art and Design course when the students ridiculed most of the psychological research I presented them about perception. This was a tough class because it consisted of art teachers who had been in school all day. Not only were they tired, as was I, but they had spent their day trying to keep control of their own classes. They could relax at the Poly; in some cases that meant simply going to sleep, and in other cases it meant fidgeting, rolling their eyes, interrupting and making my life difficult. I really wasn't sure whether I could tell them anything relevant from experimental psychology but this was one of the places where we had some good arguments about psychoanalysis. There is plenty of psychoanalytic interpretation of art products, and you could be sure that there would be some in the class who would lap it up – I suppose they would be the ones who were happy to make psychoanalytic ideas work within the frame of the psy complex very broadly understood – and there would be others who would declare that it was nonsense. At least they then participated, and argued with each other as well as with me. It was on the MA Art and Design course that I had my first experience of being on an interviewing panel, but it was conducted in a relaxed way, and the course coordinator who chaired the panel took the line that if the teachers intending to take the course had made the effort to attend the interviews then they should be given a place.

The critiques of pop-psychological ideas about crowds and the alternative Harré and Reicher research perspectives on football fans and riots went down better in BA Social Science, BASS classes at All Saints. These sessions consisted of a lecture to nearly two hundred first-year students at 9 am on a Monday morning followed by four seminar groups, one after another without a break, where we discussed the material in the lecture. Steve Stevens had lectured BASS, and he told me that they were even worse than the combined studies students we had sharing some of our lectures on the psychology degree at Gaskell. Those students might be combining psychology with biology, which Steve thought was promising, or psychology with sociology, which he thought was disastrous. If you went to the bottom of the barrel, he said, then you found combined studies students, and if you scraped down below the bottom of the barrel then you would find BASS. I quite enjoyed these classes, the first hour anyway. I think it was because I was able to teach about social issues and because I was teaching about the limits of psychology that this went down better than Steve's input had done.

This BASS course drew attention to the institutional split between psychology and sociology, one that was made worse by the service agreements over teaching. There was a quid pro quo agreement over a psychology contribution to BASS first year and sociology teaching on the psychology degree down at Gaskell, for example, that intensified the battle between the two disciplines. The BASS students were warned that psychology was dangerously reductive, that we psychologists from outside the sociology department wanted to replace a social understanding of things like prejudice and violence with an individual explanation, and they were right.

On the other side of the divide, our psychology students were pretty quickly inoculated against Bob and Dave who tried to teach about symbolic interactionism and ethnomethodology. Bob Anderson and Dave Francis from the sociology department did their best faced with a hostile audience, explaining that what the cognitive psychologist described as a mental mechanism they could describe more plausibly as a 'social accomplishment', something that was being created and maintained in the interaction between people rather than happening inside them. It wouldn't wash, and I quickly learnt that when I talked about 'social representations' or 'ethogenic new social psychology' to the final-year students that it would be a fatal mistake to connect these ideas in any way to what they had been exposed to in Bob and Dave's lectures. I had to make it seem as if our 'social psychology' was nicely accessible and in line with common sense and good science, not difficult theoretically, but in the process I reinforced the divide between psychology and sociology. This was a betrayal of Bob and Dave, sure, but, if you will forgive this bad-faith question, what could I do? We gave our main lectures downstairs. The sociologists gave their lectures to the whole first year group before they were handed over to John Stirling who taught Biological Basis of Behaviour, both in the New Lecture Theatre, NLT in an extension of E Block.

Our students who failed sociology at the first-year exams were always represented in departmental meetings as being confused, and understandably so, by the strange unscientific incomprehensible jargon. The arguments in examination boards usually resolved in favour of condoning the fails of those students, while those failing the Biological Basis of Behaviour course were treated as problem cases, and they usually had to do re-sit examinations in the autumn before they would be allowed through to the second year of the course. When we re-designed the degree in preparation for a quinquennial review of the course, the first target was sociology, with the hardline psychologists pushing to get rid of Bob and Dave. They succeeded.

Wrapped

I get the screws out and place them carefully on the carpet by the wall. I open the fire-door and then I go back to my office to collect my coat and bag, and then venture out onto the fire escape, shutting the door behind me. It is dark, and I track round on the concrete walkway laid over asphalt, round the corner to be faced with another locked door that led back into the building again. Now I was trapped on the roof. To my right is the side of the main building, to which there is no entry, to my left is the roof of the NLT. We had one of our few psychology departmental seminars in the NLT, where I talked about the paper I had given after I was appointed here, just before I started teaching at Manchester Polytechnic, at the first International Society for Theoretical Psychology conference at Plymouth. So, that was in 1985. That had been an opportunity to return to the city, and to meet again with Mike Hyland who was the conference organiser, and who had written a book on theoretical psychology which was based on the third year course he taught when I was there as undergraduate student.

One of the guest speakers was Hans Eysenck, and I was very well behaved, making no public protest at his presence. His talk was a review of how important and very scientific his own research was on the biological roots of personality differences. He referred to Soviet research, that of Pavlov and the post-Pavlovian animal researchers, which he presented as a knock-down argument against anyone who suggested that his work was politically biased. After all, he reasoned, if the Marxists said it, and he said it too, then there must be some scientific basis for it. This raises a question not only about what a 'Marxist psychology' might look like but also, maybe more importantly, what kind of institutions will house the discipline and then what shape and effects it would have. Psychology in the Soviet Union became tied to a bureaucratic apparatus devoted to command politics, a top–down power structure which realised many of the worst aspects of disciplinary culture inside the Panopticon Foucault described in his work on surveillance. That disciplinary regime is perfect for what we know of 'psychology' in the West to flower, for both the Soviet Union and the discipline of psychology were concerned with the regulation and adaptation of behaviour. It is then not so surprising that Eysenck and Pavlov will go so neatly hand-in-hand with each other. But this is not to say that what Eysenck meant by 'Marxism' was really much more than a convenient foil for his own theory, an authoritarian pretext against which and with which he could make his claim to be neutral and scientific.

The institutional support and propaganda that the Soviet bureaucracy gave to its own version of the discipline of psychology did make it too easy for many years to assume that this is indeed what Marxist psychology must look like. I had already been preoccupied with this, not able to decide whether it would be possible to develop a 'Marxist psychology', which was an argument that my comrade colleague Carolyn Kagan often made, that it should be possible, or whether that would be a dead-end that would merely turn Marxism into a form of social control. There were other attempts to develop such an approach outside the Soviet Union, and I encountered one of these at the first ISTP conference. The Plymouth conference included a strand of research I had never come across before, that of the German *Kritische Psychologie*, the KP tradition that was led by Klaus Holzkamp. These KP people at the conference, including Wolfgang Maiers, were Marxists who were aiming to develop a 'science of the subject' that would be a real alternative to Western psychology. They too drew on some of the Soviet research after Pavlov called 'activity theory', but they were unimpressed by Eysenck.

The dominant approach at the ISTP conference, however, was a 'theoretical psychology' that was concerned with model building, or, rather, stepping back from the many different models of the individual self or subject that psychologists proposed and evaluating how they were constructed. These studies of theoretical models were forms of 'meta-psychology'. They differentiated, for example, between 'intervening variables', internal mental states which the psychologist cannot directly observe which operate between a stimulus and a response, and 'hypothetical constructs'. A psychologist cannot directly observe the hypothetical constructs they posit in their models either, which is why some logical positivists and behaviourists would rather avoid them altogether, but as soon we describe personality differences or perceptual processes, different versions of these constructs appear all over the place. My paper at the conference was about how the different kinds of hypothetical constructs in psychology were mostly treated as being things inside the individual, and that our accounts of what was going on would look very different if we also referred to 'social constructs'. Things like shared social representations, or rules of behaviour or structures of power would be examples of those kind of hypothetical constructs, and not 'psychological' in the classical sense. The argument went down better at the conference in Plymouth than it did in the NLT at Gaskell campus in Manchester. My new colleagues weren't hostile, but some of them avoided talking to me much about psychology after that. We talked instead about course administration issues, what was happening elsewhere in the Poly, lack of leadership in the department, things like that. Maybe it was rubbish what I said, it was probably rubbish to them or, worse, it most likely seemed like I was attacking some basic assumptions about psychology that held the discipline together and siding with Bob and Dave, which, in a way, I was.

I slowly clamber onto the asphalt roof, over to the door leading from E Block and manage to hang down from the canopy over the entrance before I drop to the ground. I make my way round to the front of the building, unlock my bike, wheel it to the back of the campus again, and find a lower part of the wall where I could lift the bike up, climb up and lower it down the other side. I jump over, wrap up, and cycle home. Patsy, the caretaker who fed the foxes in the grounds of the campus in the morning and evening, was rather annoyed when she found out what had happened. I had managed to escape her attention when she had gone round locking up. She reminded me to tell her if I was planning on staying late next time, and reminded me many times after that.

In this chapter I told you how I was beginning to be locked into psychology. We have traced our way around the local physical architecture of the environment and you now have a better idea where I was located in it, but we need to turn to look in more detail at what images of the individual were housed in these places. I already knew that those who teach about psychology often have little sympathy at the beginning of their careers with the theoretical and methodological approaches they must pass on, and I wondered how, and how soon, new lecturers would be broken in. The next chapter focuses on what I was locked into as a series of ideas about what counts in psychology, and what I was compelled to relay to others, to the students so that they would comply, would even seem to believe it too.

10

PERSONALITY

Behaving badly

In which we learn that the more we teach about psychology, the more we speak about it, the more it enters our lives, and then we even start believing some of it ourselves. We discover something about the ease with which theories of personality can be put to work, and about the dangers of teaching people how to improve their interpersonal skills in order to become good psychologists.

The seventeenth-century mathematician and religious philosopher Blaise Pascal argued that one needs to kneel and pray, and then belief will follow. Belief in all manner of outlandish ideas can be secured by forms of practice, and that indeed is how psychology as a discipline often functions, as I was to learn as I stood in front of the lecture theatre and spoke about theories of personality. The form and content of psychological theory as an academic practice has consequences for every individual involved in it, whether that is the student who must listen to me and show that they understand what I have told them, or whether it is their teacher. I want to show you in this chapter how I could not but become part of the very didactic system of ideas that I was so suspicious of, and how they worked their way into me as I described them.

Work

After a year in Manchester I was no longer Sue Lewis, because the real one was back after her PhD study leave. I was given another one-year contract in 1986 and carried on teaching second year personality theory while I waited hopefully for Steve Stevens to retire and hand over the abnormal psychology and psychoanalytic theory lectures to me. My personality lectures were to all the second-year psychology students in the NLT. I taught some of the more classical personality theories, including Hans Eysenck's biologically based typology of 'introversion' and 'extroversion'. I covered aspects of personality theory that Sue, who specialised in work and organisational psychology, had covered. These included the difference between 'A type' and 'B type' behaviour and personalities, between those who are controlled time-urgent types heading for an early heart attack and luckier, more relaxed characters. I also taught more mainstream behaviourist approaches, including Martin Seligman's theory of 'learned helplessness', the idea that if people have no control over what happens to them, over what behaviourists call 'contingencies of reinforcement', then they lose the will to go on. Teaching went more smoothly when I was able to give everyday examples to flesh out the theories, and these stories always went down better than reports of experimental evidence. If a theory could be made to correspond with experience then it would be remembered more easily, with the risk that this banalised the theory and that the exam answers would simply repeat the examples. In the process of doing this I had myself, of course, to come up with illustrations of the theory which would at least make sense to me, that accorded with my own experience. So it was that I had to think about whether I was an 'introvert' as Eysenck described it, and then to appreciate that the link he made between behaviour – that is, for introverts, avoiding situations which cause too much excitement – and the underlying attempt to reduce cortical arousal in the ascending reticular activating system of the brain did make sense. It wasn't that I could directly feel what was happening in that part of the brain, of course, but I could easily imagine that what I felt was excessive arousal that I, as an introvert, wanted to avoid. As I noticed more extrovert types around me who seemed to crave more excitement, it made sense to imagine that their levels of cortical arousal were lower and that being with other people would be a way of stepping it up.

The distinction between 'Type A' personalities and B types was even more compelling, especially the link Meyer Friedman and Ray Rosenman, who first developed the typology, made between A type personality and coronary heart disease. What this typology spoke to for me was not so much differences in individual 'personality' but lifestyles, and when they described Type A personality behaviour patterns I could see how the increasingly hectic life I was leading now drove me into certain ways of managing my time – there was less of it, and I was become more 'time urgent' – and becoming more impatient with others, on the way to becoming a stereotypical workaholic and with a personality to match. For all the problems in the laboratory-experimental psychology experiments, there were some that did function as powerful anecdotes about how we might experience our own bodies and relate to others. This is something I started to bear in mind when I was cycling to meet someone and arrived there first; I realised that my agitation at them being late was something to do with the aroused state that my body had been put into by the physical activity, and that that arousal might then increase my sense of annoyance, an interpretation of my bodily state as if it were a buried feeling tied to a rational perception of the situation. I was learning to reason psychologically.

The Seligman 'learned helplessness' studies also easily resonated with what we already knew. The classic studies on rats showed that if the poor animal was subjected to a drowning simulation it would struggle, and if it was then saved from drowning it would struggle much longer the second time compared with a rat that had no expectation that their struggle would succeed. Reading these behaviourist studies made me wonder what kind of world the experimenter hoped for as they exposed their furry 'subjects' to these cruel and sometimes deadly conditions. The research payoff comes, according to Seligman, in the everyday situations that 'learned helplessness' illuminates. It does seem, for example, that when elderly people are forced by the authorities or by their families to move into nursing homes, when they have no say in the matter and are reduced to a helpless condition, they are more likely to give up living, they are very likely to die soon after the move.

These were big lecture groups. The classes gathered together psychology students with those taking the course as part of a combined honours course. The sun would stream in past the torn beige cloth wretchedly hanging on the broken curtain rails and light up the NLT's bright red seats. I had a hastily scribbled script outlining the theory, usually cobbled together the night before from a textbook and sometimes, if the students were lucky, an acetate slide or two which they squinted at when it was blurrily projected onto the side screen to the left of the large rolling dark green chalk-boards. Sometimes there was time for discussion after the lecture, but there were rarely any questions. Sometimes I was relieved when someone had something to say about the theory I was presenting, they broke an awkward silence, and sometimes there were awkward questions which left me wretchedly hanging onto my script. I looked at the curtains. The worst questions in my first year teaching came from one particular character, Tom Heffernan, who popped up in the first year I taught the course, and would usually begin with a request for clarification, "you say that the theory says this", to which I had to agree or disagree, and around which I had less room for manoeuvre, for blagging my way through to the end of the class. I was sometimes an introvert B-type battling against helplessness, by the end of the day a caricature of the worst examples of personality types in the psychopathology textbooks. It wasn't too bad. I knew it could be far worse. I had some control over my life, though I did have a sense that I too could quickly draw the conclusion that the helplessness I felt was permanent, that I could 'learn' that there was no point in fighting it.

I applied for a job in London, at North East London Polytechnic, NELP, and got it. Sue Wilkinson, a founder of the field of feminist psychology in Britain, was one of the other candidates. But I wanted to stay in Manchester, which day-by-day was becoming the centre of my world. I was in love with Manchester, but even more so with Erica Burman after she had started teaching in the same department at the Poly a year after I had arrived there. Ours was a partnership that began with shared scepticism about what psychology was telling us about who we should be, what we should think and how we should behave. By now it was more than that. I accepted the NELP post but deferred starting until the following academic year, September 1987, and then finally I wrote to them to apologise for pulling out of the commitment, I couldn't do it. There was anxiety, for sure, but not regret. At lunch next day I sat with the rest of the psychology staff in the canteen at Gaskell campus, and Jeremy Foster told me that it was a good thing I wasn't going, he had been external examiner there, he said, and he said he "wouldn't touch NELP with a barge-pole". It was a peculiar sensation, the shift to the north, bound up with attachments to people in the city more than to Manchester itself. In every other place I had lived I had London as my reference point, it was where my home really was, and I did for a long while see things in the rest of Britain and indeed in the world as if from the capital as my mental compass.

Manchester had, with Liverpool, grown very fast in the nineteenth century, becoming a centre of manufacturing, then known as 'Cottonopolis', working on the cotton transported across on the canal network from the Liverpool docks. A gold cotton flower still adorned the spire on Manchester Town Hall, and the industry in Lancashire – mainly spinning in the south and weaving in the north of the county – supported nearly a fifth of the British population. By the 1980s Manchester was a post-industrial city circled by poor estates and decaying mill buildings, though already starting to pull up from its decline with regional, central and European funding, in contrast with Liverpool over on the west coast. My new home city had such dramatic success a century before for two reasons; one reason was the weather, a damp climate perfect for keeping the cotton strong and supple, and the other was that its small size then meant that there were few planning regulations, and so it functioned as an early version of a free-trade zone.

Much of the early cotton manufacturing was small-scale, including home working in which women were very present. This drew in families with children from other parts of the country whose offspring could then also work in the mills, and the many 'aliens', that is immigrants mainly from Ireland. Over a third of the population in the late twentieth century were Irish or were descended from the Irish families of cotton workers or from those who built the canals linking Liverpool port with the Manchester and Salford docks. Some older communities, Little Italy in Ancoats district for example, are now almost invisible, but there are still traces of the city's diverse heritage. There had been riots against the German population, of which Frederick Engels, working at his father's factory in Salford adjoining Manchester, was a member, and there were Jewish communities, more religious in the north of the city.

Unlike Manchester University, which was technically still legally designated the 'Victoria University' – just as the university along the canal was officially the 'Victoria University of Liverpool' – Manchester Polytechnic had many local students, working-class students who were the 'first-generation' in higher education from their families, and mature students, some single parents and some students coming into education after almost a full lifetime of work. Our poly, like the other British polytechnics was under local authority control, so my employer was Manchester City Council; I had to go to a city council doctor when I got my teaching job so I could be certified fit for work. There was a noticeable difference between our students and those from the real university, those who were more likely to own cars and sometimes a little terraced house in the south of the city bought for them by their parents, and they were taller, better fed as children I assume. The Victoria

University also attracted more overseas students, and it was this that led some of us to notice that our student population was then rather whiter than that of the population of Manchester, a city that already had sizeable indigenous Asian and African-Caribbean and, then not so visible, Chinese communities.

Manchester still, at the same time as having a history of development and struggle – including movements like the Chartists in the first half of the nineteenth century and the Suffragettes in the early twentieth – had the feel of a small city, and as new funding arrived, a new city, and more so in term time. The real locals in different districts have distinctive accents, and can tell pretty well exactly which suburb you had been brought up in. I couldn't say I was turning Mancunion, but I began to identify with the place, and that identification as feeling at one with and protective of it – against members of my family in the south who would still ask me if it was really 'grim up north', for example – had an emotional charge as well as reflecting something like rational choice.

When a financial crisis in Manchester City Council, which included the kind of budget cuts that had been resisted in Liverpool – resistance led by supporters of the Militant group inside the Labour Party – started to bite into its education provision, it also began to hit the Polytechnic. When Steve Stevens retired from the psychology department he joked at his leaving party that teaching was very easy, that he carried around with him one sheet of paper; on the first side, he said, were the first year lectures, overleaf were the second year lectures, and for year three he used both sides. There was nervous laughter from his colleagues who suspected that he was telling the truth. I thought I could do better than that, but there was no money to give me a job to replace him.

Turning the NELP post down was difficult, and I was anxious about the uncertain prospect of a permanent post in Manchester, a city I had by now chosen as my home. I had reason enough to stay in Manchester, but no work. I felt myself spiralling down into a miserable pit, with the psychological theories about helplessness and introversion I knew so well but a mocking accompaniment to my distress. They were useless, and the sense that I was useless could not be remedied by reading about how I should need to take control of my life and get a job. The material conditions and existential despair were dimensions of the situation that psychology had nothing to say about, except to say that they were unimportant. Psychological theories about agency and personal efficacy that I had treated as ideological stories about the self now took on more unpleasant form as at best evident diversions from the real problem at hand and at worst nasty vindictive lies about what or who was to blame for what I was facing and feeling.

I lived in a shared house in Moss Side, claimed housing benefit, and there were days when I lay in bed or wandered around the house sobbing. It didn't occur to me to go to the doctor across the other side of Alexandra Park. I had seen him a year earlier when I had felt tired and isolated. What I liked about him most was that his name was Dr McCoy. I said to him that I wondered if I might have diabetes. He looked sceptical and asked me what I did. I said I taught psychology and he grimaced and told me there was nothing wrong with me. I dreamt that I was crying and screaming, held across the kitchen table while being forcibly injected with tranquiliser so I could be taken to mental hospital. This is what I was, and how I will fail, this is how I will fall into nothingness. This is what I fear when I read and teach about 'abnormal psychology', and why I hate those who treat those who fail as if they are no more than broken mechanisms, making it so as self-fulfilling prophecy. I knew this would happen. This was to be my bad year.

Rest

I was now, as Hilary Garrett the departmental secretary observed, "Up the creek without a paddle". Hilary kept order, not only managing Peter Banister in his role as head of department, but also instructing the students about how they should and should not behave. There were few problems with delayed essays and practical reports because all that coursework had to be handed in to Hilary, and if it was late then the student had to account for it to her when they turned up. They would need a good reason or Hilary would give them a telling off and remind them that they wouldn't be able to act like that in a proper job when they were grown up, and so on. It also meant that marking turnaround had to be on schedule too. She knew what was going on in the department and had her own psychological theories which helped her to spot when someone was lying or to beware of people with dodgy personalities. If Hilary started telling you something and then lost her train of thought, she would declare "it must have been a lie" and then briskly move on to the next topic. The most worked-out version of Hilary's own theory of personality concerned facial dissymmetry. Differences between the two sides of the face indicated personality types, she explained to us; it wasn't always clear what these personality types were, but behavioural tics, including frowns and smiles, also revealed them, and they revealed hidden intentions to her. She would notice the difference between facial expressions on the two sides of someone's face, and report this to other staff. We didn't teach this kind of thing in class, and she didn't seem to employ any of the theories we did teach, at least not explicitly, but this theory was one guide to her skilled dealing with others, with students and with us. She was part of the psy complex.

After the budgetary crisis I taught part time in the Poly for a while, worked as a tutor with the Open University, and also did some teaching in the psychology department at the Victoria University, at its campus straddling Oxford Road in the south of the city, between the All Saints and Gaskell Poly campuses. At the university John Churcher taught psychoanalytic theory and had some second-year lectures on personality that needed doing once a week, and so I filled in there for a term. That's where I could be John as well as Steve, while waiting, hoping to replace him at the Poly. I also taught some other classes at the university alongside another colleague from the Poly, a South African clinical psychologist Ian Burgess who specialised in cognitive-behaviourist approaches and whose temple veins swelled and throbbed when he got angry. The 'cognitive' bit of 'Cognitive-Behavioural Therapy' (CBT) refers to the thoughts you have about your behaviour, and the therapist will home in on the ways you catastrophise or over-dramatise your worries, for example, and correct them.

Curiously for an approach vaunted as being 'scientific' by many psychologists, the origins of CBT lie in psychoanalysis, in the work of the US-American analyst Aaron Beck who in the 1960s wanted to speed up psychoanalysis and make it more useful for health providers and insurance companies impatient with the idea that people should spend years on the couch free-associating and discovering their own solutions. Beck's 'cognitive therapy' and so-called Rational Emotive Behaviour Therapy, REBT developed by Albert Ellis, another ex-psychoanalyst, were eventually patched together to target both abnormal thoughts and maladaptive behaviour. The acronym REBT would seem to cover all the bases for a psychologist, but there was something about CBT that hit the button for service providers, and the training manuals were more straightforward, less jargonised and more attractive for those who really did expect that psychologists should know how people think and be able to put faulty thoughts right. CBT techniques themselves could be helpful.

At one team-taught session for the third-year abnormal psychology course at the university, we two Ians talked to the class about different psychological approaches. The other Ian described how he dealt with a patient who had something he described as an 'eating disorder'. It was interesting to notice how a problem that someone had with food or their weight, we did not really know which at that point, was quickly framed as 'disorder'. It does make perfect sense to talk about disorder if you already imagine that you should be dealing with 'abnormal' psychology or, the preferred term back down the road at the Poly, 'psychopathology'. These terms cue you in to what you are aiming to arrive at when you treat someone, to give 'order' to their lives, to make them 'normal' or, as an alternative to 'pathology', to make them healthy. Ian told the audience that this young woman, 'girl' was the term used, clearly had a mistaken idea about what her weight really was, for she was not, he said, 'fat'. She thought she was putting on weight, so he put her on the scales so she could see how much she really weighed. The reasoning being that if she could see the accurate measurement for herself she should then logically have a more reasonable idea about her supposed weight problem and they, the patient and therapist, could then talk about how to manage it in a more orderly way.

A student put up her hand to ask a question and interrupted Ian, and I could see the temple vein activity signal that he was not pleased. She asked him what it might have meant to the young woman that she thought she was putting on weight. There was some shuffling in the audience. Ian's veins bulged, and he said he didn't know what she meant by the question. He was concerned with the girl's behaviour and how it affected her health, and, yes, of course he was dealing with what she thought about, that's why he was putting her on the scales so she could have a more accurate perception of that. "No", the student said, "what I'm wondering is", and this phrase 'what I'm wondering' was a giveaway to Ian that she was coming at this case from a more touchy-feely therapeutic angle; he glared at her as she spoke. The student said that she was wondering what it meant to the young woman. Ian cracked and snapped back "it meant she was wrong".

Moral support from my comrade Carolyn Kagan and institutional manoeuvring kept me going during times when I was at risk at folding in on myself and feeling worse than usual. Funding for a half-time teaching post was eventually released at the Poly. I was interviewed for my full-time permanent post after I responded to the only advertisement for the post which had been placed in *Manchester Evening News*. There were two candidates, me and Dave Holmes, who had not yet completed his PhD on psychopathology supervised by John Stirling. One of the intriguing things about Dave was that though he was able to soak up information about any and every area of psychology and pass it on in interviews in the newspapers and on the radio, he didn't really believe any of it, and in unguarded moments would say so quite explicitly. That cynical distance from the misinformation he was happy to relay in the media seemed, at times, to make him less dangerous. This is a moot point. It highlighted the way that 'evidence' in psychology could be selected to support nearly every bizarre claim made about thinking or behaviour or underlying differences between people. There is no 'evidence base' in psychology because that base is so diverse and contradictory. The interview panel chose me.

So then, after getting the permanent post at Manchester Polytechnic in 1987, I was back with Ian again, back as Ian and back with the other Ian, back teaching on more courses, including the third-year counselling option. This was the most popular option along with the psychopathology course which was chosen by students who still imagined that they would then go on to train as clinical psychologists. Counselling was a keystone of the degree for those on the 'qualitative' research side of the department; Carolyn's repeatedly thwarted aim was to develop this teaching in a 'counselling psychology' postgraduate training based in the department which would link with community perspectives and carry out radical interventions around the Polytechnic. My first two years on this option I had, as I had requested, been kept off the behavioural input, which was a third of the course, and I taught the humanist approaches instead.

These humanist approaches included Carl Rogers' 'client-centred' or 'person-centred' counselling and Eric Berne's 'Transactional Analysis'. This had been a good opportunity to find my way into the humanist 'third force' alternatives in psychology, alternatives to the behaviourist and cognitive approaches that preceded arguments in the new paradigm by many years. This humanist work was very practical, much more oriented to therapeutic practice, to helping people change than mainstream psychological research was, and it was also very different, of course, from the post-structuralist theories of subjectivity that I'd worked on during my PhD.

Rogers and Berne might not have bought entirely into the mainstream psychological image of the 'rational unitary subject' criticised in *Changing the Subject*, but they did indeed aim for that as an ideal in therapy. For Rogers, 'unconditional positive regard' given by the humanist counsellor or therapist, for example, would enable the client or 'person', as Rogerians came to prefer to call their clients, to 'self-actualize' and to become 'fully-functioning'. The idea was that you couldn't bring this about simply by telling people how to think or by changing their behaviour; instead, the task was to provide the conditions in the therapy in which the client could feel the confidence to realise their own wishes and find their own solutions to their problems. The aim was precisely to overcome the 'incongruence' between how they thought about themselves, their 'self-concept', and their real wishes and feelings about who they were and what they wanted for themselves. Rogers himself was actually more influenced by pop-psychoanalytic ideas than he would have liked to admit, for the gap between 'self-concept' and deeply hidden desires owes something to the way that Freud was portrayed in the psychology textbooks and popular culture as marking a rift between the conscious mind and the unconscious that should, in therapy, be overcome.

I was happy with this teaching, but happier still when I was able to take over the third strand of the counselling option, which was psychoanalytic. It wasn't so much because it was truer than the other approaches but that it would be more fun, certainly more fun than the cognitive and experimental method courses in the first and second year of the psychology degree which were known as 'Fun 1' and 'Fun 2' because they were assumed to be fundamental. I couldn't yet think how I could bring the Marxist, feminist or post-structuralist theories from *Changing the Subject* into my teaching, but part of the counselling option might be one place to read up and prepare lectures on the psychoanalytic aspect. I still had little time to read anything much beyond what I needed to prepare for teaching, so I always tried to organise my timetable so that it would enable me to think and write a bit for teaching that I found interesting.

I did feel a little fraudulent teaching the third-year counselling option when I had done no counselling or therapy myself, and especially so because the centrepiece of the option was an assignment in which students had to find a counselling service and write about it, 'evaluating' it. This was one of the things that prompted me to start attending psychotherapy seminars up the road in the NHS service at Gaskell House and then, eventually, to start training as a psychoanalyst, a space away from psychology. We would get speakers in from services, and this gave a link with practice that was otherwise missing from the course.

Play

The bureaucratic endurance task called the 'quinquennial review' at Manchester Poly was an opportunity every five years for the psychology staff to settle scores with rivals and rewrite the degree course so that their own favourite approaches took precedence over the others. We very rarely had departmental meetings, partly because the psychology and speech therapy sections of the department were so different, and partly because we knew that a common project or agreed line for the department would shut down what creativity and innovation there was. It was better to let things develop where there was interest, to let people run with whatever grabbed them, and their enthusiasm for what they were really interested in would produce better work than research projects imposed on them.

One place where we did meet together was at the examination boards at the end of the year, and that's where I learnt that it was important to know when to keep my mouth shut when I wanted to support a student as much as when to speak up. Nearly everyone played a series of games in these boards in which, at one moment, they would be harsh in their judgement and at the next be lenient. An argument in favour of one of your own students would only work if you had earlier shown that you could be rigorous and concerned with maintaining standards. We would hear the same lecturer comment in a meeting at one moment that one student should be given the benefit of the doubt because they had worked very hard and, at the next, be told that we should, while discussing the grade fate of another student, bear in mind that for them it was clearly a case of "ninety-nine percent perspiration and one percent inspiration".

One agenda driving this upcoming quinquennial review while I was still hoping for a full-time permanent teaching post was the attempt to make a link between theory and practice, or, more accurately, to link the ideas that were taught in the degree and the students' own experience of them in their own lives. The connection would be made through Interpersonal Skills Workshops in which students would reflect on psychological ideas while playing them out in small groups. There was great enthusiasm for this among those on the 'qualitative' side of the department, those involved in counselling, developmental and social psychology teaching who wanted to work with rather than against 'subjectivity', but there was resistance on the part of the quantitative 'Fun' people who saw psychology as a science and so thought it should be neutral and so more 'objective' about the topics and results. For the quantitative positivist psychologists wedded to the old paradigm, the difference of perspective between psychologists and non-psychologists was jealously guarded; the pretence that psychologists were more objective and that non-psychologists were, in contrast, mired in a dangerously subjective understanding of themselves was crucial to our mainstream colleagues' sense of mission to discover things about psychology that no one else was in a position to reveal.

This departmental divide was also gendered. That is, most of the men in the department were in favour of objective scientific research that would only cash out later when the tried and tested knowledge could be applied to others. Most of the women were involved in what was seen as the 'soft' side of the discipline, but that included me. This gendered difference in approaches to psychology was pursued in almost every debate, whether it concerned the content of the courses or the way the department was managed, or 'not managed' Carolyn Kagan liked to say, mismanaged in order that the bad old ways of doing psychology could carry on as they were. Mostly she was right, for there was a gulf between the dominant stereotypically masculine and 'prediction and control' type of psychology and the more marginal stereotypically feminine concern with intuition and relationships.

There was a gap, however, between traditional old paradigm ways of carrying out research and the more stereotypically 'feminine' ethos that Carolyn also saw as being feminist. In one interview study involving members of the department, for example, Carolyn and Sue Lewis asked us separately to speak about what interested us about psychology. I said that my concern was with the way it worked rather than with making it accord with peoples' individual experience; this was because there was a danger that psychology itself operates as a mechanism that doesn't so much reveal what people are thinking as incite them to think and feel in line with what psychology claims about them. It was only when the article was published in a special issue of a journal on women in psychology that I realised that the point of the interviews was to gather 'evidence' that men in the discipline were less interested than women in making it relevant to their own lives, with what Carolyn and Sue referred to as 'self-discovery'. I felt deceived, and said so. The study seemed to have been set up in line with the questionable ethos of much psychological research which conceals what the real question is from its participants. Carolyn shrugged, and insisted that the findings had emerged from the data.

The problem was not so much the argument being made about the stereotypical differences in the way that men and women related to the discipline of psychology, but the way that traditional methodological approaches in psychology, including the deception that accompanies most quantitative research, were being used. In the process, despite the claims to be offering a feminist reflection on psychology, what Carolyn and Sue were doing in this bit of research was in keeping with the way that psychology usually manipulates its 'subjects'. It showed something about gender but revealed much more about what happens when you try to show that using psychological research methods.

I was also uneasy about the Interpersonal Skills Workshop plans, but faced with this choice, the division in the department over the value of either objectivity or subjectivity, I fell in with the qualitative side of the argument which valued subjectivity, a vanguard operation to change the ethos of the degree led by Carolyn. We helped draw up plans for these compulsory workshops in the first year of the degree, and the idea was that students would learn something about themselves as well as the relevance of psychological ideas about their interaction with others. Carolyn, who wrote articles and books about interpersonal skills and whose own background was in the Michael Argyle tradition of social skills training which she then turned into a more experiential and 'community' psychological direction, had inexhaustible energy and the ability to take up any cause and persuade people she was right. She was on the side of the good in most cases, a positive feminist force in the department, and in this case she managed to convince enough of us that even if the students didn't like the workshops to begin with they would realise later how useful they had been. The workshops would tick the box of professional 'development' and would also show that we were not disinterested observers of other people's behaviour. She wore the enemy down, and eventually we together got it approved for what would then be referred to as the 'new degree'. It helped that psychology was becoming an increasingly popular discipline, that class sizes were increasing, and so 'self-directed' student work was also attractive to the staff. There were presentations which needed to be marked, though we experimented with groups deciding on a group mark that the students assessed and awarded themselves, and this also promised to cut down the number of coursework essays to be marked by staff teaching on the undergraduate degree. This was in line with practice in the social work department in MMU where students were expected to engage in self-directed study, in what were popularly known by staff there as 'FOFO' sessions 'Fuck Off and Find Out'.

I got my permanent lecturing position in the department on the basis that I would run the workshops, and so then I shifted focus in my teaching from the more traditional personality theories to making people think about their own personalities as soon as they started the degree. I had to be a motivational leader of the workshops and cajole those students who were reluctant, particularly mature students who had a life history they didn't necessarily want to share with their classmates. We would take an aspect of interaction, break up into little groups, or work in pairs, play out scenarios, express ideas about motivation and hopes and goals, and share our thoughts and feelings about it all at the end of each morning. I felt I'd lost the plot, had forgotten why this was supposed to be a progressive intervention in the degree programme, and was taking on the persona of some kind of energetic presenter on a children's television programme. These exercises weren't only infantilising the students. The personal skills component of the first year of the undergraduate degree was eventually rolled out through to the second year and culminated in a third-year project presentation, and then into the master's degree programme in the form of a Personal Development Portfolio module.

It was ghastly, but, as with every academic and psychological practice, opened up gaps in which progressive alternatives could be developed. The project presentations by final year students to an audience of second years, for example, did become arenas for discussion of different methods, and some of the postgraduate students were able to write about their 'personal development' in a way that challenged the assumptions made in their portfolio module. The most challenging aspect for the students was a requirement that they should do presentations in groups in the first and second year, something that was then embedded in the 'Self-Directed Practicals' and in a 'Psychology Culture Identity' third-year module that I co-taught with Carolyn. It was particularly challenging because the students would then be awarded a group mark which would be distributed equally among the participants. This was a political intervention in line with a more 'community' ethos by Carolyn that went to the heart of individual reductionist psychology, questioning it and posing alternatives to it. I thought they had come onto the module to be taught something rather than be broken up into small groups and circulate their misunderstandings about a topic among themselves. It was not easier to do it this way for us either, for we only settled on topics for the course each year after a first meeting with the students; they chose topics and we then searched out and read the articles for them to work on. We were all challenged by this group intervention.

There were many excruciating moments in this infantilisation of psychology, and one of the worst was when we tried to connect what we were doing to the students with left politics. I was involved in planning the Socialist Movement conference in Manchester in 1990, one of a series of socialist conferences that aimed to bring the left together after the defeat of the miners' strike in 1985. I discussed the conference with Carolyn, and she suggested that we could connect the personal and the political by offering our services to the planning group, to organise an interpersonal skills training session to conference session chairs the evening before the conference kicked off. On 16 November we arrived at the Mechanics Institute with flip charts and marker pens to persuade political activists to play along with what they clearly saw as party games. The idea was they could then better reflect on what might be going on in the sessions they were chairing and so be more open and inclusive. They resisted, and they were right to do so. It was mortifying. It was one thing to make psychology students go through this to get course credits, and that was bad enough, but quite another thing to try and corral hardened activists into this rigmarole. At the conference over the weekend in Manchester Town Hall I hid, slipping into the back of different meetings while Erica sat in the dimly lit Victorian stairwell marking second-year student practical reports.

I was very relieved to be able to drop this teaching after a while, and then I would hear from my student tutees how much they disliked the experience. They would complain that tutors who took over the workshops would accuse those who refused to fully participate of being 'defensive', which at least isn't something I did during my time there. There was, in fact, a real journey of 'self-discovery' in this process which was designed to discover something about ourselves that corresponded with what psychologists said about us. I discovered that there could be something very limiting if not exploitative and oppressive about the use of psychological knowledge to frame people's behaviour and to encourage them to talk about themselves in line with that knowledge.

It is difficult to persuade people that psychology is problematic precisely because it chimes with common sense in a society that revolves around the deep-seated idea that individuals need to be separated from society in order to understand them and manage them. These individuals take on board such assumptions, and offer themselves up to be trained, offered skills that will enable them to cope with what society throws at them. What psychology tells you about the nature of human beings, about what they can and cannot do, dovetails with what human beings have come to tell themselves about who they are. Skills training keys into that intuitive grasp of psychology, and you need to step back and change the subject, change the terms in which we describe the problem. We turn to one such necessarily counter-intuitive approach in the next chapter.

11

CONFLICT

War and peace in the subject

In which we connect internal critiques of academic psychology with attempts by academics, professionals and political activists to speak out against abuses of power in the discipline. We move on from attempts to change the subject to the mobilisation of psychologists against war, and to the formation of radical support activities, protests that link psychology with politics and even to resistance.

I describe in this chapter initiatives some of us were able to take while still teaching approaches to psychology that we were very sceptical about. These were initiatives which drew on alternative theoretical approaches, which responded to institutional problems that bedevil academic work and which were prompted by events that forced us to take a stand. Running through this chapter is an attempt to link theory with practice, to go beyond academic psychology. You will see how attempts to go beyond psychology need to tackle deep assumptions about the nature of knowledge that mainstream positivist research methods encourage us to adopt, even invite us to apply to social and political phenomena well beyond the discipline.

Conflict

The first public event we organised in Manchester was around the internal disciplinary critique of the 'rational unitary subject' in psychology provided by *Changing the Subject*. There had been a meeting packed into one of the converted terrace houses at Birkbeck College in London in February 1986 to discuss ideas in the book where I spoke about the individual–social dualism that bedevilled social psychology, an attempt by one of its avid readers to explain what that book meant to me. Our Manchester day conference, also called 'Changing the Subject', was later that year. We set up a crèche in the TV room on the second floor of the Student

Union building. The conference was held after teaching had finished and while students were revising for their end of year exams in the summer term. I was also organising the new regional undergraduate psychology project conference which brought together Manchester Polytechnic, the Victoria University, Preston Polytechnic and Bolton Institute. That had been one way of making contact with colleagues in different institutions, though the local contact people for that event weren't into changing the subject at all.

They seemed, rather, to be stuck into their subject, stuck in their departments and most of them survived by staying on the margins, hoping not to be noticed. Perhaps that's why they were dragooned into an undergraduate event that was more closely tied to teaching than to research. It did make coordination frustrating, something that ratcheted up the A-type personality behaviour pattern in me. One colleague taught health psychology and was a heavy smoker with clouds of smoke around him operating as extensions of his large fluffy hair. Another, like his smoking colleague, trembled, and was able to delay decisions and, more annoying, to procrastinate over the room bookings for the event. Another wore a woollen hat and always had a little drip hanging from the end of his nose. These three specialised, in the eyes of impatient Ian your author, in incompetence, and together we comprised the disorganisation committee for the conference. In the process of arranging this event which also took place at the end of the academic year, I also discovered students in and around Manchester who were up for exploring what *Changing the Subject* was about.

There were four of us in the organising group for our Changing the Subject day conference, which we held in the John Dalton Building in the All Saints campus. Four was a good number, and perhaps that was why the way we understood the argument of the book crystallised around four theoretical currents. We each took charge of one strand in two parallel sessions in the morning and afternoon, with the plenary session at the beginning of the day designed to do little more than explain the structure of conference and the one at the end to discuss what to do next, how to take the ideas forward. I dealt with psychoanalysis and why, limited though it often was in practice in the English-speaking world, there were some progressive aspects of it that challenged psychology; Erica Burman introduced the session on feminism and the way that developmental psychology tended to pathologise women and children; John Bowers talked about Foucault, forms of knowledge and the notion of the psy complex; and Liam Greenslade talked about Marxism and the account given by the literary theorist Fredric Jameson of the 'political unconscious'. There were about thirty people there, including Carolyn Kagan and her partner the clinical psychologist Mark Burton, and some of our students.

It was a good day but it didn't really connect with what I was teaching, it seemed miles away from that, and it also seemed very academic, it didn't connect with psychologists who worked with people after they finished their degrees, only with those who had decided to go into teaching or research. And there was another problem which some people raised on the day, which was that we might not have intended it to be so, but we made it seem as if 1984 was a watershed moment, and as if, at long last, the book had shown the problems with psychology. It was as, if before the diagnosis of psychology as a problem in the psy complex, no one had noticed that there was anything wrong with this 'rational unitary subject' we complained so bitterly about. Of course, we knew that wasn't true. The group that produced *Changing the Subject* had been working on the ideas in the journal *Ideology & Consciousness* from 1977, but even then there was a danger that this earlier date would be seen as the turning point, as if before the good news arrived from France there were no complaints about psychology from inside the discipline. I knew that wasn't true either because the so-called paradigm revolution dated from the early 1970s, and it was clear that the way Harré and colleagues named the problem was very different from the way we were describing it at this meeting in 1986.

One of the public issues that psychologists were connecting with was the question of nuclear war, of the so-called balance of power between the United States and the Soviet Union and the impending threat of 'Mutually Assured Destruction', MAD. I went to meetings in London of the Psychologists for Peace group, and worried aloud at their meeting in May 1984 that their approach to 'psychological threat' and 'conflict resolution' was only focusing on using existing psychological theories about individuals rather than stepping back and asking how those theories might actually be part of the problem. A group of psychologists inside the British Psychological Society led by a clinical psychologist James Thompson managed to persuade the society to publish an edited book in 1985, *Psychological Aspects of Nuclear War*. This was a way in to a series of debates about how psychologists could intervene in policy debates, and they were connecting with politics in some way.

The resolving of political issues concerning relationships between power-blocs or concerning power relations structured around class, gender or 'race' into something called 'conflict' had been a strategy of some US-American social psychologists. On the one hand, they wanted to address political problems in the world, and so they turned social psychology to questions of violence and even of inequality. On the other hand, these social psychologists did not want to be seen as 'political', and so they fell into the trap of trying to maintain a dialogue in the discipline using psychological discourse, and with governmental research organisations that had always pretended that psychology was a science, and so ideally should not take a political stand. The over-arching problem is that the development of psychology as a discipline has always been guided by explicit or implicit political choices, and the attempts at 'conflict resolution' pioneered by Morton Deutsch in the 1970s ended up steering those who wanted to change the world into approaches that kept it exactly as it is. The conflict resolution approaches use a mixture of mathematical formulations – such as those derived from the Prisoner's Dilemma in which the experimental subject is faced with a choice over whether to betray their accomplice or not in exchange for freedom – combined with a liberal humanist appeal to people's goodwill. Both aspects of this conflict resolution approach are premised on the idea that if we can work out how to get along together then the conditions that led us to conflict can be quietly forgotten. Psychologists for Peace were well meaning, but they had their eyes on the traditional organisations representing psychology, hoping those organisations would take conflict resolution seriously. They wanted to steer rather than rock the boat, and my comments were met with stony silence.

Reflection on these issues posed by Psychologists for Peace was my contribution to our follow-up to the Changing the Subject day in Manchester, another day conference in November that year on 'Psychology, War and Peace'. It was a title that drew in some people from outside psychology, including the cultural and literary theorist Antony Easthope. Antony, who taught at the All Saints campus in the English department, had worked his way through Marxist, structuralist and psychoanalytic debates in reading groups with his comrades Rob Lapsley and Mike Westlake, during what he called his own 'long march'. Antony gathered around him a group of devotees and each year taught, sometimes with his comrades Rob Lapsley and Mike Westlake, introductions to post-structuralism in extramural studies courses with varying titles like 'Under French Eyes' covering and updating the same themes. He would puff at a cigar while explaining to you what Jacques Derrida and Michel Foucault got wrong and could be relied upon to make a reference to Lacan which would offend half his audience. One of his favourite anecdotes about Derrida concerned their brief meeting at a conference in Glasgow; Antony just had time to ask Derrida if he had been to Scotland before, to which the reply was "no". "I will be able to tell my grand-children this", Antony said. He turned up at our day conference and horrified the participants after I talked about Psychologists for Peace. He declared that we needed to take the death drive seriously and claimed that members of Amnesty International got a kick out of reading about torture in the newsletters. We had another go a few months later as 'Psychology, Politics, Resistance', a name dreamt up by John Bowers and Liam Greenslade.

There had been a 'radical psychology' conference at Keele University in 1970, and then newsletters and magazines such as *Red Rat* and *Humpty Dumpty*, and there had been a pamphlet produced in the early 1970s, *Rat, Myth and Magic* which was named after a popular encyclopaedia series on the supernatural *Man, Myth and Magic*. Many of the articles in these publications were concerned with questions of exploitation and power in therapy, with the ways that psychological theories were used to make people feel even more responsible for the distress they suffered in a sick society. One of the longest running magazines, *Changes*, which carried the subtitle *Magazine of the Helping Professions*, was the publication of the Psychology and Psychotherapy Association founded in 1973. Bob Hobson and Frank Margison, both in the NHS Psychotherapy Department at Gaskell House, were on the editorial board. A collection edited in the US by Phil Brown in 1973 on *Radical Psychology* also included many chapters on therapy; therapy itself was seen by some radicals who broke completely from psychology as being a practice which adapted people to society. The term 'therapist' was then even sometimes disaggregated to draw attention to the sexual abuse in which they were complicit as 'the rapist', a wordplay repeated by one of the participants at the Manchester events, causing gasps of indignation as audible as those caused by Antony Easthope's comments.

We were searching for a way of articulating these different complaints about psychology in such a way that would bring together academic psychologists and practitioners. We tried out different names for a group and a conference to draw people in, and we also wanted to include people who were neither academic nor professional psychologists but whose lives had been affected by psychology. If Foucault was right about the psy complex then psychological ideas and practices would be manifested in many different parts of society, and especially in the 'helping professions'. We also were aware that Foucault's own critical history of the prison system in his book *Discipline and Punish* had emerged from his involvement with the Group for Information on Prisons in Paris. That group was designed, he said, not to speak for prisoners about their incarceration but to operate as a megaphone for the voices of prisoners themselves. Foucault himself not only had a background working in prisons but knew from the experiences of his life-partner who was arrested and held during political protests how bad conditions could be in the French prison system. His book was not at all a disinterested academic account of the emergence of contemporary forms of punishment and surveillance but was born of personal experience and collective activity.

The coordination with people who had a more humanistic perspective on psychology led us to try out the name Psychologists for Social Justice and Equality, and we then held a larger sixty-strong conference in Manchester which was attended by Valerie Walkerdine and John Shotter, and where we tried to formalise membership of the group. We set out 'aims and objectives' which included that we were 'committed to developing psychological ideas', which seemed a bit bureaucratic and also a bit too tied to psychology as such. We tussled over the name, and decided that it was misleading, for we didn't at all want it to be only for psychologists. Our next attempt was in June 1989 under the heading Psychology and Social Responsibility where I gave a paper jointly with Kum-Kum Bhavnani about research in higher education, and Kum-Kum dealt with a question about our connection with political activity very quickly and sharply by saying that for us politics was something you didn't put on your academic CV.

We couldn't escape from this tangle of contradictions, of course, which not only included us putting papers that we gave at these conference on our CVs but also that we were still able to get rooms for our public events inside the university at no cost. There was still also a huge gulf between the academics who had the luxury of being paid to teach and write about these ideas and the professional psychologists who found it difficult to make space for more meetings. A key issue, which was raised by users of psychology services, was the imminent 'chartering' of psychologists by the British Psychological Society. The BPS had been given a 'Royal Charter' back in 1965 but was anxious now to sharpen the distinction between 'Chartered Psychologists' who had the right to pontificate about internal mental processes they knew nothing about and those poor dupes they spoke about. The users of psychology services pointed out that they ran support groups and reflected on their own psychology as well as their friends and comrades. They were willing enough to work with those of us dubbed 'psychologists', but they objected to the implication that we knew more than them about the subject. We did not. We were there to learn from them, and so the meeting agreed to begin a campaign against chartering, issuing a statement in which we declared that we psychologists would refuse to go along with this particular dividing practice. The campaign lasted a couple of weeks. The deadline for BPS charter registration was looming, and one by one our resistance folded and most of us complied. Psychology and Social Responsibility as a name still didn't seem quite right. It was, perhaps, a bit too moralising. After all, people were being told to take responsibility for all kinds of terrible things that were done to them, and the phrase 'social responsibility' merely gave that brutal victim-blaming operation a sugar coating.

In April 1990 there was a reminder that 'prison' in the work of Foucault, and in the lives of psychologists, is no mere metaphor. A 'riot' broke out at Strangeways Prison just north west of Manchester city centre. As with other 'riots', the gaze of the media, and the explanations that were being rehearsed there and in psychology forums were from the standpoint of those with power, the normal folk who, it was assumed, were not prisoners. There had been many grievances by prisoners, protests at confinement in cells and violence by the prison warders, and then a black prisoner was assaulted by guards and forcibly injected with Largactil, one of the trade names for Chlorpromazine, which is often used as an antipsychotic medication. The prisoners staged a protest in the chapel and then some of them went up on the roof. It would have been reductive, and rather missing the point of what was at stake, to ask what was going on in the minds of the prison managers when they refused to investigate what had been going on in their prison. This kind of psychological explanation was one that was mined by the media, but with the focus instead on what was going on inside the minds of the prisoners. I was invited onto the early evening BBC news programme North West Tonight, and pressed to say what the prisoners on the roof were thinking. When I said that they may be wondering whether they will be listened to and worrying about what will be done to them when they came down, it became clear that this wasn't the answer the interviewer wanted; they wanted a 'psychological' answer, one which would necessarily include speculation about what false perceptions the prisoners had of reality and about how their actions were being driven by feelings out of control. I wasn't invited back.

Our next push to take things forward to link people together to question this reduction of politics to psychology was to pick up the title we had used a few years before, to take out the commas between terms, and to try again to launch an organisation that we called 'Psychology Politics Resistance', PPR. We made an effort to involve practitioner psychologists, travelling up to a north Manchester Hospital one day, for example, to speak about the PPR initiative and get them involved. We got them at least to agree to listen to us in a lunchtime break, but they told us that, although they agreed with everything we said about problems with psychology, they didn't actually have time in their working day to do any psychological work at all. In this deprived part of the city they spent most of their time giving advice about welfare benefits or housing or doing practical work to support people.

We pressed ahead and in July 1994 organised the 'founding conference' for PPR which gathered 150 people together. We had guest speakers, including a psychologist working inside the prison system from Barcelona and an educational psychologist from Sarajevo. We took a collection at the conference for the solidarity group Workers Aid for Bosnia. By a stroke of luck, we had a surprise visit just before the conference, Don Foster from South Africa, so we roped him in to be a guest speaker too. The presence of these speakers was symbolically important, marking our solidarity with the successful struggle against apartheid in South Africa and now with those caught up in the civil war in former Yugoslavia.

The presence of Don Foster was particularly poignant because the academic boycott of apartheid had made contact with him extremely difficult, and, we could agree, quite right too. We knew that Don had been carrying out research exposing torture by the South African security forces, and while the boycott was still in force we organised a meeting that he spoke at in Manchester Polytechnic. While I wouldn't send him academic papers or material that wasn't directly concerned with the struggle against apartheid, I did want to organise that meeting for him to speak about his research, to publicise it. To do this without breaking the boycott meant getting permission from the ANC office in London, a lengthy convoluted procedure which eventually worked out well.

Contradiction

The early 1990s saw other opportunities to connect with radical psychologists in South Africa which were just as complicated. In 1993 Erica and I were contacted by Ann Levett from the University of Cape Town, and we met up at an International Society for Theoretical Psychology conference in Bierville, France that year. US-American social constructionist psychologist Ken Gergen was there, and looked shocked when I walked into the room wearing a multicoloured t-shirt during his talk as he was in the middle of his claim that it was time to take ownership of psychology rather than, as he put it, "kicking around the margins in weird clothes". The boycott against South Africa was just about to be lifted with the combined success of the international pressure on apartheid, internal protest and the ANC military struggle. Ann Levett was four-square behind the boycott campaign, and the question was when and how to organise the workshop in such a way as to support the resistance to apartheid in the run-up to the elections, elections in which Ann herself finally voted for the Pan Africanist Congress. She was a good comrade and friend, a lesbian feminist who testified in court for victims of abuse while challenging the way that the narrative of 'trauma' was being imported from the white Western world into the Black communities. She had come into psychology quite late in her career, having at one time worked as secretarial assistant to the heart-transplant surgeon Christiaan Barnard, and then founding domestic violence support services. She divided her time between work as a therapist and as an academic inside and critical of psychology at the University of Cape Town.

Campaigning in the first post-apartheid election was already taking place when we visited Ann and Amanda Kottler for a workshop on discourse analysis, and we met a younger generation of qualitative researchers in January 1994 that included Anthony Collins, Cheryl de la Rey, John Dixon, Kevin Durrheim, Kevin Kelly,

Martin Terreblanche and Lindy Wilbraham. At the Psychology and Societal Transformation conference in Cape Town my talk was introduced by Don Foster, who told the audience why I had refused to send him research papers. This conference was where the old Psychological Association of South Africa, PASA, was closed down and a new more inclusive body, the Psychological Society of South Africa, PsySSa, was founded. It was a historic moment that replicated some of the moves made on the wider political stage; we saw the old PASA leadership apologise for their collusion with apartheid, and then shamelessly take bundles of proxy votes out during the elections to the new PsySSa executive so they still ran the show, but now alongside some new folk. There were some strong radical currents in psychology in South Africa resisting apartheid, with many psychologists participating in the Organisation for Appropriate Social Services of South Africa and publishing in the journal *PINS: Psychology in Society* edited in Durban by Grahame Hayes. These energies spun into new directions after 1994 with a series of South African Qualitative Methods Conferences which spanned discourse analysis and some stunning art practice. I described one of the sessions to the BPS Social Psychology section conference in Lancaster in 1999 after returning from a visit to South Africa. I don't think they believed me. In one session in Johannesburg an artist, Steven Cohen, had tottered into the performance area on high heels, crouched down and spurted red liquid from his arse which he then dramatically and slowly drank, to the horror of the audience. I haven't seen anything more interesting than this in a psychology conference before or since.

After the 1994 PPR conference we embarked on a subscription drive for members, produced regular newsletters, John Cromby organised a conference with Celia Kitzinger in Nottingham in 1996, and in 1998 we organised a PPR Networks Festival in Manchester where we linked up with other activist mental health groups. We interviewed different psychologists for the PPR Newsletter, and published a spoof interview with Hans Eysenck, which social psychologist Michael Billig thought distasteful and wrote in to tell us so, and a real interview with Noam Chomsky which didn't reveal anything about the link between his linguistic research and his politics. Meanwhile, inside the psychology department there were other political battles to be fought. Institutionalised racism wasn't only a problem in South Africa, but something very present inside the education system in Britain. It was a problem that took on its own form here, included its own 'defences', we might say, against those who would try to challenge it. One of the difficulties, we discovered, was in naming the problem, racism as such. One way of tackling it would be to look at the admissions system in the department, to look at how we could ensure that there really was access to students from different communities so that our own student population did reflect better that of Manchester, our catchment population. This policy, of anti-racist inclusion, was also in line with that of Manchester City Council which technically still ran the Polytechnic, and this also gave us some leverage to get things changed in our department.

This would have to be linked to changes in the way that we taught psychology, and the way we tackled how the discipline either simply marginalised people from non-Western cultures by not including them in research studies or pathologised them when they didn't correspond to how people are supposed to think and behave. The colonial and enduring racist history of much psychological research meant that even if we did succeed in making our course more accessible by overhauling our admissions procedures, we still needed to work on the syllabus for the different parts of psychology so that they reflected present-day realities, of an increasingly multicultural society and of continuing oppression of black people and other minority communities. Two of us, Erica and I, were asked to take this forward by carrying out a review of the degree syllabuses, and that meant going through each of them and discussing them with our colleagues. It was an opportunity to look more closely at how limited psychology was, limited to a certain kind of subject, usually a young white undergraduate student.

It was extremely difficult to get our colleagues to take this seriously, particular those who were committed to a model of scientific inquiry that deliberately and explicitly excluded the standpoint of the researcher. They really believed that the way to be objective was to develop research questions, hypotheses, and set up the studies in a way that was neutral. One of them even told us that it was perhaps safer to carry out research on issues that didn't affect you, even on topics which didn't interest you much; this would ensure that you wouldn't be biased in the way you approached the topic or investigated it. Some of them were true to their word. One colleague who was successful in attracting grant money for different projects sighed as they told us at a departmental research committee meeting one day that they had just got some money for something they actually wanted to do research on.

One response to our questions was to ask why we were particularly concerned about 'race', and one of the favourite tropes was rehearsed at this point, a complaint that we were not looking at the lack of representation in psychology of the experiences of male 43-year-old pipe-smokers. There was a contradiction at the heart of the lament that we were being unfair which appeared time and again inside the department. It was a contradiction between a recognition that there were some limits to the knowledge we transmitted to the students, that were indeed issues of bias at best and prejudice at worst on the one hand, and, on the other, a worry that if we treated those limits as linked to political issues of power and ideology and began to protest against those limits this would mean that we ourselves were being biased, if not prejudiced. We could see this contradiction at work even in the way that the department functioned. For all the complaints about Peter Banister's management or lack of management of the department, and for all the history of grudges and petty squabbles, the lecturers got on with each other, often had lunch together in the cavernous cafeteria in the main Gaskell building and always attended leaving events for staff retiring or those coming to the end of their contracts. Jeremy Foster, the 43-year-old smoker who had been on my interview panel, for example, argued vehemently against me in meetings, but would apologise by way of a little note in my pigeonhole for his rude behaviour if he thought he had ignored and so might have slighted me in the corridor.

There were psychological theories aplenty around in the syllabus that reinforced a conservative way of thinking about the nature of protest and which effectively delegitimized political objections to what psychology did to people. I taught some of these theories in my second-year personality lectures. Hans Eysenck, for example, developed a series of scales which purported to show that 'communists' and 'fascists' were both 'tough-minded' types. Yes, sure, it is true that some people on the left I've encountered have been quite authoritarian, 'tough-minded' you could say, but it is not surprising to find this characteristic prevalent in capitalist society, and perhaps even more so among those who dedicate their lives to overthrowing it. Eysenck wanted to discredit any resistance to capitalism by smearing those who were against it, the communists, as being fundamentally the same as fascists who are intent on shoring it up with nationalist and racist discourse and with physical attacks on those who are different from the norm. Fascists always implement some kind of psychology, and that is why it is all the more important to argue with our comrades, to argue that we should steer clear of psychology.

Objections were then made that the 'Erica and Ian thought police', as we were known, threatened to close down free speech and scientific research in the department. Erica and I were the couple in the department who questioned what psychology said, known as such and tolerated, but only tolerated insofar as we did not intrude on what our colleagues were teaching. Now we were crossing a boundary. The objections were only half serious, but the half of it was serious enough, and we knew we had to change tack to bring those who wanted to be 'fair' and 'balanced' back on board. We were, of course, caught in group dynamic that we also had to take some responsibility for; two of us, perceived as a tough-minded couple, a unit, taking the moral high-ground against others in the department who felt beleaguered and who reached for the psychological theories they knew so well as a resource to try and make sense of what was happening.

The chief tutor on the 'Brain and Behaviour' and third year 'Psychopathology' modules, John Stirling, did eventually shift over to our side in the argument, an argument posed in such a way that it seemed as if the question of tackling racism could only be posed as a struggle between us and them. John had taken me aside in my first term teaching in the department and told me that he was impressed that I had offered to organise the undergraduate project conference, that this was exactly what the department needed, and then I guess he was not so happy when it was clear that I wanted to link critiques of psychology with political debates. He was a popular lecturer, and we missed him when he disappeared for a year on a staff exchange with a university in the US. He was replaced during that time by George Parrott who told us that there were no alternatives to mainstream psychology in the US, nothing like what we were teaching, and showed us how to keep the laces on our trainers tidy by tucking them in the end loop. Like Jeremy Foster, John Stirling was a very fair person and wanted to be known to be a fair and rational person. And, like Jeremy, he was.

John shifted in response to us, the anti-racist thought police, because we stopped talking about 'racism' in the curriculum or institution and about how important it would be to have a departmental 'anti-racist' policy. Instead, we used the very terms he used, about being 'fair' to all applicants so that they had a chance to get a degree and about having a 'balanced' perspective in the debates in psychology, recognising that there were arguments in some parts of psychology that reflected the experience of different cultural perspectives. We learnt something about the importance of framing issues in different kinds of language in the process, something we should have already realised. It was a lesson we were learning about the nature of 'discourse', and about the way the discursive battleground had been operating made it seem as if we, anti-racists, were arguing against those who were positioned as racists. It was an aspect of group dynamics in the department that was to reverberate in later years.

There were other arenas in the politics of the department where we tried and failed and tried again to no avail. One arena was the Gaskell branch of our union, which was the National Association of Teachers in Further and Higher Education, NATFHE. The old branch leadership were retiring, and they managed to persuade Carolyn Kagan to be branch chair and me to be secretary. We two discovered that the only way to get our colleagues along to union branch meetings was to put 'car parking' on the agenda, but after a while even this hollow trick didn't succeed in mobilising people. Colleagues realised it was a ruse, and that there was little we could do about car parking. Union work could have been a place where we could come together, transcend the differences we had over the nature of psychology and in the process engage in collective action that would, in itself, also transcend the kinds of psychological argument that some colleagues were deeply committed to. Some colleagues in psychology joined the union, but others bought into the psychological assumption that it was up to them as individuals to speak out for themselves, separately, not as a group. I became disenchanted too when it seemed as if only economic self-interest would motivate people, and fed up when I was shown salary slips by older staff in other departments on the Gaskell site who were complaining about their wages when they were getting four times what I earned. They seemed to want this remedied on an individual level rather than through collective action, and certainly not through collective action that included other workers in the university – porters, kitchen and reception staff – who were not on the teaching staff. The branch structure in the Poly was reorganised, and Carolyn and I put our energies elsewhere for a while.

We needed to know how to navigate discourse that structured the department, and realise when we were pushing a little too far up against the limits of what these psychologists, people who embodied some of the core ideas and images of the person that they themselves taught about, could bear. I suspect that we pushed them a little too far at times, and the lines of division were sometimes about the limits of psychology as they understood it from their own degrees and research and sometimes about the political challenges we raised which weren't always about psychology at all. It was quite difficult at that time, for example, to get access to different traditions of psychology, and the 'cross-cultural' research tended to simply repeat the way that Western ways of being human were privileged as if they were the correct and normal models of thinking and behaving, as if they should then be the benchmarks against which the psychology of people in other cultures should be compared and, usually literally, measured.

This situation in the department meant that, when we reported on our research links with people outside Britain, we used the reports as opportunities to draw out lessons for the limits of our own dominant traditions of psychology. Then our reports were treated as if they were no more than propaganda, just more of the same political complaints against experimental psychology. One of the long-running intermittent 'memo wars' was over reports of conferences, things that Erica and I felt we should produce to give account of what we had been doing when we were away. John Stirling would comment and highlight passages in our conference reports to draw attention to things he could not understand and then post the annotated report back to us. Eventually he asked us not to post such reports in his pigeonhole. Again, the response and counter-response, the different moves in the game were usually friendly and respectful. We were among people we profoundly disagreed with, but we at least shared our disappointment when we failed to understand each other. There was most times the shared sense of truce, even peace. But there were exceptions.

Action

In November 1989 the terrible news came through that the psychologist Ignacio Martín-Baró had been murdered in El Salvador. Martín-Baró was a Jesuit priest who was carrying out research, quantitative opinion-polling research into the voting intentions of the Salvadoran population. He was hated by the regime, dangerous to it because he worked among the indigenous people and publicised their suffering. He did this both through traditional psychological research, questionnaires and suchlike, and through a kind of inquiry that develops its questions in alliance with people treated as participants or 'co-researchers'. This approach was known as 'action research', and instead of pretending to be neutral, it made a virtue out of working with the collective experience of people and the issues that concerned them. This was a quite different kind of 'psychology' to what we had been taught as undergraduates, and for many researchers in the English-speaking world it wasn't seen as psychology at all. We didn't know much about it, though Carolyn Kagan had been linking her work with that tradition in her studies of community psychology. Here was a more radical version of community psychology that was sometimes, with reference to liberation theology developed in Brazil, known as 'liberation psychology'. Most of our colleagues didn't know what it was, but they knew they didn't like it. Action researchers in El Salvador paid the price for their involvement in political conflict there, for working at the contradictions in society. On 16 November troops broke into the campus of the Universidad Centroamericana in the capital San Salvador and murdered six Jesuit priests and their housekeeper and her daughter. One of the priests was Martín-Baró.

Prompted by the social psychologist Charles Antaki who was based in Lancaster, we prepared a letter of protest and took it around the department so that it could be sent as a collective expression of our shock and anger to the regime in El Salvador. A dramatic event of this kind and the call for a human response takes us beyond the limits of psychology. Everyone but one signed it, a refusal on the grounds that it still was not exactly clear how Martín-Baró and the other seven had died, on the grounds that we needed more evidence before we made such a statement. Yes, we wanted evidence too, and the response of the one person who refused to sign is entirely understandable, but we can reflect on this for a moment to mark the way in which most of us in the department broke from a strictly psychological conception of evidence under the impact of the murders, were impelled to act, while one remained committed to the kind of neutral position that the discipline had trained us to adopt in our research. I want to mark this difference as two positions here rather than individualise the issue by naming names. I cannot say exactly what the one who refused to sign the letter thought, neither can a real psychologist. Let us stick to the terrain of the debate over what evidence in research is and what it could be.

Here we were at the heart of different conceptions of knowledge. On the one side was a very traditional logical positivist view of knowledge that has been dominant for many years in Anglo-American psychology. In this dominant tradition which aimed to give a quantitative representation of the world – something I had learnt to see as the old paradigm – knowledge was a description of reality, and as we accumulated 'findings' we needed to be very careful about what we claimed to find, cautious about knowledge that said it was statistically probable that this was what the world was like. Because we didn't yet have enough 'evidence' about what happened in El Salvador, for instance, we shouldn't prejudge the situation, this one individual who refused to sign the letter said. Better, from this point of view was a judicious silence rather than say something now that would pre-empt investigation and so make it more difficult to arrive at the facts.

On the other side was an alternative tradition, a different approach to knowledge that saw the claims that we make about the world as always, whether we like it or not, having effects, functioning to ratify already-existing representations or questioning them. From this alternative point of view, staying silent was itself something that would have effects; silence was collusion. It is not clear whether the so-called new paradigm inside psychology went as far as this, and there had been some complaints, by the social psychologist Michael Billig, for example, that the 'new social psychology' had a rather too liberal approach to research that made it difficult to appreciate the consequences of carrying out research into fascism. Billig's research had involved interviews with members of the National Front, but he had been clear that he did not at all plan to put their views of the world alongside those of anti-fascists, either into one complete account or into a series of accounts in which the fascists would have an equal voice. Billig's colleague at Birmingham University, Ray Cochrane, was one of our external examiners on the undergraduate degree, and he told us that when members of the National Front were interviewed for the research into fascism, Billig, whose name they would have recognised as being Jewish, had to conceal his own identity from them. He carried out those interviews in Ray's office down the corridor. Yes, there was an element of deception in this research, but, unlike most psychological research, Billig did this in order to expose power rather than endorse it. Billig's concern was that if new paradigm research was always committed to balancing different perceptions of reality and piecing together a big picture, the ethical dimension would be lost. Action research took these debates further.

Our protest letter at the killings in El Salvador was not neutral and neither did it have one fixed view of what the facts were. It was an intervention very much in line with the alternative view of knowledge and its consequences in the world, within the frame of what Martín-Baró was doing in his own action research. By preparing the letter and collecting the signatures and sending it, making it public, we wanted to put more pressure on the regime to come clean about what had happened. Our intervention would be one that would press for the truth to emerge, emerge as part of the very process of asking questions and demanding that action be taken. We had learnt from our meetings in Manchester, and from our encounters with the radical psychologists in South Africa, that the knowledge we needed to challenge psychology would need to have a very different form as well as content from that of the discipline. The discipline of psychology is concerned with prediction and control, as if it described aspects of our lives and our minds that are fixed in place, essential and universal to us as human beings, and as if neutral objective scientific description should not disturb what it described. We wanted to disturb psychology, and bring the debates into the public realm, standing with those who had paid with their lives for speaking out against power, to shift focus from power to resistance.

Murder, a reminder of brute reality, also reminds us that it is not sufficient to either adopt a neutral position with respect to knowledge or to treat all accounts of reality as relative, as if they simply presented different stories that we could choose to believe or refuse. Resistance to the forms of truth that the discipline of psychology is committed to – a positivist fake-scientific accretion of facts about individual behaviour – entails not a rejection of truth as such but a different relation to truth, one in which we are actively involved in making it, making it appear while those in power are intent on telling us lies. Facts are strung together on stories about who we are and what we could be, and one of the lessons of this chapter is that a psychological approach to ostensibly isolable facts in research fails to do justice to the world. The next chapter shows the value of treating the psychology that is taught inside and outside the academic world itself as series of stories, fairy tales with moral force and with consequences for those subject to them.

12

DISCOURSE

Tall tales about power

In which we discover a new way of noticing how psychology tells stories about individuals that are structured and can then be unravelled. The discipline can itself be treated as a series of discourses suffused with power, and these discourses are woven into institutional practices and patterns of dominance and submission that maintain and sustain psychology in the institutions that house it.

This chapter is about how we can teach psychology differently, but also about how we can carry out research in a way that is more compatible with an approach to the discipline that is a little more sceptical about the truth claims psychologists make about their objects of study. This way of 'changing the subject' shifts attention from the individual human subject of experimental investigation to the discourses about thinking and behaving that frame all psychological research questions. We turn the gaze of the researcher onto what psychologists are saying and writing about people, and so we can then teach about psychology as if it was a collection of stories rather than deep immutable truths. This approach to teaching is also a convenient bridge to research for it is then possible to formulate what you are doing as respectable empirical study. This, as you will see, brings us up against the limits of the discipline.

Framing

People tell stories about themselves, and psychologists have long noticed this. The question then is how to make sense of those stories. Psychology has, from its beginnings as a supposedly scientific discipline in the late nineteenth century, framed accounts given by people about their experiences to others, and to themselves as they reflect on what they are doing. Psychology frames them within its own stories about human behaviour. Students are also taught another set of bigger stories about the origins of scientific psychology in the laboratory set up by Wilhelm Wundt in an attic in Leipzig University in 1879. They are not usually taught that Wundt had to teach his 'subjects' to speak in a certain kind of way about their experiences as they engaged in 'introspection' into their thoughts, nor that the experimenter and subject often swapped places so that the early accounts would become all the more the kind of stories that psychologists would easily recognise and would like to be told.

The scientific framing of this early history of psychology as it broke away from philosophy and became an 'empirical' discipline – gathering evidence rather than simply speculating about how people might think – also cuts out the other side of the story of Wundt's work. This other side is also missing from most psychology textbooks: Wundt saw his laboratory-experimental studies as less important than his grander project of *Völkerpsychologie* which focused on shared collective thought in culture. This collective folk psychology was close to what some social psychologists were now beginning to study again as 'social representations' of different phenomena like sickness and madness. The new social representations research helped us to make connections in the 1970s and 1980s between research inside psychology and the cultural-historical accounts provided by Michel Foucault, accounts that referred to these shared representations which organise the stories we tell as 'discourses'. One problem facing those who try to describe their behaviour to others, as we could see in different accounts of personal experiences of distress, 'madness', was that some stories are more powerful than others. We realised that we needed to study 'discourses' and we needed to link those discourses with a study of the institutions that gave some discourses power to describe reality and implement that description, to define what was real and what was not.

We had one good example of how we might go about studying discourses in the chapter of *Changing the Subject* by Wendy Hollway in which she showed how the heterosexual couples she interviewed narrated accounts of their relationships and how the narratives were structured. She took this account of her research further in 1989 in *Subjectivity and Method in Psychology*. The three discourses she described were more than simply patterns of meaning, for they drew on and then reinforced stereotypical ideas about what men and women should think and feel about their relationships. The 'male sexual drive discourse' attributes the man's needs to biological forces out of their control, and this is in tension with what Hollway calls the 'have/hold discourse' in which a belief in monogamy demands commitment by the woman to the man, and with the third 'permissive discourse' which tells both partners that they must express and enjoy their sexuality. What was most important in Hollway's account was the way the three discourses locked together, locked the partners together, and, in a manner that family therapists might describe, set up different 'double-binds' for those involved; at one moment there is an injunction, particularly for the woman, to be free with their sexual desires, for example, and, at the next, there is a demand that she restrain herself for the good of the relationship. The discourses are both about personal experience and also about social structures.

Between Hollway's book chapter in *Changing the Subject* and her full-length book which discussed in more detail her approach to discourse and her own intuitive methodology for interviewing the couples – moving backwards and forwards between the interviews and her own personal diaries – another book appeared that was influential for those of us wanting to speak about 'discourses' inside the discipline. This was Jonathan Potter and Margaret Wetherell's *Discourse and Social Psychology* published in 1987. This book provided a stepping stone, from the 'turn to language' in qualitative research that Rom Harré had argued for as a new paradigm to the fuller incorporation of many more of Foucault's ideas into psychology. A little network of radicals inside our department working with colleagues elsewhere who were already sensitive to the power of language to shape reality knew that incorporation of Foucault into psychology would also create its own problems; we knew that there was a risk that Foucault, who himself had broken from psychology in order to be able to step back and do his historical research into the psy complex, could, in the process, be sucked back into psychology itself. But we had to take that step, and the argument in *Discourse and Social Psychology* was one way of moving from 'new social psychology' in the early 1970s through the *Changing the Subject* arguments in the 1980s to a new tradition of work closer to a Foucauldian approach to discourse and power.

In *Discourse and Social Psychology* Potter and Wetherell pointed out that traditional attitude surveys and questionnaires neglected 'variations' in the accounts people gave of their beliefs. That is, what someone says to a psychologist is very different from what they say to members of their family or to their close friends. They do not express underlying beliefs but manage what they want others to believe about what they think, managing this through what Potter and Wetherell called 'interpretative repertoires'. People construct an account of what they think and give a performance of what they are thinking in order to do things; the varying constructions then 'function' in relationships between people or in what people speak about or write for different audiences. The shape of these interpretative repertoires thus depends on context.

Variability in discourse also has consequences for the way we should understand what scientists say about what they do. The argument here applies not only to pretend scientists like psychologists, but also real scientists who at one moment use an interpretative repertoire of 'discovery' through empirical research and at the next use another repertoire which refers to 'hunches' and speaks of attempts to discredit rival researchers. Here the authors drew on Jonathan Potter's PhD research at the University of York on the 'sociology of scientific knowledge' – a specific field of research that examines exactly how it operates in practice instead of relying on the tall tales of scientists which clean things up for public consumption – to show how real science is a messy contradictory enterprise saturated with discourse.

Potter and Wetherell also drew attention to a problem with the attempt in ethogenic new social psychology to piece together accounts given by people about the little social worlds they inhabit as if those different pieces were like bits of a jigsaw, and as if we could thereby arrive at the overall 'structure' of roles and rules that held that social world together. I had tried to show in my PhD thesis that the new social psychology was influenced by 'structuralist' ideas that were current outside psychology, in the work of Saussure in linguistics, Lévi-Strauss in anthropology and Barthes in semiology, for example. Here, in *Discourse and Social Psychology*, was another way of showing that there were limits to these underlying structuralist assumptions in qualitative research in psychology. We could now see more clearly, for example, that in the classic study *Rules of Disorder* the different stories told by the football fans do not fit together. There are deep contradictions between the way the fans talk about violence and reality, one striking contradiction being very evident in the piece of interview transcript where a 'hooligan' tries to persuade the researcher that when they catch fans from a rival team they would kick them in the head until they were dead, which was patently untrue. Little social worlds do not neatly hang together but rather consist of different competing interpretive repertoires, and so we need to move on from the structuralist-inspired 'turn to language' to a 'turn to discourse'.

This argument for a 'turn to discourse' was the cue for us in Manchester to link these debates more explicitly with so-called post-structuralism, and so, in line with some of the ideas in *Changing the Subject*, our work on language was concerned with the way it was bound up with social institutions and power. Instead of describing patterns of meaning as comprising intersecting 'interpretative repertoires' we referred to 'discourses', and we reworked the three elements that Potter and Wetherell drew attention to – that is, variability, construction and function – and we spoke and wrote instead about 'contradiction', 'constitution' and 'power'. This was an opportunity for us to turn the gaze of the researcher back on the discipline in which they worked. Instead of focusing on 'non-psychologists' and reframing what they said in terms that would be understood by psychologists, we wanted to treat the discipline of psychology itself as a set of stories or discourses that had power to define what counted as good behaviour and correct thinking, to define what was healthy and what was psychopathological. Our discourse analysis was also therefore an analysis of institutions, and we knew this was important, of course, because we were ourselves constrained over what we could say by the institution we were working in. We knew there were other approaches to the study of discourse in other departments, in other universities, but there was a peculiar paradoxical combination of institutional pressures that made our work difficult – psychology is institutionally resistant to an approach that is not explicitly concerned with observable behaviour or with what is going on inside an individual's head – and made it possible. This situation calls for a word about the particular conditions of possibility for discourse analysis in Manchester.

Manchester Polytechnic, like the other polytechnics in the UK, was aching to be treated on the same level as the universities. There were attempts to break from local authority control, and from the financial and political restrictions this control entailed. The Thatcher government set the overall political context for the way these attempts were managed and for the vision that the polytechnics had of their future. The 1988 Education Reform Act instituted these changes, and the Polytechnic became a separate corporate body independent of Manchester City Council in 1989. However, unlike the established universities, there was no senate or any other governing body accountable to the staff or students in this new institution. In fact, it was the Board of Governors that was constituted as a company which would then direct the rest of the Polytechnic, and this brought to a head the drive for complete financial autonomy and the push for staff to engage in 'income generation'. The Department of Psychology and Speech Pathology, for example, was told by our new Dean of Faculty in the 1980s that we needed to bring in money either through research bids to funding bodies or by putting on courses which would be externally advertised.

This pressure on staff to 'income generate' had some paradoxical effects, including on the 'discourse group' Erica and I had set up inside the department. A couple working closely together in any academic department already has effects on the dynamics of the department, as we have seen. It had positive effects here, but we will see in a later chapter how this played out in a way that was more problematic in relation to personal-political issues concerning staff and students. The Faculty management committees and the new 'conference office' liked the fact that we did arrange public events, but they didn't like us charging nominal fees to attend. We did the kinds of things they wanted us to do, but we weren't turning in much profit for the institution, most of the time hardly 'covering our costs' as the managers would say. We were fortunate in having support for this at departmental level; Peter Banister was reluctant to pass down directives from higher up in the institution and his laissez-faire approach to departmental management protected us from the impetus toward the free-market competition that was being implemented across the Polytechnic. Another paradox was that this early push to marketisation of higher education opened up some space for alternative approaches in psychology. The same dynamic applied in other polytechnics and in other disciplines, and this was one reason why the polytechnics then became sites where 'radical' sub-disciplines of the human sciences flourished; meetings of the British Sociological Association theory group were often held in polytechnics, for instance, and the journal *Radical Philosophy* was based at Middlesex Polytechnic.

When we proposed new courses or new lines of research, the concern was now not whether or not this was really psychology, but whether it would attract students and, if possible, whether it would make money. Perhaps things were particularly relaxed in our department, and it is true that Peter was shielding the staff, to the annoyance of the Faculty administration, and it was also a bit easier for us because Peter saw himself as being on the 'qualitative' side of psychology, willing to tolerate us putting on day conferences on politics and resistance and so able to tell Faculty that some of his staff were at least doing something that might count as external activity. The history of our institution under local authority management made us more susceptible to the mixture of intense control of everyday activities – micromanagement – and the imperative to generate income, to be 'sustainable'. The Polytechnic was pulled in two directions, authoritarian and individualist, top-down management and self-directed activity that was of a piece with some transformations in British capitalism that were just then being named by some critics as 'neoliberalism'.

Some of us jumped as these new demands on us to make money kicked in, and we really were worried for our jobs. Erica Burman had supervised a small research project on education case conferences, the forums in British schools where professionals were brought together to decide whether to 'exclude' difficult children from school. A disproportionate number of boys were excluded, and many of these boys were black. Clearly, the way the specific decisions were being made in the case conferences were replicating a more general problem of institutional racism. It seemed as if discourses which relayed stereotypical images of gender and race were at work, and this was the focus of a research bid we put together for a research assistant who would, in the process, be funded to do their PhD on this topic. We wrote the bid together on my Amstrad 8512 computer, the luminous green flickering letters on the black screen was a sign that we were at work, and, as classical conditioning theory would predict, an associative link was forged between this glowing colour-tone and exhaustion such that we eventually stopped going to Chuni's Indian restaurant in Rusholme for dinner after teaching when they started using the same lurid colour for their fluorescent displays around their windows and food counters.

This was our first successful research bid, and we appointed Deborah Marks as our first PhD student who started in 1989. One candidate at interview had spent most of the time complaining bitterly about her current place of work and how she was looking forward to getting out, which rang warning bells for all of us. So, Deb it was that joined the 'discourse group' which was, up to that point, for undergraduates Erica and I were supervising, those who were carrying out qualitative research for their final year dissertations. We were in quite a strong position, tasked by Peter to devise the first qualitative 'self-directed' practical exercises for the second year of the degree, practical reports using interviewing and discourse analysis. We needed this discourse group as a place where the students could support each other and where we could support them against attacks from other members of the department. Student marks were often collateral damage in dispute between staff, and we wanted to ensure that methodological differences would not be played out at the students' expense.

Psychologists seem to take these differences very personally, and it does not solve the problem to play the relativist card, to tell a psychologist that truth is relative in a bid to get them to accept an alternative conceptual or methodological framework that itself threatens their deep-held belief that they are neutral objective scientific researchers. Some of our colleagues would tell students in class that the only empirical research that counted was quantitative, and even – and this was the real frightener – that students who carried out qualitative studies for their dissertation would never be accepted for clinical psychology training. We knew from our own experience and from our clinical psychology friends in radical psychology networks that neither of these claims was true. Not all of the final year projects were carrying out discourse analysis in our little unofficial research group, and we had students who were doing interview projects about identity or even studies, for example, of constructions of subjectivity and power in the plays of Harold Pinter.

I was asked to be an external examiner for the psychology degree course at Humberside College of Higher Education, the place where I had failed to get a job and been told that I should think about teaching in sociology. The letter asking if I would take the job on came from Gill Aitken, but she had left the College by the time I took up the post, as had Julie Dickinson, who had got the teaching post I had applied for. There were usually two or three external examiners for psychology degrees, and appointment of staff from other universities was supposed to operate as a form of quality control over the teaching and to oversee the marking to ensure that the students were being fairly assessed. We students never saw the external examiners at Plymouth, I don't know who they were, and as lecturers we often treated them in Manchester Polytechnic with a mixture of respect and contempt, respect in the examination boards, and contempt as we humoured them in face-to-face meetings and worked out how to avoid implementing their suggestions for improvements to the course in our own staff meetings and in the 'pre-boards' where we rehearsed how we wanted things to go at the main event. We were a little worried at the end of each year, waiting to be noticed, singled out for praise in the examiners' report on our students' progress or questioned about shortcomings or, more dangerous still, deviations from mainstream psychology. We were more worried if we were teaching and supervising qualitative research, but we had external examiners who were sympathetic to different methodological approaches.

The examination board was the place where this work would be judged, and we knew that the current external examiners on the psychology degree were sympathetic to qualitative research. Halla Beloff, who was one of the external examiners, made this clear in her report to the end-of-year examination boards, something which was both pleasing and which caused occasional ripples of anxiety as we waited for the backlash from our quantitative-research fixated colleagues. Halla was supportive of interdisciplinary research, including in undergraduate psychology projects, and said so. To their credit – and in line with what the sociology of scientific knowledge might expect to find – our colleagues managed the contradiction between two quite different firm-held accounts about what was going on; they kept their fierce objection to what we did academically separate from their friendly cooperation in our day-to-day lives in the department. John Stirling did value good scholarship, for example, and was clearly torn between our adherence to what he viewed as quite wrong, dangerously anti-scientific ideas about schizophrenia, and friendly acknowledgement of us as colleagues when our paths crossed in the library. We were usually able to rally together to defend ourselves and our students when there were attacks on the department. The chat around exam boards renewed acquaintances and shared gossip, external examiners bringing news about other departments and the outside world, sometimes outside the academic world. Richard Stevens from the Open University who succeeded Halla Beloff, for example, had previously worked as a television director and spoke of the classical conditioning response he still had to the music of the police series *Z Cars*, spikes of adrenalin and fear from the time he had been responsible for the programme when it was broadcast live. Discourse is embedded in institutions, and suffused with affect.

At Humberside I was treated to a view of the other side of the game, for it became clear very early on that I had been invited in by someone who taught qualitative research – Gill Aitken left her lecturing post to begin clinical psychology training in Manchester University, and was co-supervised by Erica Burman for her doctoral dissertation – to a department that included many mainstream cognitive and behavioural, quantitatively oriented lecturers. I was able to see first-hand how an external is handled; given selections of student work unless we impossibly insisted on seeing everything, told that our suggestions were being 'discussed', provided with ambiguous bland report-backs on the progress made at the end of each academic year. It was also my first opportunity to compare a whole staff group meeting in another institution with my own, comforting and disconcerting to see the same types playing out the same kinds of script. Some of the guys shambling into the meeting in track-suit bottoms yawned and made it clear that attendance at the board was a chore. Younger keener staff teaching new material blushed at each mention of their course, waiting for this terrible ordeal to be over. Officious managers rolled in from lunch and kept time, kept things on the same track, the same schedule, geared toward outcomes that they could report to the next committee up in the institution. The etiquette of the examination board meant that it would be bad form, and counterproductive, to single out courses that seemed to be badly run, and most of the staff were able to stall any proposed changes until the three-year external examiner contract was over. The next examiner would come in cold, and take a couple of years to work out what was going on before their own term was up.

Education

Back at Manchester Polytechnic, there was outright hostility to our discourse analysis PhD application for our research assistant from some staff, and from researchers in other disciplines. The university ethics committee – the body in the institution that dealt with postgraduate research – included chemists, engineers and physicists who had no idea what qualitative research was. This became evident as we tried to steer Deb's PhD proposal through that committee, and since the psychology department's representative on the Polytechnic Research Degrees Committee was a quantitative researcher, we guessed that we would have a hard time getting it through. We did. The problem was compounded by some contradictions between explicit rules governing the committee and implicit rules. Again, we saw played out exactly the kind of discursive contradictions in scientific practice that Potter and Wetherell had described in *Discourse and Social Psychology*.

When Deb's proposal came up for ratification by the committee the first time round the supervision team – that is Erica and me – and the student were invited to attend. We turned up for the meeting, but were asked why we were there, and were eventually told that it was expected that we would acknowledge but then not take up the invitation, we should have kept away. The committee was very bad tempered at this meeting, and it wasn't only because of our unwitting infraction of the rules. They told us the research was not empirical, and that the proposal needed to spell out what 'hypotheses' were going to be tested. Here was a clash between the discourse of predictive 'hypothesis-testing' and 'results' pitted against a more open interpretative approach that was mainly retrospective. Potter and Wetherell had defined discourse analysis as being 'a sensitivity to language', described learning the method as being like riding a bike, and they pointed to 'fruitfulness' as being the main criterion of good research. This didn't cut much ice with our ethics committee. Eventually, after another rewrite and resubmission of the proposal they sent it out to external reviewers, and Valerie Walkerdine came to our rescue, confirming that, yes, this was one way of carrying out psychological research. The condition placed by the committee was that, because this was our first PhD student as well as dabbling in some strange new unscientific methods, we should also have an external supervisor on the team. This was Wilf Carr in the Education Department at Sheffield University, an affable partner who was willing to be visited once in May 1990 by the three of us and then left alone.

Valerie Walkerdine, together with John Broughton and David Ingleby, was co-editing a new critical psychology book series for Routledge and in 1989 my first book, *The Crisis in Modern Social Psychology, and How to End it*, was published in that series. That book was written on the green-glow Amstrad, much of it rewritten from my PhD. David Ingleby was by now in Utrecht after having lost his teaching post at Cambridge University in 1980 after having fallen foul of medical psychiatrists. Peter Sedgwick, who wrote a critical review of approaches in psychiatry and 'anti-psychiatry' in his 1982 book *PsychoPolitics*, a ground-breaking Marxist book about mental health published a year before he took his own life, had been one of those asked to write a reference evaluating Ingleby's application for tenure at the university, but discovered later that his glowing reference for Ingleby had been misrepresented at the assessment board as hostile, this in line with a scathing report from the Professor of Psychiatry Sir Martin Roth. Every member of the Social and Political Sciences Committee signed a letter of protest at the decision of the board to turn down Ingleby's application, and students carried a symbolic 'coffin of academic freedom' through the streets.

I had seen Ingleby speak at an event organised by *Radical Science Journal* in London in 1982 on why we should study the history of psychology, and sat at his feet, literally so five years later. He sat in an armchair, an Abraham Lincoln seated figure with a cravat, and I gazed up at him from the carpet in Valerie Walkerdine's flat. It was an audience in which two of the editors of their Routledge book series confirmed their invitation to me to write a book based on my PhD thesis. When the book was published Valerie arranged a launch event in April 1989 at the ICA on the 'Individual and the Social'. Nik Rose was on the panel, and shook his head throughout my contribution; I was vaguely aware of him exaggeratedly shaking his head from side to side as I spoke, and afterwards it transpired that he had shifted a long way from his early days as a radical into a kind of Foucauldian analysis that was hostile to Marxism.

My 'crisis' book included some more explicit links with 'discourse' and with the argument for discourse analysis in social psychology that had been made by Jonathan Potter, who had now moved down to Loughborough University, and Margaret

Wetherell relocated to the Open University in Milton Keynes, also in the East Midlands of Britain. Michael Billig had already moved from Birmingham across to Loughborough, and those interested in language linked up with researchers on language to set up the Discourse and Rhetoric Group (DARG). This was an important reference point for us, and a source of support for our work. We visited DARG in June 1990 with Deb to talk about the education case conference research, and it was an occasion to discuss some of the differences in our approaches. DARG was concerned with how people actually interacted in conversation, while we were concerned with broader processes of power in society and with the production or 'constitution' of subjectivity. There was some overlap, for Michael Billig was trying to connect his study of 'rhetoric' with the notion of ideology, and we read Foucault as providing a way of analysing power and knowledge functioning as ideology, even though Foucault himself had made it clear that he would prefer to steer clear of the term.

In 1990 we renamed our discourse group the Discourse and Resistance Group and then Discourse Unit, and started running courses and conferences devoted to discourse analysis. We styled the Discourse Unit, in its subtitle, a Centre for Qualitative and Theoretical Research on the Reproduction and Transformation of Language and Subjectivity. We organised our meetings inside the department and our external events under this heading, and most of the time no one else in the institution noticed and no one prevented us doing this. We slipped under the radar of the institution and then flourished because the department was happy that we were at least doing something above and beyond our undergraduate teaching. This also meant that we had no resources to fund the Discourse Unit, and it had no material existence beyond the title on advertisements for the meetings printed out on the Amstrad and duplicated on the Gaskell campus photocopier. We had our meetings in room E16, but we always kept the curtains closed over the one-way mirror that opened onto it from E17 next door.

The arrival of computers on our desks, and then email, flickering white lettering on a blue screen, most messages sent back and forth to colleagues down the corridor, began to cut into our time, but most colleagues initially refused to use the email system, and it was an event to get an email from outside the Polytechnic, from Erica's PhD student Ángel Gordo López who was still based in the department at the Victoria University, for example. Ángel, who was working on gender, told the psychology department he wanted Erica to be a supervisor, and so the head of the Victoria department wrote a bizarre letter to our department which indicated how much they got of what Ángel was doing, or of the concept of 'gender' more generally. The letter said that because Ángel's research had a 'sexual dimension' he would benefit from Erica's expertise. Psychology routinely reduces the very different ways that 'gender' as a social category is constructed over history and in different cultures to 'sex' as something seemingly fixed and universal. It is partly the confusion between the dimensions of gender and sex (and femininity and masculinity as the experiential dimension of social and bodily difference) that makes the questions about 'sex differences' that pop up at the end of seminar presentations so absurd.

Men and women are thereby reduced to their conventionally sexed bodies, and when most traditional psychologists usually refer to 'gender' in their research they mean observable fixed sexual difference, sometimes vice versa, as if you can directly read off one dimension of difference from the other. Now, however, feminist psychologists attentive to the contest and fluidity around sexual identity and gender were beginning to roll their eyes at such crass questions.

Most of our time in our department was spent on face-to-face teaching, supervision of student dissertations, marking and examination boards, and, before that, exam invigilation, which I found almost as stressful as taking an exam myself. Carolyn Kagan argued that the male and female students should be separated because the men went to the toilet more often and so they disrupted everyone else's concentration. It wasn't a serious suggestion; she was making a point about the way that even the examination hall operates as a gendered space. I was told off for wearing my Bart Simpson 'Underachiever and proud of it' T-Shirt to one invigilation. Erica commented that it was insensitive. We were not supposed to mark exam scripts during invigilation, but most of us did this, and it only made a minimal impact on the piles of marking we had at the end of the year.

There were distractions. In 1989 Erica and I were invited to speak at a conference on Postmodernism and the Social Sciences at the University of St Andrews. There were clearly parallel developments and internal battles going on in other disciplines, but in psychology we faced hostility not only on the basis of methodology but also because we were challenging the individualist focus in our own discipline, a reductionist focus upon which most research was premised. St Andrews was my second conference invitation, the first was in Lincoln earlier in the year at a BPS History and Philosophy of Psychology conference where I talked about 'discourse' and was told by the sociologist of scientific knowledge Steve Woolgar, the discussant for my paper, that the French theories I was using – work by Michel Foucault primarily – were like good wine, "they don't travel well". St Andrews counted in the English academic imagination as a 'national' rather than an 'international' conference, but it was the first major conference we had been invited to, so it was a big deal. Jonathan Potter and Margaret Wetherell had already moved on from St Andrews to their new posts south of the border by that August, so I wasn't able to test their reactions to what I called the 'discourse discourse' of postmodernism, that is, the hyper-reflexive playful use of language as a discourse about discourse. This 'discourse discourse' was, I argued, commenting on the phenomena it playfully described as if at an ironic distance, effectively a way of reproducing power relations while refusing to take responsibility for them. Erica and I rehearsed giving our papers to each other as audience the night before, and nervously awaited our time to speak on the big day, very impressed by the social geographer David Harvey leaning nonchalantly on the lectern as he spoke without any notes and by socialist-feminist Heidegger specialist Joanna Hodge correcting her script as she spoke.

John Bowers, who was now at Nottingham University, was there, and we could hear how nasty things could get in the paradigm debates. The head of the psychology department, Ian Howarth told John that there was something about him that he didn't like, something that reminded him of John Shotter, who had recently left for a new post in the Netherlands. Shortly afterwards, John Bowers was called into Howarth's office to be told that there was a problem with the teaching, that Howarth had heard that the lectures included post-structuralist theory; Howarth told Bowers "these people, Foucault, Derrida, are bastards, don't teach them". John Shotter, now stranded in the Netherlands, meanwhile, was unable to get back to the UK, unsuccessfully applying for jobs in psychology departments here. He told me that a traditional developmental psychologist Peter Bryant, who was the external assessor for a post in Sussex University, had apparently written of John Shotter's publications that they were 'lamentable'. I should say that most of the psychologists I met were decent human beings, and some of them held true to that first desire of most psychology students, to help others. Somewhere along the way, however, something unpleasant happens to those good intentions as the professional psychologist is forced to ally themselves with the disciplinary machinery that pathologises other people. Psychological discourse is disciplinary matter.

One lunchtime the departmental secretary Hilary Garrett stopped me in the corridor as I was on my way to the cafeteria after teaching all morning, and told me there had just been a phone call for me from, she thought, Puerto Rico. She told me that as it was an international call, and, as these calls were blocked on our office phones to save money, I could call back from her office. I spoke to Maria Milagros López on a crackly line who said that she had seen my *Crisis* book, and that she wanted to invite me to speak at a conference on the 'social imaginary' at the University of Puerto Rico in February 1991. They would pay for the flights and hotel. This was my first international conference invitation, and it was to a part of the world I had never been before. I had never been outside Europe. I threw myself into planning for the conference, writing the paper about the crisis in social psychology and on representations of psychoanalysis treated as forms of discourse, and resumed learning Spanish. This was also an opportunity to connect the 'paradigm' revolution arguments with work I was beginning on 'psychoanalytic discourse'. The focus here is not on whether psychoanalysis is right or wrong, whether it should or should not be viewed as an alternative approach inside psychology, but how the ideas are threaded together on compelling series of stories about human beings. Psychoanalysis claims to reach the parts other kinds of psychology cannot reach, and so it is attractive to some psychologists who want to turn it into a kind of psychology. They thereby overlook the way it also functions as a powerful discourse, and when psychologists evangelise about what they have found in Freud and his followers, the framework becomes just as problematic as the other theories that comprise the discipline.

The book *Psychoanalytic Culture* was really my first book, for I had started writing it while I was teaching my third-year option Psychoanalysis and Society in the late 1980s, even though it was published in 1997, well after *The Crisis*. It took ten years to assemble the notes from my option teaching and to link them together with an argument about the way that psychoanalytic discourse in various different forms was pervading Western culture. John Shotter said I should read Gillian

Beer's book *Darwin's Plots*, a marvellous analysis of how evolutionary theory in the nineteenth century worked with existing tropes about the ascent and descent of humankind, and how Darwin's writing then shaped the way that novelists like George Eliot reconfigured narratives of development. I pushed my book on psychoanalytic discourse, enthusiastic and still hopeful, but it got a cold response from some colleagues which, if I had to guess, had something to do with the first chapter on groups in times of crisis which was, among other things, about the responses of university departments to the problem of male staff using their position of power to pick which female students to bed. Though there were such stories about lecturers in Manchester who had since moved on to other institutions, we had hoped that nothing that like that was happening in our department.

Assessment

One reason I published the different components of my psychoanalytic culture book as journal articles first was that we had been warned that books weren't taken very seriously in psychology. We were told that there was going to be a 'Research Assessment Exercise' in the universities and that Manchester Polytechnic would submit the publications produced by its research staff. The RAE exercise was a long process inside each university during which departments selected researchers who would be entered on the basis of their publication record. It was all the more difficult because departments were also told that the final RAE score might also be affected by the percentage of researchers they entered. It was a calculated risk to enter researchers like us from a department that historically had little research going on, and there was much speculation as to whether it was worth it financially. Journal articles would count because psychology was, rather incredibly, deemed to be a science, and it was through the journals that knowledge was evaluated through peer review. Books would count for almost nothing, and book chapters would, we were told, count as less than nothing. Our discourse was disciplined.

This injunction to publish, to try our chances in the RAE, ran alongside the demand that we generate income for the institution, and I did obediently submit articles to journals, though sometimes receiving scathing rejection letters. A peer review usually consists of a brief summary of what the article is about, and an evaluation of whether the argument is sound and whether the right range of existing literature has been referenced in it. A journal editor chooses which three or more reviewers will be sent the article, so there is always already a decision depending on whether the editor likes the look of it and who they think is competent to judge it. Then, depending on the reviews, how positive or hostile they are, the editor needs to make another choice, whether to accept or reject the article, and whether to impose any conditions on acceptance, amendments to the structure or additions to the argument.

It was when I was also asked to review articles that had been submitted to journals that I realised how important it could be to conceal your identity, and to do this very thoroughly. Sometimes the papers I was sent for review still had references to the author in them, and sometimes it was patently obvious that the manuscript had been rejected by another journal and the comments rubbed out or scribbled over before it was sent off again to somewhere new to have another try. Sometimes it was possible to rub off the Tipp-Ex over the author name, hold the sheet up to the light and see who had written it. The same caution applied to hostile reviews, copies of which were sent through to the author with a rejection letter. A first article I submitted about the history of social psychology using Foucault to speak about the laboratory experiment as apparatus of power, for example, was rejected after a reviewer complained that these ideas from continental Europe were now finding their way to what the reviewer called 'our island kingdom'. I never found a place for that article. Maybe it was rubbish. Another article on power and group psychology was rejected with comments by one reviewer saying it was the worst article he had ever seen submitted to a journal. I kept a copy of the photocopied fax of that review which I could see, if I turned it sideways and then did a search of telephone codes, was sent from the Australian National University where one of the key figures from the Tajfel tradition of research into minimal groups was based.

The conference I was invited to in Puerto Rico was also, I thought, where I should give the paper in Spanish because Puerto Rico was still a colony of the United States, technically a Free Associated State in the Caribbean. It was a testing ground for Depo-Provera contraceptives that were used in population control programmes directed at 'Third World' women, and for Agent Orange herbicide that was used by the US to destroy arable land during the Vietnam War. Speaking Spanish would, I thought, be a form of symbolic resistance to US imperialism. I took some lessons with Ángel Gordo López. We practised different grammatically distinct versions of "I was playing my guitar when Franco died". I tried to translate the paper myself, gave up, and then a friend translated it. It was snowing in Manchester when the plane took off. I changed planes in Miami, and arrived, shattered, unable to think or speak in English let alone Spanish, in warm humid San Juan the next day. The two main conference organisers were Mili – Maria Milagros López at the University of Puerto Rico, and Heidi – Heidi Figueroa Sarriera who was based in a university college on the south of the island. Mili said after my talk that she appreciated me giving it in Spanish but couldn't understand all of it, maybe because of the accent. John Broughton was there, as was John Shotter, and another invited speaker was the US-American social psychologist Ken Gergen.

In San Juan, John Shotter and Ken Gergen ran down the side road next to the hotel to the beach and swam in the evenings after the conference had ended and seemed the best of buddies. But not so much during querulous exchanges in the back of the car over what each meant by 'realism'. Ken seemed to have a more typically US-American pragmatic take on theory; he absorbed ideas that would work for him caring little for the niceties of argument in the original texts, whereas John was more diligent, complaining to me afterwards that "Ken doesn't really read Derrida". John was just as irritated by some criticisms I made of him for citing the work of the seventeenth-century Italian Enlightenment philosopher Giambattista Vico, telling me after a seminar on narrative therapy that we attended together in

Helsinki on 'providential dialogues' that I was being lazy with my claims that this kind of philosophy tangled with religious ideas, that "You ought to read your Vico, mate".

Several speakers had pulled out of the San Juan conference because of threats to air travel during the first Gulf War. There were some radical students at the conference, and we tried to get a joint statement agreed at one of the sessions opposing US intervention in Iraq. Ken Gergen blocked this statement, intervening with an impassioned plea for us to recognise that there were no good guys or bad guys, and that this statement made it seem as if the United States were the bad guys. David Gergen was director of communications at the White House under Presidents Ford and Reagan and then a senior advisor to Clinton; Ken dedicated his 1991 book *The Saturated Self* celebrating postmodernism in modern culture to his elder brother David with admiration.

Now, across the Atlantic in 1991, and with complicated changes to my travel involving three flight changes, I wanted to get home. I had teaching commitments, and I was also course leader for the part-time undergraduate psychology degree which involved 'franchise' meetings with local further education colleges to validate the first year of the course before the students enrolled at Manchester Polytechnic. I arrived back with T-shirts emblazoned with slogans marking the upcoming year, 1992, as 500 years of resistance against European and then US-American colonialism. It had been difficult enough to get my teaching shifted around so I could come to the conference, and we were arranging other events in Manchester that needed working on. The best thing about the Puerto Rico 'social imaginary' conference, apart from free travel and hotel accommodation somewhere warm during the winter, was meeting Mili and Heidi, and they agreed to come over to Manchester in July when we planned a conference on discourse analysis. In the early summer term, after teaching had ended and we were preparing for the summer exams and the examination boards I travelled to Barcelona to meet Tomás Ibáñez and the radical social psychology group at the Universitat Autònoma de Barcelona. People there taught discourse analysis and they were also influenced by Foucault's work. In addition, Tomás was an anarchist activist, and this combination of radical psychology and radical politics was something I wanted to find out more about. I also met Teresa Cabruja who was also part of the social psychology group, though based in the newly founded Universitat de Girona. The group in Barcelona seemed to operate, and sometimes referred to themselves as the 'family', helping each other out not only with research projects but with writing up each other's PhD theses. One of the upshots of the Barcelona visit was that two of Tomás's students, Lupicinio Iñiguez and Joan Pujol, also decided to come to our Manchester July discourse analysis conference.

Within the space of a few months, in the first half of 1991, I had been to an international conference, made a research visit and now we had our own international conference. We had little money and we didn't pay for any travel or accommodation for our speakers, even for our international visitors. Mili and Heidi stayed in Erica's house, and they participated in the conference as guest commentators on the papers. Charles Antaki, a social psychologist from Lancaster University, came to the conference but was very perturbed when Mili gave a marvellous paper putting Foucault to work to describe the observation of populations in Puerto Rican society. She drew attention to the gulf between the Anglo-American tradition of 'empirical' research in psychology and other traditions which value theoretical analysis and even speculation. Mili finished her paper by saying that she didn't have time to describe the findings from her research, but that basically what she found confirmed everything she had just described about the history of colonialism and contemporary regimes of surveillance and fear. Charles was shocked; surely, he said, discourse analysis must mean doing some analysis. There were clearly some expectations about empirical work that he was carrying over from the old paradigm into this new research on language. Charles included a chapter by me in his edited book on 'everyday explanation', one of my first publications, and I liked him for his openness to new ideas and for his active engagement with the politics of research in Nicaragua under the Sandinistas, but there still were limits for him about what should count in psychology.

At the second discourse analysis conference the following year, 1992, we had Valerie Walkerdine as our guest speaker, and this is where there was an incursion by an enthusiastic representative of the old quantitative paradigm in psychology. We had most of the conference in E17 and the NLT in Gaskell campus, but our evening talk with Valerie was held in Raffles Hotel, a decaying building just round the corner from Hathersage Road on Upper Brook Street. We suspected there would be trouble when a Mr Wedgewood turned up on the first morning of the conference. A thin grey and grey-haired balding man in his early 60s, he wore a brown suit, perhaps the only suit in the conference, and he told me as he registered that he wanted to see what the enemy was up to. When I asked him what he meant by that, he said that he was concerned that psychology as a scientific discipline was being undermined, and that he saw this new interest in 'discourse' as particularly worrying. In the question time after papers during the day he intervened making the same point, asking for hard evidence for the claims, and disputing any evidence that was offered in reply. In the early sessions the students giving papers were rattled by this, but as the day wore on they realised that nothing anyone said would satisfy him. These disruptions did make chairing the conference sessions difficult though, and by the evening people were rather fed up with it.

At the evening session in Raffles, Valerie talked about origins of recent discourse research, and she described key ideas in *Changing the Subject*, the influence of Marxist and feminist ideas, and the role of post-structuralist and psychoanalytic theory. These were four theoretical strands that informed our work in the Discourse Unit, though it was clear that people made their own combinations as appropriate. By no means was everyone in the Discourse Unit a Marxist, though I still was, and we had some fractious discussions in E16 over whether we needed all four theoretical frameworks, or needed other approaches too. Mr Wedgewood bided his time, and then, when Valerie had finished, stood up and read from pages of notes complaining about this new-fangled nonsense, "this was no better than unscientific quack medicine with no real basis in experimental studies", and so he rambled on as the audience sighed and groaned, some exasperated and some amused. He got to the point in his intervention where he said that the question we needed to think about was "whether we want to be scientists or quacks". The audience quickly responded with "quack, quack quack", quacking, first hesitantly as one or two people took it up, and then almost the whole audience quacked until he sat down. We weren't sure afterwards whether this was an example of popular power or mob rule, but it did the trick, and Mr Wedgewood didn't return for the next day of the conference.

The same strategy couldn't be used to deal with Charles Antaki when he took up the role of external examiner for our psychology degree. It had seemed like a good idea to appoint him to the role at the time but turned out to be very problematic. Charles objected to what he saw as 'loose' criteria in qualitative research final year dissertations and wanted to lower all the marks for those dissertations by a full grade, something that would have had disastrous consequences for the final degree of the students concerned. Carolyn Kagan was in tears beforehand. This was a moment when the department came together to support the students. We managed to get the examination board to agree a procedure by which the marks were effectively taken as if they had not been lowered by the external examiner, and Charles sat glumly as we went through the marks and eventually agreed the final degree grades. Terence McLaughlin, one of our postgraduate students in the Discourse Unit who was doing some teaching, attended this dramatic examination board, and told us that Charles had showed him during one of the breaks how to get rid of the sweat from shirt armpits by manoeuvring the men's toilet hand-drier to blow in the right places.

1992 was the anniversary of the 'discovery' of the Americas by Christopher Columbus, and we commemorated it with a November Saturday conference called '500 Years of Resistance' which focused on the legacy of colonialism and racism in psychology. The speakers included Suman Fernando, a radical psychiatrist who had produced some sharp critiques of the way the mental health system addressed questions of culture. Liam Greenslade, who turned up late with Valerie Walkerdine, spoke about the way mental health services in Britain targeted Irish people – an ethnic group that has almost as great over-representation in mental hospitals as the Black community – and argued that they would be better off if they were not represented in the hospitals at all, if there were no specialist services for them.

And, lo, the Research Assessment Exercise was upon us, the 1992 RAE, and those who had registered details of articles which were published in peer-refereed journals were rewarded, eventually. The distribution of funding came first to the institution and it was then funnelled down to the subject areas that had submitted research. The process was even slower because university charter status had been granted to the polytechnics in September, and so the new Manchester Metropolitan University, MMU, was trying to configure itself as a research as well as teaching institution. It had slipped out from City Council control as part of a covert privatisation measure in higher education, and from the Council for National Academic Awards which were previously responsible for accrediting degree provision. There was confusion in Manchester for the next year over the change in name, not least by the attempt of the old university up on Oxford Road to differentiate itself from the 'Metropolitan' university by retrieving and using its own original name, the 'Victoria' university. One glitch in the name change and the old university's response to it was that, partly because the names for the rival institutions were associated with the London Underground Metropolitan and Victoria lines, some student applicants assumed that it was this new 'Victoria' university that was the old poly, and that MMU was the old university.

So slow and tentative was the funding, discussed and ratified at each level of our new university that the Discourse Unit, which, to be honest, most of the time comprised Erica and me, wasn't sure when we could be certain enough to celebrate the rumours and then promises that we two would get 0.425, nearly half of our contractual teaching time 'bought out' by the RAE money so we could carry out research and publish more journal articles for the next research assessment exercise. By the time we knew for certain, which was later in 1993, Deb had got her PhD with Valerie as external examiner, and the co-edited book of our 1991 conference, *Discourse Analytic Research*, had been published. We didn't function as a tight-knit research group like the 'family' based at the Autonomous University in Barcelona, and we had no official status within our own new university, and still no funds to bring over international visitors for conferences.

We didn't have funding to invite speakers to the Discourse Unit or for travel. Visits overseas we paid for ourselves or they were paid by host departments and conferences that invited us to speak. Funding for travel was also often difficult for colleagues from other countries to get hold of. The next, and it was the last, time we saw Mili from Puerto Rico was at the ISTP conference in France in 1993 where lack of financial support for colleagues from outside the old colonial centres was a real issue. Mili was on the editorial board of *Theory & Psychology*, a journal linked to the ISTP, and was very aggrieved that they had not found some money to support her to get over to Europe. Heidi and Mili were speaking in our symposium at the conference when Hank Stam, editor of *Theory & Psychology* came into the back of the room. Mili left Heidi to carry on speaking while she got up and stalked around to the back of the room to deal with Hank, to resign from the editorial board in protest. She then returned to her place at the front table to join us again, hissing with satisfaction "mission accomplished".

Back home, we slowly built the Discourse Unit as a research base. We had visitors who asked us how we set up the Discourse Unit, and we showed them the print-out of a leaflet from the Amstrad. Sometimes they were disappointed; they even felt deceived when we could not show them the purpose-built office block that they assumed was our dedicated home. We often sat together in E16 with our new postgraduate students, Brenda Goldberg and Terence McLaughlin, who were also funded by this new deal RAE money, and then with others who joined us in the 1990s, wondering what alternative name we might choose that best described what we had in common. We had taken our cue from the 'turn to discourse', but already the approach was being incorporated into the discipline, turned into a methodological approach rather than a critique. We were stuck now with this discourse, with this 'discourse discourse' that had become part of the story we learnt to tell others in order to explain to them who we were.

We were still teaching psychology, but with a twist, with a little distance from its truth claims, and with a little more space to do something different. This opened the way to questions about research that could not only be 'discursive' but also be 'critical', and the Discourse Unit connected more explicitly during this period of research with other traditions of 'critical psychology' that were often more certain about what they were doing than we were. The next part of the book, the next four chapters, traces some of our strange encounters with other traditions of critical research, some of which attempted to break the boundaries between academics, professionals and users of psychology services. That is the part of the journey that eventually led me to call myself a critical psychologist.

PART IV

Going critical

13

DEVELOPMENT

Cults and discourse units

In which we encounter groups more tightly organised than the Discourse Unit, and discover a radical take on the work of Russian psychologist Lev Vygotsky. We explore the way that 'cult' phenomena draw people in and the way outsiders spawn a psychological discourse which misleads everyone about what is going on, including about the relationship between sex and power inside institutions.

In this part of the book I take you into the world of critical psychological research, and that necessarily means reflecting on how we position ourselves in relation to institutions that operate, sometimes competitively, on the same terrain. I will describe how the institutional constraints on research take on a peculiar form when they are infused with psychological discourse, when they are populated by and resisted by those who wield psychology as a weapon. In different ways the following four chapters also tackle the boundaries that divide academic psychologists from those they want to speak to and work with, and you will notice a tension between how we 'critical' people define ourselves inside the academic world and how people in the world outside try to define themselves. We begin in this chapter with the Discourse Unit and work through some surprising connections with group psychology and psychotherapy.

Groups

The Discourse Unit from 1990 was a space where students could reflect on their discontent with mainstream psychology and find alternative theoretical frameworks. For some of us it was also a place to link these theoretical frameworks with political critique of the discipline, even to turn from discussing radical concepts to action, either as action research or as political change. That connection between psychology and politics was contentious in discourse analysis, including among our own students, and we each had different political allegiances. These competing allegiances surfaced from time to time as we discussed the importance of class and 'race' in structuring theories of personality, 'intelligence' or social relationships, for example, or of gender as playing a role not only in theories of psychology but also methodology, how research should be carried out.

I carried out interviews with discourse researchers in other universities who were members of different 'DARGs'. What this acronym DARG had in common was that 'D' stood for 'Discourse' and 'G' stood for 'Group'; the 'A' was the little link word 'and'. I wanted to draw out what the consequences might be for the way the researchers thought about what they did when the 'R' stood for 'Reflexivity', as it did at the York University, 'Rhetoric' at Loughborough University, 'Representation' at the Open University, or, very briefly, 'Resistance' in our own DARG in Manchester before we transformed it into the Discourse Unit. I wrote a paper 'DARG! Putting Discourse on the Map' which was going to be the first chapter of my 1992 book *Discourse Dynamics*, and circulated the paper to my interviewees for comment in the different places who were, in addition to Erica Burman who I interviewed in Manchester, Malcolm Ashmore at York, Jonathan Potter at Loughborough and Margaret Wetherell at the Open University.

They didn't like it. Margaret commented that I had marked the hesitations in speech in the bits of the interview transcript in the 'rival' groups to my own DARG more harshly, she felt, to make the others look more stupid; Malcolm and Margaret both wondered why I wanted to 'reify' the groups, covering over the differences of perspective within them. I treated the 'R'-word in each case as a signifier that pretended to sum up what each member of the group thought, as if for each and every one of them the term 'reflexivity', 'rhetoric', 'representation' or 'resistance' meant the same thing. Even within the 'structuralist' or 'post-structuralist' terms in which I was couching my analysis, there was a problem in the way I was going about this, for when we trace the connections between signifiers we cannot thereby deduce what 'signified' or concept or, even less so, what thought inside the individual head really is attached to it. Margaret also pointed out that I was effectively marginalising those researchers doing discourse analysis who were working independently of these four so-called competing traditions of research. She was right.

Jonathan objected that by bringing these differences between the DARGs to the surface I would be giving ammunition to the old paradigm laboratory-experimental psychologists, that now that discourse analysis was starting to make some headway in the discipline, I should not "rock the boat". My pretend 'genealogy' of the different strands of discourse research was, he said, "more Rob Farr than Michel Foucault", a reminder of how I had ended up doing something very close to the traditional ways of writing history carried out by Farr while he was making the argument in Britain for Serge Moscovici's studies of 'social representations'. I got the message, and pulled the chapter from *Discourse Dynamics*. It has never been published. But the process of carrying out the interviews and assembling the chapter and then discussing it in the Discourse Unit did draw attention to the way that a 'group' of researchers can take on a reality for those who are members of it, and, in a very different way, function for those who are outside the group and who feel threatened by it. Psychological discourse generally is suspicious of group phenomena, and routinely warns us against 'mob' and 'cult' mentality, effectively promoting an equally fictional image of the robust individual who depends on no one.

Research into 'group psychology' goes back to before the discipline was founded, feeding on fears that individuals in large groups or crowds could be overtaken by some strange phenomena and lose their minds. The main historical reference is still Gustave Le Bon's classic book *The Crowd: A Study of the Popular Mind* which drew on the author's own experiences as an ambulance driver working for the government forces during the 1871 Paris Commune. Le Bon came from an aristocratic family and was already hostile to the attempts of the commune to take the city under democratic control, and he was busy for years afterwards warning that people in crowds become reduced to the psychological level of savages, women and children. The book is a marvellous expression of popular fear of crowds and of the threat they pose to private property, and of the intimate link in emerging psychological discourse between racist and sexist ideas which infantilise people who protest against unjust conditions and would work collectively to change them.

Some of the first experiments in psychology were devoted to examining the influence of others on the work of an individual, the most bizarre of which flourished in the 'social facilitation' research of Bob Zajonc in the US. Zajonc and his co-workers carried out experiments on cockroaches running up little corridors alone or in the presence of their friends, experiments which purported to show that even animals with no higher mental functions could be susceptible to the effect of the social on their individual behaviour. US psychologists studied phenomena they identified and named 'group think' and 'risky shift' that also occurred in groups. A whole raft of social psychology experiments conveyed the message that other people were bad for you, unless taken in moderate doses, even buttressing the suspicion that the 'social' bit of our lives was necessarily problematic. If others got a 'foot in the door', as one strand of experimental research had it, then it would all end badly. When psychologists did countenance 'social' activity as something positive, it was at the reduced level of interpersonal relationships, they were still very suspicious of collective behaviour. Groups were bad enough, and organised groups were worse.

I soon came up against a group that was much more tightly organised than ours. That encounter drove home how powerful psychological categories are when they are used to discredit ideas that challenge the status quo. I had come across a journal published in New York called *Practice* while searching for alternative approaches to psychology. The subtitle for the journal, *The Journal of Politics, Economics, Psychology, Sociology & Culture*, was promising, but we couldn't work out exactly what the 'social therapy' it often referred to was. We wanted to find out, and in June 1991, just before our discourse analysis conference in Manchester, Erica and I were able to visit New York en route to the International Society for Theoretical Psychology biennial conference which was being held at Clark University in Massachusetts. We made contact with Lois Holzman, a developmental psychologist involved with the journal. She invited us to come and visit the new Castillo Cultural Center where the Institute for Social Therapy was based near Greenwich Village.

We prepared by reading material produced by the group, including an important article originally published in *Practice* in 1983 called 'Tools and results: Understanding, explaining and meaning (three sides of one dialectical coin)' which was co-authored by Lois under her previous-married name Lois Hood, and Fred Newman. Hood and Newman begin the article with the provocative statement that 'while social therapy is Marxist, it is not socialist', and then unroll a complex contradictory argument for, not only a new kind of therapy but also for a theory of psychology that aims to transcend the opposition between the individual and the social. One of their key theoretical resources was the work of the Russian developmental psychologist Lev Vygotsky. Many of the later articles in *Practice* and other publications produced by the social therapists insisted that Vygotsky was misunderstood by the Western psychologists who translated and wrote about him. In fact, they argued, to describe Vygotsky as a developmental psychologist already misrepresents the radical account of personal and social change that he was developing in Russia in the 1920s. What that description 'developmental psychologist' does is to reduce what he was doing to psychological categories. This problem of reductionism was something Erica pointed to in her own writing, and at length in *Deconstructing Developmental Psychology* which was already starting to take shape; it was a caution that applied to much developmental theory in the psychology textbooks.

In the psychology textbooks the Piagetian account of childhood development is usually set out as a complete psychological theory, which Piaget never intended it to be, and, in the process, other aspects of Piaget's work are screened out. The fact that Piaget trained as a psychoanalyst and was a member of Freud's International Psychoanalytical Association is rarely if ever mentioned, as is his active membership of Christian Socialist organisations. Instead, Piaget is portrayed as if he really did believe that the stage of 'formal operational' thinking was the highest stage of cognitive development, and that Swiss children were the most advanced in the world because they had attained that 'stage'. Piaget is often seen by psychologists as a theorist who prioritised thought over language, as if it is the internal cognitive processes that then enable the child to speak, while Vygotsky is assumed to prioritise language, to assume that children develop their cognitive processes from hearing others speak and then by speaking themselves, including about themselves. Now it became clear that Vygotsky was also badly misunderstood in the psychology textbooks, texts that made it seem as if his own theory of the relationship between thought and language was a developmental theory of temporal sequences that could then be pitted against Piaget's. Rom Harré knew this was wrong.

For the social therapists in New York, Vygotsky provided a new way of conceptualising thought as something that was always already bound up with *practice*, hence the name of their journal. A child, they argued, does not learn by turning the language around it into thought, internalising and then perfecting that inside their head. Instead they develop through participating in Zones of Proximal Development, ZPD, and that development continues in different kinds of ZPD throughout life. Vygotsky died in 1934, perhaps lucky to escape the worst ravages of the Stalinist bureaucracy in the Soviet Union, not subjected to the purges and show-trials suffered by many of his colleagues. But that also meant that it was possible for Soviet psychologists to sanitise his Marxist account of development as entailing personal and social trans-formation, to turn Vygotsky into a proper psychologist in the years after his death. Hood and Newman focus on that sanitising process in the English-speaking world carried out by psychologists who discovered Vygotsky in the early 1960s. Those social therapists, in contrast, wanted to retrieve what was most radical, most authenti-cally Marxist about Vygotsky's work, and to do this in order to produce, not a form of psychology but an alternative to psychology. So, there are objections in their 1983 article on 'tools and results', to the 'dualism' that runs through all of psychology, including in the misrepresentations of Vygotsky's work by psychologists.

Dualistic psychology separates the individual from the social, and this runs alongside dualistic separation between cognition and practical understanding. Social therapy for Hood and Newman is a particular kind of dialectical method that aims to overcome that separation. For them, Marxist method is neither simply a 'tool' which will enable the researcher to open up reality or open up the head of an individual to discover 'cognitions' or thoughts going on inside it, nor is it the 'result' of empirical research so we can tell everyone what we have found out about human beings. Instead, this method is, in Vygotsky's own phrase, simultaneously a 'tool-and-result'. Psychology is not really about what people think, and neither should it be. The social therapist does not tell people how to think or how to man-age their lives so they can be happier – 'happier' as the psychologists understand the meaning of the term – and neither do they encourage their clients to delve into their own heads to discover thoughts and feelings that are responsible for making them unhappy. For Hood and Newman, and for the Institute for Social Therapy, it is the process of change itself that is the key to Marxism, Marxist method as tool-and-result. This is also why it is not 'socialist', for that would imply that the end point of the process could be predicted and controlled by an expert who defines what it is to be happy with reference to a particular kind of ideological content – socialism as one example here – content that they thought they could inject into the cognitive processes of those they treated. Toward the end of the article, Hood and Newman also make connections between these radical Vygotskyan perspectives and Wittgenstein's critique of thoughts as if they are things in the head like beetles inside a matchbox; this critique helps people to learn in social therapy something about 'the social character of their emotionality' instead of engaging in 'conscious-ness raising' or other cognitivist strategies of so-called radical therapy. Against the promise to provide a theory about 'psychology', the social therapists provided a different kind of space in which people could break from psychological prescrip-tions for what makes them happy and create or 'develop' something in the ZPD of a social therapy group. The 1983 Hood and Newman article, as well as the other things we read about social therapy, raised more questions for us about what they actually did in practice.

The Castillo Cultural Center was on the first floor of a refurbished block on Greenwich Street, and while we waited in the main foyer we watched videos of Fred Newman speaking on the monitors that hung from the ceiling, read poems written by Fred on the walls, and looked at his paintings in the side gallery area. The Center contained a theatre space which put on plays written by and directed by Fred Newman. We met Lois Holzman who showed us around the Center, and then we met Fred. We also met Bette Braun who had trained as a psychoanalytical psychotherapist in a broadly 'object-relations' tradition – that is, an approach that took early relationships between the child and its care-givers as seriously as unconscious fantasy – and who was a key figure for the Institute in brokering accreditation with local education authorities. Bette was responsible for the therapy training programme at the Institute. We travelled to Harlem further north in Manhattan where we met Barbara Taylor, a member of the Institute for Social Therapy who ran the Barbara Taylor School. This school was run as what the social therapists called a "zeepeedee", in line with Vygotsky's ideas, even though he had never used that exact phrase 'Zone of Proximal Development' himself. Barbara took us to a community meeting and talent show project hosted by the clinical psychologist Lenora Fulani, and we saw her working with black youth, telling them at one point in no uncertain terms, for example, that taking drugs was "dumb dumb dumb". Lenora ran as a candidate in US Presidential elections for Fred's own political party, the New Alliance Party.

I gave a talk one evening at the Castillo Cultural Center which raised the question as to why there was such emphasis on Vygotsky in the social therapy literature, someone who was clearly not a Stalinist, but silence about Trotsky who had explicitly opposed Stalin. It was a mischievous talk, for by now I knew that Fred's outfit had its origins back in encounter group politics in 1968 as Centers for Change and that it operated for many years as a Maoist group called the International Workers Party with, as its name suggests, global ambitions before officially dissolving but carrying on as what Fred himself referred to in our meetings as a 'core collective'. Maoists, as a rule, dislike Trotskyists, viewing them as counterrevolutionary. There was silence at the end of my talk, and the audience tentatively commented that I had raised some interesting points. Someone eventually wondered aloud if Fred had any thoughts. Fred, who had been sitting in silence at the back of the room, took over the discussion in the friendliest possible way – "I want to share this with you" kind of thing – rehearsing why Vygotsky was so important. The key to Vygotsky's work, he said, was not the theorist, or the tool, or the result, but the method we wanted to build together. At the end of a long day, and after more discussions about social therapy, Mary Fridley interviewed us in the group therapy room for a piece that was published soon after in the New Alliance Party newspaper. It was well after midnight. We were jet-lagged. It was an exhausting debriefing. We noticed there was a circle of chairs and one bigger chair in the centre. We were told by Mary that it was Fred's.

This was our first time in the United States, and it was difficult to disentangle what struck us as so strange about the social therapists from a more general culture-shock. I expected to hate New York, the heartland of imperialism, but it was a vibrant place, more immediately communicative perhaps than British society; a bustling lively to-and-fro of banter and busyness on the streets and in the stores that contrasted with the more polite, restrained, even distanced etiquette we were used to at home. The social therapists told us that the reason most people didn't give to good causes was because no one asked them, and so the social therapists made it their business to go ask. We saw rows of activists in the Castillo Cultural Center on phone-banks calling for donations, and this noisy pushy operation was as disturbing as it was inspiring. Yes, we were told, Fred is pushy, and we have to be pushy too if we are going to bring about change. This was the United States. It wasn't easy to make sense of all this. Things didn't get easier when we tried to triangulate our observations of the social therapists at work with other people we trusted.

The other accounts we got from those outside social therapy didn't function as any kind of reality check. Instead they muddled the picture we had even more. We went to the Pathfinder bookstore of one of the longest-standing left organisations in New York and spoke to activists there. They were tired, worn out, and they were hostile to what they referred to as the 'Newman Group'. What seemed to annoy them more than anything else was that the Newman Group was successful while they were failing. We spoke to other US-based developmental psychologists like John Broughton who was one of the co-editors of the Routledge Critical Psychology series. He told us that they were dangerous, and that they destroyed everything they touched; we should steer clear of them, and we should beware their attempts to 'recruit' us or to enable them to expand into the UK. I talked to the historian of psychology Ben Harris who told me that they were a 'cult', and that we should not view them as Marxists.

These were warnings we wanted to heed from people we trusted, but surely this outright hostility also needed to be weighed up. The social therapists touched a nerve. We were intrigued but kept them at arm's length. They did want us to provide contacts for them and set up meetings, and we did sometimes do that. This included arranging one bizarre meeting in Manchester in July 1993 for which Fred was driven up in a huge shiny limousine from his apartment in Park Lane in one of the wealthiest parts of London. They invited us to other closed meetings in New York which reviewed the history of their group and open conferences in Long Island and White Plains, at one of which Fred told me he loved me, which was nice. But we didn't deliver what they wanted. We wouldn't build social therapy for them in Britain, and that was always disappointing to them. Our refusal confirmed to them, I think, that we were, underneath it all, underneath our radical critique of psychology, still treating them as a psychologist would, assessing what they did and trying to work out what they really thought. Instead of launching ourselves into their method as 'tool-and-result' we wanted to work out what the conceptual tools were that they were using and what the results would be. We didn't get it.

Sex

I wrote a long 'evaluation' of social therapy which I published in 1995 as '"Right", said Fred "I'm too sexy for bourgeois group therapy"', a joke they never got. I should have told them that the British band 'Right Said Fred' had a 1991 hit with a song called 'I'm Too Sexy', which included the plaint that the singer was too sexy for his shirt, "so sexy it hurts". In one of the interviews with Lois I asked her why their group, a leftist group, seemed to have one powerful man at its centre. She replied by asking me if I could name a leftist group that did not. I asked about some of the accusations that Fred had many sexual partners in the Institute and predecessor organisations, and what that said about his power as a man. She replied by saying that they had written openly about that in their journals, and she asked what it was about sex that was so special, what there was about it that made it function in bourgeois society as if it were "the bottom line". Lois wrote a tetchy reply called '"Wrong", said Fred', and things went quiet on that front for a few years.

They were not, I think, a 'cult'. When people left the 'Newman Group' they sometimes wrote bitter accounts of how they had wasted years of their lives promoting social therapy, and the same kind of angry regret can be found among ex-followers of any and every disappointing discarded belief system. People gave the group money and time because they wanted to believe and did so willingly. There is no evidence that the Newmanites ever physically prevented anyone from leaving. The term 'cult' is a lazy psychological way of dismissing the ideas of a group that an outsider strongly disagrees with. To understand what a cult is, rather than look at the group that is targeted with that word, it is worth looking first at those who use the word as a term of abuse. The word cult doesn't help us understand what people are really thinking, but the word does function as a powerful signifier as part of a discourse, a political discourse which makes it seem as if you are safe in your little private self and that groups are bad for you. You could just as well say that the Discourse Unit was a cult because many people spent years of their lives reading and writing and producing a PhD thesis, and that they were only then able to escape the cult and get an academic job, or do something better with their lives. Or, why not, you could say that about universities which draw people in with the promise of a career and then demand that you devote your waking lives to their own teaching, research and funding agendas.

The five years from 1990 to 1995 saw a number of political debates in the department of psychology. At the beginning of the 1990 academic year there were strikes called by our union NATFHE over a significant change in teaching contracts which followed the reorganisation of the Polytechnic as a body financially and politically separate from Manchester City Council. There were only two of us – me and Carolyn Kagan – on the picket line at the main entrance to the Elizabeth Gaskell campus on 22 November when the news came through that Margaret Thatcher had resigned as Prime Minister. Three years earlier Thatcher had given an interview to *Woman's Own* magazine in which she declared that "There is no such thing as society", insisted that "There is no such thing! There are individual men and women and there are families". That declaration operated as an implicit, and sometimes explicit, background assumption in much political-economic government policy under the Conservatives.

There had been increasing suspicion of collective decision-making or accountability in Britain and a focus, instead, on the activities of individuals who were expected to take responsibility for themselves and their own family, for each and every aspect of their lives. This attempt to erase society and replace it with individual responsibility was evident in different aspects of social policy. Section 28 of the 1988 Local Government Act, for example, prohibited teachers from 'promoting', as it put it, 'the acceptability of homosexuality as a pretended family relationship'. The aim of Section 28 was both to shore up the heterosexual family as an essential social unit and to put pressure on individual teachers who risked being sanctioned if they pointed out that heterosexual coupling was not the only option. Local authorities, support organisations, including those working around HIV/AIDS, and also individual teachers were thus induced to censor themselves. There were national demonstrations, and large protest marches against Section 28 through the centre of Manchester, where there was a thriving 'gay village'. There were no prosecutions under the new Act, and it was repealed in 2003, but it marked a split between collective activity to defend the rights of different communities to organise themselves and some sense of 'society' on the one hand, and, on the other, a retreat into thinking about human beings only as individuals separate from each other with responsibility only for their own families.

Psychology as a discipline benefitted from the Thatcher years, and applications increased for places on the degree course as a new generation of students appeared who thought of themselves as being separate individuals rather than as members of society. Correspondingly, the psychology degree expanded, with a huge increase in student numbers leading to some small increase in teaching staff. Paradoxically, the size of the teaching groups at undergraduate level meant that the atmosphere in class was less 'personal' even while students were told to address 'personal' issues in the Interpersonal Skills Workshops, which they often resented. At a postgraduate level there were smaller classes and we were able to address questions of subjectivity and reflexivity linked to research, and this meant that the obligatory 'presentations' of student work did have a different feel, sometimes more playful and ironic, able to satirise as well as work with the demand to be more 'personal'. These were the first signs of neoliberalism in everyday life and in the academic institutions. The shift from local authority control to being an independent corporate body was beginning to pitch the Polytechnic into the free market where it had to compete with other teaching and research institutions. This was in some ways a return to the economic liberalism that had seen Manchester grow rapidly as an industrial centre as a key player in the burgeoning capitalist economy of the nineteenth century. Rolling back the state now not only meant a return to those days, to a century when there was little public health or welfare or education provision, but it also intensified individualism, it told people that they should turn their backs on their communities and stand on their own two feet. Psychology today is neoliberal.

These changes energised psychologists in our department who had always valued individual attainment and been suspicious of those of us who spoke about the importance of group activity, membership of communities or participation in society. This was one of the reasons why it was so difficult to get them to join the union, let alone go on strike to defend their collective interests. The changes also put pressure on those of us who organised together inside the department, and, friendly though the debate often was, it boiled down to an accusation that we on the 'social' or 'qualitative' side were not respecting the right of individual students to strive or take decisions for themselves. One instance of this was the worry by the more traditional psychologists that tackling racism would increase the power of the Orwellian Erica and Ian thought police in the department as an arm of the local authority. Another was the claim that women students taking Erica's third year Psychology of Women option were, as a result, organising themselves as a group against the rest of the department, claims that circulated at one point in the complaint that the option was effectively operating as "a witches' coven". Individual women students were even contacted by one male member of staff by phone at home to see if they had any complaints about the way the option was taught that might be aired in a course committee.

After the sociologists Bob Anderson and Dave Francis were excluded from the psychology degree – a decision which was as much to do with the internal privatisation of the Poly in which different departments, including the library, were configured as separate 'cost centres' as ideological disagreements over their focus on the social over the individual – Carolyn Kagan took charge of this teaching and creatively reconstructed it as a new course called 'Societal Psychology'. This laid the basis for taught modules devoted to community psychology which she put her energies into after we both abandoned our attempts to keep the local union branch in the department going. Her hope was that in this way social problems could be addressed through psychology, and she was still hoping that there might be a forum in the department, even, under her leadership, of the department itself at some point, where a different kind of psychology could redeem itself. The department had, after all, and even despite some internal conflicts, maintained itself as a space where we could talk things through. Even those who referred to the Psychology of Women option as a witches' coven calmed down.

Dogs

One day Carolyn came into my office very upset, shocked by something one of the students had told her, that the 'boundary' between staff and students had been broken; some of the male staff, it seemed, had been sleeping with students. The student had apparently not told Erica because they suspected that her feminist reaction would be too harsh, indicative of how this situation induces a sense of pathology in everyone involved, and so the student had confided in another female lecturer instead who then relayed the news to Carolyn. The toxic question as to whether a 'relationship' was traded for better essay marks was alive in discussions about what was going on, among staff and among students. Perhaps the exchange between lecturer and student was indirect, but the effects on the other students were quite evident. All of our relationships in the department were affected, including between students and between staff. One thing she had been sure about, Carolyn said, or thought she was sure about, was that, unlike many other academic departments where this kind of behaviour was rife, it didn't happen here. That's what I told you earlier in this book. Yes, there had been a few cases in the department before I had arrived, I was told. There were stories about serial offenders, according to which women students would be seen crying outside this lecturer's office door after he moved on to a younger newer companion, but this guy had left. But since then, no, it was impossible.

The problem was not so much that sex was traded for grades, but that, as the rumours spread around the student group, all of the other students suspected that preference was being showed to some students over others. This was not only a breach of trust about fair treatment but it also threw some of the power relations in the department into relief, power for men as a group of lecturers and an attempt by women as students to individually get access to that power. Carolyn and other women lecturers asked around. One culprit who had complained about the witches' coven was shameless and shifty about what was going on. The main offender, otherwise a nice student-centred lecturer, naively insisted that it was a real relationship he had forged, not an exploitative one. That could be dealt with at least by ensuring that he did not mark this student's coursework or exam scripts. But the inquiries led to a sadder series of revelations, to the story that one of the women students had begun the first year of the course by telling her friends that she wanted to know which of the lecturers was single and so who she should focus on to get into a relationship with and so then get a good degree. The story could have been a fantasy circulating among the students, speaking more of rivalries and jealousies than anything more sinister, but suddenly the personal and political dimensions of academic and institutional life were connecting in alarming ways. The story focused less on male power than manipulative femininity.

Whether or not that story was true, it led to the accusation that a key figure in the examination board process was involved. One lecturer was made the scapegoat – it was convenient for everybody, especially psychologists, to locate the problem in one individual – he was confronted, and he admitted it, insisting that it didn't affect either the marks he gave or the treatment of the student in the exam board. An emergency meeting of the course committee, and then the examination board, decided to exclude him from these meetings. The student concerned did eventually finish her degree, and soon after ended her relationship with the lecturer, and the lecturer left the department to join another university outside Manchester. The 'boundary' issue was resolved by enforcing the rules concerning fairness and neutrality in marking and examinations, but with a cost, which was that it became more difficult from then on to discuss particular student problems and to take personal circumstances into account when deciding on final degree grades. The examination board from then on acted less as a collective decision-making body than as a committee ratifying collections of individual results in which the students were referred to by number rather than name. That is, a political problem about the relationship between gender and power was dealt with bureaucratically, and the rational ordered process of deciding grades then excluded discussion of things we knew about the lives of those we were assessing.

A first reaction to the revelations by some other male staff was to say that perhaps it wasn't the case that a relationship necessarily corrupted teaching and assessment, that perhaps it was an innocent liaison. It was always possible, another argued, that a liaison between a lecturer and a student could lead to what they described as "a normal healthy relationship". Others complained that they were "just being friendly", and that some of us were bringing the shutters down between staff and students in the name of respecting boundaries. They were just being friendly, and yet again the thought police was looming over them. Already, they pointed out, the good old days, when staff and students would work together on the Christmas pantomime or drink the bar dry at the end of the year when there was a separate bar in the campus leading off the staff office quadrangle, were over. What we were doing, those of us on the 'social' side of the department, was treating the students as if they were children, and we should, instead, treat them as adult human beings who could decide for themselves when and where to have relationships with whomsoever they liked. Some of us on the more social and feminist side of the argument began to refer to the little pack of unrepentant male lecturers who defended their rights to enjoy the women students as the 'the dogs'.

We still all got on well most of the time. I gave two of the dogs a karaoke cassette tape of Sinatra's 'New York, New York' because they liked to sing it at the terrible Christmas pantomime events that I avoided. They were nice guys one by one, but we imagined them roaming the corridors, their tongues hanging out as they waited for fresh meat to arrive at the beginning of each academic year. You will notice once again how women are often sidelined in the psychology departments I describe; this is a reflection of the dominant position men are accorded in the discipline, and I know I risk reproducing that in my own narrative. It was, no doubt about it, easier for me as another boy to maintain these relationships across the sub-disciplinary and personal-political boundaries in the department through matey banter. Identity, as a man or as a psychologist, is not so easy to disavow in this kind of context.

One of the more bizarre aspects of the affair was where the argument about 'boundaries' was turned around by the dogs, and they identified the real threat as itself being something collective that restricted their own individual freedom as well as the freedom of individual students. Surely, they argued, if we were going to prohibit relationships between staff and students on the basis that it might lead to unfair treatment, we should also prohibit relationships between staff. The main target here, of course, was Erica and Ian, seen by many in the department to be operating as a 'unit'. The two of us had already ensured that we did not double-mark each other's student work, but these events did increase the pressure on us to defend what we were doing. It also meant that meetings of the Discourse Unit were treated with more suspicion. Another consequence of the problem with the dogs, the way it erupted and the way it was solved, was that Carolyn's grumblings about departmental management became sharper, and complaints about 'lack of leadership' were becoming more bitter and personalised. The complaint that we were a 'unit' chimed both with a particular suspicion of groups threatening the implicit shared culture of the department, and a general suspicion of shared collective activity that psychology as a discipline elaborates in its fear of 'cults'. We were still a group inside a group, a situation that was about to change dramatically as we began to also operate across different departments and then as a 'trans-disciplinary' and 'trans-institutional' research network.

You need to remember, and we could never forget it, that each and every institutional and political issue we had encountered and were to encounter was framed by the discipline of psychology's insistence that it knew the difference between good and bad behaviour and could trace that to normal and abnormal development, personality, and ways of thinking about the self and others. That arrogant reductive endeavour can take on very unpleasant forms, as we will see in the next chapter when we turn to still prevalent conceptions of pathology and how it should be put right.

14

PSYCHIATRY

On the campus

In which we move beyond academic psychology to the domain of distress and treatment, and we discover how clinical psychology and psychiatry work together to treat our responses to difficulties of living as something pathological. We also learn how patients are organising themselves locally and internationally to demand not only better treatment but completely different theories and services.

I cannot pretend that I was ever anything but an academic psychologist based in an academic institution with all the privileges that brings. That gave me a particular vantage point from which to view how psychologists, whether they were educational or clinical psychologists, attempted to put their theories in to practice. Teaching and supervising students in those domains made me all the more convinced that to move over the academic-professional boundary would be a mistake, that I would, if anything, be more compromised than I was already. I stayed put in the university, trying to learn about connections with psychological practice there, and making the resources I had available to those who were trying to challenge psychology in the outside world. This chapter is about some attempts to do that.

Construction

We will hover here now in July 1995 for a moment so we can take stock and look back over some dramatic challenges to the way that psychologists deal with mental health, with problems of living that they now try to resolve into 'wellness'. This was how I learnt not only how bad things were in the psy complex, but also about some of the astonishing attempts to make things better. We are in the main hall in MMU Gaskell Campus. It is getting late on a Saturday afternoon. Unusually for Manchester, it is a warm sunny day, and inside the hall battle is taking place between supporters of two different spiritualist churches. The argument revolves around whether the voices of spirits should be seen as always accompanying a person who has the special gift to hear them, or whether the voices only appear at times of spiritual crisis. The audience is transfixed. The protagonists have clearly had this kind of argument many times before, and the stakes for them are not so much over who is right – mostly they agree that the voices should not be viewed as a problem as such – but as to whose church will prevail. This is a battle of institutions, apart from providing unexpected afternoon entertainment. There is a lesson for all of us about the relationship between theory and power.

Many of us are beginning to wonder if this should be seen as the high point of the day, the culmination of the conference as we had hoped, or as the moment when everything we had carefully arranged is beginning to disintegrate. It is an important debate that resonated through the conference, one which is now being inflected through the question of spiritualism, as to whether people who hear voices were spiritually inclined or not. The key question really is whether the voices we seem to hear in our heads are 'normal', part of our everyday experience, or whether they are the sign of something out of the ordinary, of a crisis of some kind or a turning point in our lives. The danger is that this kind of opposition, between what is normal and abnormal, can lock us very quickly back into an opposition between wellness and sickness. For some people who are labelled as schizophrenic after saying they hear voices, things may well lead to them being locked up.

Because I helped to organise the conference I feel responsible for this mess. The day does seem to be disintegrating, but I've been here before, been at these kind of events, and what feels disastrous, chaotic disagreement and almost complete break-down of communication, is often a sign that something at least has changed on the terrain of the debate. That's what we aimed to do at this conference, to change the terrain of the debate, to make it into a place where we could together work through the 'deconstruction' of experiences that had been constructed for us by the discourses of medical psychiatry and reconstructed by psychologists with much the same archi-tecture. Some new voices are emerging to argue against the ones that are usually dominant, against the voices that speak loudest and condemn everyone else to silence, at best, or even consign them to 'madness'. In his book *Madness and Civilization* the historian Michel Foucault had argued that the language of psychiatry is a monologue of reason about madness. Such an academic study of the history of madness does, of course, itself risk falling into the trap of repeating that kind of monologue. It risks reinforcing the idea much-beloved of most psychiatrists and psychologists that they are providing rational explanations of experiences that are not only mistaken but profoundly irrational, that cannot be taken on good coin, perhaps should not be listened to at all.

There were crucial theoretical stakes to this historical deconstruction of mad-ness that were rehearsed in debates between Foucault and Derrida and then played out in the Hearing Voices movement and in radical mental health politics. This may look like fancy academic language, and inside the academic world there had been attacks on it three years earlier at Cambridge University when renowned philosophers signed a letter objecting to the award of an honorary degree to what they saw as the French charlatan 'deconstructionist' Derrida. But amongst psychiatric system service-users, there was much interest in Foucault's work on prison regimes – this work chimed with their own experience inside mental hospitals – and on the possibilities of deconstructing the bizarre medical world that had been constructed for them and that prevented them from moving on with their lives. Derrida argued against Foucault's history of madness, argued that modern-day philosophers such as René Descartes were not as clear-cut in their dismissal of madness as a form of unreason as Foucault made out. Instead, Derrida claimed, Descartes struggled to find a way to make sense of the opposition between reason and unreason, much as every other philosophical system had over the course of history. Foucault's history of the emergence of the modern form of madness was, therefore, no such thing, for the conceptual and political struggle to make sense of madness was timeless, universal.

Foucault, on the other hand, did want to mark out how certain kinds of exclusion were historically constituted. Only if we saw them as historical could we act to change the course of history. In his preface to the first edition of his book, Foucault pointed out that there were three forms of division and exclusion that inaugurated the modern culture we now lived in that he could have written about. The first, he said, was the division between the West and the 'orient' that divided the so-called civilised world from the barbaric or exotic 'other' part of the world that the West could barely comprehend. Research on 'orientalism', most notably by the Palestinian scholar Edward Said, took up this idea. A second division marked out strange deviant forms of sexuality that normal civilised heterosexual adults were repelled by and found it difficult even to speak or think about. Foucault himself picked up this line of work in a series of books on sexuality before he died. The third division was that between reason and unreason, a division that today excluded what we called but could not fully define as 'madness'.

For us to speak about the experience of madness, and specifically about what it meant to hear voices, would be to challenge that exclusion, and also to engage effectively ourselves in a form of what Derrida called 'deconstruction'. He may have been sceptical about Foucault's historical account, but Derrida still gave us conceptual and practical tools to tackle what had been constructed, to 'deconstruct' it. For Derrida, analysis is bound up with its effects; you could say that deconstruction was a 'tool-and-result' approach. Back to MMU.

Today we have been trying to listen. The conference has been about the hearing of voices, which in the Diagnostic and Statistical Manual of Mental Disorders produced by the American Psychiatric Association is treated as a first rank symptom of schizophrenia. If you hear voices you must be mad, so the story goes, or, in a gentler version of that diagnosis that psychiatrists and psychologists are still taught today, you suffer from a mental disorder which can and should be treated. We put together a call for papers through a group of mental health activists called the Hearing Voices Network, many of whom have been in the mental health system as users of services. We made it clear that this was an academic conference that was open to everyone who had something to say about their experiences and theories of hearing voices. As for any other academic conference, we asked people to send in titles and 'abstracts', short accounts of what their paper would be about, and we had so many responses we had to organise the day into four parallel sessions. Now we are in the final plenary session where some of the threads of the day should be drawn together, but where instead things are unravelling even further.

Spirituality is one hot topic. One of our guest speakers from South Africa, Tholene Sodi, had trained as a clinical psychologist, but spoke about the work of traditional healers. Tholene had been working with indigenous Sotho faith healers, Ngaka, in the Northern Province, and his phenomenological approach took seriously the meaning of the experiences of these healers. His research, which was supervised by Don Foster in the University of Cape Town, was also on the way that the Ngaka made sense of the voices heard by people who consulted them through divination practices, throwing bones to make the voices of ancestors present, for example. Phenomenology, which aims to get inside the life experiences of people and describe the meanings of those experiences from the inside, is very different from traditional psychology and psychiatry as it is practised in Europe and US-America, which already at the outset categorises and 'others' what it doesn't understand, often as disordered. This isn't to say that the Ngaka themselves were more open about what they heard, and Tholene described how they also aimed to drive out the voices.

In contrast to this culturally specific account, another paper was given by a shaman. This shaman, someone who has privileged access to the world of the spirits and can use that access to guide others, was a tall white man wearing a suit who had the appearance of a bank manager. His talk began with a description of the voices he could hear in the other rooms, and other buildings, cities and parts of the world. The voices, he said, were in this world and beyond it. He could hear the voices from other planets and those of starship captains, even of other galaxies, even from other dimensions. He had a large hard-backed notebook which he consulted, and as he turned the pages he was reminded of other things that he could do. Not only could he hear voices but he could see things, and could even produce objects from other dimensions. He could hear voices from the past and from the future, and, if for example, he had wanted to make a red rose appear now in his hand, he could do that. No one in the room interrupted him and asked to do it. And, he said, to be able to do all these things was a gift; but, he said as he closed his book, it was not a gift that was his to keep. Anyone could do this, he said, and he could tell us how. There wasn't much time for discussion after this stunning paper, and we had to roll on to the next session.

Reconstruction

This series of debates didn't all begin in Trieste, but that was one of the places written into our history of radical alternatives in the field of mental health. In Trieste in north east Italy, a city that had been the fourth largest in the Austro-Hungarian

Empire, a city that was now right next to the border with Yugoslavia, a radical psychiatrist called Franco Basaglia inspired a movement called Psichiatria Democratica in the late 1970s and closed the San Giovanni mental hospital. The movement, which involved members of revolutionary left organisations and which was eventually able to gain the support of the local members of the rather staid Italian Communist Party, pressed for a referendum that would shut the asylums down. There had been scandals about treatment of patients, the number of those housed in the hospital was actually falling year on year, and so this movement for democratic psychiatry was then in a strong position to argue for these places of confinement to be dismantled.

The Italian government moved fast to head off this reform process, passing a new law in 1978, Law 180, which called for the closure of the large psychiatric hospitals throughout the country. Defeat over a referendum would have forced the government to resign. The new law was brought in very quickly without any discussion in parliament after Psichiatria Democratica had gathered three-quarters of a million petition signatures. However, this victory was very ambiguous, and the new Law 180 did not put in place any practical procedures or resources for enabling this transformation. In Trieste where the movement was strong, the law was implemented; San Giovanni was closed almost completely in 1980, and a series of community mental health centres around the city set up. It was not an easy task, and there had been some resistance to the closure by nurses working there who were organised in a trade union linked to one of the main fascist parties. For all of the problems and mixed results in Italy as a whole, Basaglia showed it could be done. The mental hospital had been constructed, and so it could be deconstructed.

The example of Trieste as showing the potential for radically changing the mental health system, even if the hopes were not fully realised, was very important. It spread as an alternative model of mental provision around the world, inspiring democratic psychiatry movements in Latin America and even providing the basis for the development of mental health services in Brazil. And it struck a chord in Britain. A new quarterly publication, *Asylum: A Magazine for Democratic Psychiatry*, was founded in the north of England in 1986. This magazine explained in the editorial of its first issue that the idea for such a magazine had come from discussions of what we now called 'the Trieste experience' two years before at a conference which had been held in Wakefield in West Yorkshire to discuss plans to close mental hospitals. A Conservative Party Minister for Health, the notorious racist Enoch Powell, had made a famous speech back in 1961 known as the Water Tower speech in which he stated the intention of the government to close the old asylums, buildings he referred to as being isolated, majestic, imperious institutions. These were not, he insisted, like the pyramids, but just as they had been built, so they should now be pulled down, and alternative provision would have to be made in the community for those he still referred to in his speech as the 'subnormal'.

While many of the terrible old mental hospitals had indeed been closed, very little had been put in their place in the community, and all the while the 'subnormal' were still treated as objects. They had been shut away in the hospitals in the past, and now they were isolated and stigmatised in the community. The Wakefield conference therefore had to tackle not only the closure of the hospitals, but to work out how to intervene to change the terms of the debate. The Trieste experience became a central reference point in those discussions, and *Asylum Magazine* was launched with initial funding coming from a conference surplus provided by its main editor, Alec Jenner, a psychiatrist at the Royal Hallamshire Hospital in Sheffield. Other editorial contacts for the magazine listed in the first issue were in Chesterfield, York and Manchester; this local contact was Nigel Rose in the Chorlton suburb of south Manchester, Nigel who I shared a house with in the late 1980s. The first issue of *Asylum* included articles about Franco Basaglia and the Italian mental health reforms, of course, news items about the British Network for Alternatives to Psychiatry and the Campaign Against Psychiatric Oppression, about the boycott of South Africa, and about the trial for conspiracy under the Prevention of Terrorism Act of an Irish Republican activist and psychiatrist Maire O'Shea. There was also a long interview with R. D. Laing which made explicit some of the contradictions inside the radical or democratic psychiatry movement.

There were two driving forces at work in *Asylum*. One was a history of self-organised activity by patients inside the hospitals. There had been a Mental Patients Union in Britain from the early 1970s, and in the mid-1980s another group, Survivors Speak Out, was formed after a Mind conference. Mind had been going from just after the Second World War as the National Association for Mental Health operating as a federation rather than as a centralised organisation, and its local branches were quite autonomous, in some places providing information, in others there were services such a telephone helpline, and in other parts of the country there was a stronger focus on campaigning. Manchester Mind ran a telephone helpline, but was one of the more activist groups; Nigel Rose and Erica Burman had both been involved in this branch. Nevertheless, there was always a tension between volunteers and patients still caught inside the system, or ex-patients who sometimes called themselves 'service-users', 'system-survivors' or even consumers of psychiatry. The Mental Patients Union and then Survivors Speak Out became the most prominent national forums for the patients, though there were a number of other local organisations.

The other main force was composed of radical psychiatrists. One of the paradoxes of the so-called anti-psychiatry movement was that it was always led by psychiatrists, whether that was Thomas Szasz in the United States, Laing in Britain or Basaglia in Italy. It was often a crisis of conscience inside the medical system that led a psychiatrist to break from that system and look for alternatives. Alec Jenner in Sheffield was another case in point. Jenner early on in his career as a psychiatrist noticed that circus trainers sedated their tigers to make it easier to control them and get them to perform their tricks. He wrote to the Swiss pharmaceutical company Hoffman La Roche suggesting that he could run trials on the drug for them to treat anxiety. The company agreed, and in 1963 the drug, Valium, became the first of the benzodiazepines marketed around the world. Even after helping found *Asylum*, and he was listed as an editor of the magazine until his death, Jenner gave medical advice to Roche, the company now marketing Valium. In 1988, after the UK government's Committee of Safety of Medicines recognised the problem of benzodiazepine dependence, Jenner told Roche that the complaints by patients of memory loss, mood swings and epileptic fits could well be a result of the 'addictive personalities' of these complainants.

Alec was, on the one hand, an inspiring figure, often invited to Asylum events when he was still well enough to travel from the farmhouse where he lived outside Sheffield, a psychiatrist who was willing to support patients so that they could speak for themselves about their experiences. A bumbling rounded bald man, Alec cultivated the air of an absent-minded professor, engaging and friendly in conversation but then throwing in the odd reactionary medical bombshell in a reminder about the importance of biology and the limits of anti-psychiatry. He was very unpredictable, and colleagues in the Asylum collective had to judge very carefully whether it would be a good idea to call him as an expert witness in support of a patient under 'section', compulsory detention under the mental health act. Laing was another example of a psychiatrist who had turned against the medical model. But for many radical mental health activists he was as much a liability to the broader project of democratic psychiatry as a voice on their side. Laing disliked the term 'anti-psychiatry', and it had such a bad press that activists came to prefer 'democratic psychiatry' in the Trieste tradition. Laing, in the interview in the first issue of *Asylum Magazine* also attacked Basaglia, claiming that his Italian rival had "with no depth of experience" and "imbued with a Marxist ideology of a rather sentimental kind" been able to "sneak in" Law 180. Thomas Szasz was even more vehement, arguing that this Italian form of 'anti-psychiatry' was effectively still psychiatry because there was state provision of accommodation for those in distress. Szasz was very much for stand-on-your-own-two-feet robust individualism, and against public provision of welfare. It is understandable that he would dislike anything that reeked of social support, collective activity or, his worst nightmare, the involvement of communists of any kind in formulating what that provision looked like.

Psychology's approach to questions of power and resistance usually reconfigures what is going on in mental health services as a collection of individual responses. It positions those who become its victims as always already the kind of beings who will want to subject themselves to others, for which psychology can then supply a variety of explanations that drum in that victim status as a result of traumatic early experiences. This psychological explanation thus conveniently leaves the role of the psychologist out of the picture. Those who resist, on the other hand, are then congratulated as being 'resilient', even as showing 'mental toughness'. The focus on individual weakness or strength often flips from the one side of the equation to the other, following fashion; in wanting, at one moment, to treat the poor victims as deserving psychological support when there are strong enough public mental health services, and, at the next, in wanting to justify the rollback of the welfare state on the basis that people should learn to take responsibility and stand up for themselves. This second option, intensified under neoliberalism, is unfortunately what has always been the dream of some of the right-wing critics of psychiatry like Thomas Szasz.

When Szasz visited Manchester for a conference in June 2010, I asked him what he had to say about the cuts to state benefits to those on 'incapacity benefit', benefits that were being cut by the government as part of its austerity drive. Szasz was 90, but on good form, he stood up and raised his voice so everyone would be sure to hear him, and seemed in his element, loved this knockabout debate: "Why would you want the state to provide benefit", he growled, and continued, "we should be against politicians like Obama and Hitler telling us what to do". He had already drawn gasps from an audience that included psychiatric system survivors after reading out from a letter a young man had sent him saying that he had been compulsorily detained in mental hospital. The young man told Szasz that he had told his parents about his problems, and they had called for the ambulance; "why is he complaining?" Szasz declared, "It is clearly what he wanted" – and then the conservative psychoanalytic punch-line – "otherwise he wouldn't have told his parents in the first place". Some-one came up after the talk and asked him for his autograph, and since they didn't have anything else to hand I offered a copy of *Asylum* for Szasz to sign. He refused, saying that he didn't want to sign something that had the word 'psychiatry' printed on it.

In May 1988, ten years after Law 180 had been passed in Italy, a small group, about ten of us, mental health nurses, academics and activists led by Nigel Rose, travelled from Manchester to Trieste to speak to people involved in the community mental health centres. Nigel spent his time on the plane with freshly unwrapped Italian language cassette tapes preparing for the negotiations when we arrived. We arrived on the train from Venice in Trieste late at night to find San Giovanni and the accommodation arranged for us by Mark Greenwood, a mental health nurse who was still back in Manchester. San Giovanni was at this point functioning as one of the community centres, which included a café, and a work co-operative. There was no accommodation; either nothing had been arranged or the message hadn't got through, and the workers in San Giovanni were surprised to see us. We sat and waited in Trieste railway station, and eventually very late we were found some-where to sleep. This set a pattern for our time in Trieste, and we spent more time waiting to have meetings than anything else, which at least gave us good opportuni-ties to wander around the old hospital grounds and visit some of the community mental health centres on the outskirts of the city.

There were still patients in the hospital, those who had been living there for many years and who would not be able to cope outside. Their predicament drew attention to one of the problems the service faced, which was that although there was alternative provision now, with over ninety percent of the budget given to the community health centres, there was still great reliance on what was called the 'community' but which effectively came down to the families taking people back home to look after them there. The centres were open 24 hours a day, but there was a strict rule that only one overnight stay at a time was allowed, the rationale being that otherwise patients would turn each of these units into a little hospital, and so the 'institution' would be reproduced inside the community.

Basaglia had made 'deinstitutionalisation' the conceptual centrepiece of his argu-ment against the hospital; the argument was that not only would the continued existence of the hospital as a place of last resort mean that there would always be a temptation to use it, but also that there was a danger that this institution operated well beyond the bricks and mortar building. Basaglia's argument here was quite close to that made by Foucault concerning the psy complex as a network of theories and practices that could operate as a kind of apparatus inside the community, effectively 'psychiatrising' people in their own family homes. There were organisations of families of ex-patients campaigning for the hospital to open again, to relieve them of this burden, and there had been attempts to counter these calls with the Marco Cavallo 'blue horse' anti-stigma campaigns in which patients gave out horse-shaped biscuits to people in the city centre.

We observed some staff meetings, and noticed that in these 'democratic' spaces, the psychiatrists, including the tall moustachioed Giuseppe Dell'Acqua, a charismatic presence, did most of the talking. We didn't need to understand Italian to be able to see that certain kinds of bodies spoke, gave the directives, and others remained silent, obediently taking instruction. Those who spoke were taller, wore white coats, and were all men. Those who listened were women, the nurses. Giuseppe spent some time explaining to us how the services worked, and the nurses participated by asking for clarification rather than contributing to the discussion. Basaglia was also, and this would also be in line with Foucault's views, suspicious about psychotherapy, and preferred collective activities to an approach which tended to individualise treatment. When we asked Giuseppe about psychotherapy, he replied that there was some interest in psychoanalysis in the community mental health centre on the edge of the city where there were more Slovenes, but this interest might be connected in some way with a concern about 'identity', he said.

We were told that European funding was tied to the provision by the doctors in the community mental health centres of figures concerning DSM diagnoses, but that these diagnoses were constructed after decisions were made concerning the needs of the patients, not before. This meant that the figures concerning prevalence of schizophrenia, for example, were completely useless, but they confirmed the idea that it was the schizophrenics who needed more support. There was also still in the hospital grounds the University Psychiatric Clinic functioning independently of the San Giovanni centre, the centre still presided over by Basaglia's successor Franco Rotelli, who we met and had a cup of tea with but who didn't speak much English. Nigel's language tapes hadn't yet brought him up to translator standard.

Erica and I stumbled across the University Psychiatric Clinic during one of our rambles around the old hospital grounds. The buildings were crumbling. There was some graffiti on the walls, including scribbled complaints from some visiting French anti-psychiatrists that Basaglia had released the mad from chains in the asylum only to then shackle them with the chains of work. This was a sarcastic reference to the 'work co-operatives' that were designed to integrate patients back into the community. These co-operatives then had to compete on the marketplace to sell their products, and opponents of the reforms claimed that this meant that these patients were effectively exploited or, as is the case with so many co-operatives, were induced to exploit themselves. Entering the clinic was like entering another world, perhaps even at the same time having travelled back in time, to a nightmarish world of polished linoleum floors and steel bed frames, and of staff in white coats who quickly hustled us out again. No, they said, this is nothing to do with San Giovanni, and they told us that they were a completely independent medical unit. Among the many contradictions in Trieste, this coexistence of a medical approach with the radical reform experiment headed by Basaglia was one. Compared with this little island of medical psychiatry inside the old hospital the Trieste experience was still a striking success, and even though the figures for diagnosis given to the European Union could not be trusted, Basaglia and then Rotelli were able to show that the level of medication had gone dramatically down after the reforms.

We returned to Manchester impressed overall by the experiment, but also more aware of some of the difficulties faced by Basaglia. There were dimensions of the Trieste experience that were problematic, and these included the lack of attention to questions of culture – the throwaway comment about the Slovenes and identity was the closest we got to a discussion of this issue while we were there – and gender, an issue that was clearly important in the power relations within the staff teams at the very least. Curiously, despite Laing's own scornful reference to sentimental Marxism in Trieste, we found little discussion of social class, and it seemed as if it was assumed that putting patients back to work would solve their problem of integration into 'the community', whatever that was.

I was keen to do more teaching about these issues, and since I was supposed to be a lecturer in social and abnormal psychology, and having now taken up a post which included some of that teaching, I had a good claim to teach on the third year Psychopathology option. The option was run by John Stirling, who continued the thread of lectures about the biological basis of 'mental illness' that began in the first year of the degree, 'basis' as singular foundation, not 'bases'. John was enthusiastic about his topic, evangelistic even about conveying to the students how important it was that they understand these biological underpinnings to psychology and psychopathology. John was carrying out research on EE, Expressed Emotion, and was convinced that he could detect schizophrenia by studying how people moved their eyes. He asked me to look at a training video on the topic which would, he said, persuade me that there was something in it. The other tutor on the course was Ian Burgess, a cognitive-behaviourist clinical psychologist from South Africa with a pock-marked sallow face. The first year I taught the last third of the course, and this included some lectures on the history of the anti-psychiatry and democratic psychiatry movements. I also covered the way that women were treated in the psychiatric system, including the much higher levels of electroshock given to elderly women, and on racism, the way that there was, for example, a four-fold over-representation of black people compulsorily detained under the mental health act. That was an opportunity to talk about Frantz Fanon and more recent trans-cultural psychiatric work by Suman Fernando.

At the course review for the module John and Ian explained to me that there was a problem, that because I taught this material at the end of the course, the students had more difficulty recalling the biological and cognitive-behaviourist lectures at the beginning and this had been evident in their exam performance. It would be better the following year if I taught at the beginning of the course. At the end of the next year, I was told that the problem was that I was having an undue influence on the way that the students approached the rest of the material. My lectures framed theirs, and so this then had a bad effect on their exam performance, on the questions they selected and what they wrote. Psychological discourse which refers to 'primacy' and 'recency' effects was wheeled out to explain to me how this worked. A discussion of essay double-marking with the other Ian had already gone very badly, and his temple veins throbbed as he told me that the material in the essays was Marxist. The word 'Marxist' was swallowed as it was spoken, as if this difficulty in naming it was itself an indication of how serious a problem it was. Ian's veins pulsated with rage when I said that they were not being taught to write about Marx but about Foucault. He looked bewildered, never having heard of that French guy, and quickly brought the conversation to a close. John told me that I should be clear that this was not censorship, he was a very fair man, but that my material would be happier somewhere else. Despite protests from the student course committee representative, I was removed from the psychopathology option. This was the year after we brought 'Hearing Voices' into the department.

Deconstruction

In July 1989, when we organised a 'Manchester Hearing Voices Conference', we also organised a meeting in the department for the Dutch psychiatrist, Marius Romme, to speak about his work on hearing voices. Marius, a tall imposing white-haired man who spoke very slowly and clearly in a deep resonant voice, told the story of how he had taken a quite traditional psychiatric view of hearing voices until challenged by one of his patients. This patient was Patsy Hage, now sitting with us at the front of room OB116, a low-tiered lecture room in the Gaskell campus 'old building'. Patsy had pointed out to Marius that he, as a Catholic, must surely hear the voice of God. This was a moment of revelation for Marius, and he issued an appeal on Dutch television for anyone who heard voices, whether or not they had ever had anything to do with mental health services, to come forward and to speak about their experiences. There was a big response, with many people saying that they heard voices and were very happy with that, and some saying that they had never told anybody about what they heard in their heads because they were frightened that it would be seen as a psychiatric disorder. From this the Hearing Voices Movement in Holland was set up, bringing together people to share their experiences and so to de-stigmatise the hearing of voices among those who had been treated in hospital for schizophrenia.

John Stirling sat in the front row of the meeting and was keen to ask Patsy Hage during the question time whether she had ever felt that the voices she heard were sometimes a problem. No, she said. She smiled and explained that the voices have never been a problem, though yes it was true that she had sometimes felt uncomfortable talking about the experience to other people. But surely, John asked, surely it must sometimes have been a problem, and surely this must be an experience you would rather not have. No, she said, and repeated that it was a part of her experience of what it is to be her, and she went on to explain that she would not want this experience to be missing from her life. This was one of a series of meetings that launched the Hearing Voices Network in the UK, a Network that had its headquarters in Manchester and which became closely linked to *Asylum* through the work of student and activist Terence McLaughlin, and 'experts-by-experience' like Mickey and Sharon de Valda. Terence was part of a team of people who saw this network as a new wave of democratic psychiatry, and he argued for dismantling the way this experience was treated as a 'symptom' as part of the psychiatric system and psy complex. What we needed to do, Terence insisted, was to 'deconstruct' psychopathology.

A small group of us, including Terence, were working together at that time on a book *Deconstructing Psychopathology* which was published that year. David Harper was working on paranoia, Mark Stowell Smith on personality disorder, and Genie Georgaca on psychosis. This group was one of what Brenda Goldberg, another PhD student in the Discourse Unit, called the 'book clubs'. Brenda was involved in another book project with Erica Burman and other researchers, on books that were published the following year as *Psychology, Discourse, Practice: From Regulation to Resistance* and *Challenging Women: Psychology's Exclusions, Feminist Possibilities*. The book projects were places for intense debate, and in the deconstructing psychopathology group, we argued fiercely over, for example, whether we should call psychiatric discourse 'psychotic', whether that would be a good way of turning things back to label those who labelled the patients as being the ones with the problem, the ones who themselves spoke a strange pathological language. Among our undergraduate students were several who had direct experience of psychiatry, some of them were even inpatients at the psychiatric unit in the Manchester Royal Infirmary just over the road from Gaskell Campus. They used to come over the road for supervision and even take exams in their pyjamas.

The 1995 Hearing Voices conference in Manchester was one expression of this deconstruction of pathology, insisting, with Foucault, that just as the binary opposition between reason and madness had been historically constructed, so it should be possible to dismantle that construction. Asylums and then these institutions renamed 'mental hospitals' had been built to contain people, and these institutions could be closed, the walls between the patients and the normal people outside broken down. We structured the conference as an event that was not only concerned with language, with what Foucault called the monologue of reason about madness, but with institutions, with forms of power through which people were diagnosed and incarcerated. We were concerned with the 'discourse' of madness, but always saw language as bound up with 'discursive practices' that included the architecture of power. The separation of the hospital from the university, and the enclosure of each to keep some people in and others out was part of the problem.

Some psychiatrists and clinical psychologists also responded to our call for papers, and we were happy to have them there. The psychiatrists like Phil Thomas, who was a good friend of the Hearing Voices Movement and Asylum magazine, knew, as did most of the clinical psychologists who attended, that the rules of the game on the day were going to be slightly different from other academic conferences. Phil spoke at this conference of psychiatry as an institution that operated as a present-day slave-ship, with patients as prisoners trapped in the hulls. Instead of having the top table, and being able to define which theories were right and which were wrong, the playing field was levelled so that clinical psychology, psychiatry and spiritualism and shamanism pitched their stories alongside descriptions of the mind as being like a faulty computer or, as one historical-materialist user-survivor participant Rowland Urey put it, as an ensemble of social relations. In this way, we aimed to turn deconstruction into a process of dialogue in which the old binary oppositions could be broken down and new ones constructed.

Deconstruction was one motif for the kind of critical work we wanted to do, but it didn't mean that we wanted to be tied to the mixture of approaches that were put under the label 'post-structuralism'. Our first use of the term 'deconstruction' in the title of a book *Deconstructing Social Psychology* was tactical, returning to some of the questions raised about social psychology in Nigel Armistead's *Reconstructing Social Psychology* published in 1974. The term neatly combined a critique of assumptions in the mainstream of the discipline of psychology with our attempt to sidestep the too precipitous aim of 'reconstructing' the discipline again. Although many of the contributors to the *Deconstructing Social Psychology* book I co-edited with John Shotter in 1990 were not into post-structuralism of any kind, they were also quite suspicious of social psychology as such, as had been many of the contributors to the original book. Nigel Armistead left psychology and was a devotee for some time of the 'orange people' around Bhagwan Shree Rajneesh. Some other cognitive psychologists also went orange, including Guy Claxton who wore very subtle shades of ochre and tan when he addressed a meeting of the Psychology and Psychotherapy Association at Gaskell House in November 1994 on the role of reflexivity in the politics of psychology and told us that his response to the demand that we get up and do something was to insist that we stop doing things and sit down instead.

I was always surprised when I heard criticisms of deconstruction as being negative, as tearing existing theories and practices down and putting nothing in its place. This complaint came from traditional psychologists who worried that there was nothing being built as an alternative for the poor people who suffered from their psychopathology, and the complaint also came from some radical psychologists who had their own favourite models of psychology that they wanted to put in place of the models they didn't like. We should, Isaac Prilleltensky argued when he visited us and spoke to the Discourse Unit, move on from 'denunciation' to what he called 'annunciation' of an alternative; it was an argument he rehearsed in his 1994 book *The Morals and Politics of Psychology: Psychological Discourse and the Status Quo*. We were accused by others of being heartless, of caring nothing for what could be done to help people. The 'deinstitutionalisation' process that Basaglia and the Psichiatria Democratica movement built was at one and the same time a 'deconstruction' of existing practices and a reconstruction. We saw deconstruction itself as an ethical practice of questioning which enables all of those involved to question who they have been told they are and so, instead of being treated as objects, be subjects of their own lives, human beings. They already, and more immediately and effectively, not only produce new kinds of critical statements about what is being done to them, but also 'enunciate' many alternatives. This enunciation of alternatives is an active process by which the speaker is realising something of their experience, something of their being as they speak. It is simultaneously, dialectically, a 'tool-and-result'.

So, here we are in the hall on campus. The squabble between the spiritualists is maddening. If only they would calm down and let us agree on how we might respond to voices and what we should do to take our understanding of the limits of psychiatry and psychology forward. They are, even so, doing us a favour, for they are showing us how the struggle between psychology and psychiatry – between a 'cognitive-behavioural' explanation of distress and a medical model of 'mental illness' – is itself only one of the battles between different institutions wanting to maintain their own power. It provokes for me a question as to whether a battle between these two churches is qualitatively different from the battle between different parts of the psy complex, and through the day many participants have been learning that it should not be up to any one institution with power to define how our experience should be understood. Not only did I well know that performance in a psychological task could entail real or imagined effects on those involved, but we could already see how 'experts by experience' were being recruited onto mental health service panels on condition that they keep repeating their story of how they became a system service-user. When they stepped aside from that role, they would lose their paid consultancy positions.

Just for a moment, inside this hall, the terrain of the debate had shifted from normality versus abnormality or health versus psychopathology to voices as gift or sign of crisis. For some it was neither and for some it was both, and the day opened a space as a form of 'practical deconstruction' for people to think again about what they thought they knew about other peoples' experiences and about their own. We couldn't agree on how to speak about these things, and that was the point. We would live with that. Instead of a cognitive-behavioural approach which does claim to know what is correct and incorrect about how we think, and instead of a humanist approach which aims to bring all of our experiences together into one wholesome single self so that 'voices' are integrated into who we are, we were learning to live with interminable deconstruction of the self so that we could talk together as what we are, divided subjects. Not psychological subjects but contradictory divided subjects.

My main concern now is how to bring this day to a close. The sun is going down, and the janitors who have been brought in to open the building at a weekend are keen to get us out and get home. I have rolls of black plastic bags ready for us to collect up polystyrene cups and paper plates. Every time we have a conference here I worry that it will be the last. There is muttering from the Dean of Faculty that we never charge our delegates enough to recoup the costs. This time I had been told that we were being too 'generous' by setting the registration fee at 10 pounds, and there was some delay before she agreed to sign the forms. Each time there is more pressure to take the event through a 'conference office' which will take a cut which it uses to keep itself going, a little self-funding institution inside the institution. I go out through the double-doors into the reception area where one of the young janitors is standing looking into the hall, waiting for us to finish and leave. "Well", he says, "another psychology conference?" Yes. "But this is an odd one isn't it, do all these people hear voices? I was talking to them in the breaks and, well, we do, a lot of us, don't we" – he hesitates, and seems unsure about whether to say this to me – "we hear things and people tell us we shouldn't talk about it". I smile. He is awkward. He has said enough, and we hurry on to get things cleared up and shut up.

This was one of the good times at MMU, an institution that taught psychologists, and facilitated psychological research, including forms of radical psychology that connected with the tradition of action research. Research is always an intervention, whether it pretends to be neutral, keeps things fixed where they are, or whether it embraces change. In the next two chapters I describe my four years in a different research environment. Here you will see a smaller institution struggling for status and nervously attempting to give space to critical work. That space opened up, and I thought I could jump into it and make use of it. The struggle in and against an academic institution, however, is always over how far you can make use of it and how far it can make use of you.

15

CONSTRUCTIONISM

Assessment and appointment

In which we move further out to the edge, further north west, and here we discover how smaller teaching institutions, through a peculiar effect of their own construction of the social world as psychological, set limits for themselves. We look at Kelly's Personal Construct Theory along the way, at surprising connections between psychology and Marxism, and at attempts to construct the world differently.

There have been plenty of attempts to develop a radical critique of psychology and a radical alternative to the assumptions that the discipline makes about people. We connect with some of those attempts in this chapter, and I want to show what the limits of those forebears of contemporary critical psychology were. I have to admit that I was tempted out of MMU, my academic home, by ambition, and I persuaded myself that it was more an ambition to do something different in the discipline, to change the subject, than a concern with academic status. I hope that becomes clear in what follows, and as I tell you about what it is like to move from one place to another I describe how and why I imagined that the dead weight of a fairly traditional teaching institution could be lifted. We live in hope.

Esteem

It is autumn 1995. I am puzzled. Not so much by why I am here, but why these people want me here. The Tower Block at Bolton Institute of Higher Education is a six-storey concrete and glass brute block of a building. The main tower looms over an inner courtyard containing a rectangular slab of murky green water. Perched at the rim of it is a plastic heron. This main campus is little more than a roundabout, a large square traffic circle edged by four main roads; on Deane Road to the south is a Sainsbury's supermarket which functions as the cafeteria for many of the staff.

On a good day there is a view from the upper floors of the Pennine hills separating us from Yorkshire to the east, and from the other side of the block we can see the outskirts of Manchester about fifteen miles away. North is the Business School. We are in the north west of the North West, in a teaching institution aiming to become a university, hoping to skip a rung that will join this college of higher education to the polytechnics that were awarded upgraded status three years before. Ranged around the room on low chairs are members of the Department of Psychology and Biology, here for an informal meeting to meet the candidate for a new Chair.

This will be the first Chair of the department and the first externally appointed Professor post at Bolton. This is the first step, another first step the Institute takes, to persuade the government that they are already at university level. Another first step because there have so far been many false starts. It takes a short while to work out why that might be. There is a Professor of Engineering and a Professor of Poetry who were promoted from the ranks, and there are different tales told about why this new position has been created. One story hinted at by the Principal, affable trim Bob Oxtoby, who is about to retire, is that he was in the bath one night, and the thought came to him that he would like to have a Professor of Psychology. So, one puzzle is over the possible status of 'psychology' as a discipline that might impress outsiders who will give Bolton Institute their just desserts, sunshine desserts. Another story that circulates around the staff group is that the head of the department Alec Bagley is just about to leave and that his retirement gift to his old institution will also, perhaps, be a little time bomb he leaves behind. I hear this from my inside source Dave Nightingale who is keen for another social constructionist to support him there, and he thinks it could be me. Alec rests in his crumpled jacket in his very small office, slowly clearing it for when he goes, and very slowly and thoughtfully administering his team.

Another story is that Alec suggested the idea to the Principal, who liked it a lot, but that Bob Oxtoby had no idea what kind of psychologist the new appointment would bring. So, another puzzle is why someone who is known to treat psychology as a social construction rather than as accumulated scientific knowledge about people should be sitting here now. The lecturers who are now eyeing me up suspiciously are also, I guess, wondering the same thing. There have been comments about large research grants that I might be bringing to the Institute, comments that are clearly geared to fishing for the reason why I might be in the frame for the post. There is some amused musing over how my work would connect with the study of lemurs in the biology section of the department, which, alongside some respected experimental research on decision-making, is pretty well the only research going on here. The lemur people are great; when they can they go to Madagascar to study lemurs in their natural habitat, but most of the time they have to make do with Chester Zoo. The decision-making people are friendly but I'm not sure they would have decided to appoint me if they had been asked. I'm not sure what to say, and I'm about to ask the one question I should not ask.

If I can think of one precipitating cause, one event that started me on this path to the professorship interviews at Bolton, it would be a conversation with Nik

Chmiel, a cognitive and occupational psychologist who was with us at Manchester Polytechnic for a while in my first few years there. One thing I remember about Nik is that he had the kind of ergonomic office chair with a slanted seat on which you balance while your front calves rest on another backward facing cushioned plate. He believed in this ergonomic occupational design, and made a good case for it, and he also believed in self-advocacy as a good cognitive strategy for yourself and for others' perceptions of you. There was once promotion in our department and Nik applied, even though he had no real expectation of getting it. I asked him why he did that, and he told me – his little raisin-black sharp eyes peering into mine – that it was important to "put down a marker". I followed his example. The next promotion round we both applied, and failed. The new Dean, David Pyle, who seemed to model himself on a supermarket manager, was the one who frightened us into playing the income generation game, putting on high-fee short courses for people outside the university as an alternative to bringing in money from research council grants. This David with the light brown trimmed moustache leafed through his Filofax during the interview; the message was that I was wasting his time, but it wasn't a waste for me.

Nik found promotion somewhere else, but had prompted me to put down a marker. There are dangers in this strategy of course, and one of the dangers is that your superiors will view your applications as ridiculous and construct the kind of 'moral career' for you wherein you are known to always apply and always fail. This serves to stop many people from ever putting themselves forward. There are two other dangers that have less to do with the perceptions of others and more to do with the way you come to perceive yourself, aspects of the institutional process of career-advancement in higher education that works its way into your own being, into what you think of as your own psychology. One danger is that putting down a marker is an indication of what in psychology is referred to, and often valued as, 'self-esteem'. Confidence in yourself is an indication that you have the ambition to succeed, and that just as you have pushed so far to apply for a post, so you will continue pushing and so do well, if that's what pushing amounts to, in the post when you are appointed. You mentally and emotionally ratchet yourself into the post you imagine should be yours, the post you believe you are entitled to, and the danger is that you don't stop. This is the career mentality that afflicts academics of all kinds.

One underlying problem with this kind of careerist mentality is that self-esteem isn't actually always good for you, and one of the traps that psychological measures of personality always make is to simplify their account so that what they think they have identified as a causal factor can then be observed and measured in a variety of different situations. Psychologists routinely forget that different situations, different contexts, give rise to different phenomena. So, high self-esteem in one context, where it amounts to having a little more confidence in your own abilities, can very quickly turn into self-esteem as overweening arrogance in another, self-belief that entails contempt for others. It is difficult to generalise about what 'authoritarianism' is exactly as a personality characteristic, but it does seem as if self-esteem plays its part there. Career-path management which separates those who aspire to higher

status from those who are willing to carry on with the drudge-work is thus a feeding ground for self-esteem and for those who are then tempted to coerce others
to work harder so that the results can then be presented as evidence of leadership.
This is quintessential psychology in practice; it is what happens when you configure yourself as a psychological being and convince yourself that everything is
down to how you behave and how you think. I mention this now because one of
the delightful and frustrating things about Bolton Institute was that there was little
evidence that there was anything of this career-path management in place there. I'll
tell you more about that as a problem in a moment.

The other problem with putting down a marker is that it incites a belief in one's
abilities that can rapidly spin out of kilter with what one can actually do. Here it
locks into the interminable process of accounting for oneself that is at the heart
of evaluation of work and worth in higher education. While the Teaching Quality Assessment homes in on course-team paperwork and 'evidence' of learning in
the classroom, the Research Assessment Exercise, the RAE, makes each individual
speak about their success and their ambition for future success. We had done well,
relatively speaking, at Manchester Polytechnic in the 1992 RAE, mainly because
psychology was one of the few 'units of assessment' there that submitted published
work, and because some of us had pushed ourselves forward by publishing and
organising. And we did it by being able to account for ourselves, promoting ourselves as if we were good, even the best researchers. To plan for the RAE involved
preparing endless narcissistic vignettes about how good we were and how we were
going to succeed, exercises in self-love that must then be all the more convincing
when you are making applications for jobs in other institutions.

And I'd learnt that, as well as making your own institution love you nearly as
much as you love yourself, you needed to put a little pressure on them by threatening to withdraw your love by applying for promotion elsewhere. Now, at the time
of this informal interview with the staff group at Bolton, we academics were all
coming up to the 1996 RAE, and one question was whether MMU would keep
my publications and so love me enough to promote me there or whether Bolton
Institute would buy me and my publications so that they could impress the Higher
Education Funding Council with their new Professor. For this circuit of cynical
and narcissistic self-promotion to function I had to believe in myself as much as my
institution pretended to believe in me. In this there is also the question of evidence
which in research includes not only writing and empirical research but also bidding
and funding. I made no claim to bring big research money with me, and that's what
the jokes at Bolton over coffee and biscuits as we sat down to talk were about; no
I would not bring a large team of researchers with me to the department.

There was a treadmill of grant applications to bodies like the Economic and
Social Research Council, for example, and I had once stepped onto that, getting
A-grade evaluations for research funding to work with the Hearing Voices Network
but no money, and then stepped off it again. I had friends in other departments who
spent their lives preparing such applications, partly because they were told that
'income generation' would count in the next RAE more than publications, and

becoming disappointed exhausted shells of themselves. That isn't what I did. So, it seemed rather ludicrous that I was in the frame for this post. It was partly who else that was in the frame that made me take this seriously, but also wonder what on earth was going on. I sat waiting for the meeting to start and smiled to myself as I thought of the last large empirical project, if we could call it that, that I had been involved in. It had rolled on for many years and was just about to bear fruit in a book that was designed to be called *Psychology and Marxism*.

Radical

The project was carried out with Russell Spears, who had finished his PhD at Exeter University the same year as me and then spent a year in Manchester in a post-doctoral research post at the university. Marxists working in psychology were hard to find, and Russell, who was working on quite different kinds of social psychology to me – I would call it 'old paradigm' quantitative research – participated in the first radical psychology meetings with us. It was partly because we had different perspectives on what it might mean to be a 'Marxist psychologist' that we decided to work together in the first place and then to carry out a global survey in the discipline. From that we planned to put together a collection of writings which would at least show the variety of different ways that Marxism and psychology could be linked. We knew of the attempt by the Frankfurt School, for example, to connect psychoanalysis and Marxism in the collective project that became known as Critical Theory, and we had come across friends and colleagues in the discipline who were sympathetic to Marxism but hostile to psychoanalysis, no problem with that, so we wanted to know more about how the different possible connections might work out.

The questionnaire we posted around the world in 1991 was long, too long, and it was also rather intimidating, as some of our respondents pointed out. Was it really helpful, they asked us, to expect people to say exactly when they became a Marxist and to specify what kind of Marxist that would be? We asked for thoughts about different kinds of Marxism, different kinds of psychology and, of course, we wanted more names of people we might approach. Many questionnaires, most of them, weren't returned at all, though some likely candidates, Jerome Bruner the developmental psychologist who worked within a broadly Vygotskyan framework being a case in point, did take the trouble to reply and ask why on earth we ever thought they were Marxist. I had tried to learn from these kinds of mistakes. I was coldly put right by Ivana Marková when I invited her to come and speak at a seminar in Southampton in December 1984, that the fact that she wrote a book about Hegel was not reason to assume that she was a Marxist. She was not. At the 1993 Bierville ISTP conference, the grandson of the famous Soviet psychologist A. N. Leontiev paced up and down angrily insisting that his work had absolutely no connection with Marxism. Some colleagues politely returned the questionnaire, telling us that they feared that under the Conservative government there was a threat of a revival of McCarthyism and that filling out a questionnaire now about their political beliefs was the last thing they wanted to do. We decided that we would include self-defined Marxists in the book, that even though we might ourselves have qualms about whether these people were all bona fide Marxists, we would leave that to them to say.

We had chapters on the usual suspects and some unusual ones too. There were a few psychoanalytic contributions, rather evangelistic pieces, which goes with the territory. There were also chapters on the German tradition of *Kritische Psychologie* revolving around Klaus Holzkamp's version of activity theory, and on the revolutionary Vygotsky rediscovered by Lois Holzman and Fred Newman. J. J. Gibson's ecological psychology of perception was, it seemed to some, Marxist, as was, more surprisingly, the radical behaviourism of B. F. Skinner; Jerome Ulman who wrote that chapter tried to persuade me and Russell not only that there were Marxist therapeutic communities in Mexico run on behaviourist lines but that Skinner wasn't the reactionary he was sometimes painted to be, sending over copies of letters written by this 'Fred' in which he grudgingly accepted that Marx might have something useful to say about the human being as an 'ensemble of social relations'.

We did, however, slowly accumulate a large pile of questionnaires, and while these arrived in the post, faxes flew backwards and forwards from Manchester and Amsterdam where Russell had now got a teaching post. I flew backwards and forwards too for discussions about the project while we sought out publishers for the work. This was a next major hurdle, and most publishers replied saying that the volume we were proposing would both be too large and too specialised. There were, after all, not many Marxists in psychology, and even the left-wing publishers we approached were cautious because, they said, they were publishing too many psychology books already. They were not publishing many, but the problem was that psychology had not gripped the imagination of the general population and, even less so, that of the left. The expansion of psychological discourse was just then taking off. Some publishers sent the proposal out for review, and we got from those reviews more contacts for the project, people working in psychology who identified as Marxists, but no contracts.

There was another lesson in this process about who one might suggest as a sympathetic reviewer for a proposal and how favourite phrases might give you away when you intended to provide an anonymous review. One reviewer, for example, complained of the proposal that parts of the argument were not easy to understand "even when read with the finger moving along the lines". We had not suggested Halla Beloff as a reviewer to this publisher, had not at all imagined she would consider herself to be a Marxist, but she was our external examiner for the degree in Manchester, and when she used exactly that phrase in an examination board one day to complain about a badly written final year dissertation I tackled her about it. We laughed even so, and she congratulated me for being "a good sport" for not holding a grudge against her for having advised the publisher to turn the project down. Well, it was true, no grudge, and by that time I too could be generous, able to keep the academic frame in this interaction for we had finally found a publisher for the book.

Pluto Press, a publisher that had once upon a time been linked to the post-Trotskyist International Socialists group eventually agreed to publish the book with the subtitle *Coexistence and Contradiction*. The 'Coexistence' part of the phrase was a reference to the attempt by the Soviet bureaucracy under Stalin to engage in 'peaceful coexistence' with the capitalist world, even to the point of using the local Communist Party in each particular country to suppress rebellions there if it was necessary for diplomatic reasons; 'contradiction' signified in some way the importance of dialectical materialism in the project. We had Ernest Mandel, the Belgian economist and revolutionary, lined up to do a review of the arguments in the book, and in early 1995 we were negotiating with him over the questions we wanted him to address in his final chapter. On 20 July 1995 we had bad news from Brussels that Mandel had died. Only shortly before I had spoken to him on the phone about his chapter and the format of it through which we would signal some of the key arguments about psychology in relation to politics. He was quite ill, and commented on the way this was restricting what he could do, this bodily process to which he was subject was, he said, "a law of nature, more powerful than a human being". The same day of the bad news about Mandel we had a message from Pluto that they thought that booksellers would not sell the volume with 'Marxism' in the title. They wanted us to keep the subtitle, *Coexistence and Contradiction*, but change the main title to *Psychology and Society*. That's where we were at with it while when I visited Bolton.

We hadn't managed to persuade one apparently good comrade, David Pilgrim, who had been in different Marxist groups and who did radical work in mental health, to participate in the book. I had worked with David briefly a few years before on an article about Michel Foucault and psychology, but the pages that David contributed before he got bored with the idea were mostly about the existentialist philosopher Jean-Paul Sartre. I eventually wrote the paper myself, but the encounter gave me some insight into an important strand of radical clinical psychology in Britain that filtered ideas from France, like Foucault's for example, through a humanist-individualist frame of reference. That's where the link with Sartre came in, I guess. This was the radical tradition that was influential in the Psychology and Psychotherapy Association and in the organisation's *Changes* magazine from the early 1980s, one that included Craig Newnes, who went on to become the editor, and David Smail and David Pilgrim. The main shared point of reference for that circle of academics and practitioners was an approach in psychology called Personal Construct Theory developed by George Kelly, an approach that had been picked up in the UK by a clinical psychologist Don Bannister.

A very successful book published twelve years earlier by Don Bannister and Fay Fransella called *Inquiring Man* popularised Kelly's theory. The motif running through Kelly's work was 'man as scientist'; he argued that human beings, whether they were actually scientists or not, developed and employed a system of personal constructs to make sense of the world, and used those constructs to predict what was going to happen next. This approach humanised clinical practice, according agency to clients and also broke down the distinction between the expert 'practitioner scientist', which was the term Hans Eysenck used to describe clinical psychologists, and normal people. This was one almost home-grown tradition in British clinical psychology that was radical, involving other clinical psychologists like David Winter and Miller Mair, who extended the construct approach into a study of narratives and stories that we tell about ourselves as, for example, lacking or confident, as having low or high self-esteem. This approach treated each and every individual as a social constructionist, constructing their reality, reducing the process to what each individual chose to make of it.

The theory was, particularly in the hands of these radical psychologists, an interesting take on psychology. It played the phrase 'prediction and control', which was defining the work of clinical psychologists, against psychology itself, insisting that the people who were already engaged in prediction and control of the world were the patients rather than the practitioners. In this way, the subject of psychology was viewed as an active inquiring subject, according them some dignity for being themselves 'scientific', and it also made psychologists think in a different way about what science itself was up to. The theory could also, at the same time, be used as a tool for psychological diagnosis, and that's how the Kelly 'repertory grids' were sometimes used. In these grids the patient specified what was important to them and noticed connections and patterns. The grids could identify which constructs people were using, and how 'tightly' together they were organised, that is how strictly a system of constructs might err on the side of controlling rather than predicting the behaviour of others. The danger with this was that some standard notions of psychological expertise were retained, even when the notions were used against the enemies of the personal construct people. I remember one of them telling me, for example, that Eysenck had 'tight constructs'. We laughed. Halla Beloff also drew attention to some problems in the phrase 'man as scientist', when she once asked if 'models of man' were also models of women. Perhaps there was not one way of relating psychologically to the world or to other people, and perhaps the theory risked becoming a normative account. One of the contributions to the pamphlet *Rat, Myth and Magic* had the rather unkind title 'George Kelly: Another Nasty Liberal'.

Most of the personal construct people I knew in the UK were radicals, and critical of psychology, and of traditional scientific method. Some of them tried to make explicit connections with politics, but something of the 'personal construct' approach did still place limits on how they related to other rival theories. David Smail was one of these researchers who, as a clinical psychologist, had done valuable work in putting critical perspectives on the agenda of different services. He once gave a talk at Gaskell House NHS Clinical Psychology and Psychotherapy Centre where he described Foucault as setting out a model of concentric circles in which society was on the outside, the community further in, and then the family inside that, and then, in the centre, the self. I objected that this was a humanist model, and diametric opposite of what Foucault argued. For Foucault, I pointed out, the discursive practices that constituted the subject ran through these different 'circles' and it was these practices that made them appear as if they were 'layers' of existence nested one into the other. The idea that the self was a centre of different layers of meaning that surrounded them was historically constituted and it precisely led to a warrant for the kind of individualist psychology that Smail said he wanted to question. He was very annoyed, and that was the last time we spoke to each other. We invited David Pilgrim to speak to the Discourse Unit, where he was nonplussed by Erica's claim that what we dealt with in psychology was entirely socially constructed, and became most exasperated by Terence McLaughlin's claim that 'mental health workers' work in the sense that they labour to produce mental health. We had a confused discussion, and David could not see the Foucauldian and Marxist point that Erica and Terence were making, that the phenomena that psychology described were to some significant extent constituted, created, produced by psychology itself.

There were two candidates shortlisted for the new Professor of Psychology post at Bolton Institute. One was me, and the other was David Pilgrim. I wasn't really sure that I wanted the job, but I wanted to be offered it so that I could go back to MMU to tell them, and my cunning plan was that they would then be worried enough about losing my publications for the 1996 RAE to give me promotion there. David wasn't sure whether he wanted it either, and he advised me to do the same as him when he was appointed at a dodgy institution – he clearly had more experience of this kind of thing – which was to keep notes from the start about the mistakes they made so you could use this information against them later when you wanted to make a complaint. As well as these informal meetings and the formal interviews, we were each required to give a presentation to the staff group on the title 'My model of leadership', and then talk about how we would manage research in the department. These events, the informal interviews and presentations, were organised so as to keep me and David separate from each other. David's approach, I learnt later, was to tell the staff how he would lead them, while mine was to question what 'leadership' was in an academic context.

It is time for my bad question. "So", I asked the staff group, "I'm curious about what this shortlist tells us about psychology at Bolton Institute". The psychologists and biologists leaned forward expectantly or back into their seats rattling their teacups. Dave Nightingale stared at me, eyes glazed through steel–rim glasses that reduced the size of his pupils but curiously magnified the size of his eyes in his shaven bony head. Alec made himself more comfortable in his chair. "Why", I asked, "have you shortlisted two Marxists?" Some of the staff glared at Alec while others protested that they had had nothing to do with the shortlisting process, even that the advertisement for the post had appeared out of nowhere with no consultation in the department. Dave tried to sidetrack the conversation onto the social constructionist perspective that me and David Pilgrim shared, as if this would be a better bet and would better bring them all on side.

I liked these people, and, it seemed, they liked me well enough, little choice that they had in the matter, and I was telephoned shortly after the formal interviews with an offer. I had settled down to watch television while eating chocolate. This, I had promised myself, is what I will do when I am a professor. Then David Pilgrim phoned to ask if I was going to accept it because he was in the middle of some negotiations at his current job, presumably also involving some mixture of inducements and threats around his publications. I told Sandra Burslem the Vice-Chancellor at MMU, and she sent me a nice letter wishing me good luck in my new post. Bolton it was.

Fog

It was a cheap post, paying much less than other professorships I had applied for, and had even got as far as interview for in the previous year or two, and Bob Oxtoby cheerfully told me over a cup of tea in his office when I asked for a higher salary that it must really, for me, be like winning the lottery. He was right. It was a significant increase in what I had been paid at MMU, but for that I would have to get up much earlier in the morning and commute to Bolton, a forty-minute journey around the M60 ring road. There was almost immediately a muddle in the department over whether the post was a professor 'of' psychology or 'in' psychology and what 'chair' meant. It was a time when a fog of confusion seemed to settle over the department that stopped us from thinking about what was going on, and not for the first time. I often thought of David Pilgrim's advice, and should have kept more notes about this and other strange things about Bolton. There are some distinctions in other countries that could have helped clarify this. In the US, for example, teachers in school are 'professor', while in Spain there is a distinction between the teachers in a university who are 'professors' and a 'Catedrático de Universidad' who is usually chair of the department. Bolton, a town with a population of about a quarter million people, however, was making things up as it went along. A meeting about 'internationalisation' in the Institute shortly after I arrived included a brief discussion about provision of train travel-passes to Manchester.

Instead of any career-path management structures, and this is a point in its favour, there were alliances of people who had been in the Institute for many years, but, not so much in its favour, they seemed to spend most of their time preventing things from happening. Because I had been appointed as professor with an unclear but high status in the organisation I was put on the Institute ethics committee and on the professorial appointments committee, and on a number of other committees that never met and that I lost track of my membership of. One of the lecturers in management, Mike Humphreys who did research into organisational culture, had his proposal turned down at ethics committee before I was able to attend a meeting because he was wanting to carry out an ethnography and the committee couldn't work out how he would be able to get written permission from everyone in the company he was intending to work in. I was often notified of meetings of this committee after it had met.

Joe Whittaker, who ran an action research centre about disability rights in the Institute, told me that I should be careful overusing the postal service because there had been threats of disciplinary action against researchers caught using it for 'political' purposes. Leaders of the local union branch were closely allied to management. I found it difficult to imagine that 'Human Resources', the personnel department, could take any kind of action because it hardly seemed to exist. I was in the HR office shortly after I arrived because I needed their help in trying to organise the publicity for my inaugural lecture, and one of the secretaries helpfully showed me my file, which included letters of support from my referees. Shortly after I arrived in Bolton there was a nasty case of victimisation of gay men; they had been arrested during Operation Spanner for taking part in sadomasochistic parties and prosecuted for causing actual bodily harm even though they were all consenting to what took place. Prompted by Peter Tatchell, I wrote a letter of complaint to the *Bolton News* about the case, supporting the men and protesting against the way they were being vilified. Bob Oxtoby told me that he had received letters calling for me to be dismissed, but this was told to me with amusement, after he commented that it was good that I hadn't put on weight after my appointment because it was a sign that I was working hard.

We only discussed one case in the professorial appointments committee before either it folded up or I was no longer notified of its meetings; a lecturer in art who had applied for promotion to professor had practically no publications or research experience, but argued that in his field it was the quality of the paintings that should count. Bob Oxtoby and the professors of engineering and poetry stood around and shuffled through a pile of canvases which had been submitted for our evaluation along with his application letter. "Yes", Bob said, "some of them are really quite good". The guy got his promotion. The internalised lack of confidence in what Bolton was and what it could do was sometimes helpful for those who had sharp elbows, but mostly the lack of what psychologists call 'self-esteem' was painful, and held everyone back. I had to rewrite some of the paragraphs to be submitted for the RAE in 1996 because they were so self-deprecating. They had appealed for understanding by the psychology panel, pointing out that we didn't have many resources, and included the claim that we had been doing our best "for what we are" being the crunch phrase. "I think for what we are", Rob Ranyard who did research on decision-making said to me, "we're not doing too badly". I rewrote the paragraphs in the language of exaggerated self-promotion that the RAE panel expected, emphasising our strengths and keeping quiet about the lousy context and high teaching loads. Rob, a nice guy, changed them back again.

The disadvantage of loosely defined informal networks of people running an institution like this is usually that there is a 'glass ceiling' which prevents women, say, from progressing in their careers, or 'glass walls' which box workers into certain roles. At Bolton Institute the problem was, rather, a 'foggy ceiling' in which any suggestion I made, or any good ideas for improving things from anyone else seemed to disappear, slowly, imperceptibly, was made unthinkable. The foggy ceiling in psychology consisted of Mr Foggy Rob, Mr Foggy Paul who also did experimental research in cognitive psychology, and the Dean of Faculty Mr Foggy Peter, and meetings involving the three of them and me used to last for ages before they invariably succeeded in agreeing that it would be better to leave things as they are. The Principal was not a Mr Foggy, but he seemed happy to beam on us from time to time and to have no foggy idea about what was going on. They wanted to get university status, and mobilised the staff and students around this hope, but by consulting on questions related to it in the most counterproductive ways. At one point, for example, and unlike anything that would have been attempted at universities in Manchester, they commissioned alternative logos for the new 'University of Bolton' they aspired to become, and set up a display for staff and students to view and express their preferences. The exercise merely succeeded in guaranteeing that whichever logo was eventually picked would be mocked by over half of the university, and it drove home the fact that this was a symbolic choice empty of content since every application so far for an upgrade of status had been rebuffed.

It often seemed hopeless, but at the same time there were people doing amazing work, ranging from Mike in organisational research and Joe in disability action research to Tom Philips and David Rudd working on literary theory, and Jill Marsden who I already knew from a conference we organised in Manchester on 'cyberpsychology', and another inspiring professor in a field I had never heard of before called 'critical management studies'. This was Heather Höpfl, a Christian feminist post-structuralist who was really the star academic of the Institute based in its Business School. The umlaut over the 'o' in her name made locally accented staff accentuate it with an even longer Lancashire open vowel, and her contribution at every meeting was framed as 'hopeful'.

And inside psychology itself, there was Dave Nightingale who was energetically pushing the social construction line and was able to keep us linked with a group at Huddersfield University led by Viv Burr and Trevor Butt, who also had a background in Kelly's Personal Construct Theory, helping to organise the first Understanding the Social World conference in July 1995. There was also a strong strand of theoretical and philosophical teaching by Ronnie Mather who took no prisoners in debates over Foucault and Marxism. He was up for setting up our own version of the Human Sciences Seminar, which we organised on a Thursday afternoon, the same time as the one that took place in the philosophy department back in MMU.

We also set up meetings of the Discourse Unit, and so now the unit existed on two sites, and we began to refer to ourselves as a 'trans-institutional' site for research. We added 'practice' to 'language and subjectivity' in the subtitle of the Discourse Unit. Together with Heather in the Business School and other researchers in English we set up the 'Bolton Discourse Network', putting together a book which pulled together the very different approaches we took to spoken and written texts, and more. The 'social constructionist' argument made by David as well as the emphasis on what he called 'embodiment' led us to look beyond analysis of naturally occurring conversation, beyond the speciality of 'conversation analysis' forms of discourse analysis or focus on written texts and images that 'semiotic analysis' took us to. In our book *Critical Textwork,* which eventually came out in 1999, we included analyses of television, film, gardens, cities, organisations, bodies, silence and action.

We ran versions of the three-day Discourse Course that we relocated from Manchester, expanding the scope of discourse to include visual representation and to also even engage with questions of embodiment and biology. Lucy Yardley came up from Southampton University as a guest lecturer on our May 2000 course, for example, speaking on the way neurological processes that attended physical disorders like Meniere's Disease could be framed in terms of Derrida's deconstructive notions of 'difference'. There is always a temptation to respond to the dizziness that characterises Meniere's disease by keeping still, but it is necessary to keep moving, to keep re-adjusting to the internal differentiation that occurs inside the perceptual-balance system in relation to the outside world. We tried to give the new courses a distinctively Bolton feel by treating participants to bowls of the locally produced Uncle Joe's Mint Balls, sweets that were briefly renamed during the Operation Desert Fox December 1998 bombing of Iraq 'Saddam's Balls'. The *Bolton News* photograph of soldiers gleefully sucking Saddam's Balls was good for some rather obvious discourse analysis.

A first major project we undertook at Bolton Institute was taking forward discussions we had in Manchester about 'criteria' for qualitative research. A joint paper by John Stirling and Sarah Grogan produced for the psychology department at MMU in November 1995 was on 'science criteria for psychology projects', produced as a response to 'concerns' about criteria raised by our external examiners on the undergraduate psychology degree after the kerfuffle over Charles Antaki's attempt to reduce all final year project marks by 10 percent. These concerns chimed with a backlash against the growing popularity of qualitative research among postgraduates and, worse for the mainstream, among undergraduates in British psychology departments. John and Sarah's 'science criteria' were not too bad, and they had clearly taken on board points made in collective discussion in the department, but we knew that we needed to address this with colleagues from other departments, so in November 1996 we held a Qualitative Psychology: Criteria for Research Practice working meeting in Bolton. From that developed a series of guidelines that were designed to be flexible, to take seriously the different contexts in which qualitative research was being developed; we argued in my document circulated after the day that 'we should value each criterion and each exception'. I elaborated this idea in a more 'deconstructive' direction in the criteria I published in my book *Qualitative Psychology* where I identified different criteria and, following Derrida, put them 'under erasure' to deconstruct them; that is, I marked them as issues to be taken seriously but not treated as fetishes, for there were rules we should know how and when to apply and how and when to break them.

The first open day conference I organised at Bolton Institute was designed to put Bolton on the map. I was accumulating a series of facts about Bolton. I learnt that it was the birthplace of the inventor Samuel Crompton who invented the spinning mule crucial to the development of the textile industry during the industrial revolution, for example. And I discovered that 'Worktown' in the Mass Observation studies of the 1930s was Bolton. The conference in June 1997 brought up Dorothy Sheridan from the Mass Observation Archive in Sussex, and Halla Beloff down from Edinburgh to talk about the Worktown photographs taken by Humphrey Spender.

I had the time and space to do what I wanted, and involving other people in research, which we did through visiting speaker seminars and the Bolton Discourse

Network, was exactly what they expected. We had critical psychology meetings in which we could connect with radical mental health politics. Sharon LeFevre came and talked about self-harm, describing how she would give talks to groups of psychiatrists put on as part of their training, learning from the patient, and start cutting herself slowing with razorblades to see how and when they would react so that this could then be talked through with them. Sharon didn't do this in front of us, thank goodness.

The main activity of Psychology Politics Resistance while I was in Bolton was through another group we set up called North West Right to Refuse Electroshock. This focused on the question of ECT, Electroconvulsive therapy – 'Electroshock' – and the human rights of those subjected to it. We knew that some users of services said that they benefitted from ECT, as they did from their drug treatments, and we wanted to build the broadest possible alliance of people who would campaign at least for the right to choose whether to have it or not. There had been a scandal concerning some of the machines used in hospitals, and we had a meeting with a psychiatrist from Salford who told us that he would have ECT "even if the machine was faulty". Helen Spandler, who was one of Erica's PhD students, and I pointed out in another leaflet with the heading 'Psychologists Against the Nazis' (formed after British National Party involvement in racist attacks in nearby Oldham) that ECT had its origins in fascist Italy – the technique was first trialled in 1938 after a professor of neuropsychiatry noticed that pigs shocked before slaughter were more docile – and that mental patients were among the first to be confined and exterminated in Germany. Helen, who still has a load of the badges, remembers that Carolyn Kagan, the community psychologist at MMU, was one of the few psychologists she knew to buy one. The issue here is not over whether or not Electroshock and psychiatric drugs have an effect. Of course they do. Rather, the question is what effect they have, and the problem is that they often cause worse so-called side-effects than the distress they claim to clear up. Many of those on long-term medication, for example, attended meetings of PPR and the North West Right to Refuse Electroshock, shaking with the often incurable tardive dyskinesia caused by the drugs, and shaking with anger at what at been done to them without their consent.

Psychology Politics Resistance organised a Networks Festival in London in December 1996, and grew to over 600 members. We also campaigned for the release of Isabel Rodriguez-Mora, one of Maritza Montero's students at the Universidad Central de Venezuela (UCV) who was arrested in October 1996. Isabel, who had won a student prize from the Interamerican Society of Psychology for her undergraduate research project, had the bad luck to be carrying out research on prisons from a university that was a thorn in the side of the regime. I had met Isabel when I went to teach a course in Caracas earlier that year, and we together left the class with Maritza and other colleagues including Esther Wiesenfeld and Euclides Sanchez to join a protest march against police violence. It was one of the few demonstrations I have been on where one of the chants was the name of a university, in this case 'U, U, UCV'. Isabel was accused of various subversive activities, and an international petition and letters might have helped in securing her release from prison in January 1997. Following further threats that she might be re-arrested, she left the country to live and study abroad.

Apart from my time and a little office on the sixth floor of the Deane Road Tower Block, which I decorated with curtains from home and plastic grape vines, we had no resources. With the retirement of Alec Bagley as head of department – he waved goodbye pretty soon after I arrived – things settled into the fog, until the excitement of the new head, the arrival of Patrick McGhee. Now it was finally clear that the 'chair' to which I had been appointed was not chair of the department. Patrick's presentation to the staff group was dazzling, using PowerPoint as they had never seen it before, not only brightly coloured slides but images that swooped down into the screen and lines of text that announced their entrance with the noise of revving and braking sports-cars. I had met Patrick years before on the registration desk of a social psychology conference, the one on attribution theory at Oxford, and seen him intervene at other seminars in Manchester, a young urgent man with a rapid-fire Scottish accent. Now twice the size and with twice the energy, he was here to take charge of psychology at Bolton, drag it into the future and make it a platform for one of our defining strengths that, he told us, would be 'critical psychology'.

I am not giving away any secrets to say that I thought I could do something more radical in this place and that I failed, and so the next chapter traces the journey to critical psychology as an approach that is just as limited as its predecessors. If this chapter was shadowed by personal ambition – the place was a step down but the promotion was a step up – then the next chapter is about institutional ambition, the attempt to make a mark as doing something new using the rubric 'critical' as the password to success. You might ask yourself why I would think that the problems that had been put in the way of radical research in other places would be any less for us in the mid-1990s, or now. I was optimistic, and learning how to channel this optimism with the energetic support of those who thought they could make the psy complex work for them.

16

EVOLUTIONARY

Realistic and critical too

In which complaints about what the discipline gets wrong are crystallised as critical psychology, an approach which pretends to provide something completely different. Critical psychologists insist that what has been constructed can be taken apart again, and so they quite rightly shift focus from a concern with knowledge to a concern with what psychological knowledge does to people.

It is tempting to tell a story about the emergence of critical psychology as being the end point of a necessary evolutionary process in which the discipline of psychology develops a reflexive conscience about its shortcomings and allows practitioners to step back, take stock and chart a better path forward. Some of the self-representations of critical psychology as a separate sub-discipline spin a narrative of that sort. Unfortunately, this is not the case. What I will show you in this chapter is that this latest version of attempts to voice qualms about what the discipline does to people is just as susceptible to being turned into part of the discipline again, with critical psychologists engaging in often futile debates, debates which serve as spectator sport for the rest of their colleagues. The new identity we assumed in this spectacle was a trap.

Relativism

We learnt to call ourselves critical psychologists. This rubric 'critical psychology' started to gain traction about five years before, with the Routledge book series named for it and then one of the editors of the series finding an academic institutional base in a new Centre for Critical Psychology at the University of Western Sydney based in the Nepean campus on the outskirts of the city. Here Valerie Walkerdine took up what was called a 'Foundation Chair'. Different existing strands of 'radical psychology' and also feminist critique of the discipline began to be brought under this umbrella term. This new approach presented itself as a brand that could explain to the traditional psychologists what we were complaining about, and we were then told to market critical courses to psychology students.

I circulated an outline for an *International Journal of Critical Psychology* in 1995, and pitched it to several publishers, and at the Huddersfield Understanding the Social World conference I tried to persuade the discourse analyst Jonathan Potter to join the editorial board. Jonathan told me that he wasn't into 'critical' research at all but was only interested in what people said, with how they talked. There were divisions opening up between those who would see social constructionism as a critical tool to dismantle psychology and those who only seemed to want to tinker with the internal mechanics of conversation. Alexa Hepburn, who had got her PhD that year, gave a paper defending 'deconstruction' and 'postmodernism', and, in line with the overall theme of the conference, 'social constructionism' of different kinds was advocated by a number of leading psychologists who would sometimes by now be described as 'critical'. It was sometimes difficult to grasp what was critical about it, beyond the argument that we should relativise the stories told by the discipline about what people outside it were thinking. That itself, however, was a step forward as a critique of a discipline that either pretended to give explanations that were universal or that segregated and compared cultures in 'cross-cultural psychology'. I didn't really appreciate how important postmodernism was as a progressive influence in the margins of psychology until I attended a session at a social psychology conference in San José in Costa Rica after having delivered a keynote in which I had attacked postmodernism for its relativism. I arrived late at the session and found a seat at the back of a darkened room where the speaker was helpfully projecting the complete text of his talk – it was in Spanish – and complaining about the 'anglosajones' – that was me – who couldn't or wouldn't accept that postmodernism was marginal precisely because it was the postcolonial, anti-colonial voice of those at the margins, outside and against the West. This was a reality check.

At the Huddersfield conference Ken Gergen employed again one of his favourite motifs of those years, which was to shuffle sheets of paper to illustrate his point, that there was nothing that should lead us to put the sheet which told a psychological story about our behaviour on top of the others. Gergen had been a reference point for a parallel version of new paradigm arguments in the US from 1973 when he managed to get a valuable critical article called 'Social Psychology as History' into one of the mainstream journals of the American Psychological Association. There he argued that the 'facts' about behaviour that the experimental psychologists pretended to discover were changing so rapidly that it would be more honest to view what social psychologists were doing in their research as a form of journalism. Then the question was whether what we did was the bad restricted journalism of the experimenters or something better as we traced how our experience went beyond what the traditional psychologists could comprehend.

Ken Gergen finished his talk in Huddersfield by saying that there were more important things in our lives that were beyond words, but he didn't mean power or resistance. He held up a pocket cassette player on which he played some Western classical music. Some of the audience walked out, bemused or insulted by this slide from relativism – the argument that all stories were equal – into a hopeless appeal to common sense Western aesthetics, common sense for those brought up to value one particular tradition of music. Rather like psychological claims about the universality of the models of the mind they described, here was another universal, the claim that this is what we all, all human beings must value. At one and the same moment, then, there was a critique of the sway of Western psychology as being but one story and a reassertion of the importance of Western culture. Cultural difference was certainly around at the conference, though it was rarely noticed, let alone turned into a topic of debate.

Another US psychologist, the radical Ed Sampson, had another, better stab at the relativist argument in Huddersfield where he read out a paper that, he told the audience, had been rejected by the journal *American Psychologist*. There were more sophisticated accounts of human experience than those given in psychology journals, he said, and then he described examples from Buddhism, Pentacostalism and feminism, claiming that these belief systems attended to our nature as relational rather than as confined to separate individuals. In very different ways these traditions drew attention, he claimed, to the importance of our psychological being as being located not inside the head but in what he called an 'acting ensemble'. It was the first time I had met Ed. I admired his work. I went to the conversation session after his talk where we had a difficult discussion about what I saw as the limits of what he was proposing as a full-fledged alternative to mainstream psychology. It seemed to me that in popular culture this more extended idea of psychology had run way beyond research in the discipline, and here was evidence that we should heed Gergen's point about us as journalists tracing changes in experience; television programmes like *Star Trek*, for example, were always already organised around an acting ensemble in which two or three characters worked out a problem between themselves, and the relationship between them was invariably configured as crucial to who they were. This objection got a very frosty reception, and I couldn't help feeling that, as with my conversations with Ken Gergen, there was a cultural-political gulf between the rather liberal perspectives of the US Americans and what might count as critical elsewhere.

What they seemed to get right, and this applied to Ken and Ed and to the discourse analysts around Jonathan Potter, was that there was a clash of accounts, discourses, narratives about where 'psychology' really was and how we should study it. The psychologists had different models and strategies for doing what they thought was scientific research, but if you looked closely, you could see that the stories they told about other people reflected not so much what was going on inside their subjects' heads but their own institutional position. The problem was that psychologists, and the same caution applied to some of the social constructionists too, found it difficult to appreciate how their ability to tell their stories was bound up with questions of structure and power. It was not simply that some people spoke about who they were and what they did differently from others, or that some stories were on the top of the pile of sheets of paper by accident so that they were noticed first or taken more seriously. Stories about our individual psychology were organised in institutions, in academic institutions and in the other institutions of the psy complex where certain people had rights to speak and others were ignored, or were told they were wrong or even mad. To insist on a psychological story, to make it stick, there needs to be a dangerous edge of certainty to the argument combined with power to implement what is right against those who are deemed wrong. The flipside of psychological demonisation of low self-esteem, for example, seems to be overweening arrogance, something which is sometimes turned from defence into attack.

I saw this happen in psychology departments and at conferences. I had once been invited to give a seminar at Liverpool University, for instance. My colleague, Sandy Lovie, who had prompted the invitation for me to speak there in October 1994, was a historian of psychology who focused on the way that statistics were developed in the discipline and how they were misunderstood and misused. But when I arrived to give my talk I discovered that Sandy was away on 'sabbatical' – occasional leave from teaching that was one of the privileges of teaching in one of the 'old' universities – and the young lecturer who met me seemed anxious about how my talk would go down. I asked him if there was any research on psychoanalysis taught in the department. No. That was to be expected, and I was going to speak about psychoanalysis not as a theory of mind but as a story that we told about ourselves, a story that was pushed away by mainstream psychologists but that kept returning unbidden, reappearing in hidden ways to inform the way psychologists talked about what they did. Erica Burman, in *Deconstructing Developmental Psychology* described the way that psychologists try to avoid psychoanalysis and do that with such energy that we could view psychoanalysis, whether we liked it or not, as being, she wrote, the "repressed other of psychology".

What was perhaps a more important question to ask before my talk at Liverpool was whether there was anyone in the psychology department who taught or researched in the qualitative tradition instead of the quantitative experimental one. No, not apart from Sandy, perhaps, who was away, I was told. And, he said – I had to guess what the connection might be – "David Canter might be attending this seminar." I knew this wasn't good news. It was all happening too fast for me to get depressed about it, but I was certainly apprehensive. I had encountered David Canter a couple of years before when Erica and I visited Surrey University in Guildford, where he was then based, for informal interviews about two teaching posts there. We were worried about the market–ethos that had appeared at MMU and were exploring other possible jobs. We had felt the pressure piling on in Manchester, and though we had managed to work the system there just a little bit by putting on short courses about discourse analysis and a series of different day conferences on different topics in critical psychology, we clearly weren't raking in enough money. There were rumours at one point that each staff member had a price on their head and that they should be bringing in double their salary in external income. We felt the writing was on the wall for us there.

It turned out that Guildford was too comfortably middle-class, and quite a white city, and we decided not to apply for jobs there, but we had some interesting conversations which reminded us how lucky we were to be in Manchester. Erica was told by Glynis Breakwell that what she, Erica, did was writing and not research. We were familiar with this line of argument from our own university. When it was a polytechnic and at something like the Bolton-stage of nervousness about research, a ripple of horror swept through a training day when someone said that there was a difference between 'research' and what many staff at the Poly were doing which was re-circulating what they had read in the journals, that was 're-search'. Another more optimistic session was led by a professor of engineering up at the All Saints campus who had succeeded in attracting some grant funding, and who told us what we needed to do before we could sit back and, he said "watch the lolly come rolling in".

It was David Canter who made explicit what our research at Surrey should look like, and we had a rather difficult cross-paradigm crossed-wires conversation with him about what the department expected of us. David told us that the university had just taken over a nearby college of nursing and that he had concerns about exploiting the students there as subjects in psychological research. We agreed that, yes, this was a concern, before realising that his 'concern' was not that this exploitation would be a bad thing but rather that his department should be able to exploit this new opportunity.

David Canter since then had founded a Centre for Investigative Psychology at Liverpool University. This centre focused on criminological and forensic research, a strand of research that became more popular under the Conservative government. Forensic psychology succeeded in hitching together two motifs important to Margaret Thatcher. One was the reduction to the level of the individual signalled by the word 'psychology'; the other motif was an increasing concern with the discipline identifying those who were not normal and who may pose a danger to law and order, this was a motif that the term 'forensic' exploited. Psychology as a discipline always adapted itself to changing political-economic circumstances, and there was an emphasis first on one and then on another aspect of research, focusing on the identification or correction of abnormality. The discipline flourished as organisational or work psychology in industry in the beginning of the twentieth century, but then devoted more attention to intelligence testing when migration and unemployment became more important, before shifting focus again to clinical and educational projects which would aim to adapt people to society toward the end of the century.

These conceptual developments are what are tracked by the historians of psychology, and their research reminds us how our own psychology today operates relative to particular prevailing cultural and political-economic conditions. These broad-brush characterisations need to be complemented by detailed study of how contrasting strands of work dispute the mainstream or try to join it, and how old forms of research appear under new labels. That is where historical research in critical psychology has been so useful. It already seemed in the 1990s that forensic psychology which targeted those who did not want to be part of society ran alongside a burgeoning 'health psychology' which aimed to educate people who could be fitted in. That is, with the arrival of health psychology, targeting deviance was augmented by the claim that psychologists could educate those who exhibited bad behaviour to come back into line again, in line with the norm psychologists constructed in their research. This brings me to my encounter with Canter in Liverpool.

David Canter arrived shortly after I began delivering my paper in Liverpool. He walked to the front of the room where he took his seat directly facing me. There were some worried glances in his direction, and when I finished there was silence. The audience were waiting. David said, "this is nonsense". At times like this, we can grasp for psychological explanations, and they can be a comfort. I already had enough cues to suppose not only that he often did this kind of thing but also that other people there would know that too, that they might also use a psychological explanation to put this kind of thing down to his peculiar aggressive character, say. My heart racing and trying to sound calm, I said that this was a challenging response and it would be good to know more about why he'd said that. From that we had a discussion, if you can call it that, which for him seemed more than anything else to be an occasion to describe his own research. It was an argument which eventually petered out. One or two people then nervously asked varieties of the 'were there any sex differences?' questions, and then it was over. In the corridor afterwards I commented to David that his first response was rather harsh, and he smiled and said that it was just a way of "taking the floor". This is fine enough, but it was clearly the case that someone else in the audience, a junior lecturer or a student say, would not have been able to say such a thing, and this was not just one story jostling alongside another. This kind of 'debate' about psychology was structured by relations of power in a particular kind of institution that accorded rights to speak to some and silenced others. In this case, because I had been invited as a speaker, I had no choice but to speak.

As psychologists started to notice critical psychology it was from time to time included in conference programmes, but this was not merely to indicate a generous broadening of the scope of debate, but also to mark out a new internal enemy to be spoken about and, if possible, dispensed with. I was included in one panel discussion in a conference plenary event, for example, where I was told that I was to speak for critical psychology alongside a social psychologist and an 'evolutionary psychologist', a specific disciplinary upgrade on sociobiology of a few years before. The social psychologist, George Gaskell from the LSE, had, I guess, looked up 'critical' and declared that this supposedly new approach was just a revival of out of date critical theory from the time of the Frankfurt School. That was the tradition from the 1920s in Germany that had tried to link psychoanalysis and Marxism and had then underpinned authoritarian personality research inside social psychology in the US after the Second World War. The evolutionary psychologist on the plenary panel, a young guy with a ponytail, was more cynical. Evolutionary psychology combines anecdotes from experimental psychology with Just So stories about how selection strategies have given rise to certain kinds of biologically wired-in behaviour. It is psychology in one of its purest forms in the sense that it not only describes present-day behaviour in Western society as if it were universal and always the same over the course of human history – its account of aggression and sexuality is breathtakingly Neanderthal and sexist – but it also keeps drumming home the message that this is the way things were from the dawn of time, back in our biological heritage, and always will be. Afterwards I was told by several audience-members that they enjoyed the session, but they wanted more "blood on the carpet". Why? What kind of spectacle was academic debate being reduced to here?

What I liked best about this evolutionary psychologist was that he was quite open about why he studied this kind of psychology. The social psychologist talked about improving communication and progress, I talked about stepping back and finding alternatives that were politically better, but the evolutionary psychologist argued that his approach was growing in influence and so, logically, it was the smart thing to do to follow it if you wanted to advance your career. These moments when the psychologist unwittingly or deliberately replicates in their own lives the kind of approach they take in their research can be valuable opportunities to notice and reflect on what this knowledge does, who it is for. Those rare moments complement the more difficult and usual situations when the psychologist can tell us that he knows how we think and does this unthinkingly, then it seems they are able to do this just because that's what they've been employed to do, and because they have the power to make it so.

Realism

The Discourse Unit hosted a day conference at MMU on 'social constructionism' in April 1996 which reflected on these kinds of questions, and which was one of the bridges for us from discourse analysis to critical psychology. The book of the conference appeared afterwards as *Social Constructionism, Discourse and Realism* and included other contributions that were starting to line up with the critical camp. The conference was ostensibly about one of the most ridiculous debates in social psychology, between 'relativism' and 'realism'. One of the axes of the debate was, it seemed, between the Discourse and Rhetoric Group at Loughborough University and the Discourse Unit in Manchester. However, that version, which was often used to frame what we said, was itself very misleading, for there were full-blown relativists in Manchester and researchers who tended toward some kind of realist position in Loughborough. The polarised debate also made it seem as if there were no social constructionist researchers in other places who had their own take on these questions, which there certainly were. The relativism-realism debate thus tangled us in its many contradictions and false oppositions and threatened to marginalise our friends in the two institutions, and in other places.

Anyway, to briefly set out what were perceived to be the battle lines once again, on the one side were the relativists. These were researchers who took seriously studies of scientific knowledge and cultural-anthropological research, and some of the post-structuralist arguments from deconstruction and postmodernism. They drew the conclusion that we need to shift focus from the claims to underlying truths that structured mainstream psychology to, as some of the discourse analysts liked to say, 'respecify' psychology as a conversational accomplishment, or as something that had not much reality beyond the ways it appeared in speech and writing. This approach was relativist because it relativised the claims made by psychologists and showed that each of the claims was relative to the host society, to a community or to a smaller more local context in which such claims were made.

On the other side were 'realists', that's us, but it was a snag-word that makes it seem as if we were a more coherent group and clearer about what we were up to than we were. On the one hand, 'realism' in scientific research is an alternative way of conceptualising reality outside language which is very different from that posed by the dominant logical positivist tradition. Rom Harré advocates a new paradigm for psychology as a realist, and one of his students Roy Bhaskar was inspired by Rom to elaborate a complex philosophy of science that posited an 'intransitive' real dimension of existence, a world of objects, structures and powers that are modelled and studied by scientists. When Rom argued that we should treat people as if they were human beings, for example, he was arguing for a conception of our object of study that was structured in such a way as to have the power of what he referred to as 'second-order monitoring', a form of power which we respecified in qualitative research as reflexivity.

Discourse, and all the things in psychological discourse that are socially constructed in different cultures and points in history, rest on these underlying structured objects which are real. And, in addition to that, there are, Bhaskar argued, 'emergent structures' which also have powers and which impose constraints on our action, structures that we need to take seriously when we analyse discourse in relation to politics, ideology and power. Some of us on the realist side of the debate objected to relativism when it seemed only to be concerned with language rather than things under the surface of language that made language use possible, and some of us were also concerned with the way that language itself was structured so that it operated not so much as a level playing field of communication as a power apparatus in which some people could and should speak in certain kinds of ways and others were silenced or told to speak when they were spoken to. We often slid between these different conceptions of what was real.

The Loughborough-Manchester version of this squabble about relativism pitted those who were seen as simply interested in the way that people speak against those who wanted to locate what people said in relations of power. Or, to put it another way, it pitted those who wanted to carry out rigorous academic research on transcripts of conversations against the finger-wagging political activists who rocked the boat and really wanted to do something quite different. Our political anger became channelled into attacks on the relativists, and there were some easy and obvious targets. The kind of discourse analysis that many of these academic rivals were carrying out reduced political phenomena to conversations, and their own brand of conversation analysis seemed to be an excuse for avoiding analysis of power and ideology. The context was rigorously stripped away so that they conversation could then be rigorously re-described in 'conversation-analytic' terms.

In one conference presentation, for example, Jonathan Potter introduced a piece of transcript of an interview between a social worker and a young married couple at risk of having their child removed into care. In this case the context-stripping was not so rigorous; it was one of those moments where it became clear that if the audience was to make any sense of what was going on there needed to be a little framing of it, and so some leakage of the external world into the analytic description. Jonathan cued us into the character of the husband by telling us something about the way he spoke that was not marked in the transcript; this guy had an 'evocative sniff', we were told, and Jonathan imitated this sniff for us. The question of social class became present as an issue but was not explored in the analysis. I asked about the power that may have been structuring the interaction, and how conversation analysis could pick that up, and Jonathan pointed out, quite correctly, that 'power' had not been mentioned in the transcript. He was empirically correct and wanted us to look only at what could be directly seen in the text. Charles Antaki once gave the same kind of reply to a question about power in a presentation, but more dramatically, holding up the transcript and peering at it, saying that he did not see power there. Loughborough students were schooled to defend themselves against this kind of question about power with a little mantra that this was an interesting point but that it was not their research question.

This kind of analysis and circumscription of 'research questions' was well-suited to academic institutions, and to psychology which had struggled with the turn to discourse as a threat to empiricism, a discipline only concerned with what could be directly observed and reported. In this way, discourse analysis in the hands of the conversation analysts was being turned into a kind of 'textual empiricism'. Notwithstanding the compatibility between this kind of analysis and research careers, we were keen to engage with these approaches within the scope of discourse analysis, and invited a colleague from the university up the road who had done their PhD at Loughborough to speak about the way that conversation analysis might respond to some approaches to language from within that tradition that did take power and ideology seriously, the work on so-called Feminist Conversation Analysis developed by Celia Kitzinger and Sue Wilkinson. We wanted to take forward some of the links between feminism and discourse analysis we had explored in day courses a couple of years earlier. The response to the invitation to speak at a Discourse Unit event was first 'yes' and then 'no', the reason for refusal given was that the event would be geared toward masters level students and so, the email said, would not be of benefit to the speaker's academic career. We had to change the event at the last minute into a transcript analysis session in which we together analysed the email exchange comparing different methodological frameworks to try and make sense of it.

The 'death and furniture' defence of relativism co-authored by three of the Loughborough folk – Derek Edwards, Malcolm Ashmore and Jonathan Potter – written in 1992 and eventually published in 1995 horrified some of their friends there as well as us. The realists, the authors said in that article, were intent on stopping the flow of conversation, including academic conversation, by reducing the debate between realism and relativism to what they called 'Bottom Line Arguments' in which seemingly self-evident 'facts' would be summoned up to prevent debate. Banging on a table to prove that it was there was the 'furniture' realist move, and referring to the Holocaust was the 'death' move. The danger, of course, was that this academic argument against realism thereby served to relativise historical facts, to reduce politics to a language game in its most trivial sense. They spoke for relativism as if there were no stakes to that, as if they spoke from no particular position at all, disinterested in the context or effects of their argument, advancing a quintessentially academic position.

It was made to seem as if we were obsessed with power as something real. Maybe we were, but there is plenty of power around nowadays, enough to be concerned about it. At an April 1993 conference on 'critical social psychology' in Barcelona, Jonathan idly scribbled a little diagram of the way I treated the relationship between discourse and power; a jagged angry mouth of power loomed over language threatening to eat it up. It was neat, and he was happy to give me the image at the end of the session. For us, discourse was intimately linked with power and ideology, and the students we taught who were from marginalised communities already spontaneously carried out a kind of 'discourse analysis' themselves in their everyday lives when they noticed how they were caricatured, misrepresented and mocked in advertising and then even in the depictions of them in psychology textbooks. It was working class, black and minority ethnic students, and those with non-normative sexual preferences who 'got it'. Discourse analysis was a way of formalising their objection to ideology and how they were positioned within it, as lacking, stupid, deviant or uncivilised. A good proportion of our students were 'mature' students, which included those with practitioner experience of some kind. We had some fantastic students who wanted to get into psychology precisely because they wanted to change it. Discourse research became a way for these different non-normative students, and those in solidarity with them, to speak back, to find a place in the academic world where they could be taken seriously.

The trap we fell into in our objection to the way that relativism was being promoted in some social constructionist and discursive research was to make it seem as if we agreed with the claims that psychologists had already made to describe things inside the head that no one could directly observe. Appeal to things under the surface of language was something that mainstream psychology had always made, and the discipline told us that it really was describing real things like intelligence or personality. Then 'intelligence' and 'personality' took on their own reality for those who used this language when they were still really no more than moves in language games, moves which, as Jonathan Potter rightly pointed out, needed to be explicitly 'respecified' as such. While some of the liberal relativists who only wanted to look at language threw those appeals into question, however, they didn't want to buy into the accounts of power and ideology that some of the radical realists were attracted to.

Between the social constructionist 'relativism-realism' 1996 day conference and the 1998 book, things were starting to go pear-shaped on the realism side of the debate, and I began to realise that I had been quite wrong. The 'realist' argument was attractive because it had always been part of the argument made by Rom Harré against the false science that was psychology in its laboratory-experimental guise, and even more so in the argument made by Roy Bhaskar who connected his 'critical realist' theory of science to Marxism. I went to a 'critical realism' weekend conference at Warwick University at the end of August 1997, and began to wonder whether this was the right way forward. Carla Willig, a revolutionary socialist who contributed from the realist side in the social constructionism debates was there, and she had a fierce argument with one poor academic, Tony Brown from the education department at MMU. Tony made the mistake, while ordering drinks one night, of commenting to Carla that he was only interested in the ideas and not in their political consequences. There was blood on the carpet in the bar, but not in the more reverent academic sessions. Critical realists from different academic disciplines sat in a semicircle around Roy, a beneficent figure with long flowing black hair down to his waist, against each side of his chair carrier bags full of papers, which made him seem all the more to be sitting on a throne. He nodded and beamed as the participants each began their account of how they had used critical realist ideas by thanking Roy for his invaluable contribution and guidance.

Then there was indeed an eruption of the real. The death of Diana Princess of Wales hit the news, and hit the conference on Sunday morning. Participants began to try and make sense of the event in realist terms, and there were references to things beyond words, beyond language. Alison Assiter read out pages from her book on critical realism, kept returning to the question of the crash, distracted from the narrative of her talk. Margaret Archer, a critical realist professor of sociology who was also a devout Roman Catholic, even acting as sociological advisor to the Pope, gave a talk which didn't include religion but did refer in rather religious vein to some of the most traditional developmental psychology research to account for how it is that children learn to use language. Shortly after this conference Roy Bhaskar announced that not only was there something he called 'transcendental realism', something which Harré had not followed his path to, but that he had also decided that God was transcendentally real. The conceptual car-crash that was realism, in this form and in relation to psychology, made me realise that we could not simply decide by fiat what was and what was not real outside language. What political differences we had with some of our colleagues at Loughborough were being fought out on the wrong terrain. In some important ways they turned out to be right – referring to something as real does not make it so. Others noticed this.

There were radicals on the relativist side of the argument who were very close to the Discourse Unit. A group of researchers led by Wendy and Rex Stainton Rogers were making playful interventions in psychology that not only relativised psychology but disturbed it. They sometimes connected that disturbance to political critique, one example of which was in the work of one of Rex's PhD students, Celia Kitzinger, on the social construction of lesbianism. Their research group, mainly based at Reading University, and with links to the radical social psychologists at the Autonomous University in Barcelona, was called 'Beryl Curt'. This name was a sarcastic transformation of a powerful signifier in British psychology, Cyril Burt.

In their 1994 book *Textuality and Tectonics* Ms Curt is described on the back cover as having 'congenital acorporality' whose critical polytextualist writings have been made possible by a group of devoted amenuenses, of which seven are listed. Beryl described in her book a 'climate of problematization' in psychology which she clearly wanted to make worse, and she did this throughout the book in dialogue with an 'interrupter' who opened up the text to a series of contradictions and riddles. There were joint meetings of Beryl Curt and the Discourse Unit in Reading and Manchester in 1994 which were as chaotic and playful in form as they were in content, and they productively disturbed our assumptions about discourse and reality, ahead of the game in terms of what it might mean to be critical. When you are a relativist, Beryl told us, it doesn't at all mean that everything goes; rather, it means that nothing goes; you question everything.

This approach might have also saved us some of the difficulties we had with students who wanted to study discourse because they assumed that it directly reflected something underneath or outside language. Some of them were happy with the argument that discourse consisted of patterns of meaning shared between people, not reducible to things going on inside the head of individual speakers or listeners, writers or readers, but they often clung on to the idea that the study of what people said about things was an accurate description. This was not a question of avoiding or wishing away the world – as it threatened to be in the case of the 'death and furniture' arguments – but of conjuring up strange new worlds that seemed to exist because they existed in discourse. I had one student writing a master's dissertation on UFOs, for example, who gathered together reports people gave of seeing flying saucers, and was intent on linking this in his 'reflexive discussion' to his own similar experiences. We spent many hours in which he tried to persuade me that these accounts must have some basis in reality, and I couldn't persuade him that there was a difference between the accounts, the discourses and their referents. He wouldn't put that into question, but doing discourse analysis does put every account into question, attending to the texture of language, noticing how images of the world, and of minds, is constructed in it. This was in the spirit of the way we had understood 'deconstruction' ourselves, in my case reframing it in a way that was more congruent with Marxism. Deconstruction does not mean dissolving reality into the play of language, but rather, as Jacques Derrida himself argued, taking account of what he called the 'lines of force' that structure our readings of a text.

This was high theory that was also eminently practical. There was a tradition of Narrative Therapy in Australia at the Dulwich Centre around Michael and Cheryl White which connected the therapeutic process of questioning how the problem had been constructed with deconstruction and with analyses of power provided by Foucault. There were other parallel strands of therapy in Aotearoa/New Zealand with David Epston in Auckland, and Taimalieutu Kiwi Tamasese and Charles Waldegrave, an Anglican priest, at the Just Therapy group in Wellington. They took the same line, encouraging questioning of dominant narratives. I had met Michael and Cheryl as well as David, Kiwi and Charles at a Discursive Construction of Knowledge conference organised by John Kaye in Adelaide in 1994. This was also my first encounter with Ian Law and Vanessa Swan, and with Maria Nichterlein and John Morss who were into the work of Foucault's friend, the philosopher Gilles Deleuze. Yet another parallel strand of critical therapeutic work was represented at that conference by the psychiatrists Eero Riikonen and Sara Vataja from Helsinki.

I hallucinated most of the content of the conversations I had that week in Adelaide, spent most of the time recovering from a disastrous flight. I had arrived at the airport in Manchester on Friday, to find that I needed a visa for Australia, the furthest I had travelled, a bureaucratic border obstacle that had never occurred to a Brit. A Saturday arguing in the travel agent led to a compromise over the cost of rebooking an outward flight and then a journey on Sunday night, arriving on Monday morning just in time to go into the first conference session where I was to give my paper. The conference was in a hotel, in the windowless centre rooms, and as I spoke I felt as if I was standing on a trampoline. What these folks said to me about the connection between discourse and psychotherapy was quite weird and practical at the same time. I was able to bring them together in the edited book *Deconstructing Psychotherapy* along with the Irish therapists and psychiatrists Nollaig Byrne and Imelda McCarthy who developed an approach called 'Fifth Province'. There are four historic provinces in Ireland – the British-occupied statelet in the north east of the country consists of six counties of the province of Ulster – but what Byrne and McCarthy did was to use the narratively-imagined fifth province as a place which broke up Ireland into one which valued multiple identities. They deconstructed Irish identity and, more importantly, the search for individual identity which preoccupied so many of their patients. Those therapeutic deconstructions attended to power, treated it as something real.

As the term 'critical' started to gather force, and different discursive, radical and feminist researchers were gathered together under that label, some of those processes of structure and power became more evident. Psychology departments in the 1990s began to employ one or two lecturers who were expected to teach about 'qualitative' research. Then this rubric 'qualitative' was assumed to include discourse analysis, and then the feminist arguments against mainstream psychology also began to be ghettoised and rendered invisible, treated as part of the 'critical' corner of the department.

Masters

These were issues we grappled with as Patrick McGhee took charge of the psychology department in Bolton and encouraged us to develop a new MSc, the first Master's Degree in Critical Psychology. Dave Nightingale was, of course, centrally involved from the beginning of this project. There were new members of staff who were doing radical work, such as Dan Goodley who had been an undergraduate student at MMU, and who I had taught on my third-year elective option Psychoanalysis and Society. After he graduated in 1993 he did his PhD at Sheffield, and then came to Bolton, bringing a radical disability activist approach with him. Most published research at Bolton was in the field of cognitive psychology, based on experimental studies of decision-making of strange tasks in artificial situations constructed by the experimenter, and usually ending up with data concerning speed of response. Critical psychologists aimed to question this, an aim that had already been quite explicit in the title of the 1995 South African Critical Methods conference which was 'A Spanner in the Works of the Factory of Truth'.

In a presentation to the department before interviews for a new psychology lecturer – such presentations were the accepted norm here as well as at MMU – Dan Goodley asked one of the candidates who had been enthusiastically describing experimental research on reaction times – how quickly someone responds to an image flashed up on the tachistoscope screen – what reaction times had to do with psychology. The candidate froze. They had never been asked this question before, clearly never even thought about it. The rest of us, rushed to help, and so did Dan, offering different possible reasons why speed of response told us about our own psychology. That lightened the moment again, but we all ended up laughing, including the candidate, because each answer to the question failed to answer it. Dan and I made a pact that that neither of us would leave Bolton unless we both decided to do that and had together found a way out. For the moment, it looked like this was a place where we could get things done, though we were unsure for how long. Patrick McGhee brought people like Rod Noble and Tom Liggett into the critical psychology team and managed to get through the foggy ceiling to gain agreement from the administration to back the new course. Patrick was adept at bureaucratic management of courses and at preparing paperwork for reviews of teaching; during one exhausting session preparing for the dreaded Teaching Quality Assessment, the TQA at Bolton Institute, he got carried away and declared "I love this". His enthusiasm drove us.

There were some uncertain moments, as when Patrick reported back from the Dean of Faculty that it was very possible that the degree could go ahead, and that he could give it the 'amber light'. Patrick pointed out that in a British traffic-light sequence red and amber showing together was followed by the green light, but then followed by amber alone before giving way to red as stop. Really, the 'amber light' on its own should have meant that the course would be brought to a stop. To get the go ahead we had to configure the MSc Critical Psychology as a 'distance-learning' as well as a 'campus-based' degree, and that meant producing detailed course handbooks which would lead the student through readings and assignments. Dave Nightingale pushed for more information technology support, but this was repeatedly blocked, and instead we produced four volumes of course handbooks which we would then post out to the students. Bolton Institute had been bedazzled by Patrick's appointment presentation, but the internet was viewed as a mysterious realm, it seemed, rather like international work. Dave met with the head of IT services with detailed proposals for a website which would support the MSc Critical Psychology programme and promote the department, to be told that perhaps we shouldn't move too fast, that it perhaps was not a good idea to "clutter up the internet". Dave had already been told off for airbrushing away the Tower Block from an image of Bolton Institute and popping in an image of a nice lake in draft publicity for our new programme.

We realised that speaking out against the abuse of power in psychology – that's what we were attempting to do in our critical psychology – was very different from objections to psychology in the right-wing press. I gave a talk at the British Association for the Advancement of Science in September 1998, for example, which attracted the attentions of *The Daily Telegraph* which reported my talk with the headline 'Psychology a fake science that deceives public'. Mr Wedgewood, who had bothered us at our discourse analysis conference six years before, reappeared but in more sinister mode, harassing one of the other speakers, Ann Phoenix, beforehand by email. He objected to the critical work that Ann was doing on gender and 'race' and wanted to speak out for science. The conference organisers and chair of our session were alerted, and things were unpleasant for Ann but proceeded without disruption. I received letters congratulating me on speaking out against the mollycoddling of people rather than getting them to take responsibility for their actions, another warning that complaint at psychology comes from the right, those who want to disregard the personal aspect of political questions, as well as from those of us on the left who see in psychology a betrayal and distortion of our individuality.

While there was some anxiety about the blossoming of new forms of virtual interaction on the internet, there was much enthusiasm, something we were also trying to tackle in a way that would avoid a psychological framing of the issue. I was putting together an edited volume on *Cyberpsychology* with Ángel Gordo López, the argument being that these forms of technology created anthropological spaces in which we could see being born new forms of subjectivity that escaped the kinds of psychological description that the discipline had given so far of memory and cognition. We wanted to move fast to try and seize the possibilities that were opened up by a kind of psychology in cyberspace that would serve to unravel all the traditional claims about psychology inside the head. We didn't really want to put cyberpsychology in the place of old paradigm laboratory-experimental psychology, any more than we wanted to build a 'critical realist' psychology that would improve on the old kind. We wanted to move fast because we suspected that psychologists themselves were planning to move in on this new territory. We were right, new journals devoted to virtual networking were already in production by the very year we published our book. Ángel had already given a talk for us at MMU about cyberpsychology when he was an Erasmus student across at the Victoria University, and dressed up for the talk in rubber wellington boots and a silver top. The book launch in the cold desolate upstairs room of Fuel bar in Withington in November 1999 was just as weird.

For the MSc Critical Psychology course we assembled teams of writers who were assigned to write the introductions to the readings and formulate the essay questions. The first modules and handbooks were ready in time for a first run of the MSc from September 1998 following a 'validation' of the programme for which the external assessor was Carla Willig. Alongside this we began a series of annual international lectures on critical psychology. We got funding from the British Psychological Society for Gordana Jovanović to visit from Belgrade University. This was a marvellous opportunity that turned into a complete disaster. Shortly after

Gordana arrived in February 1999 NATO bombing began of Yugoslavia, at the end of March, with the aim of preventing further Serbian attacks in Kosovo. She watched reports of the bombing of Belgrade, of the bridges near the house where her parents lived, and she couldn't return home. Bob Oxtoby had retired, and a new Principal of Bolton Institute, Mollie Temple, had taken over in January that year. Mollie supported the development of the MSc Critical Psychology, attended Gordana's lecture, and provided additional financial support when Gordana was stranded here with us, staying for some time in our house in Manchester. Some sections of later stage MSc course handbooks were written by Gordana during this time, who managed to return via Budapest in July that year, just after a conference on Critical Psychology and Action Research. We held that conference at MMU because Bolton Institute closed its main buildings for repair work and refused to negotiate over our plans for an international event.

This was the conference where we launched the first issue of *Annual Review of Critical Psychology*, *ARCP*, on the theme 'Foundations'. Papers from the action research conference were published in the second edition of the journal, and reflected one of the unexpected emerging themes during the conference, which was the impact of the work of Augusto Boal in his 'theatre of the oppressed' that had been developed in Brazil. We had talks about the theatre of the oppressed, a community intervention in which the audience were invited to act out different scenarios themselves and explore possible political courses of action. Boal returned to Brazil in 1996 after the dictatorship fell, and became active in the Partido dos Trabalhaldores, using theatre of the oppressed events to enable communities to discuss 'participatory budgets'. He spoke in the conference room in Manchester Town Hall in October 1998. James Thompson from Manchester University spoke at our conference about his work using Boal's approach in prisons in Brazil, and organised a workshop one evening at Friends Meeting House. James set up a stage scene with some members of the audience in which we played prisoners and guards. Notice how different this is from the classic Zimbardo study where participants were locked into their prisoner and guard roles. There was a key moment where the prisoners had to work out how to confront a violent situation. The idea was that together on the stage the performers would work out how to manage things, and that the audience would watch and learn and discuss what had happened afterwards. Jane Callaghan, one of Erica's PhD students, was in the audience, and grabbed the hands of fellow spectators to storm into the stage area to support the prisoners. This broke the frame of the play, broke the frame of the Boal technique, and took us a step further into thinking about what action research should really be about.

My time at Bolton Institute was marked by two deaths. It began just after the death, in November 1995, of Klaus Holzkamp, a founding figure of the German tradition of *Kritische Psychologie*, KP. I never met Holzkamp but was invited to speak at the commemoration of his work in Berlin in January 1996. His partner Ute Osterkamp told me that at the time of his death he was reading *Deconstructing Developmental Psychology* and was becoming more taken with Foucault's work.

Gordana's understanding of critical psychology was shaped by this German tradition, and Holzkamp's death prompted publication of more of his writings in English, as well as some splits in the German KP, between those who adhered to a stricter Marxist project of developing what their founder had called a 'science of the subject', and those influenced by postmodernism, those who wanted to loosen the truth claims made by any kind of psychology concerning how peoples' minds worked. My response to the German KP work was always really more in line with the 'relativist' argument than the 'realist' one. That is, it did seem as if the goal of German KP was to construct what they then took to be a scientific model of the human subject that would be real, and this model would then limit our capacities to relativise psychological stories about who we were and could be. I saw this psychological realist tradition of work as being quite conservative despite its Marxist theoretical reference points.

Closer to home, as we were putting together the first issue of *ARCP* in early 1999 the sad news came through of the death of Rex Stainton Rogers. Rex was a large genial man with a booming voice. He examined one of my PhD students in February 1996, concluding the viva with a loud declaration to the stunned Mark Stowell Smith that "If you were a dog you would be worried now, because you've been doctored". I could forgive the student if they didn't immediately hear this as good news. I examined two of Rex's PhD students, Nick Lee and Carol Owens, and it was on one of these occasions that I asked Rex about the unconscious. "Freud?" he replied, and then he wondered aloud, "Has my childhood affected who I am today?", posing it as a question to himself which was followed by a brief silence while he performed carrying out a little mental inquiry, and then came the answer, "No, never really thought about it", so that was that. At seminar talks he would be accompanied by Wendy Stainton Rogers, who sat eating bananas and interrupting, or she would speak and he would playfully disrupt the talk. The bananas were a source of quick nutrition. Wendy said coming north of Watford "gave him hives" and she travelled up once on her own to do a seminar for us in Bolton in October 1996. She was chewing nicotine gum. I have never smoked, but took a bit and felt sick throughout her talk. I learnt that, as with other psychoactive substances, nicotine has physiological effects, but no predictable psychological ones. Rex died quickly after complications arising from diabetes, a problem he refused to take seriously as a medical condition; he detested doctors, believing in critiques that emphasised the iatrogenic effects of medicine, the ability of the medical system to 'story into being' new maladies while it pretended to cure the old ones. The humanist funeral in the parish church at Long Wittenham in February 1999 brought together the critical polytextualists of Beryl Curt, and we included a tribute to Rex in the first issue of our journal.

Our slow-hatching *International Journal of Critical Psychology* mutated very quickly into *ARCP* at almost the last minute, after our first announcement of its launch. Valerie Walkerdine sent me an email congratulating me on the initiative but also saying that while she didn't want "to rain on my parade", as she put it, the *IJCP* title had already been signed up by her with Routledge. There was clearly some rivalry over how critical psychology would be defined and where it would be located which was also expressed in the almost simultaneous launch of an MSc Critical Psychology at Valerie's Centre in Sydney. Nevertheless, she came to our 1999 conference where we launched our journal and she participated in the final plenary session. Bolton had provided a base for developing some forms of critical psychology, but we needed to connect with other places to develop it further and being at Bolton made that difficult. To do that, we had to regroup in Manchester. We will be back in Manchester for the last part of this book.

One of the lessons of the fruitless and stupid 'relativism-realism' debate – a debate neither side wanted and which was conducted in terms that neither of us chose – was that there is a big difference between psychological experience and the discipline of psychology. 'Psychological experience', if we agree to refer to our subjective sense of ourselves in that way for a moment, is multi-faceted; it is relative to time and context. There is amazing diversity and variety to psychological experience, how we think about ourselves and others, this despite the increasing success of the discipline of psychology to define and regulate how we think and speak about ourselves. There is no 'real' that could be detected or enforced by professional psychologists, and we should not allow them to pretend that this is what they are doing. The discipline of psychology is grounded in a certain kind of society, capitalist society, and a relativist social constructionist account can be used to show how it parades as truth while only providing a very partial limited account of what it is to be human. But, at the same time, we need to acknowledge that the discipline of psychology is itself locked into this society, repeats and reinforces it. There is something real in that, something that can only be grasped through an analysis of forms of power and control; we can grasp the possibilities that relativism offers – to cut against the truth claims of the discipline – and also attend to the power that psychologists have to define what is real. Let us relativise power in order to dismantle it, and to speak truth to power is to speak as human beings who are marked by the contradictory nature that the use of language bestows upon us. That is a concern of the last part of the book; the final four chapters shift focus from teaching and research to the nature of contemporary institutions and trace the eruption of institutional crises that speak of power and of resistance.

PART V
Institutional crises

17

QUANTITATIVE

Administrative and personal

In which we return home, now part of the apparatus, to discover that there is more to psychology than teaching and research, a bruising context in which we try to find out how people think and what they will do next. We assess students and each other, and try to resist getting recruited into some bureaucratic manoeuvres that will change the balance of power in an academic department and university.

This looks like a new beginning, but it was the beginning of the end. This book has tried to show how the discipline of psychology is a problem in and of itself, but also how the discipline is curiously intertwined with institutional processes which corrupt it further, which exacerbate what is already, at root, psychology's alienating and destructive nature. This part of the book illustrates how psychology is like and unlike other academic disciplines which are subject to similar institutional processes. It is worse, for it promotes precisely the very forms of discipline and subjectivity that power in contemporary capitalist society routinely mobilises against us. We begin to see in this chapter how the chain of command in a psychology department is infused with psychological conceptions of leadership, personal responsibility and power.

Transgression

Once again the Research Assessment Exercise opened a temporal window. I moved out onto the ledge. The next government census of academic work carried out in higher education was due in 2001, and I wanted to return to Manchester Metropolitan University. I was tiring of the commute. I had continued supervising PhD students at MMU during my time away, organised the 1999 Critical Psychology and Action Research conference at the Elizabeth Gaskell campus, and was keen to again work in the city where I lived. The new Dean of Faculty, Leni Oglesby, unlike her predecessor, was keen on research, and so in 2000 I wrote to MMU Vice-Chancellor Sandra Burslem to tell her that I would like to come back if that were possible and to ask her advice about what I could do to make that happen. Sandra, who had sent a cheery response four years before to my letter advising her that I was about to leave, didn't reply.

The particular names are fairly unimportant in the machinery of the institution. What matters more than the personality or idiosyncratic behaviour of these people, or the other characters that replaced them soon after, is the political context to which they bend as they try to maintain their positions. If they fail to bend then they are finished, and must retire or move on to try their luck elsewhere, but when they succeed they serve as role models for a host of littler wannabe leaders lower down the apparatus. There is an intimate link between administration and personal relationships that should be of interest to psychologists, but it is precisely that link between the two that is repeatedly overlooked while reinforced by the discipline. It is not really psychology as such that is in charge in this wider scheme of things but the play of power, as we shall see, and here psychology plays its distinctive part in present-day institutional processes.

When a new post of professor in my old department was advertised a few months after I had written to Sandra I put together my application and visited my colleagues there to talk through with them what the institutional context now was for this job. I knew I would need to pitch my covering letter to address debates that had been going on there, and knew that, as in every department where this happens, there would be competing expectations about who might be appointed. The situation was quite grim, for the university had recently been subjected to the Teaching Quality Assessment and research had been put on the back burner. Now it was lurching back again toward the idea that it should focus on publishing and on obtaining research grants, with the complication that those researchers with strengths in one activity were not so devoted to the other. On top of that, there was some anxiety about whether psychological research in MMU would be viewed well by the RAE panel that oversaw this discipline. Qualitative research, community action research and feminist research were still not seen as 'scientific' by psychologists enrolled as gatekeepers for assessment and funding, and we suspected that discursive and critical research would be even less well received. The panel was supposed to evaluate four publications, ideally to be refereed journal articles by each member of staff submitted, but the proportion of staff in the department publishing in journals was still low.

There was another complication, which was that there had been plans to develop a 'counselling psychology' programme in the department, and Carolyn Kagan, who had pushed for this over many years, had been promised that there would be a new appointment devoted to that project. Counselling psychology was emerging as a teaching and research field sympathetic to qualitative research and political critique of the rather dehumanising practices of its host discipline. This was partly because humanistic psychologists were attracted to counselling and psychotherapy generally, and so they seized this opportunity to connect their agenda for personal change with changing psychology itself. However, in order to persuade the British Psychological Society that the new approach was different from counselling and psychotherapy outside psychology they had to claim that they drew upon an accumulated corpus of scientific knowledge about the development of emotion, thinking and behaviour. To get students to pay for a university course longer and more intensive than most other trainings they had to promise something in return, which was the cachet of empirical proof that the techniques worked, as well as offering higher professional status than those positioned as rivals in the marketplace.

Carolyn argued that instead of conforming to this mainstream model of what counselling psychology was, MMU should make it clear that it was doing something different, more radical and closer to action research and community social psychology. She had plans to expand the remit of the speech therapy clinic as a community resource as a base for a counselling psychology practice that would transform this new sub-discipline. This would mean opening up systemic family therapy perspectives in counselling to frameworks that had emerged from feminist research, and change the way that counselling psychologists thought about what the aim of therapy was. This would be congruent with what Carolyn called 'critical community psychology', and, for all the limitations of community psychology, she was right. Community psychology as such was now being instrumentalised and institutionalised in contexts where it became even more obvious that that approach was devotedly psychological. Carolyn knew this. Now she felt betrayed, for the new post that was actually advertised was more general, and even if I could claim to have some interest in psychotherapy – I was well into my own psychoanalytic training – the BPS required teaching staff on an accredited course to be registered as 'counselling psychologists' rather than any other competing brand. This was part of an increased drive to standardise courses and inspect provision according to the 'bench-marking' of degrees across Britain. So, there was a tension between what was being opened up by counselling psychology as a new field of practice that could connect with critical work and the attempt to regulate, that is, to administratively define what made counselling psychology distinct as a training that could charge high fees to prospective students. I met Carolyn and Sue Lewis who was also involved in the counselling psychology plans, though not qualified as a practitioner herself, and they reluctantly gave me some of the course document proposals, clearly not happy with what was going on, aggrieved at what they characterised as lack of direction and leadership in the department.

There were interviews, of course, and I was lucky that my main competitor for the post did research on language and nonverbal behaviour, on 'discourse' he claimed during the poorly attended presentations of our work to the department, and he had no interest in the broader traditions of critical, feminist and community action research that MMU psychology was known for. There was a long-standing tradition in the department that other lecturers should have the right to at least attend presentations by shortlisted applicants for posts. Peter Banister, who was still head of department, used to encourage staff to look through application forms and feed in their views to the appointment panel. This practice could have led the department to appoint people who would fit in, a problematic issue for equal opportunities and could serve to exclude people who were different. As it was, this most minimal staff participation in candidate presentations did ensure that the competing aims of the different sub-groups were balanced out and feedback was often ignored completely by the panel bound by a more rigid set of agreed criteria and overseen by Human Resources representatives. Voluntary attendance at candidate presentations did make the process more transparent. I had undertaken appointment panel training in MMU before I left, a process that included us interviewing actors brought in to test whether we could deal with applicants who were intent on misleading us, and I had sat on selection panels here in this institution and acted as an external assessor at other universities. It was a fairly transparent fair process.

I was phoned by Bill Hallam from Human Resources at MMU to say that they wanted to offer me the job. Bill had been appointed by Manchester Polytechnic Vice-Chancellor Ken Green as Director of HR, jumping across from being head of NATFHE, the staff union. Union activists at lobbies of Governing Board meetings would then shout sarcastically "Good old Bill, you won't let us down will you" as he walked into the building. He was known as 'little Ken'. I was surprised and relieved to be given the post, and felt I should tell Mollie Temple, my Principal back in Bolton. She wrote to me saying that Bolton Institute would raise my salary to match that offered by MMU, which was a good deal higher than what I had been earning, but the letter was dated after the deadline for me to sign contracts to return home, and I did anyway want to get back to Manchester.

MMU was, for all of the problems I relate here, very loyal to its staff, and that provoked grudging loyalty in return. People in the department didn't seem surprised when I turned up again. It was as if I hadn't been away, and a warm welcome was accompanied by the comment "well, you're back". I was very happy. My old office in E Block had been taken over by Erica Burman, and so I was given a tiny room with bars over the window in the ground-floor speech therapy corridor in the main building, an office formerly inhabited by Maye Taylor who had just left the university. The cafeteria on the ground floor of E Block had been closed and replaced with vending machines in a little room called 'Café Almost', and the waiting area adjunct to the 'New Lecture Theatre' which the toilets fetched off was also used as a classroom, a rather smelly one; we would rather teach in the Portakabins installed in the car park than there.

This year, 2000, was when we finally had the PhD viva voce examination for Terence McLaughlin whose research was on the history and politics of the Hearing Voices movement. Terence was a scholar, but a very unusual academic who combined his work in the university with activism for *Asylum Magazine* and many other aspects of mental health politics. This mental health movement, he used to say, was now the revolutionary vanguard force, and he threw his energies into it. At some moments he also saw the Discourse Unit as part of that force, and occasionally used to ask how we could 'recruit' people to it. We continued to have our meetings together in room E16, as Erica had continued to do after I left, and we used the little lecture theatre E17 on the other side of the one-way mirror for Terence's viva one June Friday. The external examiner was Marius Romme, the Dutch psychiatrist who had inspired the Hearing Voices movement, and so I was apprehensive about how it would go. The thesis combined a historical account with personal and political reflections on what hearing voices might mean for psychiatry and society, and I knew it would challenge Marius as much as it did the mainstream approaches that treated these voices as signs of pathology. I was apprehensive, not only because I worried each time a PhD student went into examination, whether I had made the right judgement as to whether the work was ready, and I agonised each time about whether this or that particular examiner would behave like a decent human being.

I used to attend every viva, in accordance with MMU regulations, taking notes about the process so I could discuss them with the student afterwards, knowing that they were likely to be in such a high state of anxiety that they would not themselves be able to remember what the examiners had said to them. There was a format in the rather strange private enclosed viva examinations for a PhD in Britain that was often a mystery to the student before they experienced it themselves. I realised how strange this was all the more after being on tribunals for PhDs in Barcelona, travelling there and back from Manchester in one day several times, events that were public and in which, after a presentation of the research by the candidate, examiners were expected to give a talk about how the research reminded them of issues that interested them. These were set-piece events in which the decision about the quality of the thesis had been made beforehand by committees in the university, and so the formality of the ritual was balanced against the sure knowledge that everything would eventually unroll as planned. The tribunal would, after the presentations, meet briefly and one member would usually suggest that the thesis was so good that it should be marked as 'cum laude', awarded the degree with distinction, which indeed it invariably was. This public process also meant that the candidate who had attended other such events by friends knew what to expect.

Our PhD vivas were more precarious affairs, something I already knew from my own, but what I learnt from seeing my own students through the process was that each stage was fraught with dangers, from the choice of the examiner to the way the student approached the event. Our first viva for Deborah Marks in Manchester in 1993 with Valerie Walkerdine as examiner had, perhaps, been the most nerve-wracking, and we, Erica and I, both felt on trial too as we searched for signs of Valerie's approval or dislike of what she had read. As time went on, the arrangements became even more complicated as we formed networks of researchers doing similar work, but these were researchers who always had histories of friendships and jealousies which could be played out at the expense of the student. There was, in addition to the external examiner, an internal, but that appointment of an internal could also be hazardous. Often it was extra work that would be taken on as a favour, and one could run out of such goodwill just as quickly as one could run out of sympathetic colleagues who were also skilled enough to negotiate with the external and, in some subtle way, advocate for them. I would examine PhDs for colleagues and then, in return, they would act as examiners for my students, but each time there was implicit close examination of the supervisor almost as much as of the student. There were institutional limits on the number of times we could use the same examiners, and there were some examiners we vowed never to ask again.

For all the checks and balances in the submission of preliminary reports by the examiners before the viva and the discussion between examiners, and sometimes with an independent chair for the event, there was an element of chance which could lead to some nasty surprises. While the normal outcome for a PhD examination is 'minor corrections' that can be carried out fairly quickly, examiners sometimes take offence if their own work isn't cited by the student, and they might then ask for amendments or additional sections to be written, sometimes finding excuses for asking for this extra work. The process is mysterious and unfair. I have been brought in on a number of occasions as a 'third' examiner after things have gone badly wrong in different institutions, and in most cases the examiners were at fault, causing unnecessary suffering to the students involved.

I was even more apprehensive than usual in the case of Terence McLaughlin's viva because he wanted to exploit a loophole in the examination regulations that allowed him to invite friends to attend. This request was frowned on; students usually didn't want to cause trouble and so they invariably agreed to go along with the normal procedure in which they would be sat in a room with two or three other people and their future would be decided in that private space. But Terence argued that this was an opportunity to make the process public and visible to other PhD students so they could learn from it and, more importantly, it would be in keeping with the ethos of his thesis as an analysis and intervention, as action research. It should, to borrow the Marxist Vygotskyan terminology of Fred Newman and Lois Holzman in New York, not only be about the 'result' of the research but function as a 'tool' for future research; the thesis and the examination together should be a 'tool-and-result' turning E17 into a zone of proximal development for all of us.

Carolyn Kagan came to the rescue as internal examiner, as she often did, with Rebecca Lawthom as independent chair, always a reliable supportive ally; they were not only up for this innovative breaking open of the secretive viva space, but also had the social skills to manage Marius Romme and an audience. It was fortunate that public PhD tribunals are also the rule in Holland, so this was not such an extraordinary event for Romme, perhaps, but he could not but be aware that a long friendship and collaboration over radical psychiatry and critical psychology was also being tested. I was allowed to attend the first pre-meeting of Carolyn, Rebecca and Marius on the morning of the viva, and while they had lunch and a more detailed discussion about how they might schedule the questions, I rushed to E16 where a little crowd from the Discourse Unit and beyond had assembled. Terence was there. I tried to reassure him by saying that, from what I had heard so far, there was nothing he didn't deserve. He reminded me that he had gone to a Catholic Christian Brothers school, from which he had been expelled for being a Marxist after one of the Brothers found him reading Freud's *The Interpretation of Dreams*, and calmly told me that I shouldn't say that there was nothing you don't deserve to someone who had been subjected to that kind of moral education. Erica told me that if I couldn't think of anything really helpful to say I should keep quiet.

We filed into E17, and Rebecca told the audience that we should all keep quiet throughout the viva, act as if we were not there. Terence was told that he should not look at us, let alone address his answers to us. In this tense but transgressive atmosphere the viva unfurled for nearly two hours, with questions about method from Carolyn, and about psychiatric categories and the development of the Hearing Voices Network in the UK from Marius. There was discussion of the sections of the thesis that covered the contribution of Marxism and questions about contradictions between this and the more personal reminiscences Terence included about being in Ireland among the spirits and elves, beings that were more real to him than the things that psychology described. I was not the only one itching to intervene and clarify how this point in the thesis answered that objection by Marius. His brow was furrowed, he looked worried, lost. Straight questions were met, instead, by Terence's typical elliptical Zen-like pronouncements about the nature of activity, change and history. We relaxed the moment Marius dropped his hand to his side to rest on his briefcase, one rapid movement in which he seemed also to relax and declare out loud that, at last, he got it; "Now I see", he said, "it isn't supposed to make sense".

PhD vivas were never easy rides, and none of our students wanted to be waved through with no questions. This meant that selecting examiners was always a difficult task, balancing the need to get someone who would be rigorous enough in their questions against finding someone who was still reasonably behaved when they were handed some power. Over the years our list of examiners included more names to avoid. There were some lucky escapes. One examiner that a student was very keen to have for his viva refused to send a curriculum vitae and list of publications to the university, telling me first of all that I could look him up on Amazon and copy his book-list for the forms, and then saying, when I phoned him about it, that "well, I'm not that interested in the topic anyway". And there were some nasty experiences. One examiner filled out the initial assessment forms, which should have functioned as a safety net to pick up if they really didn't like the thesis, and then turned up on the day to berate the student over the title of the work, demanding that the whole thing be rewritten before another viva a year later. It was a mean trick, they humiliated my student and subjected the student to a year of misery and anxiety because of a disagreement over method and I haven't spoken to them since. In some cases the students behaved badly, one taking in a tape recorder to try and faze the examiners.

When the shoe was on the other foot, when I was examining PhDs, I always had that anxiety at the fate of my own students ringing in my head, as well as remembering how I too felt on trial during my own viva, as well as those of my students. There were some tricky moments when there had to be a discussion with the student in the viva about what needed to be done to turn a bad thesis into something that could be passed, and sometimes emotions ran high; mine, with some anger at a supervisor who had allowed a submission of work that was really not ready yet; and the students, disappointment that it was not as they had been promised. In one case,

I agreed with the other examiner that we needed to spend the viva time discussing what more work needed to be done, but we were so anxious about how the student would take this, perhaps, that we barely waited until they had sat down to tell them the PhD was not ready to be passed yet. We were subjected to a torrent of abuse from the student who told us that we were behaving like his parents and treating him like a child. We held our nerve and calmed things down. Afterwards the student emailed me to tell me that they were willing to explain to me how I should have handled the viva. I declined the invitation. I should have accepted it. The thesis was resubmitted, it was fine, and we passed it.

Carolyn Kagan had been a good friend and comrade from the beginning of my time in Manchester, and to Erica as a colleague while I was away. She could be relied upon to take a problem and dismantle it, testing out strategies for addressing it in the institution. This even despite some quite deep political differences over what our attitude should be to existing bureaucratic regimes that pretended to be socialist. Visiting students were sometimes shocked to find huge posters of Hugo Chávez on her office wall, and we were sometimes subjected to reports of activity in committee meetings that seemed almost as long as Castro speeches. There were jokes that she managed to deal with the bureaucracy in Manchester Polytechnic and then MMU so well because she liked order, that action research in the community for her usually amounted to turning people into well-behaved citizens who would learn better how to participate in the existing state of things rather than revolutionise their own lives. Terence tested her patience on many occasions when she wanted clear thinking and constructive answers, and this made us appreciate the support she gave him during his viva all the more.

Carolyn should have been promoted to professor before us, and we knew it. I think she didn't resent it because she didn't write much for academic journals, and, rather than play the standard research assessment game that clicked into action every five years or so, she carried out small-scale projects which resulted in reports for Manchester City Council or other non-governmental organisations that tried to improve services. Our first professor in the department was Hilary Klee, a cognitive psychologist who made the smart move of taking a year unpaid leave from teaching in the early 1990s so she could spend time in and around the research councils that funded large-scale projects. She secured funding for research into drug addiction and HIV/AIDS, burgeoning health psychology agendas, and from then on disappeared from teaching to run a Centre for Social Research on Health and Substance Abuse. She was a bright, brittle figure who directed a research programme on addiction that had a linked funded PhD studentship from 2000 to 2003. She was happy to direct the work on the programme while I supervised the appointed student, Christian Yavorsky, for his PhD. Christian made the sushi for our 2001 'Asylum in the Twenty-First Century' Bastille Day conference which was held at Friends Meeting House in the centre of Manchester. It was an unusually delicious lunch for this kind of meeting and was eaten in a flash. This was the conference at which we made the disastrous, never repeated decision to allow the Scientologists to have a bookstall; some participants gave them a hard time over their own particular normative specifications about what was mentally healthy and what was not.

Christian Yavorsky's research, which included ethnography and film analysis, connected well with our concern with psychopathology, and he served as our interrupter from the floor to move us co-authors of *Deconstructing Psychopathology* and critical friends from fragment to fragment in our collective contribution to the June 2001 *Geist Gegen Genes* Russell Tribunal on Human Rights in Psychiatry in Berlin. This extraordinary Mind Against Genes event, which was co-sponsored by the Israeli Association Against Psychiatric Assault as well as Psychology Politics Resistance and the Discourse Unit, followed in the tradition of the Russell Tribunals which had begun with public investigations into US action during the Vietnam War. The Brazilian novelist Paulo Coelho spoke in the opening plenary session about his experience of being labelled and confined by psychiatrists, and liberation theologian Ivan Illich spoke in one of the parallel sessions about genetics and medicine, this a year before his death. We rushed back into the conference in time to attend the Illich session from a demonstration against police repression of anti-globalisation protests where we sold copies of *Asylum* magazine. A bizarre dream-like presentation of the Tribunal's findings in a press conference hosted by one of the Green Party representatives in the Berlin State Parliament degenerated at points into squabbles between Kate Millett and Thomas Szasz, who thought the verdict on psychiatry was not harsh enough.

There was, at this time, a division of labour in the department that worked well, and it was a model for the way we saw contributions from different professors who were good at either funding applications or academic publishing or research reports. Erica Burman was appointed professor in 1998, a promotion that secured her support from across the university and in the feminist networks that spanned the different universities in the Manchester area as well as a good reputation for critical research in the Discourse Unit at MMU. During most of the time I was in Bolton, however, most of her time was spent in Women's Studies, a cross-departmental network and degree programme with no actual physical base. This move from psychology to women's studies teaching was one way out of the difficult situation caused by the staff-student relationship rows in the mid-1990s, and it did also mean that Erica was quite marginal to decision-making in the department.

When I applied for the post that came up at MMU in 2000, Sue Lewis also applied as an internal candidate. MMU appointed me and also promoted Sue to professor, the right decision but one which called on the department itself to provide half of the funding for my post, something which I was sometimes reminded of when someone wanted to make me feel insecure about my position there. The balance of power was very unstable, a precarious balance of promises and threats that was directed to each of the individuals involved and that shaped the interpersonal relationships. It had psychological effects for sure, but those effects were expressions, not causes, of the structured set of positions we had to navigate as we tried to work with each other, whether as colleagues and rivals or comrades and friends.

These appointments of professors with different abilities and interests left Carolyn Kagan out in the cold. In November 2000, shortly after I returned to MMU,

I prepared a letter to Vice-Chancellor Sandra Burslem which explained that we four professors were concerned that the situation was not fair and that if Carolyn was not promoted in recognition of her work in community action research we were concerned that she might leave MMU. Hilary Klee, Erica and Sue signed the letter, and in the next round of professorial appointments Carolyn was promoted. This enabled some kind of bureaucratic balancing in the academic leadership of the department, but it also, at the same time, threw long-standing relationships and delicately poised rivalries out of balance. Our head of department, Peter Banister, was not a professor, and Carolyn had always bitterly complained that he should have functioned as a manager who would lead us forward. Whether we liked it or not we were tangled up in management.

Leadership

Carolyn Kagan's plaint that we did not have an efficient manager to guide us rested on a model of leadership that was thoroughly psychological, relying on an analysis of the abilities and faults of each individual at different locations in the pyramid of power that structured a traditional institution like ours. Carolyn wanted to be the leader because she thought she could manage the department better. This ambition could sometimes be rather worrying, not because we begrudged her the opportunity to implement some of the more radical policy initiatives around teaching and research linked to the community, but because it would entail a chain of command that would repeat the worst of the administrative structures in the university. It would implement those administrative structures inside our own department. Carolyn complained that, rather than arguing for us in the university, Peter obstructed initiatives that were developed in the Faculty or at higher levels. I would always respond by pointing out that these initiatives were usually designed to undermine our own work, and that Peter was defending our autonomy as a department, was obstructing those who were intent on subjecting us to endless procedures that would waste our time and drain our energies.

The department had grown in the last four years, and the office administration was becoming more cumbersome. Hilary Garrett, our departmental secretary, left and was replaced with a series of different administrators, which meant that procedures were starting to replace people, real people that the students and staff had been able to go to and discuss what should be done when there was a problem. A series of administrative assistants on short-term contracts appeared in the office and after struggling to make sense of the job would then move on, handing over to the next one. One particularly friendly guy called Dan took charge of processing hundreds of claim forms which we found stuffed behind the radiator a few months after he left. There were endless reorganisations of teaching and research in the Faculty which Peter could not stop also being implemented inside the department, the most dramatic of which was the formation in MMU of research institutes. This was Carolyn's chance to exercise managerial control over at least one domain in the university.

There was very little funding for the new research institutes, bodies that would in some cases correspond to departmental boundaries, but, in the case of our faculty, straddled psychology, social work and health research. Memoranda flew backwards and forwards, Carolyn complaining that a budget of just over 30,000 pounds was insufficient to hold the thing together, and then producing new versions of a business plan to launch it. The Research Institute for Health and Social Change (RIHSC) was set up in December 2003 with Carolyn as director, and she began to use this as an alternative power-base in the department, claiming resources and then the right to make decisions about what research should be supported, including decisions that undermined Peter as head of department. Carolyn was intent on showing that it was possible to lead research in an agreed direction and was open about that plan.

This did also cause some problems for the Discourse Unit. Erica's and my publications addressed psychology but in a way that ran against the ambition of the discipline to provide a 'psychological' explanation not only for individual behaviour but also for people's experience in other domains like education. Four miles down the road, at the Didsbury campus, a new Education and Social Research Institute (ESRI) had been formed which not only covered the field of childhood and education research, which Erica had been working on from way before *Deconstructing Developmental Psychology*, but also broader questions of methodology. More than that, ESRI was home to a group of researchers who styled themselves as 'post-structuralists' of some kind and they had hosted a series of workshops with Valerie Walkerdine, for example, as well as seminars on deconstruction and postmodernism. Ian Stronach who headed ESRI from its formation in 2003 had visited Bolton Institute in our Human Sciences seminar when I hosted it there to talk about post-modern research evaluation, and now he asked us if we would both like to have our publications for the next RAE counted in with education rather than psychology. As far as we were concerned, what was most important was that the publications would be counted as highly as they could be, and if that was to be under the education RAE panel rather than the psychology one then this surely would be for the best for MMU. More money would then come into the university from the Higher Education Funding Council for England as a result.

Carolyn was furious. If we "defected" to ESRI, as she put it, we would significantly weaken RIHSC and this would weaken her own position in the institution. When it became clear that we would most likely have our publications for the next RAE counted with education rather than psychology or social work she began to shift the focus of RIHSC from publications, which we had both been strong on, to grant funding. She began to ratchet up the pressure on us to show that our research was, she informed us, utilising a term used by the university to allocate resources, "sustainable". Even qualitative, feminist and community action research had to conform to an institutional model that divided up the research process into separate compartments that could then be sub-contracted to researchers on temporary contracts.

Formulation of the research, the interviews, the analysis and then writing up for publication would each, bizarrely, be treated as if they could be carried out by different people. This made 'salami-slicing' of a large research project into separate thin-as-possible journal papers possible, and it encouraged the researchers to keep bidding for money to extend their contracts. Intuitive engagement with the topic and then the material and the crafting of the analysis to make an argument that flowed from the initial aims of the research became impossible, as did, of course, participatory research that worked with and alongside people. This emphasis on the mechanics of research divided into the components described in the old textbooks was profoundly positivist. In this way an institutional practice which was geared to the needs of an academic world that was being privatised was pressing back alternative methodological approaches into traditional shape, back into traditional psychology. This is not what Carolyn wanted, but what the administrative context she participated in demanded. Among other things it demanded and replicated psychology.

I had a very difficult meeting with Carolyn in my new office up winding wood-chip wallpapered stairs on the first floor of the old Brook House building. I had escaped my little cell room with the barred windows, and now had a little more room to drape the plastic vines around the old heating pipes, decoration which also neatly covered up the peeling paintwork. I pointed out that the next RAE was still a few years off and that we were still committed to RIHSC as a space for doing radical research connected with social change. Carolyn wanted to know where the Discourse Unit would be based, and I explained that we had always maintained the unit as a place outside the institution. She threatened to withdraw any administrative support for our meetings, including possibly preventing us from using Room E16. I couldn't blame her for mentioning again that my post was part funded from within RIHSC and hinting that this was not "sustainable". This term 'sustainable' was originally borrowed from ecological discourse, and it did annoy me to hear it used in a context that spoke, instead, of business models.

At times like this, we could both usually step back from this pernicious business ethos that was structuring and distorting our friendship, and we could do this because we had some shared political reference points to make sense of what was happening in the university. But it was difficult. Whatever we really thought about it, whatever a psychologist might imagine they could discover about our personal choices as we coped inside this institution, the problem lay in the discursive practices that we resisted or reproduced, kicked against or colluded in. I agreed to set up a research group that would be part of RIHSC, even if we didn't work formally within it as the Discourse Unit. Carolyn said she would be happy to resolve it like this. The agreement almost broke down in the last few minutes of the meeting; there was an edgy couple of moments when we exchanged glances, but I didn't challenge her when she told me that what was most important in RIHSC was not that people should be in charge of things, but that they should think they were. It was a friendly attempt on her part, I think, to make an alliance with me again after a difficult meeting, and perhaps it was a joke, an allusion to our shared political allegiances. I almost laughed, but didn't, fortunately. It is easy to pretend that I would not have done the same, said the same, if I was in her position. Once, when I set out my ambitions to reconfigure a research institute in another university I had applied to manage, Erica told me that if I had got the job I would have behaved like Carolyn. Erica and I kept the Discourse Unit going – I had drafted a memo that would formally close the Discourse Unit in protest but held back from circulating it – and we still took shelter in our own meetings. We still felt fairly safe, and much safer than colleagues in other psychology departments who were being told to publish traditional quantitative research in mainstream journals or risk losing their jobs.

Peter Banister's management strategies mainly relied on knowing what information circulated in the department and how. To discover that, he would drop something into the conversation, something specific, something which he could pick up again later down a chain of gossip to work out who talked to whom. It was often easy to notice what was being fed by Peter into the knowledge circuits by comparing notes after meetings. That messed up his information gathering, much in the same way that reflection and sharing of information between participants in experiments messes up those little closed-circuits of knowledge production. Peter quickly worked out what the interests of each colleague were, and he also worked on that as a private channel of communication. For John Stirling who taught psychopathology, for example, it was about Volkswagen vans. We would sometimes notice a brochure about the latest design or a relevant newspaper article in John's pigeonhole. For me, it was *Star Trek*, and this was a genuine interest for Peter as well. He attended Star Trek conventions, and so we had him speak once about *Star Trek* at a meeting of the Discourse Unit; it was all the more a strange seminar, because our PhD student and autonomous Marxist Babak Fozooni was also there, and he was something of a specialist on the political economy and imperial structures of the world of Star Fleet. Peter was flummoxed by this, as were we all.

More widely, outside MMU, there were some sharp divisions over what critical psychology was, and suspicion that those divisions also entailed a battle for ownership of the term. Things came to a head at an International Critical Psychology Conference in Bath in 2003, a conference that was organised, among other reasons, to welcome Valerie Walkerdine back to the UK. Valerie was moving from Sydney to Cardiff University, and most of those attending the conference were there to support the development of critical psychology, something she had carried on building in Australia well after I left Bolton to return to MMU. There were some surprisingly mainstream talks at the conference, and some weird ones. Ken Gergen and Mary Gergen did a joint turn in which Ken announced that, rather than give a formal paper, he would do something more subversive; so while Mary swayed around whirling a feather boa scarf, Ken got out a banjo and started strumming on it. One report of the conference published afterwards in South Africa said it was like being at a terrifying Christmas party where a favourite uncle has gone senile and no one knows what to do. But this wasn't the worst of it.

One of my PhD students, Babak, rebelled against the congratulatory mode of the conference and rewrote his conference paper the day before he was due to give it, giving it the title 'Fuck Critical Psychology'. I told him this was a mistake, but there was no stopping him, and when I arrived at the final morning parallel session where he was presenting I realised with horror that Valerie was sitting in the audience. I sat next to her, mortified as Babak spoke, and she was understandably upset. The consequences of this performance rolled on for some time afterwards. It wasn't helped by Babak's edition, number 3, of *Annual Review of Critical Psychology*, which he edited under the pseudonym 'Melancholic Troglodytes' and in which he rather insultingly categorised contributions under different headings: 'Leninist' and 'Liminal' to signal that they should be treated with suspicion, and 'Revolutionary', those that had the stamp of approval and which included other articles pseudonymously written by himself.

I had registered the domain names 'www.discourseunit.com' and 'www.criti calpsychology.com', but when Valerie found out, this after the Bath conference, she phoned me and accused us of macho behaviour and me of trying to organise what she called a "trotskyite takeover of critical psychology". There was nothing I could do but apologise again for what had happened at the conference, assure her that I had tried to dissuade Babak from going ahead with his stupid public attack which she felt was personally directed at her, and arrange to hand over the domain name to her *International Journal of Critical Psychology* which was being published by the former Communist Party publishers Lawrence & Wishart.

In early 2004 we launched a new front group inside MMU which we used to host our public seminars, the rather clumsily titled Qualitative Research, Subjectivity and Critical Theory. Wise Carolyn, who gave such good counsel, once wrote an article which was critical of psychological notions of character and friendship. She pointed out in that article that when friendships end, the partners sometimes look back and claim that they never really knew the person they were friends with. This simply overlooks the fact, she wrote, that people change, that they might know each other very well when they were friends, but then they move on. We were comrades and friends, but malign institutional processes distorted our relationship, divided us and drove us into different competitive responses to the problems we faced.

Health

For all of these complications, Carolyn was still often an ally, and there were some bigger changes coming that we both had to confront that were worse and with deeper implications for my future at MMU. Our faculty was based at Gaskell and Didsbury campuses; the faculty included Psychology, Health Care Studies and Law at Gaskell, and Social Work at Didsbury. Health care studies included nurse degree training and was also home to a small group of researchers who were working on the sociology of health. The head of the Department of Health Care Studies was Dave Skidmore, someone who helped secure funding for one of our PhD students, Ilana Mountian, and one of the leading researchers was Joel Richman who carried out ethnographic research in health settings and who was the internal examiner for my student Christian Yavorsky's PhD on addiction. Joel's research was real ethnographic research, carefully tracing the relationships in a ward in a hospital and showing how the institutional demands were managed by the different actors. He had some interesting things to say about what he was seeing in our own campus, all the more interesting because they framed things in terms of relationships and power rather than imaginary mechanisms inside peoples' heads. Christian told me that he almost cracked and thought that his chances of getting the PhD were finished, when, during the viva, Joel had told him that it looked like a good book, but the question was whether it really was a thesis. Joel was coming up to seventy years of age, and after a medical procedure went badly wrong and a spinal nerve was accidently severed, was quite disabled. He could walk, but slowly, and he used to come in from time to time as an emeritus professor doing some teaching and shambling around the main campus building.

We could feel things closing in. The reprographics department at Gaskell was barely more than an office space next to the photocopier machine which housed Mike the technician who was also a photographic artist who would give us previews of his exhibitions, and Darrell who worked a few months on so he could take cheap flights and spend months off travelling. Now there were rumours that it would close. The psychology technicians in E Block were also increasingly beleaguered. Their chief, Peter, was often called away to attend meetings, so technician Gareth had less time to chat about *Dr Who* and the other technician John had less time to talk about everything. I only knew these three by their first names, signs of power in the privilege of personal address in this kind of place.

Even exam invigilation was more fraught in 2003. MMU used a Territorial Army training centre as one of the sites for examinations, and some students and staff, most notably Paul Duckett, a radical community psychologist, contested this. Paul argued that some students with family members or friends involved in the conflict, whether or not they were opposed to Western intervention in Iraq, may find it stressful, objectionable at least, to have to take their exams in that setting. We contacted the MMU student union and were told that the students just wanted to take their exams and had no problem with it. Paul pushed the point, and it was agreed that staff who felt uncomfortable with invigilation in the TA centre could swap their shifts with colleagues invigilating in other less controversial sites. Paul also led covert resistance against the request that we each hand over to RIHSC names and contact emails of people we were working with in different mental health and other activist organisations. The request was in line with 'community engagement', and the plan was that a shared database would be a platform for mobilising partners in different projects and public events, proof that we were inclusive as a research institute in the university. This was what Paul referred to, in a choice phrase we often repeated, as "shopping our friends".

The times we escaped from this entanglement with the needs of the institution were also times of reflection on how links with the 'community', however bureaucratically and instrumentally configured they were by the university, were important to our teaching and to attempts to make psychology more inclusive. We could see a sharp contrast, for example, between MMU and enclosed elite universities in other parts of the world. Erica was invited to teach a course at the University of Michigan in early spring 2002, and we spent time in Ann Arbor, a campus town where students sipped lattes in the cafés while tapping away at their laptops, and where senators flew in every day to address meetings, to groom the new ruling class. The professor who organised Erica's visit told us that her salary was not high enough to be able to afford to send her own children to that university. We went down to the basement of the Michigan League building in the evening to check out a hip-hop concert and asked where the drinks were. There was bewilderment before they got it and then looked at us like we were winos and told us we needed to go up and around the block to the liquor store if we really wanted alcohol. One day we drove to nearby down-at-heel Ypsilanti where we gave talks about politics and psychotherapy in a private house organised by the radical anti-medical 'Academy for the Psychoanalytic Arts', and then returned to the Ann Arbor academic bubble, conscious of the privilege oozing through it. On the final day at the beginning of April it was snowing as the carillon tower filled the centre of the campus with music; the Bengali student society set up their sound system and danced in the white flakes at their 'Bhangra in the Diag' event. These were times to step back and forget and then worry again about what was happening at home.

A new Dean was appointed in 2004 to replace Leni Oglesby, and the balance of power would now, Dave Skidmore thought, lie with Health Care Studies and so with him as head of that department. As soon as the appointment of Vince Ramprogus as Dean was announced, the story began circulating from health care studies that "he is one of ours" and that "he will be under our thumb". Vince, it transpired, had done his PhD at MMU, supervised by Dave, with sociological ethnographer Joel Richman on the supervision team. Vince had a book listed on Amazon as *The Deconstruction of Nursing* and so I wondered whether he might also link up with some of the critical work we were doing, until I had a look at the book. The term 'deconstruction' was clearly being used in much looser sense than even in our borrowings of it from French theory. Vince Ramprogus, unlike his predecessor, and in line with new directives about 'sustainable' development coming down from the central administration at All Saints, was mainly concerned with how we might attract funding for research and teaching, and he aimed to win large contracts with the local National Health Service. This faculty would, he said, be "the future of healthcare" in Manchester. His first meeting with staff at Gaskell Campus was quite disturbing. Vince anxiously gripped the lectern and seemed glued to the spot as we eyed the sandwiches at the side of the hall. He said that "standing still" was not in his vocabulary and that we had to recognise that "continual change" was inevitable and necessary. Dave Skidmore reassured us after the talk that we – and by 'we' he meant Health Care Studies – had Vince where they wanted him, and there was nothing to worry about.

The campus front of house staff complained shortly after his arrival that this new Dean had demanded his own marked parking place, which didn't seem to be so much of a crime, but that he had also made them get rid of the large shabby striped ginger cat they fed and which often slept on one of the low chairs opposite the entrance. Hollywood films often remind the viewer who the good guys are by showing them stroke a cat, and we had a sense that these new performances on the campus stage did not augur well. We did worry what would happen next in this tidying up first phase of Vince's reign. Then, in a series of dramatic changes over the next few months there were rumours of what was referred to in corridor whispers as "financial mismanagement", and Dave Skidmore was sacked. The next steps in this sub-oedipal saga – a stereotypical scenario in which the humiliated boy rebels against the patronising and weak father – were messier and more drawn out. At the beginning of the new academic year, in September 2004, Joel Richman was called into the Dean's office and Vince told him that there was no more teaching for him to do, his services were no longer required. Joel refused to leave, and the front of house staff refused to remove him, so Vince called the police, who escorted Joel out the building.

Different members of our department discussed these events with Joel over the next months, and I tried to persuade him to take it up with the union. We were trying to revive the Gaskell branch. But no, he said, no one would take him seriously, "I'm only", he said to me miserably, "a poor old crippled Jew". He was the latest and maybe the last victim of a vendetta waged by the new Dean, he thought. Joel said that since he had got on well with Vice-Chancellor Sandra Burslem in the past he could strike a deal with her, and showed me a list which included an apology for the way he had been treated and the demand for some compensation. I said I doubted this would work. Eventually something was settled, hardly anything financially, it turned out, but the price was that Joel should keep quiet about the events, which he certainly didn't do in one-to-one encounters in the following years after he disappeared from MMU.

There were certainly colourful characters on stage to flesh out the script that was steadily unrolling around us, but this shouldn't mislead as to where the problems lay. New institutional demands across the higher education sector were insinuating their way into work, into our lives, so that everyone suffered and wanted to take it out on the cat. Imagined conspiracies on the part of management were countered by secret meetings where we invented scenarios in which the figures embodying the threats could be caught out and removed. A discourse of 'bullying' that began to emerge was itself an indication that psychological explanations were increasingly in command, an attempt to counter measures taken against us, and they misled many of those involved, focusing on bad individuals rather than institutional coercion.

The following year, September 2005, Sandra retired and was replaced as Vice-Chancellor by John Brooks, an engineering physicist by background who came to us from Wolverhampton University. He called a first-ever meeting at MMU of the newly constituted 'professoriate' in May 2006 which most of us attended out of curiosity and decided never to come to again. At this Wednesday morning meeting Brooks told us, with the help of some finance graphs projected on the screen behind him, that we needed to be aware of the "financial bottom-line facts". After he finished speaking, one of the professors asked him about the importance of scholarship and academic freedom, and as he asked his question Brooks stood leaning back against the desk at the front of the room swilling apple juice from a glass and pumping it around his cheeks. He leaned further back, tipped his head to the screen while watching the questioner through almost closed lids before repeating the bottom line. Later at the meeting, the same professor put up his hand to ask another question; Brooks swung round and with an outstretched arm made a beckoning gesture sneering, "Ok, have another go".

This same September was the first run of the National Student Survey, the NSS heralded in the British press as serving as a wake-up call to the universities. The idea was that the NSS would gather attitudes and evaluations by students and publicise them so that universities would have to up their game to compete with each other to attract new applicants onto their courses. Instead of the quality of the course, the catchphrase of the NSS was that it focused on the 'student experience'. The student would thus, in a move that was a logical complement to the drive to make universities market their products to their students, turn the students into 'consumers', a word which Vice-Chancellor John Brooks himself embraced and often used. We heard from Carolyn Kagan in some of her tales from the top that Brooks humiliated our new Dean in senior staff meetings, sometimes reducing him almost to tears, and that she too was worried about what was going to come next. We found it difficult to believe that at his first meeting with senior staff when he arrived at MMU, Brooks asked who the union activists were and said he intended to get rid of them. I am told that he meant the best for MMU. When Brooks did meet with union representatives he told them that he had once been a member of the union but had left on a point of principal. When they asked him what the point of principal was, he said he couldn't remember. Why assume he was the bad guy?

I describe individuals who are happy to comply with the demands of the institution and individuals who refuse because the institution is populated by individuals who develop their own idiosyncratic ways of coping with what is demanded of them. There is, of course, a trap here in this account, that I make it seem as if we are witnessing a battle brewing between good and bad people. There will be an institutional crisis at the end of this story, and I guess you know that already, but we need to track the conditions of possibility for people to make the moves they did, to track the symbolic architecture of the institution if we are not to simply apportion praise or blame. That is what this auto-ethnography of psychology, a kind of 'biography of the disciplinary field' aims to keep focused on. I, for sure, am implicated in all this, and I want to show you in the next chapter how I got drawn into the looming crisis too, how I colluded with it.

18

QUALITATIVE

Watching them watching us

In which we try to make sense of what we are subjected to in the discipline as it functions organisationally, and we are led to reflect on our sense of paranoia in a community structured by an institution we cannot control. We then notice a twist in psychological paradigms that we had not seen coming, in which qualitative research turns into a driver for psychologisation.

Psychology in its most traditional quantitative laboratory-experimental mode shuts out personal experience. But it is too easy simply to complain about the way that the discipline treats people as objects instead of human beings. Psychology is also adept at incorporating ideas from qualitative research, and then the problem is not so much that it treats people like objects but that it turns them into subjects of a particular kind; these kinds of subjects are expected to monitor their own activity and to have emotional responses that can be tracked by researchers. This also poses a risk for my auto-ethnographic study of psychology, for that kind of anthropological investigation might itself end up reducing social institutional processes to personal characteristics of those who I describe here, and might end up also filtering the account through my own personal paranoiac responses to what happened. Please bear that risk, that trap, in what follows.

Mystification

Now it is 2011, a turning point for our project of critical psychology. These last few years have led us to suspect that there are institutional processes in the discipline and in our own university that will not end well. We have begun to notice the way that paranoia operates, and we have been attempting to disentangle the sense that we are under threat from the real dangers. We sense that this is the beginning of the end.

Psychological phenomena described in the textbooks never operate in their pure state, they are always entangled with elements of the context in which they appear to us, and within which we try to make sense of them. Those contexts – whether interpersonal, institutional or international – are themselves tangled up with relations of power. They are also tangled with ideological mystification that always makes something appear as if it were something else. This is a problem that psychologists have long tussled with, trying to find methods that will directly connect what they observe in an experiment, or in what they call the field, with the way things play out in the real world, a problem they name as the problem of 'ecological validity' of research. A field experiment for a psychologist sends them out into strange territory, out of the laboratory and into a real world that they cannot control as much as they would like. The laboratory-experimental frame is still in place, it holds the psychologist within its frame, but there are a host of 'variables' to be identified and a researcher out in the 'field' is uncomfortable. They are not at home.

There are, however, some psychologists who work in communities who are able to configure their objects of study in such a way as to turn the community itself, as well as each member of it, into an object they can study. Here they have to grapple with a paradox that structures every institution and every community, the sense that they can capture everything that is happening around them and the simultaneous suspicion that things are not exactly what they seem. This is a paradox that Marx observes when describing the factory system of production under capitalism; that at one moment this world seems well ordered and transparent to each individual and at the next it obscures exactly what it does to those inside it, as well as whose interest it serves, who it is that benefits from the illusion of transparency, the fiction that everything is out in the open. We were beginning to learn of the experience of colleagues who fell out with their own institutions, and this made us all the more suspicious of those who seemed to circulate up and around the university systems with apparent ease. There were psychological consequences of these processes of institutional power, and psychology itself is operative here in the way each process unfolds.

Each revelation about the institutional manoeuvres that structure the life of a psychology department, and each new rumour that pretends to throw light on what is really going on, also often unfortunately begs for a psychological explanation, an explanation that could make things worse. Our time in the Discourse Unit at MMU from 2000 was, among other things, a time of academic visits to colleagues around the world which helped us locate better what we were up against in Western psychology. Visits by colleagues to take courses, give seminars and attend conferences cued us into some of the most important issues, some of the most telling signs that all was not right; they helped us notice aspects of the situation that we would otherwise have taken for granted or simply felt anxious about without knowing quite why. Visits to other institutions also highlighted aspects of political context that bear on the way that academic organisations protect themselves, and the way they respond under pressure. The Discourse Unit was always international, either because of the students who came from different cultural traditions in psychology and other disciplines or because of the links we made with like-minded colleagues around the world.

One important international forum was the biennial 'SIP' Interamerican Society of Psychology congress, a society with a complex history bound up with what most US-American psychologists still call South America. The first SIP congress was in Santiago, Chile in 1953, and from the beginning the congress functioned as a place where psychologists from the Spanish and Portuguese speaking countries could meet. Some of our colleagues pointed out that the organisation also functioned as an appendage of the American Psychological Association, the APA which was founded at Clark University in the US in 1892 and which is a hugely influential force on the shape of contemporary psychology globally. Over the years more critical and action research-oriented psychologists have participated, though the tensions between the APA and radical SIP members have remained. The involvement of 'military psychologists', for example, has been a sore point, and I was told that when Ignacio Martín-Baró spoke at the 1989 congress in Buenos Aires a few months before he was murdered, military psychologists from Argentina and others with links to the Salvadoran army were present at his talk, sat in the front row. They were watching him, and even though radical psychologists watched them, they were helpless to prevent what eventually happened, as helpless as they were to prevent countless other such incidents across the continent. The APA has itself legitimised torture by its members who work with the US military over the years.

The first SIP congress we attended was also in Santiago, in 1993. It was a bizarre and moving experience to be in the opening ceremony staged in the headquarters of General Augusto Pinochet's military junta, to see Isabel Rodriguez-Mora stride across the stage, her long black curls flowing behind her to receive her SIP award for community psychology action research, and then, together with our Barcelona comrades, to be excluded by the VIP-only APA cocktail party which was there to mark this event as symbol of a return to democracy. Massive steel doors slowly divided the hall into those invited and the rest of us. We could not help but recall that the 1973 coup took place in this country vaunted as the 'England' of Latin America, and so very unlikely to see its long-standing democratic institutions crushed to nothing. The coup engineered by the CIA ushered in the first country-wide experiment in neoliberal economics. Neoliberalism pretends to leave everything open to the free market, but though it entails the stripping back of state welfare support for the poor it also entails the brutal exercise of power, a strong state. The coup was the culmination of a tense political process that provoked paranoia on the side of the powerful, and on the side of the powerless, those who were trying to change society but who came, too late, to see that their paranoia had some basis in the reality of what was looming ahead of them.

I gave a paper in terrible Spanish in a symposium organised by Tomás Ibáñez from Barcelona, and Erica, who was idly listening to the translation into English on headphones while reading Marge Piercy's feminist science fiction novel *Body of Glass*, said that the interpreter gave up at points, saying that they couldn't understand what I was talking about. It was the first very large international conference we had attended, and the schedule was as thick as a telephone book, with hundreds of parallel sessions from morning to night in a continual sequence running without any breaks. We returned to Chile several times teaching courses in later years, including at Universidad ARCIS in Santiago, a university closely linked to the resistance to the dictatorship. The privatisation of higher education and other state welfare services was so important to the regime that even before Pinochet lost power he permitted private universities, like ARCIS, to set up shop. Our colleagues who taught at ARCIS described how difficult it was to fail students on the basis of poor essays or exams, how they would be told, for instance, that this or that student could not be failed because they were a comrade, had been tortured by the army after the coup in 1973. Another of the private universities, Diego Portales, was set up by a businessman who gathered together the staff one day and told them, "I couldn't decide between setting up a circus or a university, but since I never had a chance to go to university, I chose that".

At the 1999 SIP in Caracas Erica encountered Christian Dunker, a critical researcher from São Paulo, who had some interesting things to say about paranoia. At a day conference we organised in Manchester in 2006 at the Didsbury campus of MMU where we had Kazushige Shingu from Kyoto as a speaker, the discussion turned to paranoia, Chris was there too. We were reminded of the Paranoia Network founding conference that was held on this campus July two years before. A team of international visitors from Brazil, Greece and Turkey joined with activists from *Asylum Magazine* and Psychology Politics Resistance to host the event and we included, as part of the process, space for people to give testimony on video about their experience and talk about their theories about paranoia. The decision to record some of the conference took a while, and we eventually put the cameras in a separate part of the hall so that if people wanted to come and speak to camera they could do so. In the main conference hall we heard from psychologists and psychiatrists and from users of services, some of whom had once been active in different kinds of revolutionary politics, and there were contributions from researchers who studied the securitisation of society, the way in which surveillance has become part of everyday life. One theme repeated during the day was that in contemporary culture one cannot be paranoid enough. As David Harper, a clinical psychologist who did his PhD on paranoia in the Discourse Unit, pointed out, there is a powerful motif of 'paranoia' in political discourse which informs how we relate to others.

Postgraduate research in the Discourse Unit was often explicitly connected with direct action against mainstream psychology. This was the case for those who were part of the Hearing Voices Network, of course, and there were also many initiatives that brought critical psychology of different kinds in conflict with those psychologists who wanted to reinforce dominant gender roles and normative sexuality. In December 2010, for example, one of Erica's students, Jemma Tosh, was centrally involved in protests against the BPS Division of Clinical Psychology invitation to Ken Zucker to speak at its conference that month in Manchester. Zucker, as well as claiming to be able to identify children with 'Gender Identity Disorder', and so pathologise transgender people, was also proposing that men who attempted rape three or more times should be diagnosed as having 'Paraphilic Coercive Disorder'. A letter from Jemma was signed by the BPS Psychology of Sexualities section and Psychology of Women section, chaired at that time by Christine Horrocks, backed up by demonstrators standing in the falling snow outside the conference, and this pressured the Division of Clinical Psychology to allow Jemma to speak inside the conference and to challenge Zucker.

Things were not always plain sailing inside our research group. The division between mainstream quantitative methods and qualitative research had some bizarre echoes in postgraduate supervision, even in the Discourse Unit. One PhD student enrolled from the United States, and after she arrived in Manchester, she told us that she was bound by the code of ethics of the American Psychological Association which required her to carry out quantitative studies. We could not track down exactly where this demand was spelt out as an ethical imperative in the APA, and neither could she, but the argument did turn into an irresolvable conflict. We brought in the director of research in the university to try and broker a deal by which the student would transfer to another supervisor, but the student insisted that she had the right to be supervised by me to carry out the kind of studies she wanted exactly as she wished. That deadlock only ended when she decided to leave. We did tend to attract students who were more rebellious than those in other parts of the department. In one case I was sent an email from an anonymous address after having argued with a student about the process by which the thesis should be submitted and examined. We were up against deadlines and I was trying to navigate the university procedures, but my student interpreted my attempt to mediate this process as an attempt to tell him what to do. The anonymous email said "Parker, violence is coming your way", and when I emailed the student challenging him about this, he said I couldn't prove it was from him. When I wrote back pointing out that it was possible to trace emails through the Internet Protocol numbers there was silence. Moral support as well as advice about tactics from Carolyn and Peter stopped me from over-reacting. The student got his PhD, and has done some great work since.

Another theme in the Paranoia Network conference was that the separation of people from each other, and the consequent privatisation of experience, intensifies a sense of alienation. That privatisation of experience transforms alienation from creative activity that characterises work under capitalism, transforms and intensifies it so that people become suspicious of each other and then even of themselves. That is, some aspects of the structure of life under capitalism become embedded in the lifeworld of each individual, and so if we want to understand 'psychology' we need to trace back where that psychology has come from. Our individual psychology does not spring up from inside the head but is a function of social relationships, the 'ensemble of social relations' as Marx put it and as Rowland Urey, one of the participants during the Paranoia day conference, also again reminded us.

Now, two years later, at our 2006 Didsbury day conference, Chris Dunker pointed out that researchers in psychology, and perhaps the same applies to all academic researchers, come to operate as paranoiacs. He spoke specifically about PhD research where the thesis topic is present in the life of the student for three years or more, and where everything that they see, whether it is in books, or in the cinema or on television, comes to speak to them as yet another instance of what they are studying. Researchers devoted to a cause that is the topic of their work search for that cause anywhere and everywhere, and it is by virtue of that search that they come to sense that they will be able to speak to colleagues about their experience and expertise and persuade them that the phenomenon they have chosen really is important. And, yes, I do have a tendency to see psychology everywhere. That, in part, is what this book is about.

These five years from 2006 saw many occasions when we were reminded that there was much more to Michel Foucault's account of surveillance than a simple accusation that we were being watched. There was enough of that. I got a certificate from the Director of Research Development for attending a 'Chairing a Viva' workshop in February 2006, and there were plenty of other events arranged to monitor our engagement with processes through which we would monitor the progress of the students. Foucault's *Discipline and Punish* emphasised the regulatory aspects of power, and this spoke to us inside psychology about the way that the discipline had emerged in the late nineteenth century contemporaneously with the development of capitalism in Western society, and of the way that psychologists seemed intent on 'prediction and control' of individuals. Crucial to Foucault's argument is both the idea that populations are rendered into separate individuals, their specific characteristics observed and tabulated by the professional, including by the psychologist, and the idea that those who are observed know that this is happening.

That second aspect of Foucault's argument is sometimes overlooked by those who fix on his description of the design for the Panopticon and then see Jeremy Bentham's design instituted in the proliferation of closed-circuit cameras and other surveillance technologies. The central guard tower may actually be empty much of the time, but what is crucial is that we come to arrange our own behaviour and the way we think about ourselves as if we are observed. Then, as a reverse-side of Foucault's argument, an argument that we can already find in Marx's writing about capitalism, people who learn to experience the world in terms of individual agency, their own and then that of others around them, also come to explain what happens in society as being the result of individual choices and machinations. From that thought comes the other side of a paranoiac vision of the world to the feeling of being watched; the misleading cul-de-sac of conspiracy theories in which we assume that evil capitalists or evil psychologists are up to no good and that they have it in for us. At one extreme of this conspiratorial logic are the fears of the Scientologists who see in present-day psychiatry the agents of Xenu who tried to annihilate us millennia back.

In this way, paranoia and conspiracy become core elements of our own psychology so that who we are comes to mirror and confirm what the psychologists think about us, what these psychologists think we are thinking. A year after *Discipline and Punish* was published Foucault drilled down further into this aspect of the argument, in his 1976 book translated as the first volume of *The History of Sexuality*. The subtitle in French which we can translate as 'The Will to Knowledge' or, better, as 'The Desire to Know' draws attention again to the process by which knowledge is extracted from people by psychologists who want to know about others, but Foucault also explores how what he calls the 'repressive hypothesis' inducts each individual into the sense that there is something about themselves that was hidden and that they will be healthier and happier if they bring it to light. Here Foucault turns from the question of surveillance to confession, to the incitement to speak which very successfully encourages people to believe that they should talk about their innermost thoughts and feelings to others, most importantly to professionals who, listening to them speak, will thereby relieve their suffering.

There is a one-sided reading of Foucault's argument in his book on sexuality that might make it seem as if the target of his critique is psychoanalysis, psycho-therapy and counselling that invites us to spill our guts on the couch, and then it as if Foucault is there indicting these psy-professions as new forms of confession. It is then as if confession in the church has now simply been replaced with confession in the clinic. However, as with the story about surveillance cameras in the disci-pline book, things are a good deal more complicated than that. Not for nothing did Foucault once work in prisons as what we might now call a 'forensic psychologist', turning against that profession and turning back the gaze of the psychologist onto their subject population, turning it back onto the psychologist himself or herself. The two sides of the process he describes in the two books, that of surveillance and that of confession, are painted across the broad canvas of Western civilisation over the last two centuries but are reproduced moment-by-moment in the minutiae of psychological research. An often-overlooked aspect of the notorious 'obedience' studies in social psychology, for example, is that the experimenter Stanley Milgram says to the subject, after he has debriefed them when the study is over, "Now that you know, how do you feel?" This makes explicit the flipside of traditional psycho-logical research; as well as deceiving their 'subjects', the psychologists want to know what their subjects are thinking and feeling, and asking them to speak about these things is an essential part of psychology itself.

This double process of subjection to psychology, to the discipline of psychology and to its discourse about the nature of individuals in the psy complex is some-thing we had to grapple with when teaching the Qualitative Methods module on a North West Consortium training programme coordinated by Steve Stradling from Manchester University and then on the master's degree at MMU. Steve, who had a life before psychology in a rock band and who then ended up doing research on 'traffic psychology', was open to alternative approaches to research and happy to include us before the cross-institutional Consortium was wound up. It was tempting on this module but too easy to depict the laboratory-experimental psychologists as the bad guys, as if they were deliberately manipulating peoples' behaviour with no concern for ethics. There were ethical principles at work in the laboratory studies; the problem was that they were the wrong ones, the kind of ethics that justified the unfortunate bad practice of deceiving people because of the good knowledge that would come out of it. This instrumental use of psychological research, treating it as a means to an end, was only half the story. Many psychologists were very willing to complement their experimental research in the laboratory with studies in 'the field' where they were happy to be more open about what they were doing, and they really wanted their participants to contribute their ideas in attitude surveys or personality questionnaires or focus groups. The hook was that it seemed more democratic to give people a say.

We knew this when five of us – me, Erica Burman, Peter Banister, Carol Tindall and Maye Taylor – got together to write a book on qualitative methods that would be the book of the MSc module. We met a few times, but we eventually had to patch together quite different approaches within qualitative methods that were distinct not only in terms of the outline of precise replicable steps to gathering and analysing data, but also in terms of the broader methodological principles we employed. The new paradigm in psychology was broadly qualitative and set against the positivist aim of accumulating a body of knowledge that could be taken as given by next generations of researchers. We had to bridge the gap in our five-handed book, however, between those of us who really wanted to question psychology and those who wanted psychology to adapt and be improved by what qualitative methods could offer. We already had to fend off forensic psychology students who told us they hated qualitative methods but then became enchanted by the idea that analysis of discourse would be a way of reading the minds of serial killers. They would deliberately, it seemed, overlook the crucial point that discourse analysis focused on discourse itself, not on things behind it or in the mind of the speaker, for they wanted to look into pathological processes under the surface and turn discourse analysis back into real psychology again.

One of my chapters was on discourse analysis, and it did set out 'steps' to the analysis – it was a chapter that has returned to haunt me many times since in discussions of discursive and critical psychology – and the other was the introduction in which I argued two lines; that we could treat the new qualitative methods as more scientific or we could treat science itself as a social construction. Carol Tindall's chapter on 'personal constructs' included a 'repertory grid' which aimed to represent an individual's personal constructs to the psychologist and to the person who filled out the grid, and could be read as a plea for what George Kelly called 'man as scientist' or as a deconstruction of that image of the human being. Carol used to introduce the Qualitative Methods module and headed up the counselling third year undergraduate option for many years'; she was a slightly deaf, rational and quintessentially humanist presence who would lay out the possible ways of doing the work to the students and then intone loudly and clearly "It's your choice". She was a humanising force in the department who used to bring in eggs from her hens at home and leave them in the staff pigeonholes; it was a delight to see the boxes sticking out higgledy-piggledy, a messy testimony to our ability to personalise public space. There was a chapter by Maye Taylor on ethnography which framed the process in terms of observations and hypotheses, terms that would be familiar to a psychology student, and there was not a whisper of 'auto-ethnography' which would have been pushing things too far perhaps. The book *Qualitative Methods in Psychology* was used as a course text in the Open University, and so sold well, this despite the fact, as community psychologist Maritza Montero from Venezuela pointed out, that we misspelt the name of Paulo Freire, a leader in Brazil of attempts to develop a critical pedagogy, throughout.

At a departmental meeting about qualitative methods John Stirling commented with astonishment that he had read my introduction and decided that I was in favour of science. Well, I am, why not? The deeper question is what science is, and whether psychology has any claim to be scientific. Jeremy Foster decided that I was conscientious enough about science to contribute sections to a book to be co-authored as *Carrying out Investigations in Psychology*. I contributed, colluded.

Psychologisation

The failure of the 'paradigm revolution' in psychology was not, in fact, down to the quantitative psychologists succeeding in discrediting their new rivals, the new pretenders, after having dispensed with philosophers and sociologists, but in the recuperation, the absorption and neutralisation of qualitative methods. And that recuperation was made possible by broader changes in the way that their potential 'subjects' related to psychology itself, by the filtering out of psychological knowledge as a form of discourse into the outside world so that what people said to the psychologists corresponded with what the psychologists expected them to say.

Qualitative research thus became less of a threat to the mainstream, and began to function as confirmation, not only that the knowledge worked, but that deep down people bought into that knowledge and wanted more of it. Even the most radical forms of 'participatory action research' imported from Latin America could in this way be recruited into psychology, the advantage for the discipline being not only that this kind of research could ask people to pose the questions they wanted solving themselves but also that these good subjects would also willingly and actively relay what they knew and felt to the researchers. Ignacio Martín-Baró was working on quite traditional opinion-survey studies when he was murdered in El Salvador, and was dangerous to the regime precisely because he was using that knowledge tactically, conscious that some questions called for quantitative research and some for qualitative. Now, however, we were faced with the promotion of qualitative research in psychology as a good as such, applicable to any kind of question, with new converts enthusiastic about qualitative 'methods' because, they thought, it would thereby be reaching the parts that the quantitative methods could not reach. They were keen to build a corpus of knowledge of the discipline about individuals and groups, and about the communities in which they lived.

The psy complex was present in the very community psychology that pretended to offer the most thorough-going critique of, and alternative to, the mainstream. We noticed that there were a number of psychological traps concealed in the community psychology alternative that was beginning to be recognised as a loyal sub-discipline by the British Psychological Society. Just as recognition by the BPS had been important to the development of qualitative methods in psychology while also functioning as a double-edged sword – recognition seemed to go hand-in-hand with regulation, in line with what the accreditation panels understood it to be – so it was with community psychology. One trap was that the founding fathers of the approach seemed to function as totemic figures, almost as saints, and that the names of these figures were invoked by their followers with awe, which often led to an emptying out of the contents and contexts of their particular critique of psychology. The issue here was not so much that psychologists like Martín-Baró really were priests – comfortable with worship – but that the research process in successful community psychology if it really was psychological invariably seemed to rely on a charismatic, almost shamanic figure to guide it. A second problem that corresponded to the authority given to the psychological researcher entering a community was that the community was all too often configured as if it were a homogeneous unitary object of knowledge and that certain figures in the community were invested with the authority to speak for it.

Conflicts of perspective in the community could be tolerated by the community and by the researcher, but only, it seemed, within certain limits, and for the psychologist these limits were set by their need to make contact with 'informants' who could be trusted to tell them something useful. These should ideally be informants who would trust the psychologist and agree that the psychologist themselves had something useful to offer. Just as it was for those involved in anthropological and 'development' practices worldwide, the psychologist was constrained by their need to do this within a certain time period set by the research project and within the parameters of the topic that had been funded by the university they were operating from or by some other external agency. We were thus tangled back in the old problem of the psychologist functioning as an external agent who worked with leaders of a 'community' and effectively colonised it. Now, however, the motif of 'participation', and the idea that psychology itself has something to offer, a way of speaking about problems, means that coercion is replaced with soft power.

There was another aspect of this limitation of qualitative research, a limitation that turned qualitative research in psychology from being an alternative into part of the problem, a part of the problem that was even more difficult to address. Critiques of laboratory-experimental psychology had for many years been driven by a humanist impulse, by the idea that people should not be treated like objects but should, instead, be treated as if they were human beings. However many times we repeated that the new paradigm argument was for a better psychology in which we should treat people as if they were reflexive self-monitoring human beings for scientific purposes, students were liable to repeat back to us garbled reformulations of the argument to the effect that Rom Harré argued that we should for goodness sake treat people as if they were human beings. Then it was as if we were only urging the good natural voices of people to speak about what they knew and felt, to be recognised and heard.

The power of this humanist motif of individual self-conscious voice transparent to itself, speaking about what each subject really believed and wanted, was a potent reminder of how deeply embedded were the particular forms of individuality that Foucault described, a peculiarly limited sense of individuality as the result of a historical process of development in Western society. We had already noticed that even though humanist psychologists were the nicest and apparently most friendly people in psychology departments, they were also likely to be the ones who would step aside from political conflicts. We had been told how angry anti-apartheid activists in South Africa were when Carl Rogers had broken the academic boycott to set up contact meetings in which black youth were bussed in from townships to meet white students – Rogers argued that this face-to-face contact would dissolve racism – and in other humanistic psychology departments where black women colleagues had objected to racism and sexism; the response had been a complaint that they should calm down and fall in line with the ethos of 'More hugs, less shoves'. The depoliticising impulse of humanistic psychology turned social issues into personal issues, and then turned against politics as such.

The issue now, however, was that this humanist impulse was also being reconfigured through the idealisation of, for example, women's voices as being the site of truth, as if those voices were speaking out against the masculine forms of domination that structured mainstream psychology. In some sense this was necessary. Most psychology students are women, and as you travel up the career ladder you find that the proportion of men increases, until, in leadership positions, the majority are often men. Male scientists set the agenda for research projects and still aim to 'predict and control' what they study, mastering it and showing their mastery of knowledge in line with a stereotypically masculine way of dealing with the world. This isn't to say that this stereotypically masculine way of behaving is only the preserve of men, nor that men do not themselves sometimes struggle against this and attempt to connect with the more intuitive and relational aspects of their nature as human beings. Rather, the point is that the distribution of masculinity to the side of scientific rational inquiry that underpins most quantitative research, and stereotypical femininity to the side of messier and more inconclusive work that characterises much qualitative research, means that there is now all the more than ever a temptation, especially for those new to the ideas or to those guided by liberal feminists, to slide from feminist critique of science into a celebration of feminine alternatives to it. Humanism itself was thus essentialised rather than radicalised.

Most, though not all, feminist critique in psychology makes a distinction between what it is to be 'feminist' as a political position which aims to understand the way that the discipline operates to buttress the power of men in patriarchal society on the one hand, and what it is to be 'feminine' on the other. Psychologists have often been very busy defining what the difference is between masculinity and femininity, and still spend most of their energy on pinning down what it is to be 'feminine' as if it were an essential and universal characteristic of women as such. This means that feminist critique has also focused on the way that psychologists define women as feminine as well as on the restrictions that kind of definition imposes on women's lives. Qualitative research was one place where feminist work was able to find a voice, but this work was often precisely concerned with showing how actual living women did not correspond to what the quantitative research was pretending to find out about them. Now, if qualitative research aims to make people speak about themselves, to confess all to the psychologist about their thoughts and feelings, and if women are assumed to be naturally more intuitive and open about these things, then the danger is that this qualitative research will end up reinforcing those traditional gender stereotypes. The psychologist would thereby be recruiting women as 'feminine', as opposed to 'feminist', into the apparatus of the psy complex.

There is a little paradox here, which is that this supposedly more feminine intuitive and relational aspect of human experience does still tend to usefully question reductionist individual psychology. This is the way it functions in the work of the feminist psychologist Carol Gilligan, for example, who had drawn on interviews with teenage young women to show that their understanding of 'morality' was very different from the models of moral development presupposed by male psychologists and based on studies of men. Carol Gilligan argued that an intuitive and relational form of morality was hidden from the mainstream studies, and she took the risk of idealising femininity as a natural phenomenon in order to have some conceptual leverage against the traditional masculine models. Models of men were not, she insisted, models of women.

The paradox – the contradiction between critique which seems to throw psychology into question and the attempt to reinstate a psychological explanation and method to deal with the critique – is resolved by the turn to social and community psychology, or by treating who we are as always already relational, as an 'acting ensemble', as the radical psychologist Ed Sampson might say. It is an argument that seems to run in the tracks of feminist argument, but it also serves to put the discipline of psychology back on track. Then, by attending to the way that this paradox is resolved once again in favour of psychology and its own forms of knowledge, it is possible to see how and why even community psychology can turn out just as easily to be concerned with the maintenance of social order as its subversion. We could see the false resolution of this paradox at work in our own department where some community psychologists were very keen on what they called 'good leadership' and management and were suspicious of those who refused to play the rules of the game. Sometimes they were right to be suspicious, particularly when the men were behaving badly, sleeping with students, say, but sometimes this suspicion would serve those who wanted to maintain their management of the parts of the department where they had managed to seize power. Again, this isn't so much an expression of the individual decisions made by these characters as a function of the strategies that were available to them, strategies configured in the wider social field of the institution.

Foucault was one of the first to name new systems of governmentality, of the way that people were being ruled and ruled themselves, to name them as 'neoliberal'. Capitalism in the nineteenth century was grounded politically in the ideology of liberalism, and early liberal economics relied on individuals taking decisions about employment and investment in the ostensibly free market, a market that in reality was never free for those who were compelled to sell their labour power to survive.

Neoliberal capitalism is a return to this focus on the individual as the welfare state and other forms of social support are rolled back and people are thrown onto their own resources, encouraged to form their own networks to sustain themselves, either in what some psychologists like to call 'communities' or in what a Conservative Party leader David Cameron once referred to as the 'big society'. For Cameron, arguing against the legacy of a predecessor, Margaret Thatcher, there *is* such a thing as society, and his vision of society is as the complement rather than the enemy of individual psychology. It is against that background of neoliberalism that we can make sense of how it is that psychological discourse has become increasingly more important to the way that people are managed and the way they manage themselves.

There are two aspects to this intimate link between management and self-management, one which Foucault noticed and one he did not. The first aspect can be seen in what the feminist sociologist Arlie Hochschild called 'emotional labour'. Her research on airline stewardesses showed how these workers had to engage in 'deep acting' in order to reassure customers and form some kind of relational bond with them. This deep acting, a performance of their role in the work which required the mobilisation and expression of feelings, and only good feelings, as if they were genuine, and genuinely for the benefit of the company, was exhausting and alienating. This emotional labour can be seen across the service sector under late capitalism or in the neoliberal conditions Foucault described.

Foucault had noticed that individuals are required to bring something of themselves into their work and that this locks them more tightly into relations of power. The psy complex in prisons and schools and in universities thus functions as an apparatus that supplies the forms of discourse through which people make sense of themselves as the kind of beings who must perform their work and their relationships with others, their clients and their colleagues. Here also is an aspect of 'performance' of role, of course, that went unnoticed by the micro-sociologist Erving Goffman, and his last attempts before he died to formalise his model into an account of what he called the 'interaction order' was rather too focused on observable behaviour. The take-up and trumpeting of Goffman as the basis for a model of the human being that might displace old paradigm psychology in Harré's work also failed to address this question.

What Foucault didn't notice, and there is a peculiar absence of engagement with feminist analyses of gender relations throughout his work, is that it was women who were the quintessential ideal-typical subjects for the performance of emotional labour. That is, women were assumed to be able to do this kind of work better than men, and then women became the models for men who were trained in the service sector, including in professions like teaching, to learn these skills. Again, we need to attend to how patriarchal structures of power have been able to recuperate this emotional labour so that even though women are seen as having the more 'natural' capacity to engage in emotional labour, men can quickly learn it and use it to rise through the ranks and, as before, become the top managers.

The process Hochschild and Foucault describe is thus sometimes called 'feminisation', but it is important to emphasise that the feminisation of work does not necessarily benefit women; while it may play on stereotypes of femininity it is not feminist, nor is it necessarily confined to dispensing advice to women. In higher education, for example, the reproduction of power inequalities can be seen in the way that senior managers who are still usually men are able to induce their middle managers, who are now often women, to do the dirty work, to perform the emotional labour, to know how to make their staff behave and how to make them feel bad by appealing to a sense of personal responsibility for decisions and mistakes made by the organisation. The woman middle manager, then, will be less likely to use direct threats and more likely to insinuate that there is something wrong by telling their staff how disappointed they feel. This is not standard cognitive psychology but a new emotional manipulation of social bonds that is, in many organisations, a more effective and intense form of psychology in action. This use of psychological discourse as part of management applies, I know, across disciplines, but there is something more intense and fanatical about it when a psychologist uses it in their own department. There is an intellectual and emotional commitment to this discourse being true. Psychology does really become part of the problem.

Back in 2000, the second edition of *Annual Review of Critical Psychology*, the one which was based on the action research conference at MMU the year before, included a prescient paper by Ángel Gordo López on what he called the 'psychologisation' of critical psychology. We were in danger, he wrote, and this was something he often pointed to in meetings of the Discourse Unit, of using psychological categories in our critique of mainstream psychology. What we didn't seem to appreciate was that psychology was embedded in culture today, necessary to it. When we spoke about how we experienced the hold of psychology or how we felt about the bad things that psychology did, we were effectively repeating and reinforcing psychology itself. The theme was reinvented and reworked by Jan de Vos whose PhD I was on the supervision team for at Ghent University. Jan wrote about Stanley Milgram, for example, and drew my attention to aspects of the experiment that were significant not only to a historical account but also to what was happening to us all today. At the first supervision meeting in Ghent the team practised saying the word 'psychologisation'. The term became the centrepiece of Jan's thesis, and is an extremely useful way of conceptualising the network of concepts I have been reflecting on here – of the role of emotional labour, feminisation and neoliberalism – and showing how the psy complex today operates throughout Western society and, Jan insisted, as a globalising force, recruiting organisations and individuals into its own peculiar way of understanding and speaking about the world and the people in it.

The political consequences of this psychologisation are also important, for it encourages us to think about individuals in such a way as to accentuate their 'identities' as members of different groups and it provokes an emotional attachment to those identities. It means that when those identities are impugned the individual who bears one of those identities feels hurt. It also thereby encourages the bearers of identities to feel under threat, vulnerable, and even to imagine that they can only be taken seriously if they present themselves as such. In this way, there is a danger even that recognition of peoples' rights to speak about their own experience is predicated on them adopting the position of being a victim of some kind. Another paradox, then, is that contemporary forms of psychologisation that would seem to be concerned with human agency, ostensibly concerned with reviving a humanist ethos and championing the voices of each individual, actually often reduce peoples' agency; it is as if they must be victims in order to be heard. On the positive side, this focus on identities makes us take seriously a variety of forms of oppression that operate around the axes of gender, sexuality, race and disability. On the negative side, it sets conditions for how people should speak about their identities and it psychologises politics, even setting identities against each other so that there is an eventual de-politicisation of peoples' responses to social problems.

Resistance

In the 2007 to 2008 academic year we managed to get funding for a new module on the master's programme in psychology, Ethics and Mental Health. This was an opportunity to revisit many of the issues that we had taken up with *Asylum Magazine*, the Hearing Voices Network and the Paranoia Network. It was also a poignant marker of the death, just before the course began, of our dear comrade Terence McLaughlin from lung cancer. It was difficult to get the money for the Ethics and Mental Health course because Carolyn was still annoyed that we had submitted our publications with ESRI down at Didsbury campus for the 2008 RAE. In the end, most of the RIHSC publications went to the 'social policy' panel to be evaluated because there was just not enough research work of any kind going on in psychology that could be made to count. This was partly a reflection of the narrowness of psychology, and, despite the inclusion of qualitative researchers on the RAE panel, it was clear that critical, discursive and feminist research would be low-graded. Other universities that did alternative research related to psychology decided to submit under sociology instead.

Despite the emergence of qualitative methods on the syllabus of many psychology degrees, partly thanks to Peter Banister's efforts at getting it included in 'bench-marking' BPS criteria, this was running against the tide, in two respects. There was now much more psychology around, and the psychologists were more intent than ever on sealing off their own discipline against rival pretenders to theories of subjectivity. This also played out in the content of the degree. The first-year practical which had been run by Stuart Robertson when I arrived in Manchester, and which asked students examine the statistical correlation between bad performance at A-Level Psychology and good performance in a Psychology undergraduate degree, had long been abandoned. The lesson had been that it might help not to know about psychology before starting a degree. Now, this message was even more unappealing; not only did many more students have A-Level Psychology prior to obtaining a place on the course, it was assumed that the more you knew about psychology, from as early an age as possible, the better. There were also more 'access courses', a first year of the degree franchised out to local further education colleges and that fed students into MMU. Peter and I validated such courses.

The frictions over the RAE submission notwithstanding, it was also a time of truce in MMU, a time of tactical alliance and bargaining over resources, so we got the money and had guest speakers on the course from the user movement as well as from radical professionals, and Karen Reissmann, a UNISON union activist who had been sacked from her position as a mental health nurse for whistle-blowing, for revealing what cuts in services were being planned by the local authority. In these years many organisations that were set against each other as competitors became more secretive, and they enforced silence on their employees. The phenomenon of 'whistle-blowing' and of complaints about 'bullying' in institutions became more prominent. Critique in psychology thus had to connect with industrial struggles going on outside it, and even there we could see how psychology was being used as a tool make people behave obediently or to feel that they themselves had done something wrong if they disagreed with management.

It was still very difficult to get colleagues involved in their union inside the university though, and even more difficult in psychology where even members of the union said that they would prefer to stand up for themselves. Collective action didn't appeal to them, and some said that it would be a sign of weakness. Being tough as an individual went hand-in-hand with a sense of shame at being seen to need help from others. The speech therapy part of our department agreed among themselves to arrange for one of their members to have time off their teaching timetable for union activity in order to work for them in negotiations with management and in protest action. Not so, psychology. Teaching timetable meetings in our department were sometimes fraught affairs; Jeremy Foster, who was often tasked with organising the meetings, used to send memos reminding us of the time and room and to "bring your knives". There was eventually a balance of tasks across the work group, but factoring in time for union representation was inconceivable. Psychologists would not do that, and there were times when I was running the branch meetings as union representative for what had by now become the University and College Union, UCU, single-handed, sometimes as the only one who turned up to meetings on the campus.

The UCU branch at Gaskell Campus attempted to save the photocopy facilities when they were threatened with closure, but the most we could do was raise the issue in the 'consultation' meetings where the Dean fielded objections to a new policy that was being imposed on him by the central administration. There was nothing he could do about it, and little we could do by pressuring him except make him feel more powerless and defensive. Another running battle was around the impending closure of Gaskell Campus, something that had been rumoured for many years, and so which many staff still didn't take seriously. It became a more serious prospect when plans were unveiled for a new campus to be built on a formerly green-field site owned by Manchester City Council, plans which included open plan offices. Instead of lecturing staff having their own individual offices, it became clear that space-saving measures would be combined with more direct surveillance of staff. There would be no private space to talk to students, discussions which often ranged from academic discussion to the personal problems the students were having in producing work, and each member of staff would, instead, have their own desk and a little bookshelf in one large shared office. Despite the new declared emphasis on 'student-centred' learning, this collective staff space was to be one which excluded students. They would have to arrange to meet staff in separate dedicated meeting rooms.

The attempts to justify this were many and marvellous. When Faculty Dean Vince Ramprogus was asked where staff would put all the books they used for reference and lent to students, he asked in return when the last time was that a lecturer had ever looked at a book in their office. I had some sympathy with this response and was bit-by-bit moving all my books home, a place where I could be surer that I wouldn't be interrupted while writing. Carolyn Kagan, who had her own office as head of RIHSC, offered a defence of open plan offices on the basis that it would encourage collective discussion, and why, she asked me later, could that not provide better conditions for union activity? She explained that this was a perfect compromise between what management wanted and what we could turn to our advantage; this was in line with the way that community psychology was beginning to turn into an unwitting tool of management as it sought to save its skin in these new conditions.

In November 2009 MMU announced that there would be 127 jobs lost in the university among the support staff, mainly porters and reception staff. UCU organised a petition in solidarity with our support staff colleagues in the UNISON union calling for the Vice-Chancellor John Brooks to resign. It was a significant moment of disappointment and fracture in the department as one of the community and disability staff, Dan Goodley, who had joined the department as a professor, told me that he would not sign the petition because the support staff hadn't been very sympathetic to disabled students. Dan had at that point just travelled to Kuala Lumpur for a meeting to broker a course agreement with a university there, an agreement that John Brooks had also travelled over for. I joked with Dan about his friend John and tried not to be angry with him for refusing to sign the petition. Dan was, it was true, prioritising course development in a field of work which was, it was true, very challenging to mainstream psychology, but he was keeping to the academic frame to defend that work, willing to ally with those in power to do some good, to develop other forms of resistance.

I also colluded with that academic frame when I decided to let it go, unable to trust Dan so much after that for a strategic choice not to support staff paid much less than him. The protest was large enough to force the university to back down, though we heard afterwards that the decision to rescind the redundancy plans had been taken by the head of Human Resources, and that Vice-Chancellor Brooks was livid when he found out. The reception staff at Gaskell campus feared for their jobs, and they feared their own bosses. Ann, a worker threatened with redundancy, told us that they had been instructed only to use one squirt of disinfectant in the toilets that they cleaned during their additional part-time paid work on the campus. This would save money, but it would not do the job, and so the cleaners brought their own bottles of disinfectant; Ann made me promise not to tell Amy the manager who would "go ballistic", Ann said, if Amy found out. It was as if the culture of bullying was endemic, not only in the academic chains of command.

We also knew that things were difficult in other places, for some of our students who had gone on to take up teaching posts in universities around 'Manchester. Jemma Tosh who had organised the Zucker protests in 2010, for example, was able to get a job at Chester University, a college linked to the Church of England. When Jemma's book, *Perverse Psychology*, was published with an image of handcuffs on the cover, she was told to remove the cover image from the door of her office because it might offend some of the students. But she was more successful than our Hearing Voices Network activist Terence McLaughlin, who was once interviewed for a job there. The other candidates had withdrawn from the interviews beforehand, and so Terence was the only one left, but had a hard time explaining to the panel how his work fitted in with psychology; he said the only time they smiled at him was at the end of the day when he was leaving. They didn't give him the job.

So, this brings us to 2011. In that year a lecturer in chemistry, Claudius D'Silva was dismissed by MMU, this in response to him taking the university to an industrial tribunal for race discrimination. In this case UCU were beaten back. It was a bitter defeat. Claudius D'Silva had applied for promotion, been turned down because he was black, he said, and in 2005 succeeded at tribunal in winning a ruling that the university had 'directly discriminated' against him. The university put its team of lawyers to work on the case, and in 2007 the ruling was overturned on appeal in favour of the university. D'Silva carried on fighting, but UCU nationally decided that it could not match the funds that the university had to defend the case. Brooks and Bill Hallam, his Director of HR, seemed determined to stop D'Silva, and when it became clear that D'Silva would pursue his attempt to call for judicial review of the second tribunal appeal decision, he was sacked, and was out in the cold, with no support.

We had two lines of defence against management until 2011. One was the union which was very militant but weak, willing to fight but on the back foot, very aware that many of the staff were too frightened to speak out. The other was Peter Banister, obdurate against the stupid bureaucratic demands on the department to obey diktats from central administration. Peter retired as head of department in 2011 to devote himself to the British Psychological Society, of which he became President, and then everything changed; the neoliberal psychologised transformations in management accelerated.

Notice the tension between institutional demand and personal response. I have tried, and perhaps I have failed, to show that it is entirely understandable that people positioned in these institutions should play the game. We need no 'psychological' explanations for why that is so. Perhaps I have failed precisely because the pull toward individual psychological explanation is now so powerful, not only in the discipline of psychology and the frameworks it employs, but also in our everyday commonsensical assumptions about what counts. Neither do we need psychological explanations for why people refuse to go with the flow, why they take a stand when they notice that something is wrong. What I did and what I describe in the next chapter – the culmination of this institutional crisis – was more a function of the different competing sets of relationships I had with those around me than anything else, relationships configured by managerial imperatives. Psychology as such adds nothing useful to the account; psychological discourse detracts from it and is actually part of the problem.

19

STRESS

Discipline and publish

In which management changes bring psychology into play and into question. We begin on 3 October 2012, and explore how these rapid changes triggered a trade union dispute which led us from regulation to resistance, from obedience to escape. Along the way, we reflect on the nature of bullying, executive stress and feminisation in action, matters where power and psychologisation run through the body.

In late 2012 Wilko Johnson, guitarist with *Dr Feelgood*, cancelled a show and was rushed to hospital, diagnosed two months later with late-stage pancreatic cancer. He decided not to have treatment, knew he was going to die, and threw himself into a farewell tour, but curiously said that he then felt "vividly alive". After he announced at an awards ceremony in October 2014 that it was a misdiagnosis and that he would live, he said that he wasn't really sure what he would do next. In a radio interview in 2016 he said that the only way he could make sense of all this was that he had learnt to live all his life with depression – "it's my constitution", he said – and that imminent death had given him something to live for. Perhaps only an existential shock like this can wake us from the stories that psychology tells us about how we are condemned to live our lives. That is what I describe in this chapter. The institutional crisis and process by which I left MMU was gruelling but it for sure woke me up to life outside psychology.

First

Today, Wednesday 3 October 2012, I am free, and out of psychology, for good, it seems. There is some of the game to run yet though, it is not yet really yet 'for good', and to feel that there is freedom outside psychology is surely as ridiculous as to imagine that the more psychology you have the freer you will be. But this must be the last day I will claim the identity 'psychologist'. This morning I could have been seeing clients in my new office in Gaskell campus where the professors and readers were hidden away in rooms claimed from the library, cluttered rooms where another technician, bespectacled Mr Glendenning, had once photographed and prepared material for the slide projectors we used in our teaching. In the last months I have relocated my clinical practice; this place had become too precarious for that. The management campaign to clean up the campus had not yet reached into the Professors and Readers Suite hidden around the back of the library in the Gaskell 'Old Building'. This separate suite enforced segregation from the rest of the staff group that we unsuccessfully resisted. It was a losing battle, a management battle not only against the staff whose noticeboards were removed and replaced with video-screen displays in the main building reception, but also against the weather. The infrastructure of the building was crumbling, and the central administration had already decided that it was not worth refurbishing the place if we really were going to be relocated to a new campus near the city centre. The last group of intending students on open day had commented on the array of buckets on the sodden carpets following one downpour, asking if it was an art installation. The corridor walls around my office were plastered with double-page newspaper spreads of photos of animals and the natural world, some of which were drooping off the Blu Tack. We were an oasis of untidiness, and as yet the ceilings were holding up against the rain.

We have an academic visitor this academic year to the Discourse Unit from Japan, one just arrived from Chile, and this morning I took another visitor from Italy to the RIHSC office to introduce them to the administrative staff and help them obtain a library card. Just before lunchtime – but there has not really been any lunchtime for many years – I could have been packing away more of my belongings from the filing cabinets and shelves, but in the last few months I have already moved them out; one cardboard box was enough to contain all of the last things I gave to Erica, including the Indian shawls I had draped over my office chairs to cheer the place up. I know that I will never see this office again. This afternoon I should have been chairing a research seminar at which Erica's PhD student China Mills would talk about her work, but I was told by email late this morning to hand my identity card and keys to reception within an hour as I left the building; Erica is reading out a statement to the seminar explaining why I cannot be there.

The statement informs colleagues, students and our visitors that I have been suspended for 'gross professional misconduct' with immediate effect pending a disciplinary investigation. This is a very risky statement to read out, for the email from Bill Campbell yesterday afternoon instructing me to attend a disciplinary meeting specified that I should not discuss this matter with anyone. Bill, a professor in Didsbury campus, is a nice guy, always friendly and helpful, and I will ask him when I do see him why he is doing this. The suspension letter sent by Human Resources, HR, arrived twenty minutes after I failed to appear at the disciplinary meeting this morning because, as I told them, there was no time for me to find another union representative to accompany me. I could see in the email trail Bill accidentally left hanging in yesterday's message that HR – a body that the MMU union branch activists referred to as Human Remains – would advise him on the wording and that they would notify UCU, the University and College Union, something they were required to do because I was a union representative on the campus.

Events of the last year since the appointment of the new head of department had already convinced me that the department was no longer safe, and I had a draft of my resignation letter ready to polish and send before Christmas. That is why I had already begun clearing out my office in preparation for my departure. Now I doubt that the letter will be necessary. I am surprised at how fast things have moved, how management time speeded up. Some of us lobbied for this new head of department, Christine Horrocks from Bradford University, to be appointed because, we thought, she was sympathetic to qualitative research and, at the very least, to feminist perspectives. Erica knew her from the Psychology of Women Section of the British Psychological Society, of which Erica had recently been Chair before handing over this year to Horrocks; one assessment from the first moments we knew of her application for the post was that she, Erica said, was "like Carolyn, busy and socially-skilled, but without the politics". Horrocks was offered the job in 2011 but then withdrew her application. Erica met with her to try and persuade her to change her mind. Soon after the formal announcement that Horrocks would indeed be taking up the post in MMU, a mutual friend encountered one of her colleagues from Bradford who commented that she, the colleague, would soon be coming over to MMU. This was an odd comment and we didn't know what to make of it, for no new lecturing posts had yet been advertised. Everyone in the department assumed there had been some kind of deal with the university that would tempt Horrocks to join us, but we did not know what it was. There was some speculation that new appointments had already been agreed as part of the welcome package, but we were unsure how such an agreement would be squared with our hitherto quite open interview processes, so we discounted the idea. It cannot be true.

We had a few months grace at the beginning of the academic year, a crazy time during which we had an Asylum conference in September linked with the disability action researchers in the department under the catch-all heading of 'Normalcy', a US-American term that refers to the way that certain kinds of bodies are assumed to be 'normal' and the others are made to fit or are excluded from public space. The same form of reasoning and practice applies, we argued, to certain kinds of mental states, with 'normal' describing reasonable well-behaved people who conform to social norms and mad people drugged or shocked or incarcerated if they don't adapt well enough. It was a good event, challenging the boundaries that are sometimes drawn between bodily and mental states, including by activists who don't want to be treated as insane because they are in a wheelchair or treated as disabled because they are on psychiatric medication. Normalcy effectively takes up one of the slogans of the early anti-psychiatry movement, that normal people don't exist, and shows how it is society that 'disables' people and treats them as mad if they don't agree that they, the 'disabled', are the problem rather than the effect of what Foucault once called 'dividing strategies' that enforce barriers between the normal and the abnormal. There could be space for all of us if we worked together to make it so.

I met Horrocks for the first time on the 9 November 2011, the day before I was due to leave for a hectic research visit with Erica to Australia where she was a conference keynote speaker, and then to Malaysia and the Philippines into the Christmas break where we would deliver courses about discourse analysis and critical psychology. Horrocks, who had been meeting members of the department, told me how important the NSS, the National Student Survey was, that it meant that staff should be present on campus even if they were not teaching. She said that if it had been her decision, she would not have allowed us to go on this long overseas teaching and research visit. Practice in the department up to then had been that, provided you covered all your teaching and administrative responsibilities while away from MMU, academic work outside would be valued as extra work but good for the institution, agreed without question. She asked about the Discourse Unit, and I explained that we kept it separate from the university because otherwise there would be a risk of the administration interfering with the content of the website and, when it was convenient to them, even closing us down. She looked puzzled and said that she couldn't imagine why this would happen, but then, she mused, yes, that had been what Bradford had done to her own research group.

There were many emails to the department from Horrocks about NSS and, another acronym, KPI – Key Performance Indicator – while we were away. KPIs covered a host of things that included student evaluations of teaching and, closely connected to this, success in examinations, something that tempted some staff to inflate grades and pass substandard work. By the time we got back to Manchester in January 2012 the atmosphere in the teaching ranks of the department was one of mutual suspicion and impending threat. The surface impression was of busy efficient perpetual change which ranged from rapid implementation of faculty procedures that Peter had protected us against to removing untidy posters from the corridor walls. Here, at last, was leadership, but this meant that the leader should also obediently implement all of the directives from central management that had been blocked up to now.

We had already arranged a research seminar to describe liberation psychology in the Philippines on 11 January, which was well attended. Horrocks asked me to present the paper at the BPS Psychology of Women conference later in the year and seemed annoyed when I said that I wasn't sure that I should intrude on that space as a male speaker. She meant well, no doubt. The Philippines was the site of a parallel strand of 'liberation psychology' to the one that had developed in Latin America around Ignacio Martín-Baró. Liberation psychology in the Philippines was explicitly grounded in indigenous cultural traditions that were viewed as potential forms of resistance to colonialism and as prefiguring both new forms of struggle and new forms of social relationships. The approach followed in the tracks of work by Virgilio Enriquez on what was sometimes known as *Sikolohiyang Pilipino*, Filipino Psychology, and, like many other indigenous psychological theories, it oscillated between a claim that there was something distinctive about the psychology of people in the Philippines and the more ambitious political claim that we all had something to learn about who we were as human beings from this quite different way of experiencing and understanding how we thought and felt in relation to each other. I started work on a detailed account of what we could learn from Enriquez's liberation psychology, sifting through the material we brought back from our teaching and research visit, but obstacle after obstacle piled up in the way of this task as I was caught in an administrative whirlwind, increasing tasks and decisions to make about reorganisation of the department.

We had a schedule of 'critical psychology' events already arranged which seemed to be a thorn in the side of the new regime in the department rather than a selling point. At the launch event in February for the second edition of our Banister et al. *Qualitative Methods in Psychology* book, for example, Horrocks turned up to argue for the value of mainstream quantitative approaches and the importance of traditional psychological research alongside the newer methodologies. The second edition of the book brought on board many new co-authors, but already most of them were either leaving the department or itching to go. My argument at the launch that the 'new paradigm' revolution in psychology had actually failed, and that qualitative methods had been 'recuperated' – that is neutralised and absorbed – by the discipline, went down badly with Horrocks. Recuperation did seem to be the order of the day; at one moment we were being asked how we could make our 'alternative' views useful within the overall guiding mission of the department, to speak about them at a conference that would showcase psychology at MMU, and at the next we were told that we had to adapt what we said to what would sell to students and now also to their fee-paying parents.

We had to compromise over cuts to courses. As we were squeezed on student numbers, I realised that while community psychology was precious to Carolyn Kagan, and it was important for her to hold onto that masters' degree course as a separate space for teaching and action research, our critical psychology could operate across the curriculum. Some of the best critical psychology connects with community psychology, but is also critical of its tendency to adapt people to their role as good citizens, and the very term 'critical psychology' could turn out to be a millstone around the necks for some of those graduating and wanting to move into more respectable psychology posts later. I agreed to let critical psychology go from the syllabus listing in the department to save community psychology; it was a forced choice for the least bad deal we could strike with the new management intent on cuts. Just as we were forced to be more instrumental about the knowledge we offered – sold it at a price – so the students responded in kind. There had already been an increase in cheating in exams, at least in the cheating that was detected, and on one occasion a student raised their hand at the beginning of the exam to complain that these were not the questions they had been expecting. I risked disciplinary action when I replied too fast to a student who emailed me after receiving a grade mark they disliked and telling me that they had paid a lot of money to take the course. My hasty reply, which I lost sleep over for several weeks, was to type "you cannot buy higher marks". This year we had overseas students on the psychology postgraduate degree who had been recruited by external 'agents' working on a commission basis who had misrepresented what the course was about; one student from Nigeria with no psychology background thought she was here to get a qualification in education.

The dogs – male staff we imagined roaming the corridors looking for students to sleep with – were also happy because Horrocks combined jokes about women managers with quick banter that the men could relate to. There was a cost, of course, and across the department there was anxiety about how far Horrocks would push the increase in workload and demands that the staff be present in their offices in order to increase Key Performance Indicators for the department and boost the National Student Survey score. Another cost to the dogs was that the deployment of femininity in the service of power meant that while their own masculine identity was tickled at one moment it was slapped at the next. Individuals were targeted.

While I was away, one lecturer known for his sexism and incompetence had arrived late, as usual, to a lecture to find cameras rigged up which were, he was told, there for the benefit of an overseas student who was thinking of joining the course. It was a set up, and the recording was then used in evidence by HR in a case brought by Horrocks to deal with him, a case that a union representative drafted in from All Saints campus defended and won. His defence was that when he claimed in a video that he was one of the most famous British psychologists and made outrageous sexualised claims about the symbolism of the red Ducati Monster 796 motorcycle he was straddling, it was a joke, and he had no idea that the video would be posted online. There had been fury in the department when there was widespread tabloid newspaper coverage of his earlier claim to have derived a mathematical formula for an attractive female bottom, and there were complaints that he was bringing psychology into disrepute. For some of us, of course, it would be best to bring psychology into disrepute sooner rather than later. We didn't want to save him, but neither did we want to save psychology. As an exercise in divide and rule this worked well. This character was the dog who had complained about the witches' coven in the Psychology of Women course, and so he was a perfect first easy target. We didn't want to defend him, but we were worried about who would be targeted next.

Colleagues from the 'other side' of the department, that is, those carrying out mainstream quantitative research, began to speak to me about the union, something they had shown little interest in up to then, and asked me how we could get rid of Horrocks. Some were anxious that innocent bad behaviour would be treated as disciplinary offences. There were murmurings about one colleague who kept order in lectures by appointing two students who were armed with ballpoint pens and told to poke noisemakers in the arm, but, they were told, "Not so it bleeds". This nice guy – not one of the dogs – was direct in manner and, psychologists might say, concrete in thought. He broke the rules that ethnomethodology takes to be operative in everyday life, operative only when they are tacit, broke them by making them explicit; at departmental end of year drinks with academic and administrative staff we squirmed as he handed over some chocolates saying "I know it's important to give gifts to secretaries to make them like us better".

Understandably perhaps, there was a hidden reproach hidden in the question as to what the union could do to get rid of the new head, that we on the 'soft' qualitative side had played a part in bringing her here. But even then I didn't want to humour them, and told them that we needed to give her a chance. As a union representative I had to do something though, and so I sent an email to the whole department complaining about the increase in workload. One of my colleagues, Dan Goodley, commented on this and I replied to him, saying that I thought that Horrocks was inveigling us into working harder, wanted to get us to run round faster in our wheels so she could impress her bosses and that she had her eye on the post of Dean when Vince Ramprogus went. A minute later Erica sent me an email warning me that I had unwittingly copied that reply to the whole departmental list, not just to Dan, so I sent another message, an apology for my hasty observation, repeating again that we needed to work together to try and make this new situation work. Duplicitous, you may think, but tell me how I could have done otherwise, which is also, no doubt, how those with a little more power than me rationalised what they felt compelled to do. The union branch needed details about how the teaching workload in the department was being ramped up, so I wrote a personal message to each colleague asking them how this was impacting on their ability to cope. Some of them had already switched to personal email accounts outside MMU and responded with information which I compiled ready for a formal complaint from the union. One colleague, scared that Horrocks would find out, panicked and quickly sent on the email to her asking what to do. The cat was out of the bag.

I met with Horrocks, and she asked me not to do this again, and I agreed. She talked about her "disappointment" and the "hurt feelings" that this kind of email might cause, for colleagues who received the email and, of course, for her. References to feelings were prominent in the discourse she used to manage us in this and in many other meetings. This meeting with her was an important moment, though neither of us, I think, knew that it was, for this 'first email' was be one focus of the disciplinary investigation, with the claim that by sending further emails as a trade union representative I was, as HR put it later, "disobeying a management instruction". I'm not sure whether I should have agreed not to send private emails about the union after that, and it was a compromise that meant that emails were public and monitored. It meant colleagues kept quiet, hid in their offices and hoped to ride out the storm, and it meant that the 'second email' that was public had dramatic consequences. That's why I'm here, out of the building on the 3 October 2012, because of two emails.

Back to that meeting about the 'first email' about workload, a meeting typical of the ones Horrocks had with me from January 2012 onward; it was a disturbing meeting, with repeated references to what a great supporter she and her family were of unions, how she had learnt how to "deal with them", as she put it, at Bradford, and, concerning each specific matter concerning workload, the observation that this is something we would need to have a "conversation" about. We also discussed her worry that the department might be empty of staff over the summer break, be like the Mary Celeste ghost ship, she said. There was nobody around at that time of year, and we had to think about what would happen if a student's parents came in and whether this might impact on the NSS score. This worry prompted her to implement a rota for people to come into work over the summer break. I said that staff needed time to recover, perhaps to attend conferences, to have time to do research, and, why not, if that is the way they relaxed, to go to the pub. It might even be, I said, that we would find out that John Cavill, a cognitive psychologist who was a dutiful but relaxed fixture in the department, had been writing his Nobel prize-winning novel during this time. Her reaction to this was quick and irritable, and I felt a gulf open up between what she and I thought was important about higher education; "Oh no", she said, "Not in MMU time he won't". I made the mistake of saying that together we were learning these new language games required of us; "But no", she snapped back, "It's not a game".

I guessed that 'conversation' must be a keyword in the management strategy she was being trained in. Staff groaned inwardly and rolled their eyes in meetings when there was a reference to having a 'conversation' in place of a discussion and decision. It meant that the issue had already been decided, and that there would be no further public debate about it, only one-to-one monologues in which agreement with the decision would be obtained. This was 'emotional labour' in action, labour by a woman middle manager to get others to labour harder, to do the bidding of managers above her who were, of course, men. This was also feminisation in action. It could have had positive aspects, and some of us did look back fondly to times before the new Vice-Chancellor, Brooks, took over, when Sandra Burslem ran MMU and explicitly supported women staff and students. But now we were seeing what a difference there was between this organisational feminisation and feminism as such. The dogs were very worried but were being tamed, being brought on side with offers of promotion.

At one, now compulsory, staff meeting Horrocks said of them, "I know how to deal with men who live with their mothers". At another, she invited one of the clumsier more obstreperous lecturers who shambled around the department in a track-suit to come and sit next her when he arrived late to a meeting; "Here", she said while patting the chair seat, "Don't be frightened, it's not contaminated". He slunk over obediently and sat down. It was sad to see him cowed, this figure who was up to then so aggressive on email and so amiable if you asked him what the problem was face to face. We suspected that another innovation she had been coached in, along with the repeated use of the term 'conversation', was to bring cake to meetings. At nearly every departmental meeting a cake would appear, and colleagues would reluctantly approach it in the break – more wasted time away from their work – circling it like suspicious cats, our ears flattened, faint smiling with gratitude as we ate it but our whiskers tingling with irritated anticipation as to what was going to come next.

Departmental meetings were turned into relay points for instructions from faculty and central management about KPIs and the NSS and for reports about how these were being implemented in teaching. We were told that students expected a psychology degree to give them information about psychology, and that, if the course was to be 'sustainable' and result in a high measure of 'employability', we should concentrate on the core elements of psychology. We were instructed to rewrite the course outlines and stipulate exactly what the objectives and learning outcomes would be for each session. There was to be no room for surprises or for reflection, nothing that had not been programmed into the lecture, and critical approaches were marginalised even further. Even Carolyn Kagan seemed dumbfounded when she was told that the revived plans for a counselling psychology postgraduate course should include more about mainstream approaches like cognitive-behavioural therapy and be less ambitious about the 'community action research' ethos of the degree. Instead of marking itself out as doing something different, this course should, we were told, position itself in the academic and professional marketplace as a product that was offering the same as its rivals. There were meetings upon meetings to implement new structures in the department in which everyone should take on some kind of managerial role, take responsibility for what central administration wanted and what the faculty was tasked to deliver. At one 'senior management team' meeting in the department attended by the remaining professors I complained about this, and said I was not a manager, and Horrocks angrily stuffed reams of documents setting out a new managerial structure back into her desk saying that we would have a 'conversation' about this later.

I did not behave well in that meeting, and when I complained about being drawn into management structures I also railed against the proliferation of administrative meetings that drained our time and energy. At other moments I was mediating between my colleagues and the new regime, by turns collaborating with it and then feeling ashamed. It was a time when the flakier lecturers were being picked off, and their usual incompetence was becoming treated as academic failure rather than lovable foible. One colleague who was coasting to retirement did not respond to emails about course arrangements, and so, exasperated, I eventually copied in the head of department. He was called in for a telling off, his infraction of email etiquette now used as one more point against him to lever him out of work, and I had to apologise to him at his leaving drinks event in a pub after a degree awards ceremony. He had rather sheepishly been given a goodbye present by the head of department while the Dean looked on and the rest of us cringed. There was no excuse for my wretched behaviour while I was loyally obeying the always urgent needs of the institutional mechanisms. You must bear that in mind when I lapse into complaint at the collusion of others with an institution that they were merely attempting to make work more efficiently.

Our annual Professional Development Reviews, PDR sessions, were scheduled for the summer term. We arranged the dates. Then Erica and I were told that they would need to be cancelled and rearranged because this year the PDR would be with both the head of department, Horrocks, and the Dean of faculty, Vince Ramprogus. We consulted with Carolyn, who told us that she was surprised; it was unusual, she said, and Carolyn herself, as Director of RIHSC, would still only be having her PDR with one line manager. Our PDR meetings had usually been with Peter, who asked us where we were going to conferences and courses and, in a favourite Peter tram hobby moment that ran alongside his penchant for *Star Trek*, told us what train and tram systems operated in the part of the world we were due to visit. Carolyn seemed rattled now; torn between protecting her hard-won 'Institute' and the group she was nurturing there, and loyalty to 'leadership' that she liked in principle. She was by now concerned about the direction the department was now being taken in, but reluctant to voice this publicly. I had colluded already, so how can I blame her.

Erica and I were the only two members of the department to have our PDR with two line managers. Erica's was first. She was told on 6 June that she published too much, and there were angry exchanges about that. "It could not have gone worse" she said on the phone immediately afterwards. They had taken nearly three hours, running well over the hour timeslot set aside for these events, telling her that what she was doing did not correspond to what they wanted. We were anxious before this, and now I was very worried. We joked about me taking a tape recorder into my session, or taking my little blow-up Munch Scream balloon that I would bring up from below the table and ask to speak for me in a high squeaky voice.

My PDR on 10 July 2012 was more bizarre than I could have predicted. Because I had never had a PDR with Vince Ramprogus before, I printed out my CV and a list of my publications so he could see what work I had been doing over the year. I gave this to him at the beginning of the meeting and as he took it he commented "And I thought Erica's was bad". The meeting went downhill from there. When I challenged him over why he would treat us as a pair and, more seriously, what he meant by 'bad', he had no reply, and Horrocks, clearly embarrassed by his stupid comment, quickly intervened, repeating several times that "Vince was joking". My two-hour meeting consisted of complaints that when I travelled abroad MMU didn't benefit, "What's in it for us", they said, at one point folding and rubbing their fingers to indicate that they meant money.

The international dimension of the Discourse Unit that sustained us, and that we valued as crucial to our academic work, was now, I realised, a threat. As it is often with complaints about 'cosmopolitanism' in politics, so it was with this research group which was perceived as corroding loyalty to its home institution. I was then told that my trade union representative post was incompatible with being part of management of the department, which, as a professor, I clearly should be. I said this was untrue, that Vince should check with Human Resources, and that, if I were forced to choose between management and the union, I would choose the union. He said he would check with HR. The end of the PDR session is usually spent formulating objectives for the next year, and so I asked Vince what he would like me to put, and then, dictated by him, I wrote that I would reduce the number of publications, take a management role, and put in some bids for research funding. I was furious. As I left the room, they laughed.

I sent these objectives to Vince after the PDR, as agreed, and prefaced them with the observation that these had been what had been stipulated for me by him in the meeting. I was told by return email that this framing of the objectives was inappropriate and that there should be another meeting to clarify that I understood what the purpose of a PDR was. Erica had already consulted with Carolyn and put together a list of objectives that repeated back what Vince had told her to write after her PDR, objectives that she felt she could live with and she sent them off. These objectives included 'income generation', a target she thought she could easily meet through setting up a secondment to Oslo; that was an arrangement, however, that was, by turns, encouraged and then blocked in the department and the faculty. She was told that she should include reference to what she understood to be the 'cooperative' ethos of the institution, and was as amazed as Carolyn to discover that the term that they assumed to be a typographical error in Vince's email was actually what he really meant when he insisted on a re-draft which explicitly named it as 'corporate' ethos. Discourse really counted here.

I drafted my resignation letter, put it in a folder ready to send later in the year, and went to the UCU branch for the faculty down at Didsbury campus. UCU in MMU was now in the midst of a nasty dispute over the sacking of Christine Vié, a French language assistant who was also a union representative. Reorganisation of courses had been an opportunity for MMU management to redeploy all the staff except Christine, and so there had been demonstrations and petitions locally and nationally to demand her reinstatement. I told Christine and another UCU representative that I was planning to leave MMU, and that meant I had nothing to lose, but I was also willing to fight what was being done in the department. They wanted to be sure I knew what I was doing before taking this step. I thought I was. With union branch support, I wrote a letter of complaint about my PDR to the MMU head of research, Gerry Kelleher, asking for help, suggesting that my PDR should be carried out again by a manager who was willing to conduct it seriously and not use it as an opportunity to undermine my work and attempt to frighten me into being obedient.

By summer 2012 things had really heated up. In Mexico at a conference on Marxism and Psychology we were boiling, and not only because of the weather. The atmosphere in the department in MMU was edgy, and one of the effects of that was our own edginess about what these changes portended. I wanted to leave, cut my losses and coast along to retirement age, which was only four years to go after all, and I could do this relying on savings and clinical work outside the university sector. Erica didn't believe that I would do it but was clear that if I decided to do that then she would carry on as long as she could bear it, see out her time, and finish her academic career at MMU. She was carrying out more research in the field of education, and so we both had a fruitless meeting on 26 July with Harry Torrance who was the head of ESRI, the Education and Social Research Institute down at Didsbury Campus. We approached him with the proposal to move departments, but Harry pointed out that this would need the agreement of the Deans of both our faculty and of education, and that would be difficult to arrive at. Difficult because of the organisation of resources, money that came in following the last Research Assessment Exercise, money that was devolved to the department that housed the staff involved. There were already disputes, competing stories about where the money had gone, and who would lose out if we were now to shift from one 'cost centre' to another. I had been told during my PDR that the Faculty got nothing from my performance in the RAE and so they wanted me to engage in 'income generation', but Harry revealed that the money attached to our publication record had, as it should have been, been funnelled from ESRI into my Faculty. The punitive measures being taken against us were clearly more to do with issues of obedience than finance.

In Mexico, as I spoke to colleagues from different parts of the world about what was happening to us I could hear myself slide from description into complaint and then into a rant. I repeated diagnoses of the state of higher education under conditions of what is called 'New Public Management' from a useful analysis made by Chris Lorenz that year in a *Critical Inquiry* article called 'If You're So Smart, Why Are You Under Surveillance?'. The article should have soothed us, but as I read that account of how new management strategies were being implemented across the world, and recognised exactly the same moves that were now being made inside MMU, I seethed. The clue is in the title of Lorenz's article; we were not being treated as smart at all, but as fools who needed to be fed carrots and shown sticks to do anything worthwhile, to avoid the lazy temptation to say no. The fundamental shift in management strategy could be summed up in the replacement of 'efficacy' as something which could be experienced as an ability to change things – that is what academics, including critical psychologists were trained to do as the best outcome of their research and teaching – by 'efficiency'. Efficiency describes the operation of a system that runs along by itself, but without going anywhere in particular, and a key feature of this process is that it relies on the undermining of any individual or collective sense of efficacy. This kind of efficiency requires obedient subjection to the aims of the institution.

The watchword for this kind of efficiency of the institutional mechanism, again, is the fake-ecological weasel-word 'sustainability', and this Orwellian double-speak includes a concern with 'impact', a term that every university coming up to the next Research Assessment Exercise has worked over. The shift entails the rise of a managerial layer which protects itself and views the smooth functioning of the organisation as a good as such – that is what it is to be 'efficient' – and these managers in the university who are usually paid an unbelievably higher salary than the academics view those who refuse to comply as problem cases that have to be dealt with. It is in this context that HR turns from being an ally of the staff into a weapon of management. It was during this time that 'bullying' became more prevalent as a discourse among staff to try to explain what was being done by management, but also to name what they experienced when they were unable to track down the problem to one particular malevolent individual. While workload went up fifty percent during this one year, the UCU discovered during one of its own staff surveys that many staff saw increased workload itself as a significant cause of stress and saw this as a form of bullying.

The complaint process about my PDR carried on unresolved through the summer break, the time of the rota to prevent our campus turning into the Mary Celeste, which meant that the building was empty except for the two staff there each day, those compelled to spend time in their offices and fend off the ghosts. Morale was disintegrating. Dan Goodley escaped to Sheffield University, politely taking his leave with little more than a murmur of complaint about the way he had been treated as a researcher who did bring a lot of research money into the department. He left his partner, Rebecca Lawthom, who was then taking over as chair of the BPS Psychology of Women section from Horrocks, in the department. Rebecca was in a very difficult position, acting head of department while Horrocks was briefly away, and so I didn't send the 'first email' asking for information about workload to her. We felt for her, and felt our friendship come under strain. Rebecca was sometimes reduced in meetings to acting as the chorus, repeating the final few words of everything Horrocks said, a sharp contrast to the constructive thoughtful guidance she gave to students, to all of us at other times. Carolyn retired as a full-time professor, her farewell lecture a dispiriting occasion during which she told us how much academic time was wasted on bureaucratic nonsense while the managers sat silently and thought about the sandwiches. Now Erica and I were the only professors, apart from the new head of department, left. The 'first email' was about workload.

Second

The 'second email' was about the appointment at the beginning of the academic year of a new lecturer in the department who had been Horrocks' colleague in Bradford. We had already gone through an appointment process for a counselling psychologist over the summer in which we had followed the usual departmental procedure of having the staff group attend presentations by the candidates. In fact, by now the demand for presence and participation was in full force, and it was obligatory for staff to attend the presentation, something that was unprecedented. Appointment reminders were starting to ping into our Outlook email inbox, usually for events that we were not expected to contribute to but merely function as room–meat. What was most unusual about this new appointment was that, in contrast to an obligation to attend the counselling psychology post presentation, one which was only of interest to a small section of the department, and for which no candidate was appointed eventually, we were told *not* to attend this one, a general lecturing post. The decision of the appointment panel, which comprised Horrocks, Vince and Rebecca, was met with disbelief and disquiet. Rebecca would not let such a decision be made lightly, but she was bound by rules not to disclose internal panel debates. I was approached as union representative and told that the interviews had been rigged to bring in Horrocks' friend. I was not sure whether this was the case, so I sent an email asking for clarification about what had happened and pointing out that even if everything had been fair and above board, the sudden change in procedures were giving rise to rumours that the process had been unfair. Horrocks responded with a bureaucratic answer assuring me that "procedures had been followed", which was untrue, and I replied to the whole department saying that this response was unsatisfactory, copying this reply to the Vice-Chancellor John Brooks.

This was the 'second email' that triggered the disciplinary investigation and that led to my suspension, and I suspect that copying in Brooks had been the fateful mistake. The suspension letter from Human Remains on 3 October outlined the two allegations that were to be investigated; that I had "constructed and widely distributed an email, which intends to undermine the credibility of a Head of Department", fair cop, and that "the distribution of this email constitutes a failure to comply with a reasonable management instruction". That 'reasonable management instruction' referred, of course, to the request that I shouldn't send private emails investigating increased workload, specifically what now became known in the HR process as the 'first email'.

So here we are. It was a strange freedom that Wednesday when I handed in my keys. I sauntered down the stairs, down the 'link corridor' that ran through the main building, and then round by the old photocopying room, now an empty space after the technical support staff had been unwillingly relocated to Didsbury, space designated as a 'disability support resource', and continued along between the main lecture theatre and cafeteria, past a grim-faced Vince who looked ahead as I crossed his path. Then round the corner into reception where I handed in my keys and identity card to bemused Angela and said goodbye. My first thought as I walked out through the gates onto Hathersage Road was that I could wander down into Rusholme and do some shopping in Worldwide Foods. I had a few hours to spend before an early evening celebration for the latest 'anti-capitalism' special issue of *Asylum Magazine* which was now edited by Helen Spandler, the launch for which was scheduled to take place in a bar off Oxford Road following the China Mills afternoon research seminar.

This ended nine months of pressure, sleepless nights worrying about how to manage union representation in an increasingly hostile climate and how to defend my own work. It meant that I would not be able to attend the union branch meeting we had called on campus that Friday on the topic of 'bullying and workplace harassment'. We had mixed feelings about signalling the topic in that way, for it treated a series of institutional processes that increased stress at work as if they were consequences of the actions of a few bullies, it psychologised the problem. On top of that, the climate of fear was now such that it was unlikely that more than one or two members of the union would turn up. Getting out was a relief, but it was the culmination of one difficult process that now opened up a new one, one that could be worse. It was worse.

As psychologists we should know about stress, and we are certainly able to name it. My first lectures to the BAPA students had been on occupational stress. I was very familiar with the research on the topic which links the horrible things that happen at work with what happens to our health, combining the bleeding obvious with their bodily consequences. Much of the early research in psychology was on so-called executive monkeys who were subjected to systems of rewards and punishments that they could not control and who were then opened up so that the resulting ulcers in their stomachs could be observed and correlated with what had been done to them. Stress as a bodily reaction is not really psychological at all, but it becomes layered with psychological discourse as it is reframed and spoken about as if it has its origins in the minds of those subjected to it. Then 'stress' and 'anxiety' in reality is compounded by a sense of helplessness and a sense of responsibility that we have to those around us, and it is bound up with the isolation and shame that attends it, attends it often as a result of attempts by the workplace to deny it is happening, to cover it over and to blame the victim. Wednesday 3 October was a turning point.

The next day, Thursday, there was to be a newly composed compulsory senior management team meeting, with Erica, the last professor left apart from the head of department, now ordered to attend. In the morning she went to her doctor and obtained a medical note which gave her a week off work; 'anxiety'. I could not help feeling this was my fault, and together we felt under attack. Late one night there was a ring on the doorbell at home for delivery of a pizza we had not ordered, and we together briefly hallucinated the possibility that the Vice-Chancellor knew where we lived before we laughed, but our relieving laughter did not dissolve the stress. Carolyn, still active after formal retirement, got hold of keys to my office from the porters and checked that I had everything I needed, came to my house and told me I should apologise. I stubbornly refused. I think at that point it would have been futile, and there were points of principle to be made and repeated until they were taken seriously. I would not apologise for sending two emails.

Erica's medical note was extended to a month. We were lucky that there was no pressure from the doctor to explain what was happening in psychological terms, or to prescribe medication, as if what we were going through was something with a medical cause, something that fell in the domain of psychiatry. The doctor said they knew of this kind of thing from countless reports from other patients in similar straits. But there was temptation aplenty to describe what was happening as flowing from the bad personalities of those around us, and these kinds of psychological explanations would often be evoked by those who wanted to support us and understand what was going on. This was a trap we were careful to avoid, and all the more important to avoid in a context that was intent on pitting good behaviour against bad behaviour, setting good behaviour on the part of management against the bad behaviour of those who were disrupting business as usual. Reversing the terms of complaint would not solve things, and it was clear from quite early on that the advice being given to management included 'psychological advice'.

On the one hand, we knew that the new head of department, Horrocks, was, in other situations, a reasonable and even, at times, radical force, and we also knew that she was under pressure to bring about organisational change in the department. These were the terms on which she had been appointed, not evil intentions or indications of pathology that drove her to act as she did. Horrocks was not, we repeated, a fundamentally evil person, and was merely, if anything, too obedient to those who were also obediently trying to prevent the union putting obstacles in their way. Her choice was an ethical choice, to comply, made within a particular moral framework, the idea that management in the department needed to be strengthened and those who challenged it needed to be dealt with. How the challenges were to be dealt with was not under her control either. There was pressure on and from the Dean to implement the new processes as part of the consumer-focused strategy of the university which would also make it more competitive in the higher education marketplace, and there was pressure on the Dean to show results. The rules of the game had been set for him, even though it was in his power, albeit with a little leeway, to interpret how the results might be obtained. And the Vice-Chancellor, no doubt, wanted to make his mark, perhaps to succeed in an alliance with Manchester City Council to get a new campus built and so push MMU up the university rankings and leave with more than a new building named after him. That kind of pressure is not nothing for anyone involved, and it is not directly driven by personality flaws or other psychological factors.

On the other hand, there was pressure to describe resistance to these agendas as flowing from psychological problems, from an unwillingness to accept change that must surely flow from deeper problems with authority, and we also knew from networks in and around the BPS Psychology of Women section that Horrocks was having coaching from a psychologist based in Sheffield to help her deal with her underlings and to develop strategies to get them to comply, to comply with an agenda that she herself had clearly already chosen to comply with. Little shifts in argument, inconsistencies in management decisions, could, perhaps, be traced to that coaching, traced to advice that was consciously decided, between people strategising, rather than emanating from inside the mind, from the kinds of things in the head that psychologists are supposed to specialise in.

I did, as I planned to, ask Bill Campbell what on earth he thought he was doing when I attended a first 'investigation meeting' on 15 October. The meeting was moved by HR that morning from Bill's Didsbury campus to All Saints, the central campus, to take place in their own offices. Roger, the regional union representative who came into the room to support me, had to ask me to calm down before he assured Bill that we would do what we could to cooperate with the investigation. Roger told me that if I apologised for the 'second email' there was a possibility that I might get my job back. We, that is, the local union branch, guessed that Roger was negotiating with MMU management and was hoping to strike a deal. I began to think I knew what an executive monkey felt like. There were clearly some attempts by local MMU management, surprised by the press coverage and international response to my suspension, to save face, and attempts by the regional union branch to smooth things over. The MMU union branch, however, were up for a fight, and Christine Vié accompanied me to the disciplinary hearing instead of Roger.

The press coverage was sympathetic, both in *Manchester Evening News* and in the *Times Higher Education Supplement*. Nevertheless, whenever MMU was asked to comment, HR hinted that there were reasons for my suspension that hadn't been made public, and this made the campaign more difficult, not so much for the union, but for me, and I felt it personally. The secrecy surrounding the events was poisonous, for this was at a time when there had been a series of revelations in public institutions about sexual abuse which had for years been covered up. The message that you could trust nobody was a potent one, and I asked myself why people should believe me when I insisted that I was being investigated for sending two emails and said that this was clearly stated in the letter of suspension. Even so, colleagues around the world, including Noam Chomsky, had sent letters to Brooks and Horrocks objecting to my suspension, and there was an online petition – set up unprompted by a Turkish colleague Sertan Batur – with the demand that 'Ian Parker should get back to his work', a curious message that made me smile, one which was clearly supportive and which many colleagues and friends signed. There was outrage at what was happening, but some understandable caution as people tried to find out what I had done. Friends phoned, and I had to repeat that this had blown up over the sending of two emails. It was incredible, people were incredulous. Surely there must be more to it than this. Michael Billig phoned Erica and asked her if she was alright. He was, I think, fishing to find out if there was more to this than it seemed, and when he was reassured that I hadn't done something really awful he helped mobilise one of the letters of support from social psychologists.

We were sustained by the intensive union mobilisation across MMU and messages of support from across the world. Colleagues in the education department down at Didsbury campus made badges with the legend 'I am Ian Parker' blazoned across in black capital letters against a white background. Christine Vié wore her Ian Parker badge to a reception hosted by the Vice-Chancellor at All Saints campus. Some PhD students told us they were praying for us, and we knew they weren't joking, and others sent cards which included quotes from Audre Lorde on the importance of speaking truth to power. One day a package arrived from Canada with Doreen Cronin's children's book *Click, Clack, Moo: Cows that Type*, about a revolt by the cows on Farmer Brown's farm after they had got hold of his typewriter. Duck, initially a mediator and collaborator, then inspires the rest of the ducks to resist Farmer Brown too. Reading the book aloud in bed at night did alleviate the stress a bit. The stress continued, and increased, and after a few weeks I nearly knew the book by heart.

Paranoia worked its way into our perception of the university administration and what we thought Human Remains would be capable of next, and into some of the strategies we used to protect ourselves. As always, the defence mechanisms that I used were as bizarre as the threats I believed to be all around us. Again, there was a lesson here about the way that apparently 'psychological' defences against threat – paranoiac strategies to deal with suspicion directed at others – are often the result of real material circumstances that then manifest themselves in crazy behaviour. In those conditions it is then also understandable, perhaps, that my attempts to make sense of what was going on were not entirely rational. I felt myself hurtling into a series of manoeuvres to defend ourselves that made us feel worse psychologically. Anxiety and stress were directly manifested in bodily symptoms, it affected how I slept and how I ate, as well as who I met and how I related to them, but it was something that could not itself be explained in psychological terms because that was not where the problem was coming from. So, for example, Erica and I both met our postgraduate students at different locations around the city to be able to continue to supervise their work, and we had to deal with their anxiety about being caught as well as our own. We still had academic visitors. Raquel Guzzo from Brazil who came with similar stories about disciplinary processes from her own university, had a talk scheduled on liberation psychology at Gaskell campus on Wednesday 17

October, two days after my investigation meeting, so we drove her to the campus where she could be met by students at the gates, and then we collected her again when it was over.

We met our union representatives at different places, partly because we were not allowed on university premises while suspended from work or off sick and partly because it felt safer to meet away from the university, the more so when other members of staff who were supporting us also came along to show support, other members of staff who feared for their jobs if they were seen fraternising with the internal enemy. Costa Coffee in East Didsbury Tesco superstore was one favourite location where union branch officials met with me to discuss tactics, to reassure me and to check that I was able to continue, always careful and considerate about my health. At other times the locations were more outlandish.

I was contacted by a young lecturer at MMU who had already had some problems with HR. He had a legal background and wanted to help in drafting some of the union responses preparing for the disciplinary hearing, but he was afraid that if HR found out that he was helping me he would also be subjected to disciplinary action. So he arranged a 'safe house', a place owned by a friend in an estate on the edge of Manchester where we could meet to talk. He stipulated that he should arrive first, and then, after thirty minutes, we would wait for the all clear by text so we could make our way there from another location nearby. After that meeting he relaxed a bit, and we met again at his house, but we had to park away from the house, and work our way around to the yard at the back so we wouldn't be seen by neighbours. These meetings focused on preparation of a 'grievance' against management which would counter what they were doing with a detailed account of the pressure we had been subject to; this was a lengthy document that HR would be obliged to respond to, notwithstanding their new codes of practice that warned that inappropriate complaints by staff against managers could themselves lead to disciplinary action being taken.

These covert encounters to work out how best to defend myself in investigation and disciplinary meetings and prepare a grievance would have been laughable if they did not add an edge to every arrangement, an edge of concern that others would also suffer if they reached out to support us. A group of students and academic visitors went to Vice-Chancellor Brooks with the petition 'Ian Parker should get back to his work' and found him in his office, where he told them that there were things about my case that would never be made public. My letters to Brooks asking that he retract this comment and apologise were never answered. The students were defiant but now sworn to secrecy about what they knew because we knew that they would be punished for allying with us. Some of them had already had leaflets they posted in the department torn down and been shouted at, told that they had no idea what was really going on. Student academic visitors from Chile commented that this was too close to what they knew of in situations when friends disappeared; I felt fraudulent at the comparison but sensed that everyone was making such comparisons to make sense of what was going on. The porters at reception in Gaskell campus said it was "like living in a communist state".

The discourse of 'bullying' was used by the union, but I was unsure whether this was helpful, it could have been a mistake that relied on some psychological presuppositions about the nature of organisations under pressure. MMU was an organisation under pressure, and that did mean that individuals inside it were under pressure too, but that pressure set the conditions for 'bullying', it didn't simply give license to particular kinds of people who were disposed to be 'bullies'. MMU management also recognised the threat posed by the bullying discourse, and HR quickly rewrote the harassment guidelines during this time to remove bullying as an actionable offence. Instead, staff who brought a charge of harassment were to be liable to a new charge themselves of having broken the 'mutual respect' that should obtain between line manager and employee.

Heard

At the disciplinary hearing in November we presented, as part of my defence, character references from academics from around the world. I didn't like asking my colleagues to write these, found it humiliating, but the union insisted that this might help my case. I was fearful, surprised at how, minutes after speaking to a small crowd of supporters outside Chatham Building on the All Saints campus, my confidence drained away as I was led up unfamiliar stairways and then around to the room in Ormond Building where the Human Science Seminars once used to be held. I trembled, anxious; this was a ridiculous, but carefully staged event over which I had no control. The character references were ignored, and, instead, a thick pile of letters and petition signatures was put on the table with the angry comment "Look what you've done to bring the university into disrepute". HR, which was managing the case for the prosecution, included photocopies of a Facebook posting which incriminated me, evidence that I was orchestrating the whole campaign. Horrocks wore near-black lipstick and white foundation for her performance and said she had received threatening letters from those supporting me. I said that I had supported her as best I could during the first months of her time as head of department, but I heard myself whining and felt wretched. The prosecution, the head of HR, tried to get me to admit that I had been sending the union representative emails in a personal capacity, and then commented that they were considering changing the charge from 'gross professional misconduct' to 'insubordination'. Christine Vié was amused, calm, stubbornly determined. She knew how this worked. She been through this process as advocate during many other cases, sat in this refitted trial room before, and she was in the midst of her own defence campaign. I knew I had someone here with me who would fight. This is what I wanted, I trusted her, and she was well able to stand up to them.

The quite even-handed judgement came a week later in a written verdict that the charge should be reduced to 'professional misconduct', it was no longer so gross, and that while the 'first email' I sent about workload had raised legitimate concerns by me as a trade union representative, the 'second email' had indeed been designed to undermine the head of department, and I should apologise for that. Even if I did apologise, however, there would be a 'final written warning' put on my file, which would mean that I could be sacked immediately if there was any further disobedience. We decided to appeal against this ruling, for it meant that as soon as I returned to work I would be working in impossible conditions, continually under threat.

I decided to get the letter of apology out the way while we were preparing the appeal. I still don't think that Horrocks wanted this dispute over workload and appointment procedures to go beyond something that could be dealt with by a 'conversation' and soft power inside the department. Horrocks herself was caught in the middle manager role, putting a lot of work in to comply with her own line managers and engaging in a good deal of emotional labour to bring her staff into line so she could prove herself. There was much speculation among those involved in the campaign to defend me as to who was to blame, but I am not sure if this is really the right question. I am unable to say who asked HR to begin a disciplinary investigation, and our attempts to find out through Freedom of Information requests to MMU revealed little. It was true, the 'second email' I sent might have been hurtful to Horrocks, it would have been stubborn of me to refuse to acknowledge that possibility. Everyone, whatever position they held, felt threatened. I sent the letter and it was accepted, I was instructed to return to work in December, but instructed to do that before my appeal had been heard. I was told that the appeal hearing would not take place until the end of January the following year.

My struggle was very public, but friends asked about Erica as well, of course. This question was also asked on email lists by those who, quite understandably, wanted to know more about the gender dynamics in the struggle, why it was that there was public support for me, and silence about what was happening to her. She had also prepared a detailed grievance with the help of the union branch about her treatment by her managers, including in her PDR. The events had endangered her position in the department, but now, after twenty-six years there, she wanted to get out. There was an opportunity, with the upcoming research exercise, Research Excellence Framework 2014, of a window opening through which researchers could jump with their publications to another university. It was now crucial to keep quiet about Erica's link with what was happening to me so as not to sabotage her applications elsewhere.

I didn't know what to do. A return to work and another inevitable dispute when I was sacked as soon as I tried to resume my union activities would definitely create more noise and more pressure. We had so far got about half of what we wanted – lifting of the suspension and acknowledgement of my trade union role – but we weren't sure that we could mobilise public support for another campaign, and the local union branch was under immense pressure. It was militant but weak, and the university was not yielding over the much more significant case of their main union representative in the university, Christine Vié. I can't pretend I was thinking rationally, whatever that is, still less that I knew how to calculate what the next move should be. I needed Erica to tell me I was stressed, and that there was nothing to be gained by playing the strong man. She did. I went to the doctor the next day, and as I walked into the consulting room I burst into tears. There were two trainees sat in the corner. That was the point it was over for me. I had known I would never go back, and this made it real.

I got a medical note but no medication, and did not have to rehearse to my audience in my doctor's office the argument made in Joanna Moncrieff's book *The Myth of the Chemical Cure* that these drugs do not correct an imbalance but do something specific, they always make a difference. Joanna, who is part of the Critical Psychiatry Network, spoke about this argument in Manchester at an Asylum meeting back in 2010, noting the shift from the drug-focused approach to mental distress before the 1950s to the mistaken 'disease-focused' model pushed by the pharmaceutical companies. The drugs all have effects, just as nicotine and alcohol does, and the critical psychiatrists should, she argued, work with their patients to work out what those effects are. I was worried that my doctor would prescribe medication, but she was not a drug-pusher, and a medical note saying 'anxiety caused by stress at work' did the trick. We escaped for New Year to stay with an Ángel in Madrid for three days, during which time we mostly just slept. I lasted until the end of January. Erica was offered a post at Manchester University – they didn't mention the events at MMU but often commented during the first meetings, the presentations to staff and the interview that they were "a friendly department" – and the next day, on Thursday 31 January, she phoned Christine Vié to tell her the news about the post and get her advice. "Well", our Christine said, "you should go then"; and when I took the phone and said now I wanted to get out, she told me yes, I should go too.

I had one last encounter with the institutional machinery that morning, one that I was curious about, so I went along to see what would happen. It was nice to be back in ethnographic mode. MMU had said they wanted their own independent medical advice on my condition and directed me to attend a meeting with a doctor in an outsourced private clinic in a tower block by the main station in the centre of Manchester. The doctor was very pleasant, asking me to explain what was going on after telling me that I had been referred, she said, as she read from her notes, for "behavioural problems". I do not know what she wrote about our meeting.

I walked from that meeting to one of the free lunchtime concerts at the Royal Northern College of Music – the place functioned as a soothing space, as my own therapeutic clinic and as my office where I saw PhD students for supervision these last few months – and it was a rather peculiar event. The Principal and then head of the Board of Governors of the College were present, and they watched the Head of Strings conduct the young orchestra. Something was up, but we didn't quite know why the Head of Strings was in the spotlight that lunchtime. He was suspended the following week for abusing the students, one of a number of staff in music colleges in Manchester who have since been arrested and prosecuted. This was an unpleasant reminder that abuse and secrecy go hand-in-hand and that discipline and dismissal are appropriate managerial responses. Erica was waiting outside having already handed in her resignation letter. I emailed mine. MMU told us not to bother serving our notice; they would rather pay us for three months to keep away, to leave them be.

The personal accusations that were hinted at in the partial and evasive accounts offered by the institution played into an apprehension by many that institutions are places riddled with the abuse of power, and the fact that there are evil people who do wicked things makes it seem as if psychological causes should be sought. You can see from my account that my bad behaviour was indeed psychologised by those signed up to the institution, and I have found it very difficult to avoid returning the favour, psychologising those positioned as my enemies, as if their bad intentions were manifested in bad actions. This would, however, be a big mistake. Psychology as a discipline was intertwined with the institutional processes I describe, and psychological factors – whether in the form of personality types or moral character – are not drivers; we need to look elsewhere for the underlying causes of the problem.

20

MANAGEMENT

Big P and little p

In which we finally extricate ourselves from the discipline of psychology but learn that it is not so easy to escape the wider network of theories and practices that comprise the psy complex. We turn back and reflect on where we are now, continue our journey into and out of management, and find new ways of working on the management and care of the self.

I got through it, and my anthropological journey through psychology, my time as a psychologist is almost over, but in this final chapter I need to wrap things up with some reflections on the way that even when you might think that you have let go of psychology, psychology does not let go of you. The auto-ethnographic account in this book has fore-grounded my own part in what I describe, but I am still there inside this stuff and this stuff is inside me. It is necessary to step back and reflect on what we have learnt from this journey. I was lucky – that's a ready to hand explanation that I have already used to account for how I was able to get into psychology – for though they probably meant it in an unkind way the message from my managers at MMU was correct; it was time to get out, and I was right to do so.

Core

I was in a planning meeting for a series of cultural events focusing on the question of identity, three years after my last day in a psychology department. Three years is the usual span of an undergraduate degree in Britain, though there are government plans to reduce the time from three to two years, which will be an attractive option for students anxious about the size of the debt they will accumulate during their time in college, debt they will have to pay back to whichever private company buys the 'loan book'. Upgrade of the National Student Survey has increased the pressure on universities to compete with each other to attract their new 'customers'; that is a term explicitly used on some university websites to refer to their students. The process of privatisation and outsourcing continues apace. This process we call 'neo-liberalism' has a sharp side, the brutal exclusion of those who cannot afford education and healthcare, and disciplinary procedures against those inside or outside the institutions who dare to resist. And there is a soft side. This soft power includes psychology, but the insidious and pervasive influence of a discourse concerning the self, the mind, individual behaviour – in a word, 'psychologisation' – also means that lines are now even more blurred between Psychology with a capital P in the psy complex and psychology with a small p that we experience in our everyday lives.

A clinical psychologist at the planning meeting insisted that each concept we discussed – whether it was identity, memory or trauma – revolved around what he called the 'core self', and we had much discussion in the group about whether we needed such a notion as an alternative to the unthinkable idea that there was a 'void', nothingness at the heart of the human being. This guy came over to chat during the lunch break and told me that though a lot of what I was saying was what he referred to as 'anti-psychology', it was a view also shared by many of his colleagues inside the discipline. I hesitated but then agreed that, yes, I supposed I was an anti-psychologist, and wondered whether all this talk of the core self was what marked him out in the meeting as a psychologist. I am still not sure whether we can pin the problem down on this notion of the core self. After all, there are many people who would think of themselves as having core selves who are also deeply suspicious of what big P psychology wants to say about it. And even if we refuse to use the term, 'psychology', it returns unbidden, as if it must be at the centre of the story we tell about ourselves. I never shook off anxiety and bouts of depression, but learnt to live with it, and learnt to live without Psychology which offers so many false claims about what you must do and how you should live.

I could not have told this story of my journey through the psy complex if I had subtracted little p psychology from my account, not in a way that would have made it meaningful, but it is worth reflecting on how psychological discourse is carried into that story and then might configure how you read it. This has been the story of one individual, a life narrative that is structured as if there is a thread running from my first encounter with psychology to my last days teaching it. And I name other individuals who made their own personal choices about how to deal with the institution, how they come into and then trace a trajectory through the constellations of significant figures who shaped how I made sense of all this, and because they are named it is all the easier to apply psychological theories that could make sense of what went on.

One of the endless marvels of psychology as a discipline is that it is so contradictory. It is a skein of descriptions and theories, and methods to make them seem plausible, so when it is applied it will find threads of the narrative which it can hook and weave into one of its own accounts. However much I try and avoid those psychologising accounts I cannot prevent them being mobilised to interpret and then, perhaps, provide a frame by which people can either empathise with what happened to me or put it all down to being a manifestation of what the American

Psychiatric Association's bible, the current edition of the Diagnostic and Statistical Manual of Mental Disorders, calls Oppositional Defiant Disorder, ODD. It is quite possible, isn't it, given claims that ODD has an estimated "lifetime prevalence" of 10.2%, that there is a more than one in ten chance that I have this condition; the claim is that there is 11.2% prevalence for males and 9.2% for females, so it is more likely still.

MMU pushed ahead with my grievance against them even after I left, and I agreed to go to a meeting about it on 1 May 2013 accompanied by a union representative. For the union, it was a way of accumulating a public record of these events, showing that there was a problem and that staff were willing to speak out, but for management it was an opportunity to reassure itself that procedures had been followed and to confirm that those who brought complaints against them were at fault. The letter from HR detailing the results of their investigation duly informed me that they had decided that there was no case to answer, though I was told that they had started investigations against the management in the department as well. I am comforted by the thought that I am not alone. A rather surprising sequel to the struggle for trade union representation in the MMU psychology department was that a colleague on the 'other side' of the department stepped in to take up the union rep post. She lasted for six months before she too was suspended for misconduct, but went under the radar without a public campaign and found a better job in another university. She too needed support, including medical support for what we each experienced in our little p psychologies as anxiety and stress. We told her to hang on, told her that yes, she was right in her case to keep quiet, and that yes, it would soon be over and she would be alright somewhere else. Another lecturer had enough and left the department abruptly with no other job to go to. Others escaped soon afterwards. It was a 'crisis' in the meaning of the word as 'turning point'.

Another colleague who remained in the department and who had kept quiet throughout the campaign to defend me, contacted me when I was finally out, and we met in a café, a secret location where he was sure he would not be seen talking to me. He wanted to tell me about his own secret strategies for resisting, so secret that no one in power would be able to find out. Another colleague from the MMU department who contacted me after I had left had kept quiet during the crisis and shook with rage as he told me he could not, would not ever refer to the new head of department by their first name. He said he had looked up the surname and discovered that it meant a small pile of stones. To call her by her first name would, he said, be a silent victory for her, and his refusal was a silent victory for him. A director of research in the university retired shortly after I left, and called me to meet up; this was a colleague I barely knew who wanted to bare their soul about how bad things were, and how they wished they had been able to speak out during my crisis.

Support networks were formed, with people inside and outside the university that I had never spoken to before and who I would have said I had nothing in common with. Friendships with colleagues were disrupted, perhaps, who can say, broken forever as a result of the different choices and strategies people used to protect themselves. Suddenly, during the crisis, email communication was cut by some friends in the department frightened to speak out, and I knew from other friends still there that they agonised about what they were doing but feared for their jobs and careers. A colleague asked me after a political meeting we both attended a year back whether I was happy in my new job and whether I had "fallen out with my new colleagues yet". I understood this implicit reframing of the crisis as a self-protective discourse, functional to the institution, and as 'management discourse'. I remembered their own predilection for a form of politics that at one moment mobilised the 'community' and at the next wanted to be sure that there was strong leadership to take them in the right direction. It made perfect sense now that they would perceive those who did not obey to be a threat and would interpret disagreement with management as 'falling out' with everyone. One of the strategies of power is to sow divisions among those who have common cause, to pretend that when there is resistance it is no more than a difference between those who speak out and those who are silent. This is to psychologise organisational politics and obscure managerial power. This discourse goes alongside the strategy of inviting those who are silent to imagine they are part of a united whole which those who are resisting are thereby disrupting.

Vice-Chancellor Brooks has now retired from MMU, as has Dean Ramprogus, who was later listed as a researcher in Bolton. Horrocks retired after failing to get the post of Dean of Faculty in 2015 but popped up again a year later when she was appointed Pro-Vice-Chancellor of MMU's Cheshire Campus in October 2016, ready for the closure of the whole campus. MMU announced in February 2017, despite staff and student protests, that it would be closing the site in the summer of 2019. Those who want to stay at MMU will have to travel 50 miles north to the main campus in Manchester. Gerry Kelleher moved on from being head of research to take up the post of Vice-Chancellor for a couple of years nearby at the University of Central Lancashire. MMU appointed a new Chancellor, a symbolic post. Peter Mandelson, who encouraged further privatisation of the higher education sector during his time as Minister of Business, Innovation and Skills, was beaten into third place during election as Chancellor of Manchester University by the poet Lemn Sissay; shortly afterwards Mandelson was appointed, not elected, as Chancellor of MMU.

The MMU Didsbury, Hollings and Gaskell campuses have been sold off as part of the 'estate concentration strategy'. Gaskell campus buildings were turned into rubble, ready for a new private hospital development that would leech off the Manchester Royal Infirmary across the road. Hoardings around the site proclaimed 'The future of healthcare is coming. . . '. The psychology department has now been relocated at a new campus built on what was a green-field site near the centre of Manchester, where the main building has been renamed Brooks Building, also more commonly known by some staff as the Death Star or sometimes as the Bastard Building. We heard that Claudius D'Silva continued his campaign for a judicial review of his race discrimination case and reinstatement without success, and that his laboratory materials and records at MMU were destroyed.

After her retirement Carolyn Kagan has devoted her boundless energies to local campaigns, including to saving a building in south Manchester and turning it into a community centre; pictures of Carolyn and her campaign group petitioning the government appeared occasionally in *South Manchester Reporter*, and she is still a comrade I meet at May Day celebrations and other political events. Peter Banister fell ill with multiple cancers in late July 2019 – Carolyn told me she had visited him in hospital – and died of pneumonia within a few days, before Erica and I could see him. Carolyn spoke fondly of Peter's resistance to bureaucratic management imperatives at a memorial service in October at a church in Uppermill.

Patsy the caretaker who fed the foxes and the scruffy ginger cat in the reception area at Gaskell Campus, and who warned me against being locked into the building again, retired and died shortly afterwards. Also gone now are Joel Richman who died four years after leaving MMU. We have lost John Cavill, who retired from MMU after I left and then died shortly afterwards, as well as Carol Tindall, our colleague on the qualitative methods module and co-author of our book of the course, and Couze Venn, one of the co-authors of *Changing the Subject*; this is a sad farewell to him, to them all, and further afield, Maria Milagros López from Puerto Rico, Michael White from Australia, and Ann Levett from South Africa. And, closer to home again, we said farewell to activist comrades Mickey de Valda from the Hearing Voices Network, and Sharon LeFevre from the self-harm network. Michael Billig spoke at John Shotter's funeral in Cambridge in December 2016 about how badly John had been treated by academic psychology disinterested in ideas, a discipline disinterested in the very experience of being human it was supposed to be so concerned with. My PhD research topic, remember, was to be about men, and an explicit focus on the construction and experience of masculinity was taken forward by Tod Sloan with more care and sensitivity than I would have been capable of; he was a critical psychologist who offered emotional and material support to activists in Latin America, his death a bitter blow in December 2018. Max Hammerton, who inveighed against Sartre when Professor of Psychology at Newcastle University, on the other hand, was still very much alive when I saw him in December 2017; it was an unexpected encounter, but I could not fail to recognise his crew cut and check shirt in the electrical goods basement of Fenwick department store when I visited the city to do a talk about revolutionary politics, something he would strongly disapprove of.

A question was raised on a community psychology email list shortly after I left MMU about what solidarity could be shown for those who left, whether there should be a boycott of psychology at MMU. I responded on the list that, no, this would be a big mistake. I said this was not for my love of the place, but because there were still many colleagues doing good work trapped inside, making the best of it. True, the words 'critical' and 'discursive' were all but erased from the psychology programme after I left. Even the final year counselling option on which I was first recruited to teach, and which then ran for another thirty years, was axed. At one point before I left I agreed to go along with the decision to cut critical psychology as a named MSc programme in order that resources could be put into the MSc community psychology programme. After all, I reasoned to myself, students would be able to carry on doing critical work in the context of community psychology or under the overall rubric of psychology. Now the MSc community psychology degree has also been closed. However, there are new lecturers in the department doing interesting work for whom this account is history, and I hope it remains so, a curious story rather than a warning of what is to come for them. They may be lucky. The department ran for some time under the temporary leadership of a professor brought in after we left who specialised in a frightful field of study called 'mental toughness' but who was, we were told by those who remained in the department from the old times, a really nice guy. Rebecca Lawthom, who kept critical disability studies going, and Geoff Bunn, who had tried to secure the 'Conceptual and Historical Issues in Psychology' courses on the undergraduate degree as a place for critical work, have succeeded in reviving radical research.

I have met colleagues and friends from around the world who said they had signed the petition and quite a few who told me that they hadn't signed, not because they didn't support me but because they didn't know what had 'really' happened. I am inclined to respect those who refused to sign more than those who lie about supporting me. What does it matter? Such support is as much symbolic, retroactive and performative as anything else, and if people do not have some freedom to rewrite the narratives about who they are then we are all lost. This is not a psychological matter, not something psychologists can easily grasp within their linear cause-and-effect model of individual behaviour.

It is 'retroactive' in the sense that it obeys a logic in which what happens after the event then gives meaning to what went on before; people sometimes realise that they were always really against bad things when things have changed and there is a stronger consensus that will enable them to be heard. The fall of apartheid is a good example; for quite a few liberal white South Africans who never spoke out during those years, their declaration now that they were always against it is nevertheless positive. It is 'performative' in the sense that what is said has consequences well beyond what it describes, and speaking out after the event can be better than always keeping quiet, for it serves to legitimise a version of historical memory which gives a frame that defines what was right and what was wrong. These notions of 'retroactivity' and 'performativity', to give just two examples of notions developed from the more discursive, deconstructive and post-structuralist elements of social and political theory, help us understand better how individuals are formed and sustained in relation to others. We are then able to appreciate, for example, why it is that members of indigenous communities may speak about their personal experiences of terrible oppression, but sometimes turn out to be describing what has actually happened to families and friends instead of themselves. The memory is carried through what they are part of and not who they are in their own core self. The issue is not only whether this particular individual is reporting what really happened to them alone, which is the way that Psychology insists on approaching what our true psychology is.

What I remember of these events cannot be other than a reconstruction from my own perspective, of course. I know these events happened, and I can tell them to you now as honestly as I can. But I have to tell you that whatever psychologists claim to know about accuracy of recall, all they really know is that there cannot be such a thing. Psychologists have always known this, and then forgotten it again as they try to build models of short-term and long-term memory which will define how events get filtered and how details get distorted or lost. Some of the best research on memory, by Sir Frederic Bartlett, first professor of experimental psychology at Cambridge University, was published in the early 1930s before the warring trends of cognitive and behavioural research took hold of the discipline. Psychologists chase after fictions of their own making, and the best I could do here is string together some memories of how I was persuaded that psychology was important and discovered, instead, that it was important because it was powerful, and perhaps no more than that. Memory as such is a collective creative process. It is, to borrow a phrase from Bartlett's research, a 'war of the ghosts'. I conjure up ghosts from my past in this book to try and make sense of how they fit together, and to lay the ghost of psychology – the ghostliest of all of the imaginary machinery of our lives that we assume to operate inside our heads – to rest.

This crisis was traumatic, and I use that word 'trauma' with a little t that tries to keep it at a distance from the pathologising stories of how traumas bear on the construction and destruction of someone's self, stories which create victims and survivors, categories and types of helplessness and resilience. As these years since the crisis have gone on I have found myself able to react less and reflect more on what was triggered in me each time someone asked in a concerned and sympathetic way "so what really happened; what did you do?" I am now able to read this response as symptomatic, as an expression of the secrecy that enfolded a series of events that were, paradoxically, also so public. It is telling that every attempt we made to explain exactly what was going on after I was suspended and during the disciplinary process was almost immediately cloaked once again in mystery, our statements in the course of the campaign even then constituted what must lie at the heart of it as something impenetrable and inexplicable. How does that work? How, I would ask myself, can I be asked this question again and again about what I did as if it has never been spoken about before, as if they do not already know?

Time soothes all this somewhat, but the repetition of the narrative has also served as an obstacle to that smoothing over of the past and our attempts to put it behind us. The years after we both left MMU included working around that obstacle, doing some work on what remains of trauma, reframing it and discovering how it function as an element of the crisis as turning point. Erica is secure and happy in the Manchester Institute of Education at Manchester University, among colleagues that are, as they claimed they would be, friendly, and she was able to quickly confirm the arrangements with Oslo to which she travelled every now and again for four years in return for a fifth of her salary that was paid back into Manchester as income generation. Academic visitors now come to us here at this campus just up the road from our old place of work. This is where Erica runs, among other things, a Discourse Unplugged group and participates in another group called KPI – Knowledge, Power, Identity – a subtle subversion of management discourse hidden in the acronym. Colleagues still ask about the Discourse Unit, sometimes assuming that we had to leave it behind, that it was attached to our old place of work. We explain that the Discourse Unit website was always registered at our home address, and we continue it as an international network visible in its regular diary of events and sessions hosted in Manchester University, including occasional runs of our revived and renewed Discourse Course. A Discourse Unit Global Seminar in 2017 brought together friends and colleagues who visited us over the years; a special issue of *Annual Review of Critical Psychology* showcased the work they are doing.

Now our visitors meet with the new group of postgraduate students Erica has assembled, we have met our obligations to the students we had at MMU, and now all of them have completed their PhDs. Mine either transferred to work with me at Manchester University where I have an honorary post and so access to university resources, or to other universities where they continued their studies and I was able to work with them as an external supervisor. One or two who were actively involved in the campaign to support me and who remained at MMU paid a price; in one case the university told a postgraduate international student that arrangements could be made to extend her visa if she agreed to take part in a promotional video that said that MMU looked after its overseas students. Some visitors want to meet the now almost mythical figure China Mills who was a public voice of the campaign for my reinstatement, and who, after a spell as a researcher at Oxford University became a lecturer in the education department in the university at Sheffield with, among other good colleagues, Professor Dan Goodley, before moving on to a post in London.

The Privy Council finally approved Bolton Institute's application for university title in 2005, and Principal Mollie Temple retired soon after that. The Tower Block was demolished. The previous Principal Bob Oxtoby was pictured in *The Bolton News* in August 2009 in full academic robe taking his turn as a living statue on the empty fourth plinth in Trafalgar Square after having won an hour-long stint up there in a lottery. He is holding up a sign saying hello to his grandchildren. Patrick McGhee served time as Vice-Chancellor at University of East London until a financial scandal about a new campus in Cyprus cut short his time there, and he has now returned to Bolton University as assistant Vice-Chancellor, writing a column in *The Guardian* newspaper 'in a personal capacity' complaining about marketisation of higher education. Bolton University was focus of a campaign a few years back to defend two sacked staff. One was a union representative who was accused of passing information to the press about mortgage arrangements and other payments to the new Vice-Chancellor. The press said the union representative was not the source of their stories. The other victim of management was the union representative's wife who, the university reasoned, must also be complicit in the crime. There were demonstrations and a march through the streets of Bolton that ended up at the Town Hall.

The protest was an opportunity to catch up with postgraduate students in Bolton who are now lecturers in the new university there. They were on the march. It was also an opportunity to hear of the resignation of staff in protest – honourable behaviour by cognitive psychologist Rob Ranyard – against a wave of redundancies that had wiped out of the department our old critical MSc pioneers Rod Noble and Tom Liggett. I have seen Rod at conferences which he still attends for entertainment during his forced retirement, and Tom has finished the novel he was working on for many years. Dave Nightingale left a long time back to embark on a new career in photography. The Bolton trade union dispute was a nastier and more bitterly fought union campaign than mine, one which has not, despite the rumours of a 'settlement' which muzzles the two sacked staff, had a happy conclusion.

People sometimes ask me if my case was resolved by the award of those notorious financial settlements and Non-Disclosure Agreements that enable institutions to save face and ensure that the victim keeps quiet. Well, evidently not, or you would not be reading this now. Family and friends, and colleagues in different countries have been subjected to such strange solutions to conflicts at work, and usually with the effect of leaving them with some temporary respite but with a lingering sense of failure and injustice, of helplessness which intensifies the traumatic repetition of the events as they try to account to others for what happened but know that they must not tell all. One of the ways that the motif of speaking out about institutional corruption has been discoursed in the public realm has been through 'whistle-blowing'. It was a defence strategy we discussed in the local union branch, and one that the regional union favoured in my case; we might, they said, claim that I was quite legitimately breaking management instructions to keep quiet about workload and about the appointment procedures and it could be seen as a case of whistle-blowing. As far as the union regional representatives were concerned this would also be a damage-limitation strategy because they could not stop the flow of information about the case to the press. They entreated me at one point to stop protesting publicly while they brokered a deal with management. This would be a deal that relied on the issue disappearing from public view and ceasing to embarrass a university sensitive about its reputation and about the impact it might have on its NSS score.

Periphery

I moved on. In 2013, just after I had left MMU, I was invited to speak at a psychoanalytic conference in Paris organised by researchers in a field of research called Critical Management Studies (CMS), a phrase I had always mocked them for, while they mocked me in return for calling myself a critical psychologist. Our banter continued, with the question as to whether the next category would be critical prison warder. The invitation was one of the series of solidarity invitations to academic events, to speak and to chair sessions, a reaching out to me at a difficult time, a gesture that I appreciated. In Paris, I spoke about what happened, and reflected on it in psychoanalytic terms. There is another story to be told, of course, about my engagement with psychoanalysis as 'the repressed other' of psychology and as an alternative within and against the psy complex, but that is another book. While there is something about psychoanalysis that is disturbing and subversive to those who believe in a 'core self' and who want people to talk about themselves and adapt themselves to power, I have focused in this book on the way that psychoanalysis specifically operates in relation to the psychology around me in the English-speaking world.

The Paris conference was also a reminder that there are other academic spaces that run in parallel with psychology and that also enable a quite different reflection on what power is. One of the papers in Paris, for example, was about how CMS might recast 'whistle-blowing' through readings of Antigone. Alessia Contu used Antigone – an ambiguous heroine in the play by Sophocles – to draw attention to the paradoxical ethical position of those who defy the law or, in this reframing of the events, a work organisation. As Alessia pointed out, discussions of Antigone by Hegel and then Lacan and Judith Butler have also revolved around the question of what other forms of law or community are invoked by those who disobey. Antigone poses a puzzle for those wanting to know exactly what she intends by her refusal to obey Creon's edict forbidding burial rites for her brother Polynices, what her desire is and whether it is a pure desire. This is a puzzle that also, of course, itself shifts our attention from a consideration of power and resistance, to 'psychology' with a small p – what is going on inside Antigone's head – and then that account could call upon the apparatus of Psychology with a big P to try and answer it. I was sorry not to be able to discuss these issues with Heather Höpfl in Paris as I reconnected with critical management. She was now very ill. She had left Bolton, and ended up at Essex University, where I met her at a seminar there, and now she is gone, has left us to meet her maker.

A series of lucky coincidences and personal connections led me to Leicester University where the School of Management had a strong CMS tradition. The strapline and ethos of the school was 'Management is too important not to debate'. My critical psychology publications, I was amazed to discover, were not only more suitable for the education rather than psychology panel for the upcoming 2014 Research Excellence Framework census, but also, it seemed, would count as critical management. A letter of appointment from Leicester arrived in October 2013 asking me to start the following Monday, and so my work was registered there just in time to be submitted for the Research Excellence Framework, the REF upgrade of the rather ridiculous research assessment exercise.

The message of enthusiasts for psychology, which most psychologists become as they move up the career ladder, is that everything is psychology, and it is true that everything can be psychologised. Student psychologists learn to keep quiet about their personal experiences because their psychological research should be about other people, the non-psychologists. Students learn to write their research reports in the third person, as if they were not really there themselves directing others to carry out strange tasks or fill out stupid questionnaires. Later on they are permitted to speak in the first person, connecting what they have discovered with who they are, with who they have become when they have learnt to accept what psychology tells us about human thinking and behaviour. When they have really become psychologists through and through, they speak in the second person, telling you directly about how they have benefitted from what they know. Then psychologisation has triumphed. The same could be said about the way that management works. During my three years at Leicester I asked then-Head of School Simon Lilley what journals I should write articles for, and I was told I should carry on as I had before because, he said, "everything is management". Instead of an evangelical attempt to turn everything into management, however, this licensed a critical approach to the way everyday life is infused with management and with the discourse of managerial control. With this in mind, we can now give a little reflexive twist to the claim that everything is psychology and say, indeed it is, and our task should therefore be to try and explain how we have arrived at this sorry state.

There were friends already at Leicester, including former trade union activists from Manchester, and some of the component bodies that once upon a time made up Beryl Curt. These were academic colleagues who had already moved from psychology into management. Beryl had disintegrated after the death of Rex Stainton Rogers. Wendy Stainton Rogers became a professor of 'health psychology' at the Open University and became an important figure in the developing strand of 'critical health psychology'. Now retired, she was a good friend and source of support during my end days at MMU. This 'health psychology' and its sometimes critical work was a place where many social, feminist and community psychology researchers have ended up. My undergraduate tutor Mike Hyland became professor of health psychology at Plymouth University, as did my PhD supervisor, Roger Ingham at Southampton University, another source of support during my crisis.

That bad time was a good opportunity to renew links with colleagues and to rediscover the ethical impulse that lay behind many of the critiques of mainstream psychology. Colleagues in social psychology around the world sent letters of protest. One coordinated from Loughborough showed that whatever political disagreements we had in the past, we were still on the same side when it came to a shared response to injustice. I was reminded that objections to what psychology did, what it did to people, were often driven by what Rom Harré often referred to as the moral-political dimension of human action. I now had time to gather material I had written over the years into six little books in a Routledge series called Psychology after Critique which was published the same year as an edited *Handbook of Critical Psychology* for the same publisher. Rom wrote a foreword for the book series, and when I thanked him he replied that it was "a kind of crusade against the wicked".

I became wary of the term 'moral' because it can so quickly slide into moralising, that is, into a set of values to which you expect everyone to conform. Psychology as a discipline in its more confessional mode as a form of soft power, the kind of psychology that Foucault describes so well in the first volume of *The History of Sexuality*, often operates as a moral force and incites people to feel that they are bad when they fail to fall into line. I have been even warier of the term 'crusade', a signifier that is part of an institutionalised moral discourse bound into particularly brutal cultural-historical forms of Western power, and, when we reflect on it, a good example of operations of discourse that have been noticed very quickly by radical activists who are also effectively already discourse analysts outside psychology. But

Rom, who died in October 2019, was always right to argue that the forms of action we chart in human interaction follow sets of rules, and prescriptions for the roles we adopt, roles which cannot be reduced either to biological factors or to cognitive mechanisms inside individual heads.

Also at Leicester, there were colleagues who had been part of the broader strand of critical psychology, including those who had studied with Holzkamp in Germany where it took the form of *Kritische Psychologie*, colleagues who had been working with Valerie Walkerdine in Cardiff University where she was still based after she left Sydney. She was now based in a department of social sciences rather than psychology, and her journal *Subjectivity*, formerly the *International Journal of Critical Psychology*, had now dropped its subtitle – the subtitle which once specified the journal was concerned with critical psychology – altogether.

The crucial question, it seems to me, is how Management with a big M and Psychology with a big P are linked together, and then what the consequences are for the criticals in those two domains of work and beyond them. Leicester University provided me with an academic and symbolic space to lick my wounds and to move on. It was a place of transition, and functioned well as a safety-blanket in which I have learnt something more about how another discipline that I knew next to nothing about also operates very much like psychology, not surprising given the prevalence of psychological discourse now. For example, I attended the Ninth International Conference on Critical Management Studies which was held in Leicester in July 2015. This was a busy visit. Leicester is about two hours by train from Manchester, so I stayed overnight, in accommodation paid for by Leicester because I was attending the conference. I took supervision sessions with eleven postgraduate students carrying out their dissertations for their MSc in Human Resource Management. What could be weirder than that? But it turned out that most of the students had chosen to research 'emotional labour', and in most cases this was in their home countries, China, Singapore, Thailand and Vietnam. Those who chose other more recondite managerial topics explained what they were up to, and my task was to take them through the research methodology, something that is fairly common to all the social sciences. I now knew of initiatives in Latin America, first piloted in Argentina and used in Colombia, to mark the element that the university HR department judged to be the 'emotional salary' given to an employee, that is, the additional non-financial benefit that someone gained from working in a high-status job.

The issues of surveillance and confession that structure the opposition between quantitative and qualitative research in psychology were very present in these pieces of research, as was the concern with discovering what the participants in the dissertation projects really thought and really felt. This was familiar terrain, as was the format of the CMS conference. Vandana Shiva, the Indian feminist environmental activist gave an inspiring keynote talk which did not mention management and which would have gone down very well in any radical psychology forum. Her message was a profoundly humanist one, about the connection we all have with each other and with the earth. The audience gave her a standing ovation and some wept. One could say that she was making psychology, her intervention had an emotional effect, and it appealed to something deep inside each individual present, with the message that we each had a responsibility for our lives and the lives of others. I struggled with myself; not to be cynical, and how to appreciate what was progressive in her rejection of mechanistic instrumental ways of organising the world. It chimed strongly with what we have been through in psychology as people romantically embrace what they think of as authentic human experience in qualitative research as an alternative to laboratory-experimental method. I hoped that the critical ethos of the CMS conference would enable people to accept this positive message as a critique of discipline without falling into the trap of confession.

The format of the CMS conference was also reassuringly and troublingly familiar. There were keynote talks and then we separated into parallel sessions in which lecturers and some students spoke about a study they had carried out, usually one entailing interviews and records of the experience of problems and solutions in workplaces and communities. Perhaps the content was familiar because I had already chosen conference strands that covered topics that looked interesting to me, but even so I could have been in a psychology conference. There were opportunities in the sessions to rehearse debates over the value of different methodologies, the working over themes that had emerged, and even something close to the 'sex differences' question in the discussions, though here it was extended to questions about gender, sexuality, culture and history. We were also very much at the most progressive edge of a critical psychology event. One thing was different, and it was nice; something that was there in the best and most friendly of our critical psychology conferences, and this went alongside the embrace of a qualitative research ethos refracted through feminist arguments: I noticed that in every session the discussion time after a paper opened with the first question from the audience prefaced by an expression of thanks and congratulations for having presented us with something so good. Is this psychologisation too?

Psychologisation continues apace; a psychologist successfully appealed against a traffic offence in 2019 citing research evidence that there was too much signage for their brain to process in time. Meanwhile, the Department for Work and Pensions, DWP, was inviting applications for psychological studies to be undertaken, 'in a research laboratory environment', with recipients of the Carers Allowance and recipients of the Employment and Support Allowance. This follows on from the placing of psychologists in benefit offices tasked with using Cognitive-Behavioural Therapy to get people back to work and sanction them if they do not. There have been protests against the DWP at these offices by the Mental Health Resistance Network. There are good people in the world speaking out against abuse. Psychology Politics Resistance might have expired, and still could be revived, but there are still new radical initiatives bubbling away; Steve Reicher, now professor of social psychology in Scotland, told me about a 'psychology and social justice' event in January 2019 at the LSE, and we had our old argument over whether psychology could be a place to do critical research – he thinks it could – or whether we need to set ourselves against the discipline altogether. You know what I think by now.

There is a further twist to the psychologisation of everyday life that Jan De Vos writes about in his later work on neuropsychology. The neurological turn which is increasingly powerful in a range of academic disciplines, not only in psychology, effectively bypasses much of the phenomena that psychology was once concerned with. Now the message is not so much that you are your mind, but that you are your brain. Real neurological research, as with real biological research or studies of behavioural processes in ergonomics, has never really been about psychology at all. The problem was that some psychologists who did research in those areas pretended that they were carrying out psychological research, or that there were lessons for our psychology from what they discovered in those other disciplinary fields. Now, as psychologisation turns into 'depsychologisation', De Vos argues, even interior reflexive experience is evacuated and replaced with appeals to what is happening in the brain. Psychology, which fed the idea that these other kinds of research were part of psychology, is now eating itself. It is uncertain what psychology really is now, and where it stands. Many departments have divided, with the divisions reflecting the old paradigm wars between quantitative and qualitative research. In Birkbeck in London, for example, the qualitative psychologists have regrouped in their own department of Psychosocial Studies, leaving behind the unwittingly but comically named Department of Psychological Sciences. Psychology as a subject area in Manchester University was once in the Science Faculty and is now part of the Faculty of Biology, Medicine and Health, and another psychology degree in the university linked with education will be situated in an entirely different faculty. The apparatus of the discipline reproduces itself through the individual actors who are willing to take up positions within it; the junior lecturer who humiliated my PhD student at viva is now a professor.

I could see a similar script unrolling at Leicester after the appointment of a new Vice-Chancellor in 2014 and then a Dean of a 'School of Business' into which management and economics were merged soon after. David Willetts, who presided over the tripling of student fees in Britain as Minister for Education was appointed Chancellor of the University. Relations between the university administration and the union began to fracture as the union, now headed by Christine Vié after her departure from MMU, opposed an intensification of workload. Staff in the new School of Business who collectively refused to participate in online video 'lecture capture' were told not to 'reply all' to emails about this from the Dean because, they were told, it was an "individual decision" to comply or not. I was told by colleagues that they were very worried about what was happening, but one said of the new Dean that "I don't think she's fundamentally evil". After a decision to participate in school meetings, despite the union work-to-rule which discouraged such extra activities, one activist said that it was important to be there for the discussion, while adding "I won't stay for the cake". The old strapline of the merged school was changed to 'Leicester means Business', and the staff were told they would move into a new building with shared offices. A new member of staff was sent on a course on Emotional Aspects of Organisational Change to prepare him for his assigned role in identifying people who would be prepared to go in return for a redundancy package of some kind. I had seen out three years up to my sixtieth birthday in Leicester, very grateful to have had this academic post after I left MMU, but I didn't need a redundancy package to induce me to leave. It was time to go, there was nothing I could usefully do in disputes from over 100 miles away, and so I consolidated my work in Manchester in October 2016, combining my paid clinical work with some supervision in Manchester University in return for use of institutional resources there.

The individuals who occupy the various positions that comprise the academic apparatus move on after having fulfilled their function; the new broom at Leicester who turned the critical management department into a School of Business moved on in 2018 after fifty academic colleague resignations, and the Vice-Chancellor responsible for that appointment, for unit closures and for the shift of staff contracts from research to teaching, left a year later. I visited the MMU Death Star for the first time in December 2018 and then again in February 2019, to examine PhD students in social work and education, the second of which was carrying out research on the National Student Survey and the micro-managerial consequences for all staff. Some teaching and technical support colleagues and friends were still there, a reminder that it is possible to survive and resist an institution, to make it work for us instead of against us.

Out

It is surely true that the discipline of psychology, the big P stuff in the psy complex, has always been an apparatus of management. Psychologists proved their worth in the personnel divisions of the Ford car factories in Detroit at the beginning of the twentieth century, for example, finally breaking with their forerunners' background in philosophy and their dabbling with introspection to focus on behaviour, on how workers could be made more productive and how they could be made to behave themselves at work. The question for the psychologists was not so much how to bring psychology out of the laboratory, but how to make life itself like a laboratory – ordered and observed – so that the methodological procedures of psychological research could be implemented, put into practice. This world of work in which psychology was honed to shape was the industrial version of the prison system Foucault had described in *Discipline and Punish*. The system of work production in which each separate process on the assembly line was tabulated and coordinated adopted the approach advocated by Frederick Taylor in his 1911 book *The Principles of Scientific Management*, a work management process that came to be known as 'Fordism' or 'Taylorism'. It required an obsessive attention to detail, an obsessional frame of mind explored in the Indian psychoanalyst Sudhir Kakar's biography of Taylor, and then a model of the mind as comprising central command processes and a variety of working mechanisms that replicated in miniature the factory under capitalism.

Capitalism privileges mental labour over manual labour, however, and psychologists refined their models of the mind so that individual mental mechanisms would be valued over collective activity carried out on the factory floor. Cognitive psychology which flourished in the 1950s turned to the working practices of middle managers and office workers with new models that resembled filing and selection processes. It was only the rise of the service sector and the entry of women into the workplace that the role of 'motivation and emotion' began to assume centre stage, and this when the concerns with what Arlie Hochschild called 'emotional labour' started to become more important. This is the setting – it provides what Foucault would call the 'conditions of possibility' – for the paraphernalia of industrial and health psychology. The lives of workers outside production become a concern of the state, and the psychology of advertising and marketing then targets workers not only as producers but also as consumers. Management under capitalism which had called upon the services of the psychologists and found them so useful in regulating behaviour now also begins to extend into the domain of what we called 'self-management', and here it meets the new forms of psychology with a little p that we like to think operate in our own little private worlds, our own little spaces inside our heads where we make choices about where we want to work and what we want to buy.

The field of critical management studies therefore does not at all consist in turning little m management against big M. Instead, Critical Management Studies recognises that recent concern with processes of self-management indicate a deeper shift that now also becomes part of the problem. The 'interpellation' of people as separate individuals, as workers or consumers, rather than as members of collectives with shared interests is part of the broader process by which everyday life is managed under capitalism, and we experience that process now as little p, our own little psychology where we imagine that we make our own personal mix of thoughts and emotions. CMS comprises different perspectives – versions of the psychoanalysis, post-structuralism, feminism and Marxism we assembled as our four theoretical resources in the Discourse Unit – and other resources that have come on the scene since we set up shop and which we have also drawn upon, resources that range from postcolonial to queer theory, from Deleuze to post-humanism. It does that to reflect on how management works and perhaps even to resist it, to find new ways of organising that reflection outside the frame of contemporary management practices. Can critical psychology do something like that?

My bet is that it cannot. Psychologists who are dissatisfied with their own discipline often turn outwards, to other disciplines like education or management, but then meet the same kinds of obstacles to critical reflection on what it is to be human as those they had already encountered. Such is their relief at finding something a little better, a little more open to the singularity of personal experience and the cultural conditions which shape the language we use to describe ourselves, that they are sometimes willing to overlook those obstacles. Perhaps one test would be to compare the rich playful descriptions in good fiction with the mean-spirited and banal narratives that quantitative and even qualitative methodologies allow for. Compare, for example, the ambiguity and grounded description that novelists give of the comportment and contours of thought and emotion of their characters with the crass reductions and generalisations made by psychologists. I am reminded of this often while supervising doctoral students in English and American Studies in Manchester University, looking through textual web windows into alternative realities while marvelling that it is discourse itself that can give the illusion of depth and presence of a mind configured in it. The literary novel appears, of course, at roughly the same time as psychology, and is part of the same individualising ethos that accompanies the rise of capitalism, but ideological though it may be, it is surely truer to what human beings are today and even to what they may be. I have traced a path out of psychology and elaborated a way of understanding what psychology does that is grounded in my politics. I have made it clear that I approached psychology as a Marxist, and leave it as such. But there are other progressive non-psychological standpoints – whether literary critical, feminist, postcolonial or those grounded in radical disability and mental health movements – that enable a critique and distance and action. Those very different stories, about who we are, who we can be, and how psychology limits us, also need to be told. There are some better places to do academic research, it is true, but this is not guaranteed by calling them 'critical'. One thing is for sure, that psychology as an academic and professional practice is a worst case, and 'critical psychology' is too often trapped inside it.

We cannot escape if we only play by the system of roles and rules that make up the academic institutions, roles and rules that set in place a moral-political career that require the critical psychologist to be silent when there are abuses of power. To go beyond that, radical reflexive work also needs to take a step beyond itself, beyond its status as critical psychology to be able to imagine a world in which psychology as such is no longer necessary. One of the lessons that Marxist politics has almost but still not quite learnt from feminism is that the personal is political, that our interaction with others and our feelings about those interactions are also political matters, for these processes at the micro-level either reinforce or challenge the existing order of things. This means that we do not point the finger at bad individuals as if they are wholly responsible for ideological explanations, for patterns of power and institutional mechanisms that require and reward destructive and self-destructive behaviour, but neither do we lose sight of the fact that individuals do make a difference, either when they collude or when they refuse to do that. My one story is both particular and general; I have tried to connect what I saw and heard and what I did with other issues. There are elements of confession and accusation in it, but I wanted to weave these elements into this auto-ethnographic narrative so that you could see that bad though things are in psychology it is not the case that nothing can be done about it. It would seem that psychology can recuperate – that is, absorb and neutralise – anything; even the term 'auto-ethnography' appears in recent psychological research, but there it is usually reduced to being a warrant for talking about yourself rather than embedding what you are talking about in socially-structured power relations configured by institutions.

The phrase the Discourse Unit picked up from the time of our flirtation with critical realism was 'reproduction and transformation'; we are always, in whatever we do and however we speak, on the edge of a choice, as to whether we keep existing power relations in place or whether we challenge them. This means that our psychology is also always a political matter; the way we either merely describe it and try to conform to it, or question and aim to subvert it, links us with broader processes of culture, ideology and power. The crucial thing to remember is that even that separation between the personal and the political is an expression of the nature of the problem itself, one in which we treat what we think and feel as operating at a level which is different from the activity of challenging and changing our world, the world.

The term 'psychology' speaks of a domain of individual behaviour and of an interior world that has been separated off from our relationships with others, from competing contradictory forms of culture, from ideology that feeds illusions about who we are and who we can be, and from power which enforces the shape of the social world as it is today under this miserable exploitative political-economic system, capitalism. It is a reduced image of what we are as human beings, and when it operates as part of the psy complex it tells us that we are morally and emotionally wrong to resist it. Each of us take a journey through the psy complex when we encounter psychology in the academic institutions where it is taught, in the schools, clinics and prisons where it is practised and in the mass media where it is sold to us as a panacea when it is part of the sickness we must struggle to overcome. Psychology is fraudulent, you know that, and there is more to life if you step outside the psy complex and find many other ways to live together without it.

AFTERWORD AND ACKNOWLEDGEMENTS

Besides the introduction of a new subject after very momentous words have passed, and are still dwelling on the mind, is necessarily a sort of concussion, shaking us into a new adjustment of ourselves.

(George Eliot, Felix Holt, the Radical, 1866)

A full accounting for what is wrong with the discipline and how it betrays what there is of our psychological sense of ourselves needed to embed a description of the characters that comprise it in their particular institutional contexts. The positions we are assigned in our working lives, and not only there, entail obligations to behave in particular ways, and I hope I have shown you that decisions to comply or rebel are not really 'psychological' at all in the way the discipline understands these things. I hope that those who recognise themselves in this book will also appreciate the description of the roles they were assigned and their place within a wider flow of forces from which they could not easily extricate themselves, for neither could I. The book aims to indict what is done to us by Psychology and the institutions it serves, not impugn what particular individuals might still think of as their internal psychological sense of what they were doing.

Thanks to all those who helped me during this process, including those who participated in discussion of draft chapters, both those at the Sigmund Freud University Vienna and at the University of Oslo. The Discourse Unit network of colleagues and friends around the world supported me during my time in psychology and through the process of me disentangling myself from it. Specific thanks to Daniela Caselli, Artemis Christinaki, Ángel Gordo López, Brendan Gough, Athanasios Marvakis, Ken McLaughlin, China Mills, John Morss, Helen Spandler, Corinne Squire and Jackie Stacey – to those who raised questions about memory and the psychological frame that comes into play, whether I like it not, when I attempt to recall the details of what happened over these years. Special thanks to Erica Burman who lived through most of these events with me and enabled me to survive them. This book is for her.

BIBLIOGRAPHY

Abramson, L.Y., Seligman, M. E. P. and Teasdale, J. (1978) 'Learned helplessness in humans: Critique and reformulation', *Psychological Review*, 87, pp. 49–74.

Annual Review of Critical Psychology: www.discourseunit.com/annual-review/

Armistead, N. (ed.) (1974) *Reconstructing Social Psychology*. Harmondsworth: Penguin.

Asylum Magazine for Democratic Psychiatry: http://asylummagazine.org/

Banister, P., Bunn, G., Burman, E., Daniels, J., Duckett, P., Goodley, D., Lawthom, R., Parker, I., Runswick-Cole, K., Sixsmith, J., Smailes, S., Tindall, C. and Whelan, P. (2011) *Qualitative Methods in Psychology: A Research Guide, Revised 2nd Edition*. Buckingham: Open University Press.

Banister, P., Burman, E., Parker, I., Taylor, M. and Tindall, C. (1994) *Qualitative Methods in Psychology: A Research Guide*. Buckingham: Open University Press.

Bannister, D. and Fransella, F. (1971) *Inquiring Man: The Theory of Personal Constructs*. Harmondsworth: Penguin.

Barthes, R. (1957/1973) *Mythologies*. London: Paladin.

Basaglia, F. (1987) *Psychiatry Inside out: Selected Writings of Franco Basaglia*. New York, NY: Columbia University Press.

Beloff, H. (ed.) (1980) 'A balance sheet on Burt', *Bulletin of the British Psychological Society*, 33 (Supplement).

Bhaskar, R. (1978) *A Realist Theory of Science, 2nd Edition*. Brighton: Harvester Press.

Billig, M. (1976) *Social Psychology and Intergroup Relations*. London: Academic Press.

Billig, M. (1978) *Fascists: A Social Psychological View of the National Front*. London: Academic Press.

Billig, M. (1979) *Psychology, Racism and Fascism*. Birmingham: Searchlight.

Boring, E. G. (1929) *A History of Experimental Psychology*. London: The Century Co.

Bowers, J. M. (1991) 'Time, representation and power/knowledge: Towards a critique of cognitive science as a knowledge-producing practice', in I. Parker (ed.) (2011) *Critical Psychology: Critical Concepts in Psychology, Volume 1, Dominant Models of Psychology and Their Limits*. London and New York: Routledge.

Bowlby, J. (1944) 'Forty-four juvenile thieves: Their characters and home lives', *International Journal of Psycho-Analysis*, 25, pp. 19–53, 107–128.

Broughton, J. (1988) 'The masculine authority of the cognitive', in I. Parker (ed.) (2011) *Critical Psychology: Critical Concepts in Psychology, Volume 1, Dominant Models of Psychology and Their Limits*. London and New York: Routledge.

Brown, P. (ed.) (1973) *Radical Psychology*. New York, NY: Harper & Row.

Bulhan, H. A. (1980) 'Frantz Fanon: The revolutionary psychiatrist', *Race & Class*, 21 (3), pp. 251–271.

Burman, E. (2017) *Deconstructing Developmental Psychology, 3rd Edition*. London and New York: Routledge.

Burman, E., Aitken, G., Alldred, P., Allwood, R., Billington, T., Goldberg, B., Gordo López, Á. J., Heenan, C., Marks, D. and Warner, S. (1996) *Psychology Discourse Practice: From Regulation to Resistance*. London: Taylor & Francis.

Burman, E., Alldred, P., Bewley, C., Goldberg, B., Heenan, C., Marks, D., Marshall, J., Taylor, K., Ullah, R. and Warner, S. (1995) *Challenging Women: Psychology's Exclusions, Feminist Possibilities*. Buckingham: Open University Press.

Burman, E. and Parker, I. (eds.) (1993) *Discourse Analytic Research: Repertoires and Readings of Texts in Action*. London: Routledge.

Burt, C. L. (1917) *The Distribution and Relations of Educational Abilities*. London: Campfield Press.

Chomsky, N. (1959) 'Review of B. F. Skinner's "Verbal Behavior"', *Language*, 35, pp. 26–58.

Collini, S. (2018) *Speaking of Universities*. London: Verso.

Contu, A. (2014) 'Rationality and relationality in the process of whistleblowing: Recasting whistleblowing through readings of Antigone', *Journal of Management Inquiry*, 23 (4), pp. 393–406.

Costall, A. and Still, A. (eds.) (1991) *Against Cognitivism: Alternative Foundations for Cognitive Psychology*. Englewood Cliffs, NJ: Prentice-Hall.

Cromby, J. and Harper, D. (2009) 'Paranoia: A social account', in I. Parker (ed.) (2011) *Critical Psychology: Critical Concepts in Psychology, Volume 3, Psychologisation and Psychological Culture*. London and New York: Routledge.

Curt, B. (1994) *Textuality and Tectonics: Troubling Social and Psychological Science*. Buckingham: Open University Press.

De Paor, L. (1973) *Divided Ulster*. Harmondsworth: Pelican.

Derrida, J. (1978) *Writing and Difference*. London: Routledge & Kegan Paul.

Deutsch, M. (1973) *The Resolution of Conflict: Constructive and Destructive Processes*. New Haven, CT: Yale University Press.

De Vos, J. (2012) *Psychologisation in Times of Globalisation*. London: Routledge.

Dews, P. (1987) *Logics of Disintegration: Post-structuralist Thought and the Claims of Critical Theory*. London: Verso.

Donzelot, J. (1979) *The Policing of Families*. London: Hutchinson.

Edwards, D., Ashmore, M. and Potter, J. (1995) 'Death and furniture: The rhetoric, politics, and theology of bottom-line arguments against relativism', *History of the Human Sciences*, 8 (2), pp. 25–29.

Enriquez, V. (1994) *From Colonial to Liberation Psychology: The Philippine Experience, 2nd Edition*. Manila: De La Salle Press.

Eysenck, H. J. (1982) 'The sociology of psychological knowledge, the genetic interpretation of the IQ, and Marxist-Leninist ideology', *Bulletin of the British Psychological Society*, 35, pp. 449–451.

Farr, R. M. and Moscovici, S. (eds.) (1984) *Social Representations*. Cambridge: Cambridge University Press.

Fernando, S. (2017) *Institutional Racism in Psychiatry and Clinical Psychology: Race Matters in Mental Health*. Basingstoke: Palgrave.

Foster, J. J. and Parker, I. (1995) *Carrying out Investigations in Psychology*. Leicester: British Psychological Society.

Foucault, M. (1962/1987) *Mental Illness and Psychology, Revised Edition*. Berkeley, CA: University of California Press.

Foucault, M. (1966/1970) *The Order of Things*. London: Tavistock.

Foucault, M. (1970) 'The order of discourse', in I. Parker (ed.) (2011) *Critical Psychology: Critical Concepts in Psychology, Volume 4, Dominant Models of Psychology and Their Limits*. London and New York: Routledge.

Foucault, M. (1971) *Madness and Civilization: A History of Insanity in the Age of Reason*. London: Tavistock.

Foucault, M. (1975/1979) *Discipline and Punish: The Birth of the Prison*. Harmondsworth: Penguin.

Foucault, M. (1976/1981) *The History of Sexuality, Vol. I: An Introduction*. Harmondsworth: Pelican.

Fox, R. and Tiger, L. (1971) *The Imperial Animal*. New York, NY: Holt, Rinehart and Winston.

Fozooni, B. (2020) *Psychology, Humour and Class: A Critique of Contemporary Psychology*. Abingdon and New York: Routledge.

Friedman, M. and Rosenman, R. (1959) 'Association of specific overt behaviour pattern with blood and cardiovascular findings', *Journal of the American Medical Association*, 169, pp. 1286–1296.

Fryer, D. and Fox, R. (2015) 'Community psychology: Subjectivity, power, collectivity', in I. Parker (ed.) *Handbook of Critical Psychology*. London and New York: Routledge.

Gardner, R. A. and Gardner, B. T. (1984) 'A vocabulary test for chimpanzees', *Journal of Comparative Psychology*, 98, pp. 381–404.

Garfinkel, H. (1967) *Studies in Ethnomethodology*. New York, NY: Prentice-Hall.

Gauld, A. O. and Shotter, J. (1977) *Human Action and Its Psychological Investigation*. London: Routledge & Kegan Paul.

Gergen, K. J. (1973) 'Social psychology as history', in I. Parker (ed.) (2011) *Critical Psychology: Critical Concepts in Psychology, Volume 1, Contradictions in Psychology and Elements of Resistance*. London and New York: Routledge.

Gergen, K. J. (1991) *The Saturated Self: Dilemmas of Identity in Contemporary Life*. New York, NY: Basic Books.

Gibson, J. J. (1966) *The Senses Considered as Perceptual Systems*. Boston, MA: Houghton Mifflin.

Gilligan, C. (1982) *In a Different Voice: Psychological Theory and Women's Development*. Cambridge, MA: Massachusetts Institute of Technology Press.

Goffman, E. (1959/1971) *The Presentation of Self in Everyday Life*. Harmondsworth: Pelican.

Gordo López, Á. J. (2000) 'On the psychologization of critical psychology', *Annual Review of Critical Psychology*, 2, pp. 55–71.

Gordo López, Á. J. and Parker, I. (eds.) (1999) *Cyberpsychology*. London: Palgrave.

Guthrie, R. V. (1976) *Even the Rat Was White: A Historical View of Psychology*. New York, NY: Harper & Row.

Hammerton, M. (1974) *A Science Under Siege: An Inaugural Lecture Delivered Before the University of Newcastle Upon Tyne on Tuesday 26 February 1974*. Newcastle: University of Newcastle Upon Tyne.

Haraway, D. (1989) 'Metaphors into hardware: Harry Harlow and the technology of love', in I. Parker (ed.) (2011) *Critical Psychology: Critical Concepts in Psychology, Volume 1, Dominant Models of Psychology and Their Limits*. London and New York: Routledge.

Harré, R. and Secord, P. (1972) *The Explanation of Social Behaviour*. Oxford: Blackwell.

Heather, N. (1976) *Radical Perspectives in Psychology*. London: Methuen.

Henriques, J., Hollway, W., Urwin, C., Venn, C. and Walkerdine, V. (1984/1998) *Changing the Subject: Psychology, Social Regulation and Subjectivity*. London and New York: Routledge.

Hilgard, E. R., Atkinson, R. C. and Atkinson, R. L. (1975) *Introduction to Psychology, 6th Edition*. New York, NY: Harcourt Brace Jovanovich.

Hochschild, A. (1979) 'Emotion work, feeling rules and social structure', *American Journal of Sociology*, 85 (3), pp. 551–575.

Hollway, W. (1989) *Subjectivity and Method in Psychology: Gender, Meaning and Science*. London: Sage.

Holzkamp, K. (1992) 'On doing psychology critically', in I. Parker (ed.) (2011) *Critical Psychology: Critical Concepts in Psychology, Volume 4, Alternatives and Visions for Change*. London and New York: Routledge.

Holzman, L. (1995) '"Wrong", said Fred: A response to Parker', *Changes: An International Journal of Psychology and Psychotherapy*, 13 (1), pp. 23–26.

Honess, T. and Yardley, K. (eds.) (1987) *International Interdisciplinary Conference on Self and Identity*. Chichester and New York: Wiley.

Hood, L. and Newman, F. (1983) 'Tools and results: Understanding, explaining and meaning (three sides of one dialectical coin)', in I. Parker (ed.) (2011) *Critical Psychology: Critical Concepts in Psychology, Volume 4, Alternatives and Visions for Change*. London: Routledge.

Hubbard, L. R. (1950) *Dianetics: The Modern Science of Mental Health*. New York, NY: Hermitage House.

Hyland, M. (1981) *Introduction to Theoretical Psychology*. London: Macmillan.

Ingham, R. (ed.) (1978) *Football Hooliganism: The Wider Context*. London: Inter-Action.

Ingleby, D. (1985) 'Professionals as socializers: The "psy complex"', in I. Parker (ed.) (2011) *Critical Psychology: Critical Concepts in Psychology, Volume 1, Dominant Models of Psychology and Their Limits*. London and New York: Routledge.

Kagan, C., Burton, M., Duckett, P., Lawthom, R. and Siddiquee, A. (2019) *Critical Community Psychology: Critical Action and Social Change, 2nd Edn*. Abingdon and New York: Routledge.

Kagan, C. and Lewis, S. (1990) 'Transforming psychological practice', *Australian Psychologist*, 25 (3), pp. 270–280.

Kamin, L (1974) *The Science and Politics of IQ*. Harmondsworth: Penguin.

Kenyon, C. A., Keeble, S. and Cronin, P. (1982) 'The role of perioral sensation in nipple attachment by weanling rat pups', *Developmental Psychobiology*, 15 (5), pp. 409–421.

Kitzinger, C. (1987) *The Social Construction of Lesbianism*. London and Thousand Oaks, CA: Sage.

Knight, C. (2015) *Decoding Chomsky: Science and Revolutionary Politics*. New Haven, CT: Yale University Press.

Kuhn, T. (1962) *The Structure of Scientific Revolutions*. Chicago, IL: University of Chicago Press.

Kvale, S. (1975) 'Memory and dialectics: Some reflections on Ebbinghaus and Mao Tse-tung', in I. Parker (ed.) (2011) *Critical Psychology: Critical Concepts in Psychology, Volume 2, Contradictions in Psychology and Elements of Resistance*. London and New York: Routledge.

Lambley, P. (1973) 'Psychology and socio-political reality: Apartheid psychology and its link with trends in humanistic psychology and behaviour theory', in I. Parker (ed.) (2011) *Critical Psychology: Critical Concepts in Psychology, Volume 1, Dominant Models of Psychology and Their Limits*. London and New York: Routledge.

Le Bon, G. (1896) *The Crowd: A Study of the Popular Mind*. London: Ernest Benn Ltd.

Longuet-Higgins, C. (1972) 'The algorithmic description of natural language', *Proceedings of the Royal Society*, 182, pp. 255–276.

Lorenz, C. (2012) 'If You're So Smart, Why Are You Under Surveillance? Universities, Neo-liberalism, and New Public Management', *Critical Inquiry*, 38 (3), pp. 599–629.

Lorenz, K. (1963) *On Aggression*. London: Methuen.

Lyotard, J. -F. (1979/1984) *The Postmodern Condition: A Report on Knowledge*. Manchester: Manchester University Press.

Mandel, E. (1974) *Late Capitalism*. London: New Left Books.

Mandel, E. (1978) *From Stalinism to Eurocommunism: The Bitter Fruits of 'Socialism in One Country'*. London: New Left Books.

Marsh, P., Rosser, E. and Harré, R. (1974) *The Rules of Disorder*. London: Routledge & Kegan Paul.

Martín-Baró, I. (1994) 'Toward a liberation psychology', in I. Parker (ed.) (2011) *Critical Psychology: Critical Concepts in Psychology, Volume 2, Contradictions in Psychology and Elements of Resistance*. London and New York: Routledge.

McLaughlin, T. (1996) 'Coping with hearing voices: An emancipatory discourse analytic approach', in I. Parker (ed.) (2011) *Critical Psychology: Critical Concepts in Psychology, Volume 4, Alternatives and Visions for Change*. London and New York: Routledge.

Milgram, S. (1963) 'Behavioral study of obedience', *Journal of Abnormal and Social Psychology*, 69, pp. 371–378.

Minuchin, S. (1974) *Families and Family Therapy*. Cambridge, MA: Harvard University Press.

Mixon, D. (1974) 'If you won't deceive, what can you do?' in N. Armistead (ed.) *Reconstructing Social Psychology*. Harmondsworth: Penguin.

Morgan, J., O'Neill, C. and Harré, R. (1979) *Nicknames: Their Origins and Social Consequences*. London: Routledge & Kegan Paul.

Neisser, U. (1967) *Cognitive Psychology*. Englewood Cliffs, NJ: Prentice-Hall.

Newnes, C. (2016) *Inscription, Diagnosis, Deception and the Mental Health Industry: How Psy Governs Us All*. Basingstoke: Palgrave.

Ostrom, E. (1990) *Governing the Commons: The Evolution of Institutions for Collective Action*. Cambridge: Cambridge University Press.

Parker, I. (1989) *The Crisis in Modern Social Psychology, and How to End It*. London: Routledge.

Parker, I. (1992/2014) *Discourse Dynamics: Critical Analysis for Social and Individual Psychology*. London: Routledge.

Parker, I. (1995) '"Right" said Fred "I'm too sexy for bourgeois group therapy": The case of the Institute for Social Therapy', *Changes: An International Journal of Psychology and Psychotherapy*, 13 (1), pp. 1–22.

Parker, I. (1997) *Psychoanalytic Culture: Psychoanalytic Discourse in Western Society*. London: Sage.

Parker, I. (ed.) (1998) *Social Constructionism, Discourse and Realism*. London: Sage.

Parker, I. (ed.) (1999) *Deconstructing Psychotherapy*. London and Thousand Oaks, CA: Sage.

Parker, I. (2005) *Qualitative Psychology: Introducing Radical Research*. Buckingham: Open University Press.

Parker, I. (2007) *Revolution in Psychology: Alienation to Emancipation*. London: Pluto Press.

Parker, I. (ed.) (2011) *Critical Psychology (Four Volumes)*. London and New York: Routledge.

Parker, I. (ed.) (2015) *Handbook of Critical Psychology*. London and New York: Routledge.

Parker, I. (2019) *Psychoanalysis, Clinic and Context: Subjectivity, History and Autobiography*. London and New York: Routledge.

Parker, I. and the Bolton Discourse Network. (1999) *Critical Textwork: An Introduction to Varieties of Discourse and Analysis*. Buckingham: Open University Press.

Parker, I., Georgaca, E., Harper, D., McLaughlin, T. and Stowell-Smith, M. (1995) *Deconstructing Psychopathology*. London: Sage.

Parker, I. and Shotter, J. (eds.) (1990) *Deconstructing Social Psychology*. London: Routledge.

Parker, I. and Spears, R. (eds.) (1996) *Psychology and Society: Radical Theory and Practice*. London: Pluto Press.

PINS, Psychology in Society: www.pins.org.za/

Potter, J., Stringer, P. and Wetherell, M. (1984) *Social Texts and Context: Literature and Social Psychology*. London: Routledge & Kegan Paul.

Potter, J. and Wetherell, M. (1987) *Discourse and Social Psychology: Beyond Attitudes and Behaviour*. London: Sage.

Prilleltensky, I. (1994) *The Morals and Politics of Psychology: Psychological Discourse and the Status Quo*. Albany, NY: State University of New York Press.

Radical Philosophy: www.radicalphilosophy.com/archive

Reicher, S. (1982) 'The determination of collective behaviour', in I. Parker (ed.) (2011) *Critical Psychology: Critical Concepts in Psychology, Volume 4, Alternatives and Visions for Change*. London and New York: Routledge.

Reicher, S. (1984) 'The St Paul's riot: An explanation of the limits of crowd action in terms of a social identity model', *European Journal of Social Psychology*, 14, pp. 1–21.

Romme, M. and Escher, A. (1989) 'Hearing voices', *Schizophrenia Bulletin*, 15 (2), pp. 209–216.

Romme, M. and Escher, A. (1993) *Accepting Voices*. London: MIND.

Said, E. (1978) *Orientalism*. London: Routledge & Kegan Paul.

Sarup, M. (1988) *An Introductory Guide to Post-structuralism and Postmodernism*. Hassocks, Sussex: Harvester Wheatsheaf.

Saussure, F. de (1915/1974) *Course in General Linguistics*. Glasgow: Fontana/Collins.

Sedgwick, P. (1982) *Psycho Politics*. London: Pluto Press.

Seligman, M. E. P. (1972) 'Learned helplessness', *Annual Review of Medicine*, 23 (1), pp. 407–412.

Shotter, J. (1975) *Images of Man in Psychological Research*. London: Methuen.

Shotter, J. (1987) 'Cognitive psychology, "Taylorism" and the manufacture of unemployment', in I. Parker (ed.) (2011) *Critical Psychology: Critical Concepts in Psychology, Volume 1, Dominant Models of Psychology and Their Limits*. London and New York: Routledge.

Shotter, J. and Gergen, K. J. (eds.) (1989) *Texts of Identity*. London: Sage.

Skinner, B. F. (1957) *Verbal Behavior*. New York, NY: Appleton-Century-Crofts.

Sloan, T. (1996) *Damaged Life: The Crisis of the Modern Psyche*. London and New York: Routledge.

Smail, D. (2005) *Power, Interest and Psychology*. Ross-on-Wye, England: PCCS Books.

Tajfel, H. (1970) 'Experiments in intergroup discrimination', *Scientific American*, 223, pp. 96–102.

Teo, T. (ed.) (2014) *Encyclopedia of Critical Psychology*. New York, NY: Springer-Verlag.

Terrace, H., Petitto, L. A., Sanders, R. J. and Bever, T. G. (1979) 'Can an ape create a sentence', *Science*, 206, pp. 891–902.

Thompson, J. (ed.) (1985) *Psychological Aspects of Nuclear War*. Leicester: British Psychological Society.

Tosh, J. (2014) *Perverse Psychology: The Pathologization of Sexual Violence and Transgenderism*. Abingdon and New York: Routledge.

Walkerdine, V. (1981) 'Sex, power and pedagogy', in I. Parker (ed.) (2011) *Critical Psychology: Critical Concepts in Psychology, Volume 4, Alternatives and Visions for Change*. London and New York: Routledge.

Watson, J. B. and Rayner, R. (1920) 'Conditioned emotional reactions', *Journal of Experimental Psychology*, 3 (1), pp. 1–14.

Wertz, F. J. (1994) 'Of rats and psychologists: A study of the history and meaning of science', in I. Parker (ed.) (2011) *Critical Psychology: Critical Concepts in Psychology, Volume 1, Dominant Models of Psychology and Their Limits*. London and New York: Routledge.

White, M. (1989) 'The externalizing of the problem and the re-authoring of lives and relationships', in I. Parker (ed.) (2011) *Critical Psychology: Critical Concepts in Psychology, Volume 2, Contradictions in Psychology and Elements of Resistance*. London and New York: Routledge.

Williams, L. (1972) *Challenge to Survival: A Philosophy of Evolution*. London: The Scientific Book Club.

Wittgenstein, L. (1953) *Philosophical Investigations*. Oxford: Blackwell.

Yardley, L. (ed.) (1997) *Material Discourses of Health and Illness*. London and New York: Routledge.

Young, R. (ed.) (1970) *Untying the Text: A Post-Structuralist Reader*. London: Routledge & Kegan Paul.

Zajonc, R. (1965) 'Social facilitation', *Science*, 149, pp. 269–274.

Zeigarnik, B. (1938) 'On finished and unfinished tasks', in W. D. Ellis (ed.) *A Sourcebook of Gestalt Psychology*. London: Routledge & Kegan Paul.

Zimbardo, P. (1973) 'On the ethics of intervention in human psychological research: With special reference to the Stanford prison experiment', *Cognition*, 2, pp. 243–256.

INDEX